CW01671657

Mac for Beginners

Imagine Publishing Ltd
Richmond House
33 Richmond Hill
Bournemouth
Dorset BH2 6EZ
☎ +44 (0) 1202 586200
Website: www.imagine-publishing.co.uk
Twitter: @Books_Imagine
Facebook: www.facebook.com/ImagineBookazines

Publishing Director
Aaron Asadi

Head of Design
Ross Andrews

Production Editor
Sanne de Boer

Senior Art Editor
Greg Whitaker

Assistant Designer
Alexander Phoenix

Printed by
William Gibbons, 26 Planetary Road, Willenhall, West Midlands, WV13 3XT

Distributed in the UK, Eire & the Rest of the World by
Marketforce, Blue Fin Building, 110 Southwark Street, London, SE1 0SU
Tel 0203 148 3300 www.marketforce.co.uk

Distributed in Australia by
Network Services (a division of Bauer Media Group), Level 21 Civic Tower, 66-68 Goulburn Street, Sydney, New South Wales 2000, Australia Tel +61 2 8667 5288

Part of the
iCreate™
bookazine series

IMAGINE
PUBLISHING

Contents

Feature
8 The ultimate guide to your Mac

Feature
22 Back up your Mac Now

Getting started

Learning Apple apps

Welcome to

Mac for Beginners

Welcome to Mac for Beginners, the ideal guide for kick-starting your life with your new Mac. In this new Ninth Revised Edition, we'll start with the basics, taking you through setting up your desktop, and looking at what the new OS X Yosemite operating system has to offer. After that, you'll explore the apps that make the Mac so exciting. Browse the web with Safari, revolutionise your music collection with iTunes, get synced with iCloud, and get to know your assistant Siri. Once you've experienced the core apps, we delve into Apple's more creative and productive apps, where you can really get more from your Mac. Create a blockbust film trailer with iMovie, become a rockstar drummer with GarageBand, and completely enhance your business life with Pages documents, Numbers spreadsheets and interactive Keynote presentations. Plus, we'll introduce you to the delights of the Mac App Store. Enjoy the book.

iWork
Get to grips with Apple's productivity software

Introducing iLife

Using iWork

Essential apps

"Whether you're using iPhoto, iMovie or GarageBand, you'll be able to create something amazing in no time"

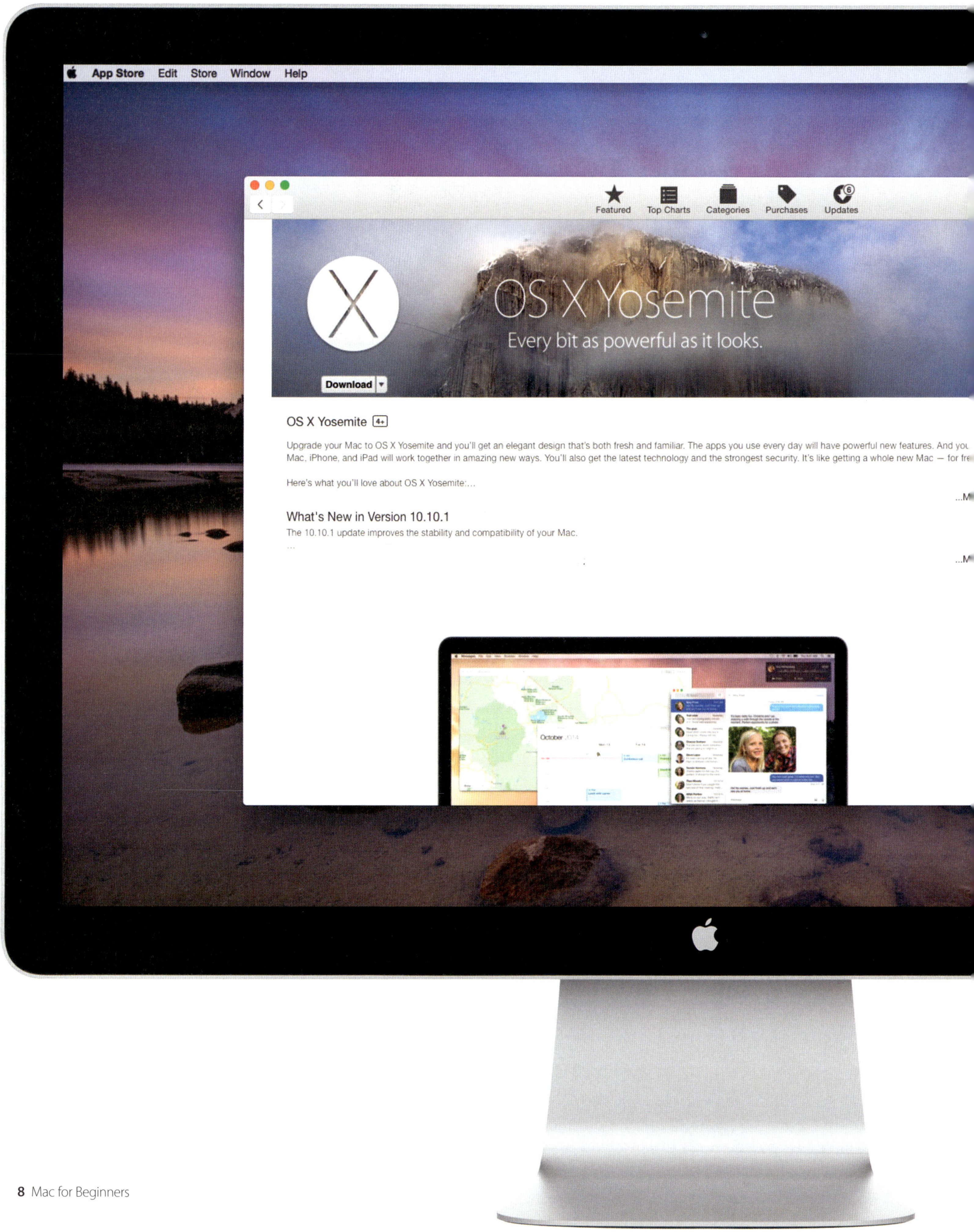
App Store
Edit
Store
Window
Help
Featured
Top Charts
Categories
Purchases
Updates
OS X Yosemite
Every bit as powerful as it looks.
Download
OS X Yosemite 4+
Upgrade your Mac to OS X Yosemite and you'll get an elegant design that's both fresh and familiar. The apps you use every day will have powerful new features. And you
Mac, iPhone, and iPad will work together in amazing new ways. You'll also get the latest technology and the strongest security. It's like getting a whole new Mac – for fre
Here's what you'll love about OS X Yosemite:...
What's New in Version 10.10.1
The 10.10.1 update improves the stability and compatibility of your Mac.

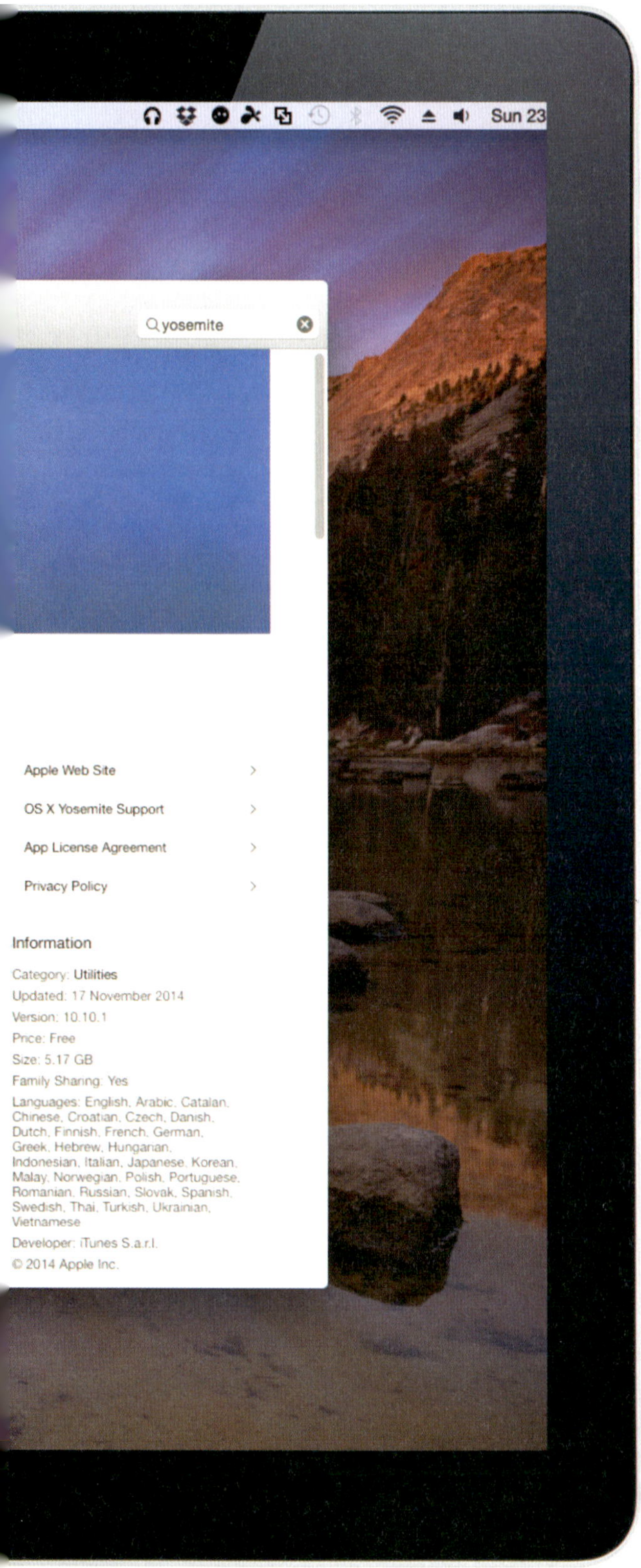

The ultimate guide to your Mac

Taking you through everything you need to know to get started on your Mac

Welcome to the Mac, and welcome to the Mac community. If this is the first time you've owned a Mac, trust us, you're in for a real treat. The Mac is a multi-talented computing phenomenon, part entertainment device, part office workhorse, part creative tool, part media hub. But among all its talents, there's one constant: you'll enjoy using it. If you're used to fighting to get a PC to do the simplest thing, you'll find your new Mac a breath of fresh air. It doesn't get in the way, and the many joys of discovering your Mac's benefits lie ahead.

"Among its talents, there's one constant: you'll enjoy using it"

However easy the Mac is to use – its reputation in this regard is well earned – it's also true that starting out on a new computer or on a new platform can seem daunting at first. Parts of it will inevitably seem unfamiliar. That's where this book comes in. Over these pages we'll take you through everything you need to get going and start enjoying your iMac or MacBook and the latest Yosemite operating system. Soon you'll be taking off with the Mac. It won't be long before you find yourself offering tips you've discovered to other Mac users – and gently extolling the benefits of the Mac to others.

OS X

The advantages of the sophisticated Mac operating system

OS X is the operating system (OS) that all Macs use to run their software – the latest being OS X Yosemite which is free to download. System updates are regularly available that boost your Mac's functionality and performance still further and can be found by going to Software Update in the Apple menu and checking for updates.

OS X Yosemite brings a wealth of goodness from iPhone, iPad and iPod touch to the Mac, which complements the features that arrived with the previous operating systems perfectly – such as Launchpad, which enables you to see and open your apps in a manner very reminiscent of the touch-screen iOS dynamics. Yosemite comes with apps such as Messages, which lets you send free messages between all Apple devices; Maps, to explore the world on your desktop; and Notes, which lets you jot down quick and easy notes that are synced to your iCloud and made available across all of your devices. Speaking of iCloud, this system now works harder to bind all of your devices together, integrating your mail, calendars, contacts, reminders, documents and more, so that whenever you add, delete or change something on your Mac,

these changes also occur automatically on your other devices too. Also making its Mac debut is Notification Center, so you'll never miss an important email or message again.

Entertainment

The Mac has made a name for itself as a creative device, but if you're just looking to relax then it will happily fill that role too. In the mood to watch a movie? iTunes has expanded from its original role as a music player and organiser, and now it can handle your video collection just as easily as it does your audio library. At the same time, the iTunes Store also holds a growing video collection that you can either rent or buy and watch on your Mac. Both current and classic films are available, and there's a good choice of television episodes too, particularly when it comes to comedy. Don't forget podcasts either. Some of the video podcasts in the iTunes Store – all free, remember – offer excellent quality.

But what's the best way to watch this downloaded content? You can play videos full-screen from within iTunes, although some users – particularly those who own big-screen Macs and an Apple Remote remote control device – enjoy sitting right back and watching their movies through Front Row. This is the Mac's built-in media software that allows you to easily navigate your iTunes music and video content or iPhoto pictures.

And, of course, AirPlay – Apple's wireless streaming technology – lets you stream video as well as audio from your Mac over a Wi-Fi network to your Apple TV. So even if you download your videos to a MacBook, you can still enjoy them on a really big screen.

Don't forget that you can also watch live or archived television footage on your Mac through a web browser. The BBC's iPlayer (**www.bbc.co.uk/iplayer**) has earned a fine reputation, but several other channels also offer either a live view or an on-demand service archive of previously broadcasted television shows.

If your entertainment interests are more cerebral, what about reading a book? As part of the OS X Yosemite update, iBooks makes an appearance in your Dock. This app works in the same way as the iOS version and all of your previous mobile purchases will be synced with your Mac and appear on your iBooks shelf. While reading, an intuitive interface lets you make bookmarks, highlight passages of text and add notes, and the store is just a click away.

Browsing

If we were to make the bold claim that the Mac offers the best way to browse the web, you would probably ask for evidence.

So here's exhibit one: Safari, the Mac's built-in web browser. It's not only one of the fastest and best-looking browsers around, but it also complies with modern web standards, which means that the latest cutting-edge websites should appear exactly as they were intended. Safari also comes with clever features such as private browsing, which hides your browsing history from prying eyes, and a neat 'Top Sites' view that presents small previews of your most-visited sites on one page and lets you visit them with a single click. Very convenient. In Top Sites view, Safari even lets you know when new content has been added to these sites, so you can stay on top of them.

> "Browsing the web on a Mac you're far less susceptible to viruses than on a PC"

Another great feature, for those of us who hate the ads that clutter webpages, is Safari's Reader mode. With a single click, webpages are transformed to show the important text in a simple scrolling, image-free window. Safari also comes with many other features, from full-screen mode to one simple search field for both search terms and web addresses.

Exhibit two: choice. It might surprise many, but Macs come with a far bigger range of web browsers than PCs do. You may not find Microsoft's Internet Explorer here, but on top of other big browsing names (Chrome, Firefox and Opera), there are niche alternatives such as Omnigroup's OmniWeb (**www.omnigroup.com**) for you to try.

Exhibit three: security. You'll be more comfortable browsing the web on a Mac because you're far less susceptible to viruses or other malware than on a PC. Especially as Apple has introduced GateKeeper, a system that provides more control over the apps you download and install and protects your Mac from malicious software. And if it's the kids you're worried about, you can rest assured that Mac OS X comes with a full set of parental controls – found in System Preferences. With the Mavericks update, there are other cool features to enjoy, such as the Sidebar, which provides easy access to your bookmarks, Reading List and shared links from social networks, and a faster all-round performance.

Music

As the creator of the iPod, the most successful music player in history, Apple has long had a special relationship with music. "Why music?" asked Apple legend Steve Jobs rhetorically in 2001, the year iTunes was launched. "We love music. It's part of everyone's life." Nowhere is this view more apparent than within iTunes, the hub of all music operations on your new Mac. It's a fantastically versatile program. Some will use it as a simple music player, either with music imported from their CD collection (stick a disc into your Mac and it will convert its tracks and add them to your iTunes library automatically), by importing digital music from another source (iTunes can automatically convert music held in Windows Media format) or by buying it from the iTunes Store, which you can reach through iTunes. Here you can browse and preview short samples of tracks, buy them with a single click and be listening to them on your Mac seconds later.

Others will use their Mac as an audio hub. iTunes can sync your music library to iPods, iPhones and iPads wirelessly by using your personal iCloud account, so you can take your tracks wherever you go. iTunes also comes with a cool feature called AirPlay. If you have a compatible device, such as AirPlay-enabled speakers, an AirPort Express wireless device or an Apple TV, you can stream your music from your Mac straight to them. Another feature, Home Sharing, allows you to share your music with other iTunes users (Mac or PC) who are connected to your home network.

The Mac isn't just great for listening to music. You can create it too, thanks to GarageBand. GarageBand is part of the Mac's bundled iLife suite and allows you to create your own music, either using the built-in instruments or by recording a real instrument by plugging it into your Mac. Even if you're an absolute beginner, GarageBand can be fun. You can drag pre-built 'loops' of audio onto tracks to build up a song, and even begin to learn how to play an instrument by downloading free basic music lessons from within the program.

Top 10 tips

01: Using Spotlight

OS X's Spotlight search enables you to find text, and image or movie files anywhere on your Mac (even if they're buried deep inside an old email that you were sent ages ago). Click on the Spotlight icon at the top right of the screen and type a phrase into the search field. Then click Show All to see search results from a variety of sources. You can also customise Spotlight to meet your specific needs.

02: Changing brightness/ volume

We all like to work in different ways, especially when it comes to sound volume and image brightness. You can control sound volume using sliders within an app like iTunes, or instead drag the master volume slider up or down from the top right of the main menu bar. To change Brightness, simply use the slider in the System Preferences>Displays option.

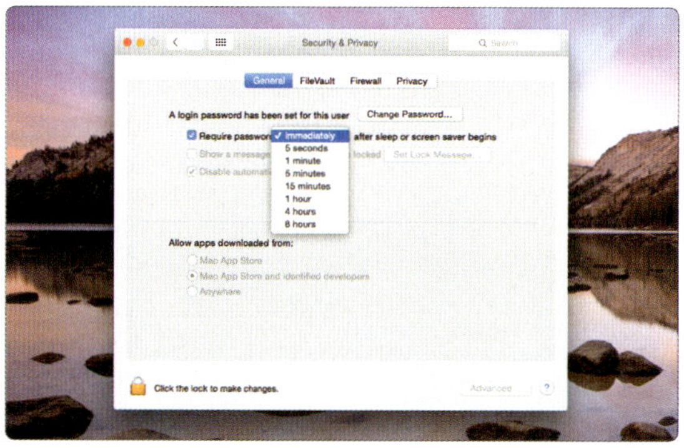

03: Setting up passwords

If you pop out of the office and leave your Mac unattended, you can get it to lock when the screensaver activates. Go to System Preferences>Security & Privacy and then select the General tab. Click the option to 'Require password after sleep or screensaver begins', then pick a time for this password protection to kick in.

04: Minimising/ maximising windows

The desktop can soon get cluttered with multiple open Finder or app windows. You can use Mission Control to tile them, then click on the one that you want to view full size. Alternatively, click on the yellow Minimize icon at the top left of any window and it'll shrink down to the Dock. The green Maximize icon will make the window expand back up to full size.

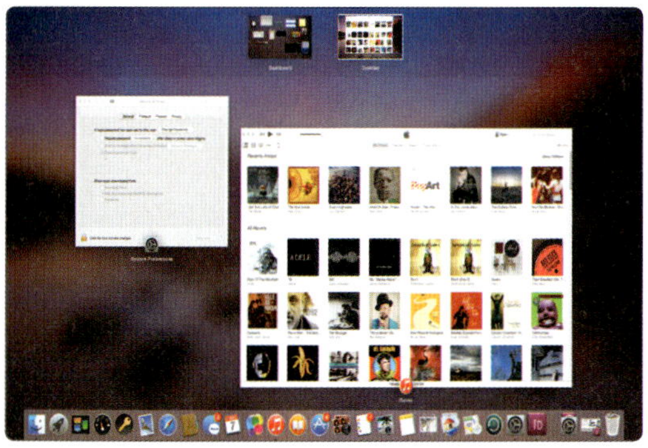

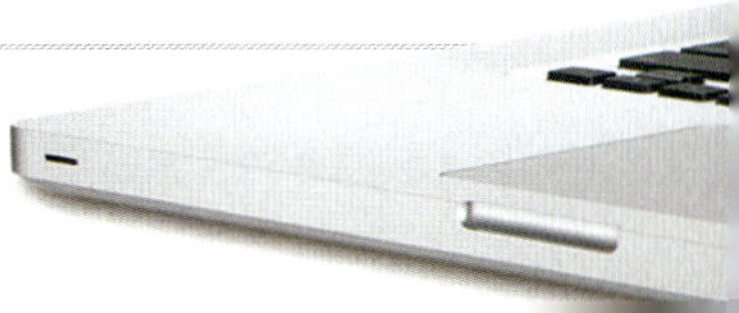

Mac OS X is a joy to use compared to Windows, with many user-friendly and powerful features that make your life easier. Here are some top tips to get started with OS X, from changing the appearance of your desktop to creating multiple user accounts and securing your system

05: Change the background

To make yourself feel more at home you can change the default desktop background. Go to Apple>System Preferences>Desktop & Screensaver. Browse through a variety of themed folders for an eye-catching image (or rummage through your iPhoto Library for something more personal). Click to select a new background.

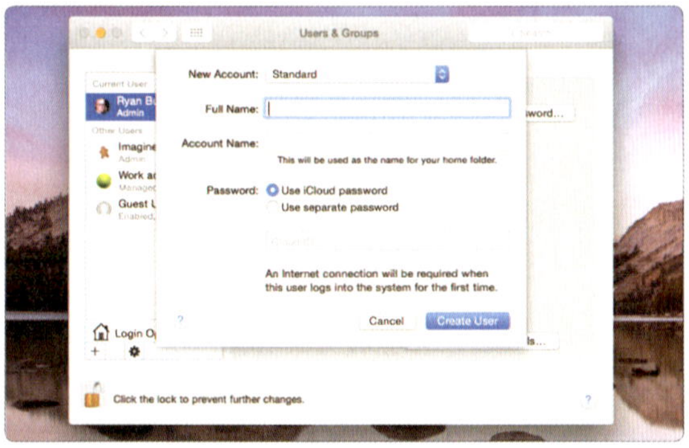

06: Set up multiple user accounts

To stop others tinkering with your files or settings, give them their own user account. Go to Apple>System Preferences>Users & Groups. Click the padlock and enter your Admin password. Click '+' to add a new account. This user can then choose their own password. Any changes they make to things like the desktop background will be unique to their account.

07: Create and rename folders

To create a new folder, click on the Gear icon at the top of an existing folder and then choose New Folder from the drop-down menu. Alternatively, on the menu bar at the top, head to File>New Folder. By default, each folder is labelled as 'untitled'. Click on the label and then type something more informative.

08: Add applications to your Dock

Docking a favourite application makes it easier to access. Browse to the Applications folder to see a specific application's icon and then drag it to the Dock. You can then launch it by clicking on its docked icon. Remove unwanted docked applications by dragging them from the Dock. They'll vanish in an animated puff of smoke!

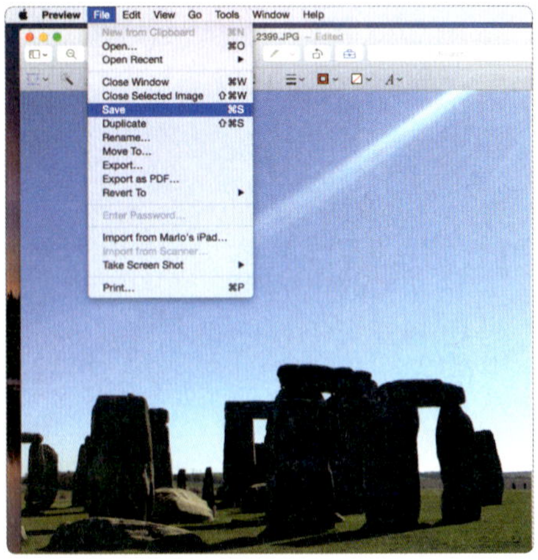

09: Save edited files under another name

Let's say you've adjusted the colour of an image using Preview. Go to File>Save As and give the file a name. Click on your house-shaped Home directory and browse to the Pictures folder. Click Save. The edited version of the shot can then be found and reopened by going to the Pictures folder.

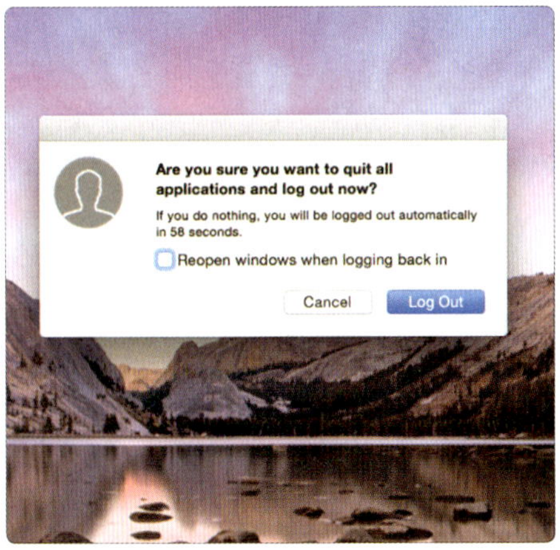

10: Log off and shut down

To log off after a hard day's work (or a fun gaming session) go to Apple>Log Out. Click the Log Out button. This will take you to the Mac OS X screen, where you can click Shut Down (or let someone else log in to use their account). Alternatively, press your Mac's power button and choose the Shut Down option.

The Dock

The Dock at the bottom of the screen enables you to access commonly used applications with ease

Mission Control
Click this icon to view all of your open files and apps, making it easy to find any files or windows currently open on your desktop quickly

Dashboard
Click here to access a variety of handy floating widgets, including a clock, calculator, calendar and even a weather forecast

Mail
Launch the Mail app by clicking here and follow the step-by-step instructions to set up an account

Contacts
This app lets you store vital contact info. With Mavericks you can update this by using all of your Facebook contacts

Calendar
Keep track of important dates and events using this powerful but easy-to-master calendar app

iTunes
Import music from disc or purchase it from the iTunes Store and play it on your Mac. You can also buy iOS apps here

Photos

If the extent of your photo organisation in the past has been to loosely organise them in folders on your PC, or even just to shove prints in a shoebox, you'll be stunned by the organisational prowess of your Mac's iPhoto application.

iPhoto gives you a whole new way to easily sort and group your photos. For example, its Faces feature automatically recognises faces in images and lets you add names to them. iPhoto learns from your choices and can suggest other photos that might include that person. After a while, this automatic recognition gets very good. You can then browse your photos in a special Faces view which gathers all photos of one person together.

In the same way, iPhoto's Places view uses location information often embedded in a digital image to display their location on a map, while an Events view groups photos by the date that they were taken. And if that's not enough flexibility for you, check out iPhoto's Smart Folders, whose contents automatically update to hold images depending on the criteria that you set.

If there's a downside to digital photography, it's the tendency for shots to be kept on your computer rather than shared. iPhoto, however, encourages you to post images to Facebook or photo sharing site Flickr. And if you're after permanent gifts, it can design letterpress cards, books and calendars that can be ordered from within the program.

Storing photos in iPhoto also makes them available in other iLife and iWork programs, making it easy to put your slideshows to DVD using iDVD, or home movies using iMovie. iPhoto isn't an all-singing, all-dancing photo editor in the vein of Photoshop, but it will happily handle the basics very well. You can crop, straighten and correct odd colours in a photograph easily and its tool to correct red-eye is almost foolproof.

Perhaps the best feature of all though is that, through your personal iCloud, you can activate Photo Stream, which automatically pushes photos taken on your iPhone or iPad to all of your devices, including your Mac, without the need to plug anything in or manually transfer files. Magic!

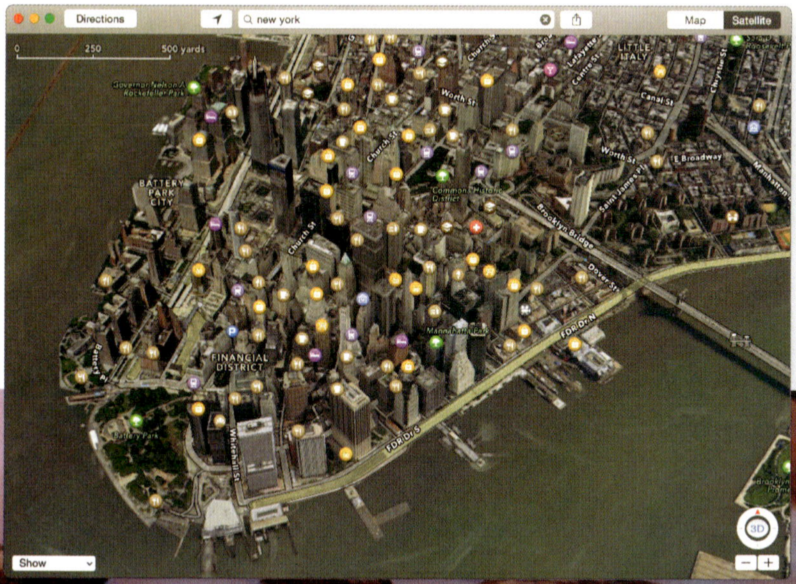

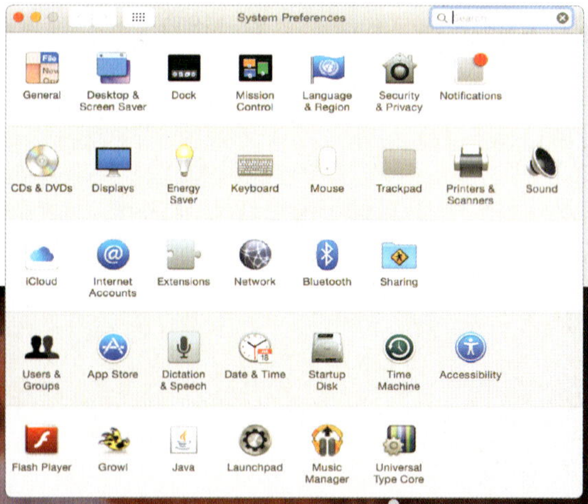

App Store
This bustling online store is where you can purchase apps for your Mac. The format makes it easy to search and browse through apps by category

Reminders
Create quick and easy to-do lists, set yourself alerts and then get them synced across all of your OS/iOS devices

Notes
The new Notes app lets you create quick and easy notes, place them on your desktop and then sync them across all devices using iCloud

Maps
Another OS X Mavericks addition, Maps lets you explore the world in full-screen and marvel at the wonder of 3D Flyover mode

iBooks
A new addition with Mavericks, iBooks lets you access all of your iOS books and read them easily

Photo Booth
The Mac is also a great place to have fun and this photo manipulation app is a big hit with the kids

iPhoto
This powerful app enables you to store and edit your photos, as well as share them through popular sites like Facebook

Time Machine
If you plug an external hard drive into your Mac, you can then use this app to back up the entire contents of your computer

System Preferences
You can do a host of things here, from changing the desktop wallpaper to modifying the size, shape and location of the Dock

Trash
Click on this icon to have a quick check of its contents, then Control-click on it to find the Empty Trash option

Video

What do *True Grit* and *The Social Network* have in common? Apart from being two box-office blockbusters, both movies were edited on a Mac using Mac-only software. It's a growing trend, and one that's becoming accessible to more people – not just professional film-makers. Ten years ago, you would have needed to sell your house and car to be able to afford that sort of editing functionality, but now you can do it using equipment costing just a few hundred pounds.

If you've got a video camera and a Mac, you already have all the hardware you need. If your camera is a relatively recent model, it's a decent bet that you'll be able to start working with it without even having to install drivers or tweak settings.

While many top-of-the-range movies are edited using the high-end Final Cut Pro on the Mac, iLife's own bundled iMovie is the gold standard of home video editing. Editing in iMovie is as simple as importing your footage and then placing it into a project area. Simply drag and drop to add transitions between scenes or titles, and there's a full array of sound effects that you can use to enhance the audio quality. Even if your original footage isn't top quality, iMovie can improve it. It has a stabilisation tool to correct shaky video and individual clips can be colour-corrected. The professional look is enhanced through iMovie 11's templates that help you quickly create short and memorable trailers for your work.

The real beauty of iLife applications is the way that they work together. With the iLife media browser, you can add a soundtrack from iTunes or images from iPhoto or even export your video to iDVD to create permanent keepsakes on disc. That's not the only export option either: you can also share directly to popular video-sharing sites such as YouTube or Vimeo.

And naturally, there's an easy transition to even more powerful tools. Final Cut Pro X isn't too expensive (£199.99/$299.99), and it is the latest version of the famous Final Cut editing suite. It imports existing iMovie projects while allowing you to work with multiple audio and video tracks.

Gaming

It used to be said that the Mac lagged behind Windows when it came to games, but that's far less true now. There are plenty of reasons for this change. The attention of games developers has been grabbed by the Mac's ever-increasing market share. Also, the Mac's transition to running on Intel processors a few years ago resulted in both performance improvements and easier porting of games from the PC platform.

The arrival of the Mac App Store has also proved critical. It has given exposure to Mac games developers who would otherwise struggle for the limelight. That has benefited the developers of games like *Call Of Duty* and *Batman: Arkham Asylum*, which have been some of the App Store's biggest sellers since it launched in January 2011.

The arrival of the Mac App Store has also encouraged existing iPhone and iPod games developers, already familiar with the App Store format and Apple's development tools, to try their hand at the Mac games.

The conversion process is comparatively simple, and as a result, titles that originally grabbed attention on the iPhone, such as *Angry Birds*, *Flight Control* and *Plants Vs Zombies*, have been ported successfully to the Mac. Crucially, in many cases, this transfer has come ahead of their arrival on PC or console systems.

And Mac users don't just have a better choice of games now. The arrival of Game Center means it has never been easier to shop for Mac games (via Game Center's internal link to the Games section of the App Store), and you can also use it to compare scores and challenge your friends online.

There's another reason for the Mac's growth: the arrival on the Mac platform of Steam, a digital distribution platform that boasted 25 million user accounts before it arrived on the Mac. However, now Mac gamers have feature parity: Steam games release simultaneously on Windows and Mac. If you're a Windows Steam user, though, there's great news: if you already own the PC version of a game on Steam, you get Mac versions at no extra charge.

Shortcut tips

The brilliant thing about OS X is the way it lets you control the way your Mac behaves with a few taps on the keyboard. These keyboard shortcuts can speed up the way you interact with your Mac, so you are able to clear away clutter, find files fast or jump between open applications in a click. By knowing the keyboard shortcut for a command, you no longer have to drag the mouse up to the main menu and rummage around in submenus!

We'll cover shortcuts that work with OS X, plus show you some generic key combinations that will work in most applications (like copying and pasting). Many shortcuts use the key with the Apple logo on it – we'll refer to this as the Command key in our tips, since some wireless keyboards don't feature the Apple logo on the Command key. The key with Alt on it is the Option key.

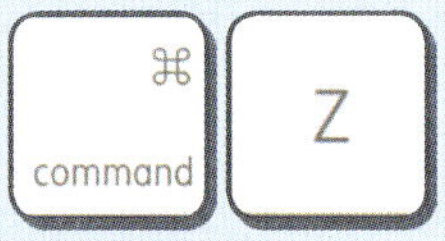

Command+Z
This is the Undo function in most applications.

Option+Shift+Command+Escape
If you hold these keys down for three seconds, you'll Force Quit the currently-open app. Only do this if an app freezes up.

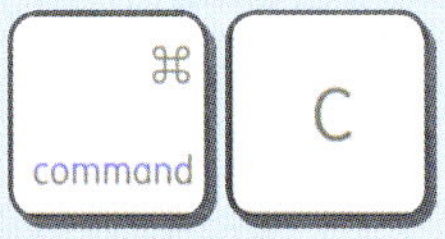

Command+C
Copies selected text, documents or even images.

Command+Shift+3
Takes a screenshot of your display and saves it as an image file to the desktop.

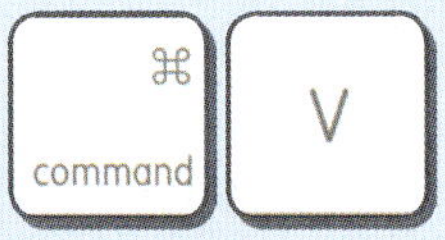

Command+V
Pastes anything you copied with the Cmd+C shortcut.

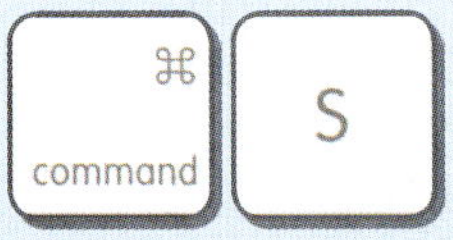

Command+S
This shortcut saves the current document, using the same name.

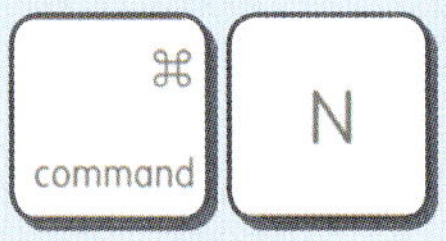

Command+N
This will give you a new document in any application you're using.

Command+Tab
This activates a handy mini-Dock. Keep pressing Tab to switch between currently open applications.

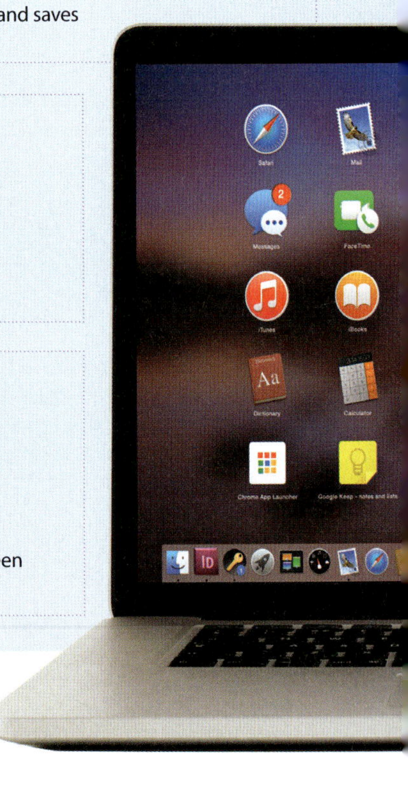

Spacebar

Tap the Spacebar when you've selected an image or document in Finder to get a Quick Look at its contents without having to open it.

Command+Space

This shortcut opens the Spotlight Search window. You can immediately start typing a search term.

F9 (or F3 if using an older OS)

Activates Mission Control to tile all open documents into handy little thumbnails.

F4

This summons your Mac's widgets.

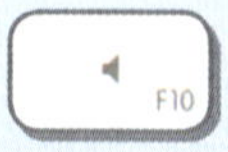

Control+F3

(or F10 if using an older OS)

This displays all the open windows in your currently active application.

Command+F3

(or F11 if using an older OS)

This command pushes all open windows to the side so you can see the desktop.

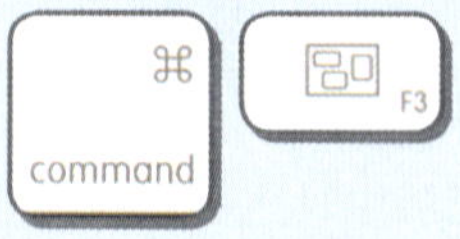

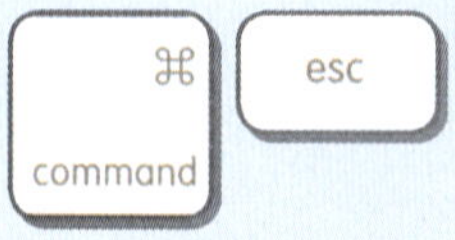

Command+Escape

This opens Front Row, so you can enjoy media like movies and photos.

Option+Command+Eject

When it's coffee break time, this will put your Mac to sleep. Push any key on the keyboard to wake it up again.

"Shortcuts can speed up the way you work"

Command+Backspace

This shortcut sends the selected file(s) to the Trash, so you don't have to drag them there.

Option+Command+D

In System Preferences, you can make the Dock pop up when you move the mouse over it, or press Option+Command+D.

MAGIC MOUSE

Right click

If you do this while selecting a word in Safari, you can choose 'Look Up in Dictionary' from the context-sensitive pop-up menu.

Scroll

There's no wheel on this mouse; just slide your finger down the middle to scroll.

Control+Scroll

This combo enables you to zoom in to get a magnified view of what's on the screen.

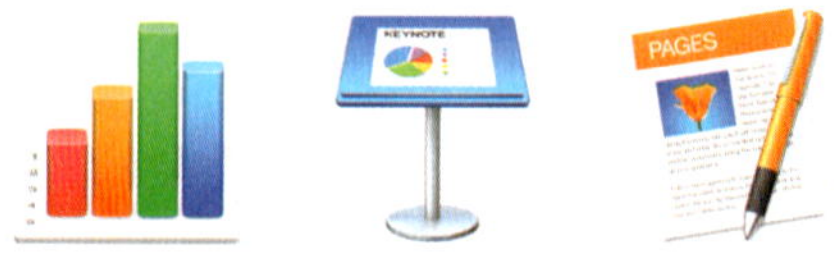

Office

If you didn't think of the Mac as an office workhorse, think again. Easy to use, supremely resistant to viruses and coming with a reputation for reliability, Apple desktops and laptops tick plenty of hard-nosed business boxes.

But what about the software? The good news is that the dominant office software is available on the Mac – and it's just as good as the one on Windows. Microsoft Office 11 for Mac has virtually the same functionality as its PC sibling, but looks better. You can swap Word and Excel files with PC users and even share Outlook calendars on a connected server. Plus, recent Macs come with built-in support for Microsoft Exchange Server 2007, so if you use Exchange at work, the chances are that you can access all your emails and calendars at home too.

Apple has been making its own steps into the office space too. Its Mac-only iWork suite, the components of which are now free to download, also features word processing, spreadsheet and presentation capabilities. If its word processing and spreadsheet tools lack the complete range of functions of Microsoft's equivalent tools, they are at least arguably easier to use. iWork's Keynote presentation software is a genuine alternative to PowerPoint, with its more polished templates and more impressive transitions.

iWork files are also Office compatible: files saved in Office on the PC can be opened in Pages, Numbers and Keynote, while you can export them from iWork in PC format too. What's more, you can sync documents to your iCloud and access them from any computer or iOS device in the world to continue working on them – and everything saves automatically so you don't have to worry about work being lost. The only thing missing in both the Microsoft Office and iWork suites is a decent database, but even here you're spoiled for choice: pick between Filemaker (**www.filemaker.com**) or iDatabase (**www.apimac.com/mac/idatabase**), which presents a budget alternative.

Office work isn't all about spreadsheets, letters and slideshows, though. What about managing your accounts? There's plenty of choice here too. AccountEdge (**www.mamut.com/uk/mac/accountedge**) and Business Accountz (**www.accountz.com**) are both reasonably priced and capable desktop applications. So you see, Macs cover all bases when it comes to personal and professional use.

Productivity

Keeping yourself organised has never been more demanding. But your Mac, and its built-in calendar application, can help you to keep on top of things. Calendar (formerly iCal) supports multiple calendars – so you can track work and family commitments separately – and you can view calendars in several ways: by day, week or month. You can invite others to events you create and set an alarm to remind you before it starts.

The calendar also lets you sync appointments with iPhone, iPod touch or iPad Calendar apps, using iTunes as a handy go-between. If you use Apple's iCloud service, you will also have the ability to sync your calendar without a physical connection, and you will be able to share calendars between multiple Macs too.

Beyond its calendar, the Mac has been built to take control of the chores while you do what you want to do. For example, every computer user knows they ought to back up regularly, but the organising of backup discs and choosing what to copy invariably gets in the way. Not on a Mac. Here, backing up is as simple as attaching an external drive. Apple's Time Machine backup utility takes care of the rest.

To be truly productive, you need to get as much done as possible while avoiding those repetitive tasks that can take up a lot of your time and become quite frustrating. Automator is a drag-and-drop tool for automating common chores. You build a workflow by piecing together actions and the saved result automates the task in the future. With some applications, you can just record your mouse and keyboard movements and save the result to an Automator workflow, where they can be stored and replayed. It's like programming without the hard work.

Another often overlooked productivity treat for many Mac users is Services, which comprises small pieces of functionality that can be shared between different applications. Accessed from the application menu (if you are in iTunes, for example, Services can be found under the iTunes menu), services suitable for the current application automatically appear – so if you're working in a word processor, you might see a service to send the currently selected text in an email. Furthermore, if you don't find a service you would like to see, you can easily build one of your own – using Automator, of course. There are plenty of options on your Mac to make you more productive.

iTunes top tips

Organise your entire music collection with iTunes, rediscover your favourite tracks from yesteryear and sync songs with mobile devices

The way that we manage music has changed dramatically since iTunes and mobile devices like the iPod and iPhone came along. Once you've copied your CDs into your iTunes app, you'll rediscover music you haven't listened to for years. Think of iTunes as your personal digital jukebox! You can use it to store and organise your music collection, as well as discover and buy new music (or movies) via the iTunes Store. Your digital tracks can be turned into Playlists (like cassette mixtapes of old!) and transferred to your iPod or iPhone to be enjoyed on the move. Here's are some of the ways you can take advantage of iTunes 12, the latest version.

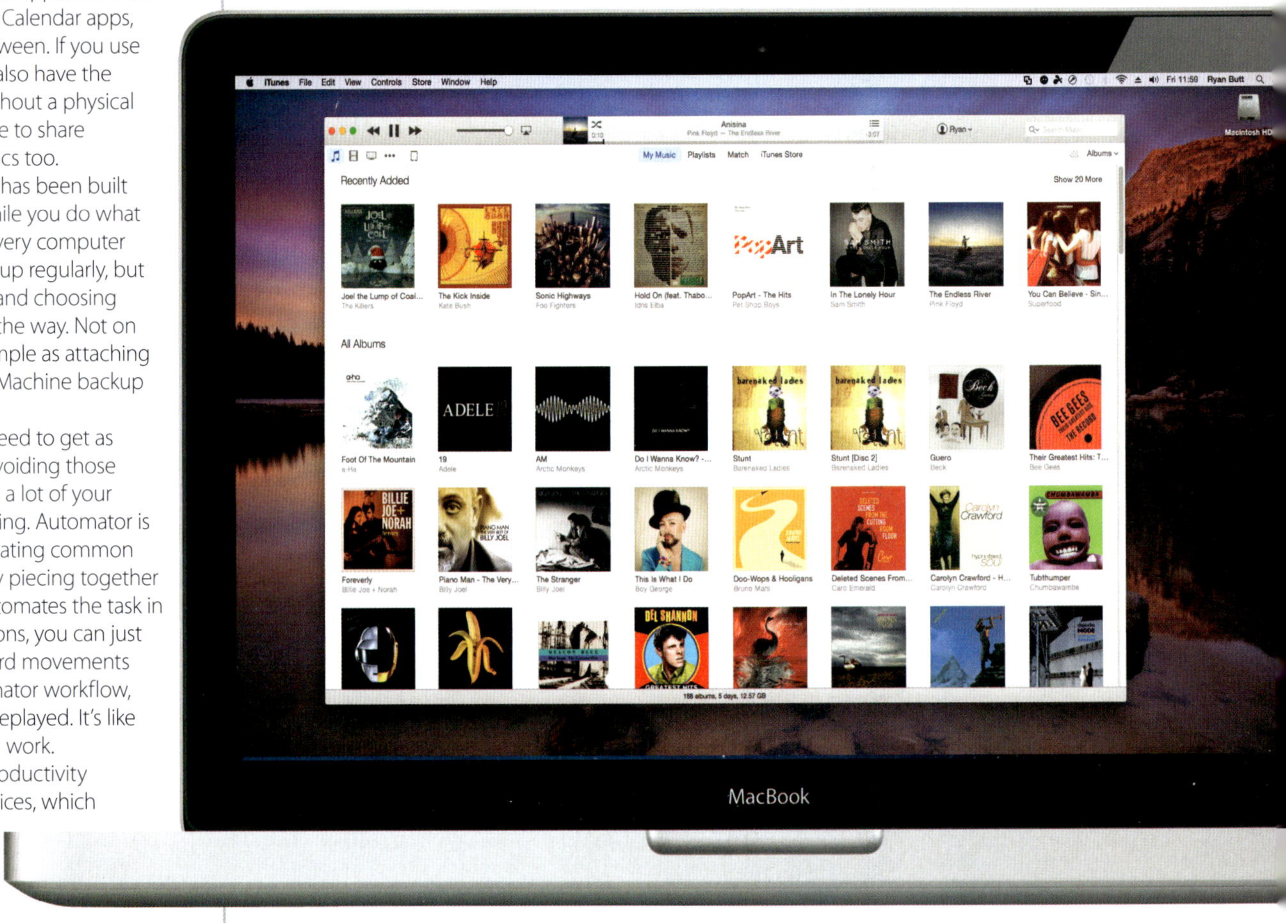

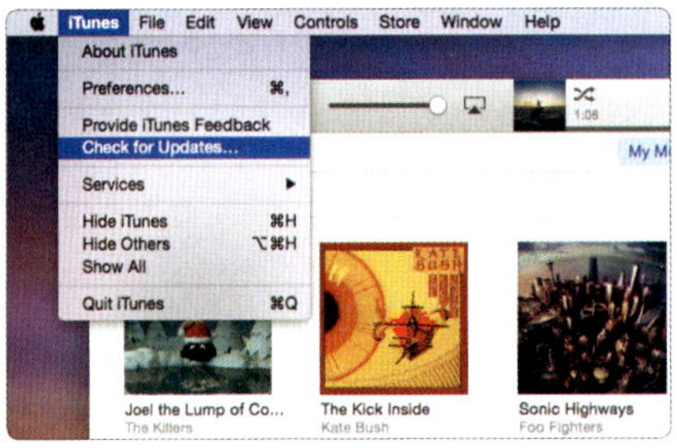

New software

Like other apps, iTunes is always evolving to include improved performance and extra features. You may be informed that newer versions of iTunes are available when you open the app, but you can also check out any updates by going to the iTunes menu (look next to the Apple icon in the top menu bar) and choosing Check For Updates. You can then download and install the latest version of iTunes.

MiniPlayer

To reduce the size of the iTunes interface, simply go to Window>Switch to MiniPlayer. This turns iTunes into a small floating mini player that enables you to perform useful commands like playing, pausing, jumping forward to the next song or even searching your library. You can adjust volume here too by using the slider in the AirPlay menu.

Create a Playlist

It can be a little daunting when you're deciding which songs to listen to from a huge music library, but thankfully, you can create Playlists. Select the Playlists tab and click on the '+' icon at the bottom left corner of the iTunes window and then name your Playlist. Click on Music in the Library section. Drag tracks from the Library into the new Playlist, which will be listed to the left.

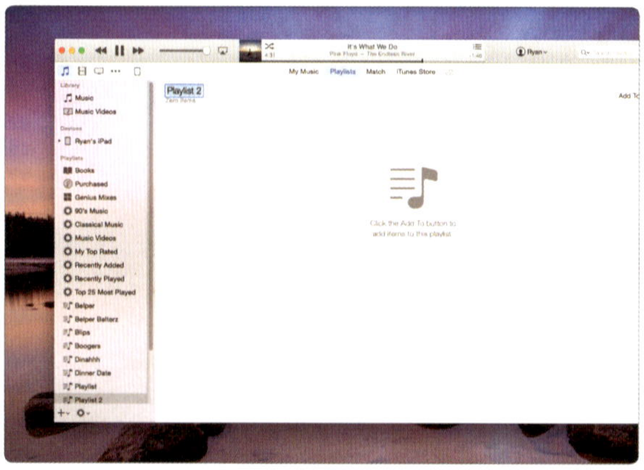

> "Once you've copied your CDs into your iTunes app, you may rediscover music you haven't listened to for years"

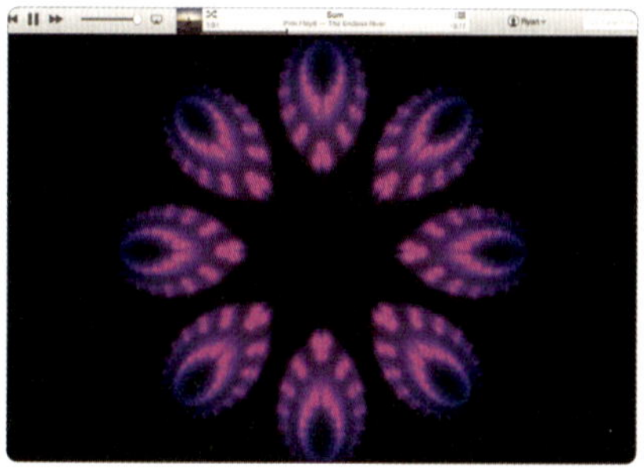

Visualizer

By pressing Command+T you can activate the Visualizer and enjoy real-time animated graphics that react in time to the track that you're currently playing. To see different types of graphics, go to View>Visualizer and then choose from the available options, like Jelly. By pressing Command+F you can also expand the Visualizer to full screen and enjoy a psychedelic light show to accompany your music. Perfect when you want to really hear the tune!

Get Album Artwork

If an album in your Library isn't displaying the cover, right-click on it and choose Get Album Artwork. iTunes will then trawl an online database for appropriate covers. If no album art can be found then you may need to adjust the info. Right-click on the album, choose Get Info and then tweak and amend the info before trying again.

Sync an iPhone or iPad

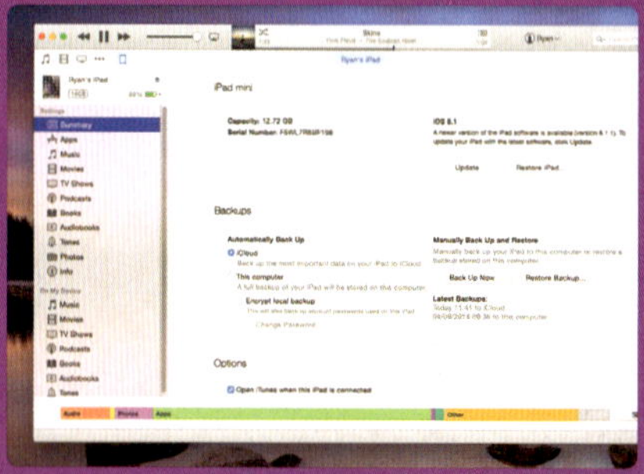

01: Plug in your gadget

When you plug your iPhone (or iPad) into your Mac via a USB cable, click on the relevant icon under Devices. Click Summary. Tick 'Open iTunes when this iPad (or iPhone) is connected'. Tick 'Sync only checked songs and videos'.

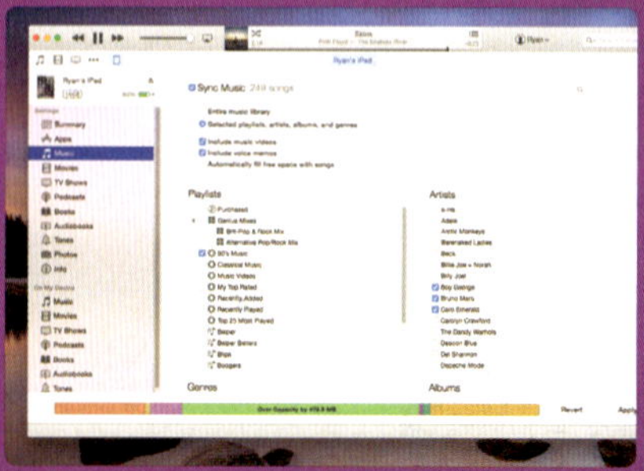

02: Choose what to sync

Click on the Music tab in the main window. Tick Sync Music to see songs on your Mac. Tick Selected playlists, artists, albums and genres. Tick the playlists or albums that you want to sync onto your iPad/iPhone.

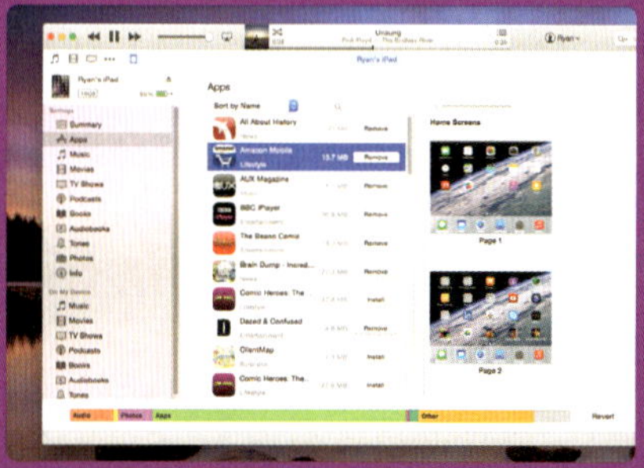

03: Sync

You can also tick boxes to sync apps, movies, TV shows and photos. Use the Info tab to sync Contacts and even Safari bookmarks. Click Apply to start syncing. This will transfer content from your iTunes Library onto your mobile device.

Mac App Store

Browse thousands of Mac applications, all located in one convenient App Store

Launched back in July 2008, Apple's original App Store was initially accessible via an app on the iPhone – and subsequently the iPod touch and iPad – enabling users of those devices to peruse thousands of downloadable apps designed for iOS devices. Apps span a wide range of categories (from Photography to Education) and let you extend your iPhone's functionality in many exciting ways. The iPhone-centric App Store has proven incredibly successful, so there was little surprise when a Mac OS X App Store appeared early in 2011. On its first day, the new Mac App Store sold a million apps.

The Mac App Store enables you to find useful software for your iMac or MacBook in one convenient place, without having to trawl the internet. To browse it, you'll need the Mac App Store app, which is available by default with OS X Mavericks (you can use your Apple>Software Update menu command to install the latest version of older operating systems). Once you've updated Mac OS X, the Mac App Store will appear in your Dock. Double-click on the app's icon to fire it up.

As there are thousands of Mac apps to explore, finding what you need can be daunting, so it's worth rummaging through one of the 21 categories first. As with the iOS App Store, these Mac app categories cover a wide range topics, including Games and Social Networking. Once you've found a category that you're interested in, you can refine your search by looking at the Top Paid or Top Free Apps to see what is popular. Alternatively, you can search the App Store with a relevant keyword. Once you've clicked on an app that catches your eye, you can find out more about it by viewing screenshots of its interface. More importantly, you can read the reviews of people who've already downloaded the app to see whether it's worth your time (and money!).

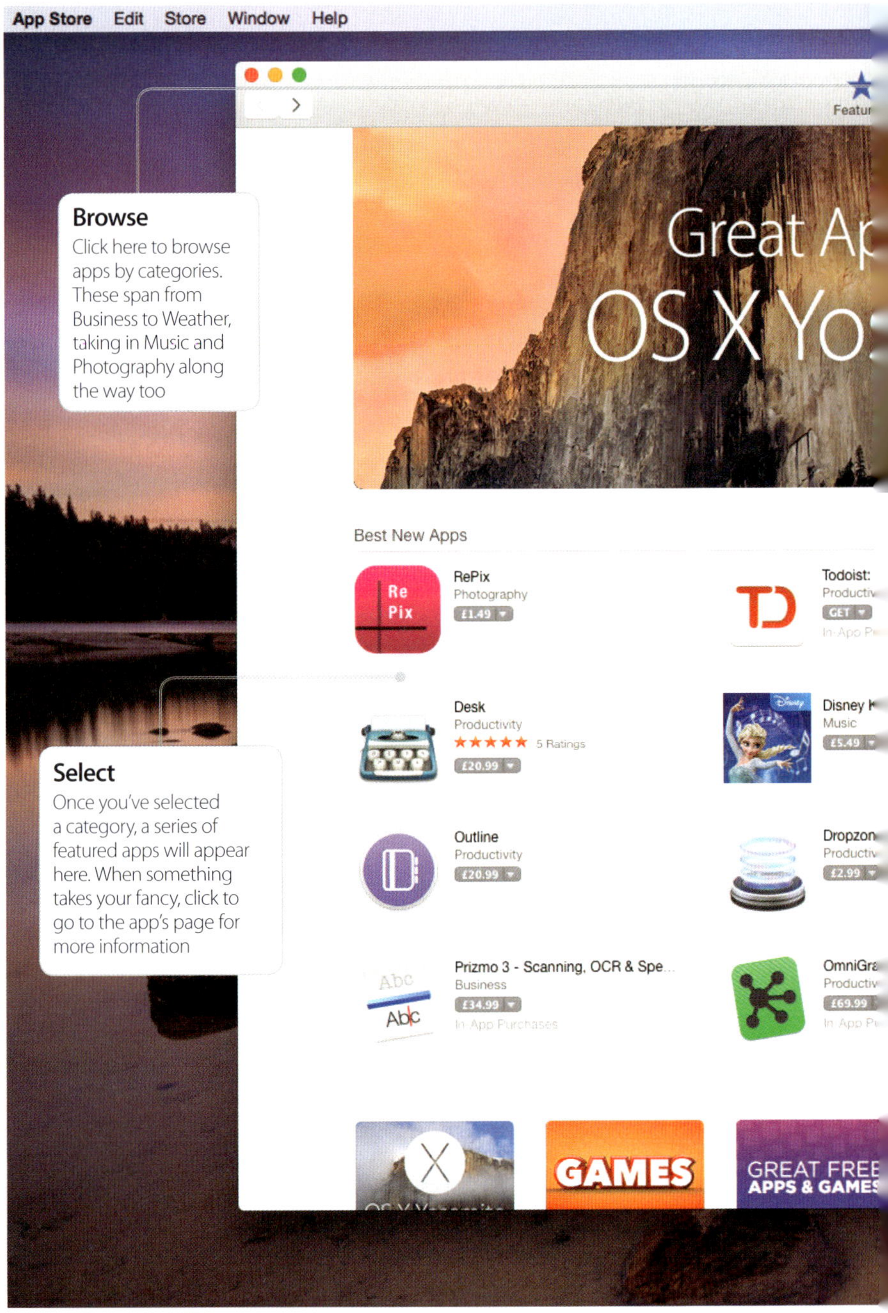

Communication

The Mac is all about communication, whether by email, text message or video. Apple Mail, the email program that sits in the Dock of every Mac, is a superb way to keep in touch with friends, family and colleagues. It can handle multiple email accounts and, thanks to the Mac's Spotlight search engine, all its messages can be searched in an instant. Want to add files or photos to your email? Just drag them over your message window or use Mail's photo browser to grab snaps from your iPhoto collection. In Mail, email doesn't need to be drab: you can style it using beautifully designed templates.

Mail is clever too, analysing the contents of incoming messages, not just to check whether they contain spam – in which case they will be neatly removed from view – but also to interpret the contents. So if you get an email asking you to meet someone tomorrow at one, you can click on this invitation to add it to your iCal calendar. And Mail

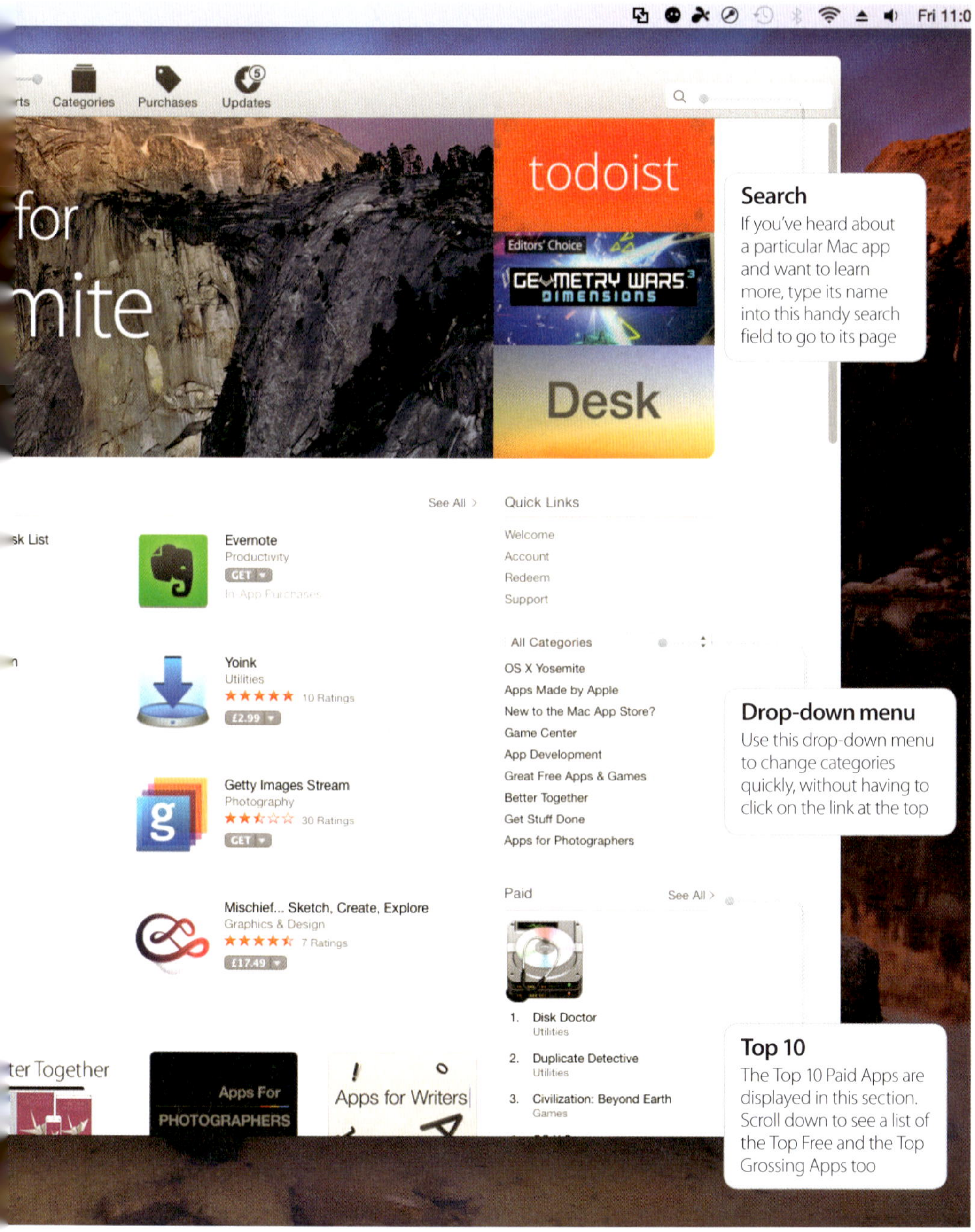

Search
If you've heard about a particular Mac app and want to learn more, type its name into this handy search field to go to its page

Drop-down menu
Use this drop-down menu to change categories quickly, without having to click on the link at the top

Top 10
The Top 10 Paid Apps are displayed in this section. Scroll down to see a list of the Top Free and the Top Grossing Apps too

works neatly with the Mac's own application for storing contacts – Address Book – which syncs with your iPhone or iPad via iCloud, so your contacts are with you all the time.

Facebook is becoming an ever more popular way to communicate and while most people are happy using the Facebook website, there are plenty of Mac applications that integrate with it. Even iPhoto offers a way to upload your images directly to your Facebook account – and comments about the photo made by Facebook friends can be seen within iPhoto. You can also use the web to keep up with your Twitter contacts – although it's easier to use one of the Mac's own applications: the Twitter application itself is a free download from the Mac App Store.

FaceTime is another cool feature that allows you to have a video chat with other FaceTime users, whether on the Mac, iPhone, iPad or iPod touch. If you prefer to do your talking via text message, then Apple's own Messages app is perfect.

But if you want to keep up with friends using other text messaging services, such as AOL Instant Messenger, look no further than the excellent Adium (**www.adium.im**). The possibilities for communication are endless.

Creativity

The Mac, at its heart, is a creative tool. It seems to have always been that way. The desktop publishing industry began on the Mac back in the Eighties and, 30 years later, today's web design industry still favours the platform. How can that be? Perhaps the Mac's ease of use has something to do with it, or the fact that creative peripherals, such as drawing tablets, are designed to work seamlessly on it.

It's as likely, though, that the quality of Apple's hardware strikes a note with creatives. And that applies from a practical, as much as an aesthetic, point of view. Those Mac screens – particularly the larger iMac displays – not only look great, but offer great colour reproduction. And the Mac's built-in ColorSync technology ensures that what's great-looking on screen will look just as good (and colour-accurate) when it prints out.

Above all, it's the software that appeals. A quick scan of the Mac App Store will reveal dozens of cool budget drawing and illustration tools – not forgetting Pages' superb layout tools – while the industry-standard design applications all work well on the Mac, from QuarkXPress to Adobe's Creative Suite, which comprises popular applications such as image editor Photoshop, drawing tool Illustrator and page layout application InDesign.

The web is the catalyst for much creative work nowadays. For those who want to put a creative site together without having to get their hands dirty with code, Pages, which comes as part of the iWork suite, is a great start. You can base your website on pre-built templates and customise it by dragging other iLife components – video from iMovie, images from iPhoto or audio from iTunes – into it. Instead of having to hand-code functionality to add features such as embedded YouTube videos, you can just drag a widget to your page. Publishing to the web is a single click away.

If Pages whets your appetite to get more serious about web development, there are plenty of more powerful tools available to help. Another Mac-only tool, Coda (**www.panic.com/coda**), offers a single window coding environment that's popular with Mac web coders and developers.

> "There are dozens of cool budget drawing and illustration tools in the Mac App Store"

BACK UP YOUR MAC NOW

Never lose a file again with these top backup tips and tricks for your Mac

No computer is completely faultless. Macs might be famous because they 'just work' but sometimes they do have issues, and those issues can be a lot more serious than a simple crash.

It's for precisely this reason that even the biggest Mac fans will tell you to keep machines backed up so that your files, photos and media are always safe no matter what happens. Laptops can be lost, dropped or stolen in just a few seconds, and if you don't have a working backup, your precious files can often be lost forever. Software can be a problem sometimes, too. Before you do any serious software update on your Mac, it's always a good idea to back up your machine. So when you see the notification telling you there's a new version of OS X available, it's worth saving the update until later and making sure all your files are safe first. Things like treasured family photos and vital documents are not easy to replace, so why not take the time to keep a backup copy safe and sound?

One of the main reasons people used to have for failing to back up was the cost, but with high-capacity hard drives dropping in price, there's bound to be a backup solution that suits your needs without breaking the bank.

In this feature we'll show you everything you could need for keeping your files safe, from simple Time Machine backups to more complex options like online backups, or off-site options for those that want to be completely covered. Read on and you'll soon be able to sleep comfortably knowing that should the worst happen, you've got duplicates of all your most vital files readily accessible.

Finder File Edit View Go Window Help
Thu 12:07 Ryan Butt
Macintosh HD
iCloud Drive
Back
View
Arrange
Share
Edit Tags
Action
Search
Favorites
Dropbox
AirDrop
Desktop
Applications
Pictures
ryan
Documents
Downloads
All My Files
iCloud Drive
Library
Music
Deleted...
Devices
Macintos...
Tags
Important...
Work files
Automator
TextEdit
Preview
Numbers
Keynote
Pages
iCloud
Ryan Butt
Account Details
Set Up Family
Sign Out
iCloud Drive
Options...
Photos
Options...
Mail
Contacts
Calendars
Reminders
Safari
Notes
You have 5 GB of iCloud storage.
Backup
3.22 GB Available
Manage...

Back up your Mac now

Set up Time Machine

Set up automatic, regular backups of your data

If you've got important or precious data on your Mac, like family photos or work documents, it's vital that you keep it backed up in the event that something goes wrong with your Mac, such as a hard drive failure or a whole Mac failure. There are several different ways you can back up your data but the most efficient way is via Time Machine, an app that ships as standard with all versions of OS X from 10.5 Leopard onwards. It's a foolproof automatic backup system that backs up your Mac every hour when your backup device is connected to it, saving you the need to remember to back up your data. Time Machine is really easy to set up and we're going to take you through the process step by step. All you need is a Mac running OS X 10.5 or newer and an external backup drive.

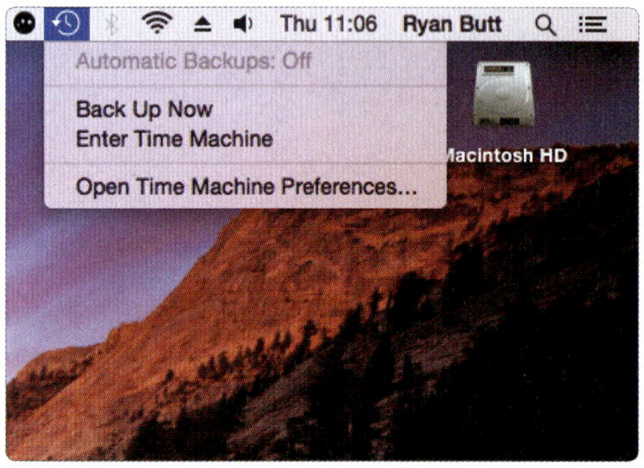

01: Launch Time Machine

Click on the Time Machine icon in the desktop menubar – this looks like a clock face inside an anti-clockwise circular arrow. Alternatively, find Time Machine in your Applications folder.

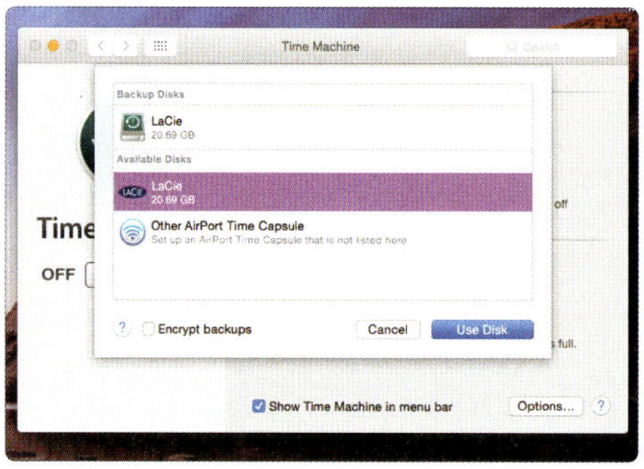

02: Turn Time Machine On

Select Open Time Machine Preferences from the drop-down menu. Toggle Time Machine to On and click Select Backup Disk. From the pop-out window, select your external hard drive.

03: Back Up Now

Your first backup will begin after a few moments. If you can't wait, click the Time Machine logo in the menubar and select Back Up Now from the drop-down menu to manually start the process.

DaisyDisk

Delete unwanted files before you back them up with DaisyDisk

DaisyDisk shows you visually where your disk space is being used on your Mac. It works in a simple way: it scans your internal or external hard drives and presents your storage in an interactive circle – the larger the portion of the circle, the more space it's using. Click on a section to view individual files, and in order to delete files, drag to the designated 'collection' area at the bottom of the interface and hit Delete.

DaisyDisk shows you which files and folders are taking up the most hard disk space

Optimise Time Machine backups

Customise your Time Machine backups to save space and time

Time Machine is designed to back up everything on your Mac. However, there may be occasions where you don't want to do this – whether that's to conserve space on your backup drive, or just to back up certain files. The good news is that it's easy to optimise Time Machine backups to save space and time.

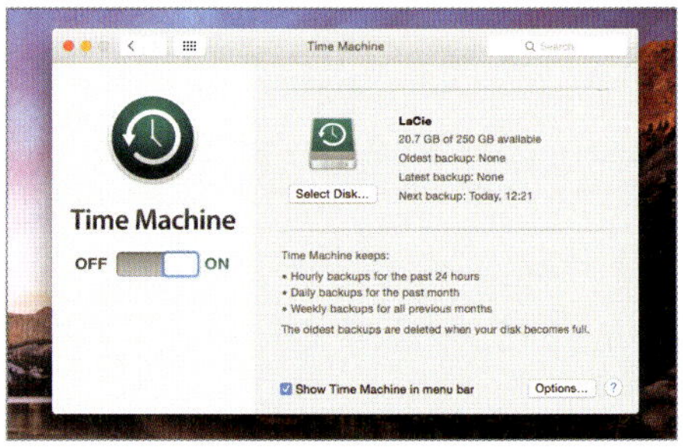

01: Launch Time Machine

Launch Time Machine by clicking the Time Machine icon in your menubar. Select the Options button in the bottom-right.

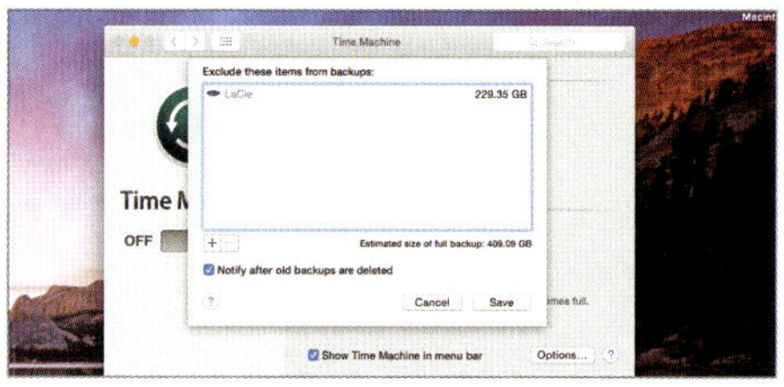

02: Browse your files

Press the '+' icon to choose files and folders that you don't want to back up. A Finder window will appear for you to browse.

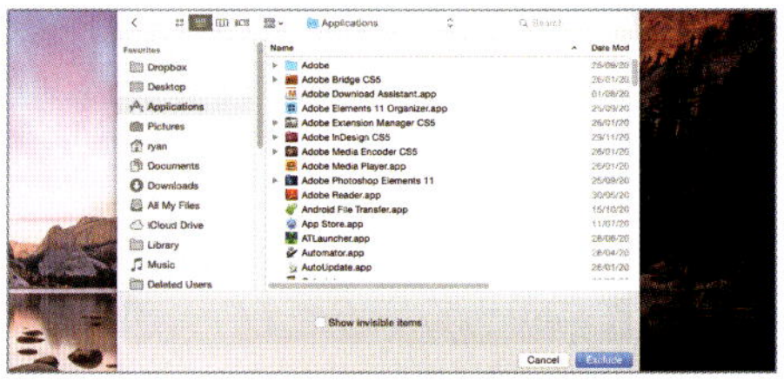

03: Exclude from backup

Navigate to the file or folder that you don't wish to backup. Repeat the last two steps until you've excluded all of your chosen files.

Choosing the right backup for you

A look at the different backup options

Apple Time Capsule £249

Apple's Time Capsule is a wireless backup solution, removing the need for cables and enabling several Macs to back up to it at once, while also doubling as a router and offering plentiful amounts of storage

SD card £12.95

SD cards are commonly found in digital cameras. Although their storage capacity is smaller and can only store limited files, most Macs have an SD card slot built in meaning that it's easy to move files onto them

RAID array/RAID drive £200

A RAID drive contains two hard disks that 'mirror' each other, meaning that your data backs up to both drives simultaneously. So if one drive fails, your data is safe and sound on the second hard drive

Portable hard drive £50

Portable hard drives are a great backup solution for people who are on-the-go frequently, such as business people. Portable hard drives are lightweight, no bigger than a passport and offer ample storage space

USB Flash drive £18.95

USB drives are built with Flash, meaning they have a lower failure rate than traditional hard drives with spinning disks. They're compact, can hang off your keyring and are perfect for storing important files

Setting up RAID

Use Disk Utility to set up a handy RAID drive

A RAID drive is the most secure and reliable way to back up your data. You can set it up in two ways. RAID 1 will copy all your data twice, once to each drive, so everything is safe even if one drive goes down. RAID 0 is much less secure, but much faster. It splits your data into two and stores half on each drive. This makes for speedy backups, but if one drive fails, all your data is corrupted. In this tutorial, we'll show you how to set up a RAID 1 drive.

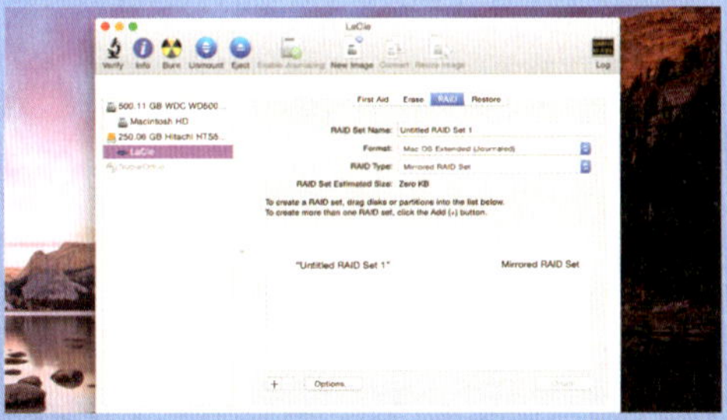

Select RAID Drive

Launch Disk Utility. Select your first RAID drive from the left. Click the RAID tab. Ensure the Format is 'Mac OSX Extended (Journaled)' and RAID Type is set to 'Mirrored RAID Set'.

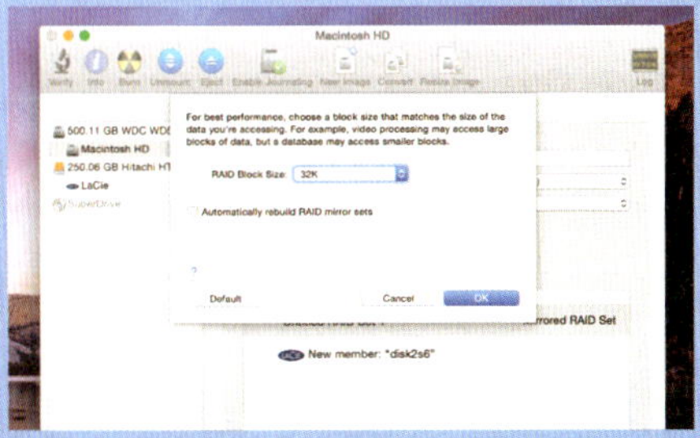

Customise RAID Drive

Drag both RAID disks into the blank box on the right-hand side. Click the Options button and set the RAID Block Size to 32K. Once you're happy, press OK.

Back up your Mac now

Set up Carbon Copy Cloner

Easily clone your hard drive onto an external hard drive

Carbon Copy Cloner is a great app for making one-off, complete backups of all data on your hard drive in preparation for tasks such as erasing your hard drive or upgrading to a newer operating system on your Mac.

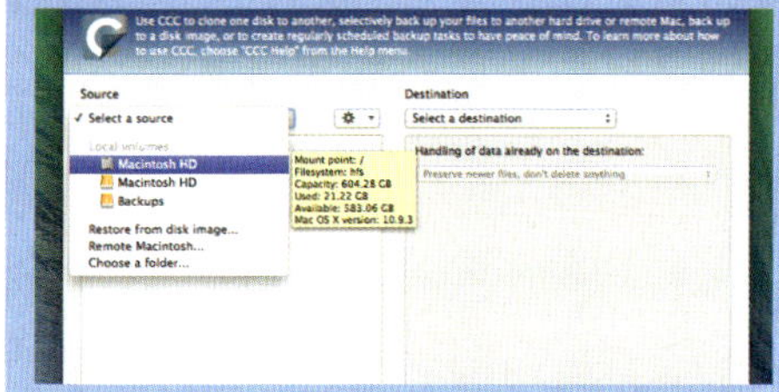

1: Choose file source

Launch Carbon Copy Cloner from your Applications folder. Click Source and select the drive where the data that you want to back up is stored.

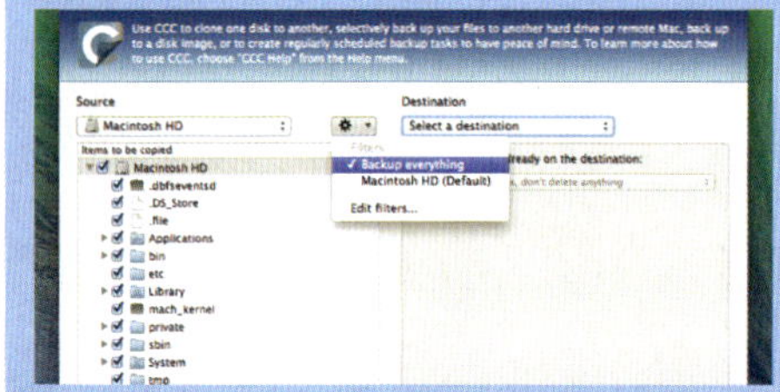

2: Choose backup drive

Click on the cog icon and select 'Backup everything' from the drop-down. Next, click on Destination, and choose your external backup drive from the list.

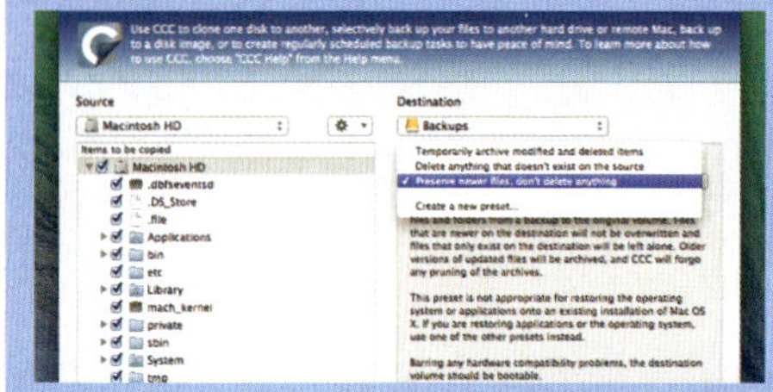

3: Start cloning

From 'Handling of data on the destination', select 'Preserve newer files, don't delete anything' – this stops existing data on your drive being deleted. Click Clone.

Back up specific files with Automator

Let your Mac back up specific files automatically

Automator is a built-in OS X app that enables you to create automated 'workflows' for repetitive tasks, saving you time and effort. There are hundreds of workflows that you can create, but the most common include renaming batches of files, setting birthday reminders and combining multiple PDFs into one PDF. In this tutorial, we're going to take a look at how you can use Automator to create a workflow that automatically backs up specific files and folders to your external back up drive.

The end result works in a similar way to Time Machine, but rather than backing up everything, it only backs up what you want it to – perfect if you only want to back up a few specific folders.

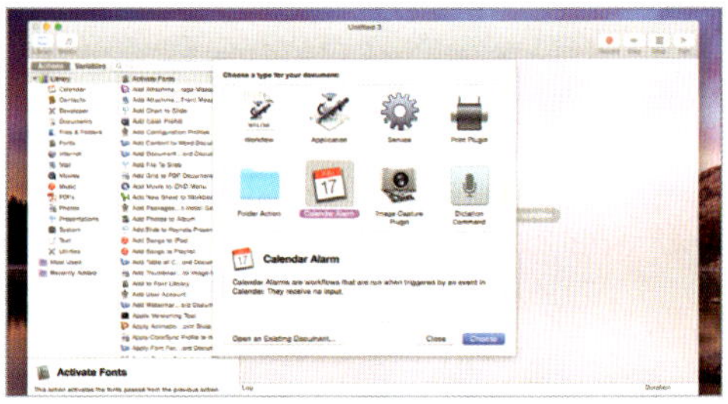

01: Launch Automator

Launch Automator. Select Calendar Alarm from the window and press Choose. Drag 'Get Specified Finder Items' into the blank space in the right-hand column.

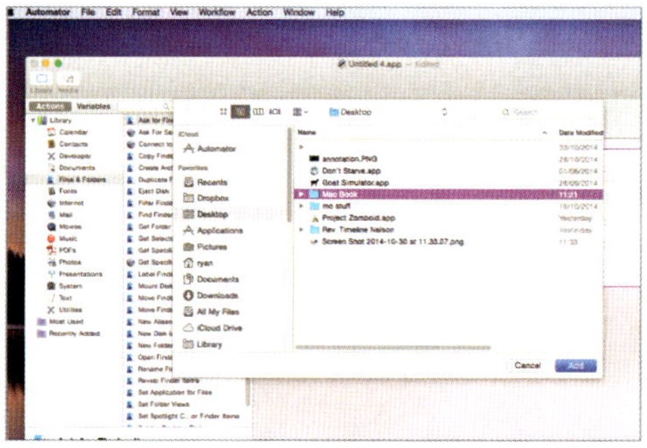

02: Add backup files

Click the Add button and choose the files and folders that you wish to back up. Hold down the Cmd key to add multiple files at once. Press the Add button.

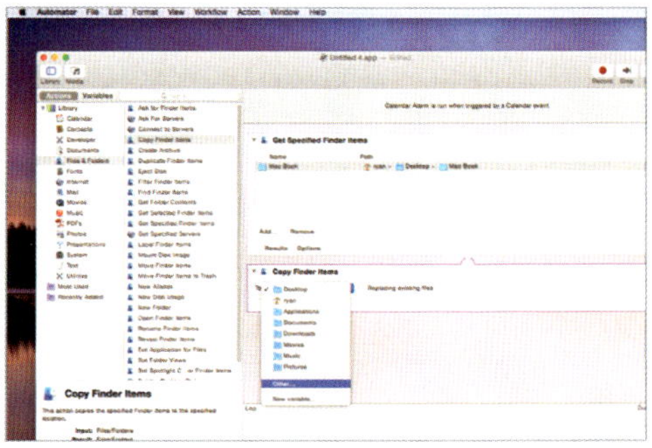

03: Test your workflow

Drag 'Copy Finder Items' to the right-hand column. In the To drop-down box, choose your external backup destination from the list. Click the Run icon to test the workflow.

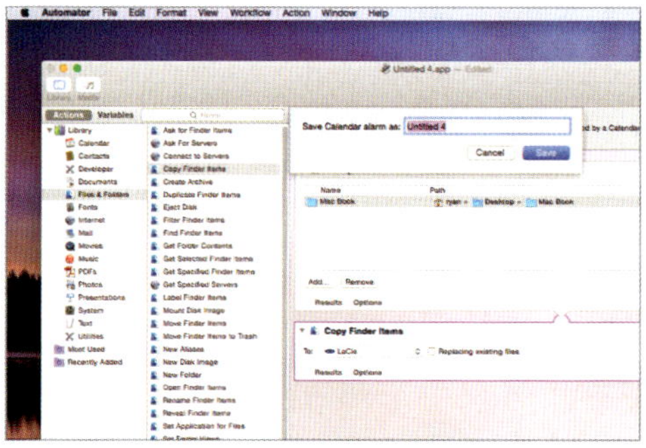

04: Save your workflow

Next, select File>Save and give a name for your workflow (this will appear on the Calendar alarm). Click Save. The Calendar app will open. Locate your new Calendar alarm.

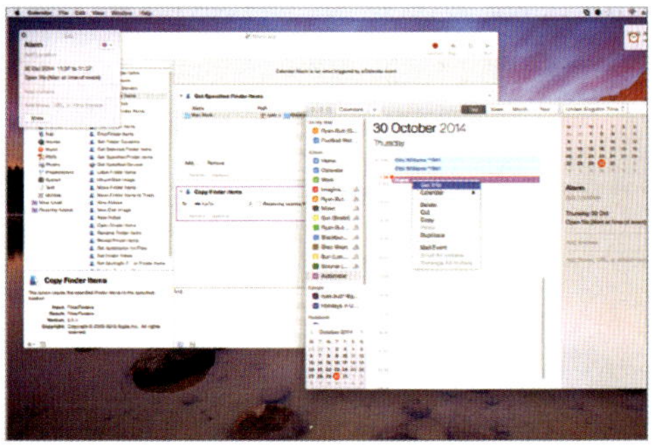

05: Repeat your backup

Right-click on the Calendar alarm and select Get Info. Change the default time and choose a Repeat time if you want the backup to run Daily, Weekly or Monthly.

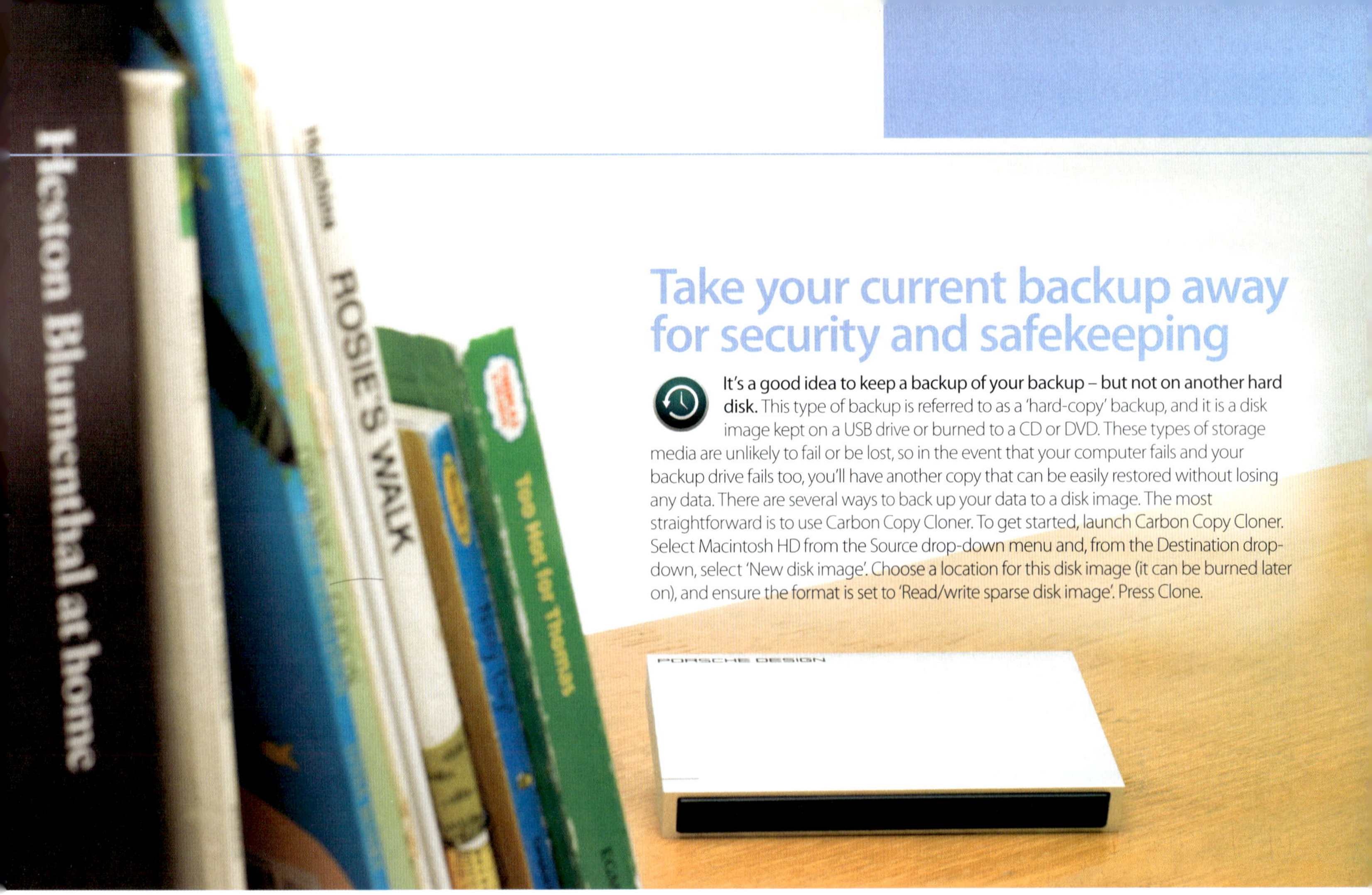

Take your current backup away for security and safekeeping

It's a good idea to keep a backup of your backup – but not on another hard disk. This type of backup is referred to as a 'hard-copy' backup, and it is a disk image kept on a USB drive or burned to a CD or DVD. These types of storage media are unlikely to fail or be lost, so in the event that your computer fails and your backup drive fails too, you'll have another copy that can be easily restored without losing any data. There are several ways to back up your data to a disk image. The most straightforward is to use Carbon Copy Cloner. To get started, launch Carbon Copy Cloner. Select Macintosh HD from the Source drop-down menu and, from the Destination drop-down, select 'New disk image'. Choose a location for this disk image (it can be burned later on), and ensure the format is set to 'Read/write sparse disk image'. Press Clone.

Back up hand-picked files

Save space by only backing up specific files

Backuplist helps you back up specific files and folders, which is perfect if you are running short of space on your external hard drive or simply don't want to back up absolutely everything on your Mac – this is a much quicker solution than excluding items from your Time Machine backup.

To get started, launch Backuplist and click Browse to add your external drive as the destination for your backup. Next, press the '+' button beneath the Source Files interface to choose the files that you want to back up. These files will be contained into a Backup Set, which remembers the files you've chosen, meaning you can back up these files again if you want to. Press '+' to keep adding files and folders. Once you're happy, press the Backup button to continue.

Partitioning hard drives for more effective sorting

Split your external drive into smaller drives for simpler organisation

If you've got different types of file to back up such as work and home files, it's a good idea to partition (split) your backup drive into smaller backup drives for better organisation of your data.

To do this, launch Disk Utility and select your external hard drive from the left-hand side. Click the Partition tab and press the '+' button to add a new partition. Give the new partitions a name, choose a size and press Apply.

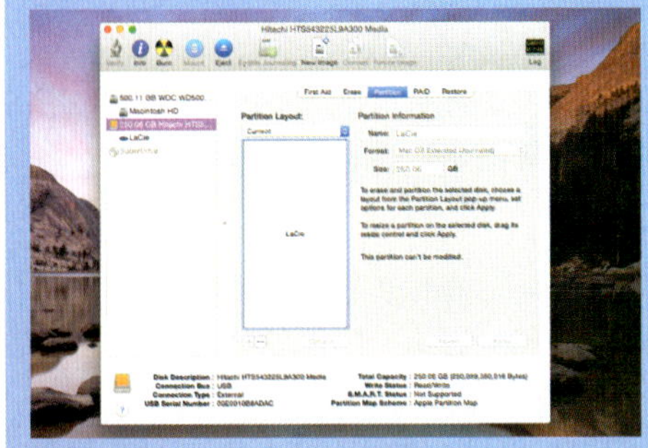

Back up your Mac now

Best online storage apps

Find the right online storage cloud solution for your Mac

If you're not looking to back up your whole Mac, an online cloud service may be the ideal solution. There are lots of services out there, so let's take a look at the most popular…

Dropbox

From £60/$99 for 100GB | 2GB Free
www.dropbox.com

Dropbox enables you to upload files or folders of your choice to your account. It offers Mac, PC, iOS and Android apps, meaning that you can access your data anywhere with an internet connection – the only drawback is that its overall pricing for storage is expensive compared to other providers.

Google Drive

From £0.99/$1.99 per month for 100GB 15GB Free
http://drive.google.com

Google Drive offers the most competitively priced cloud storage. Google Drive has Mac, iOS and Android apps so you can easily access and manage your data anywhere. Although the storage plans are well priced, the storage is shared across Gmail, Google Docs and Google+.

OneDrive

From £30/$50 for 50 GB | 7GB Free
http://onedrive.live.com

OneDrive comes with a generous 7GB of free space, which can be increased to 15GB by referring friends and enabling Camera Uploads, and the UI is easy to use. However, there's an upload size limitation of 2GB per file, or 300MB if you're uploading files via the website.

Complete online backup solutions

Back up your Mac's data automatically and securely online

Backing up your data to an online cloud service is a relatively new phenomenon and one that has become possible thanks to increased internet speeds and security technology. There are a variety of different companies that offer online backups, now with fairly competitive prices. The main advantage of an online backup is that if your computer stops working, your data is stored securely offsite, meaning that you can easily restore it back to a new computer.

However, there are some disadvantages to online backups that need bearing in mind: if the servers where your data is stored are hacked or fail, your personal data will be at risk – or worse still, lost. Upload speeds for online backups are also much slower, as it is solely dependant on the internet speed in your area. Online backups are a great solution, but should not be used alone – have a hard copy backed up to an external drive for added security. Let's take a look at two of the most popular services.

	Backblaze	CrashPlan
Available storage	Unlimited	Unlimited
Pricing	$5 a month per computer	$5 a month for one computer, $12.50 for up to 10
Number of backups	Unlimited	Up to 10 computers

Backblaze | Back up using Backblaze

01: Launch Backblaze

Launch Backblaze from your Applications folder (download a free 30-day trial from www.backblaze.com). Backblaze will begin backing up your data online automatically.

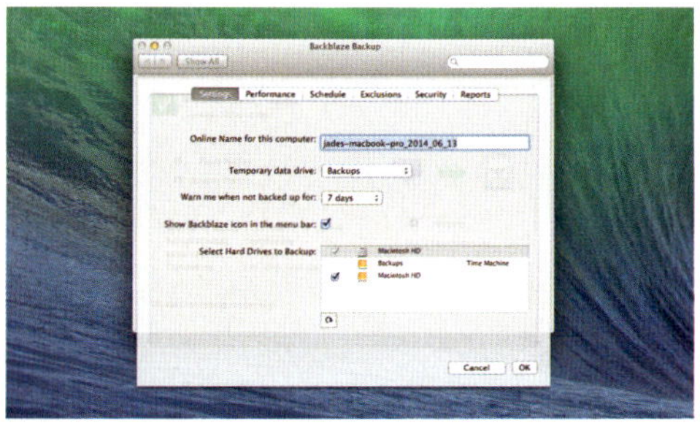

02: Customise your backup

Click Settings to choose the hard drives to back up – you can back up external drives, too. Select the Exclusions tab to choose files and folders that you don't want backed up.

Backup options with iCloud

Back up files from all your Apple devices

iCloud is Apple's signature cloud service. Built in to OS X and iOS as standard, it offers a variety of features such as iOS device backup, syncing of Contacts, Calendars, Notes and Reminders, and also storage and syncing of Documents created in Pages, Numbers and Keynote across all of your Apple devices. You can also sync your photos wirelessly between your iOS device and iPhoto for Mac. With the release of iOS 8 and OS X Yosemite, iCloud users can now update to iCloud Drive, which offers a bulkier, more versatile way to store files and access them across devices and other apps (not just the ones used to originally create the files). Let's have a look at your iCloud options in more detail.

iCloud | iCloud backup options

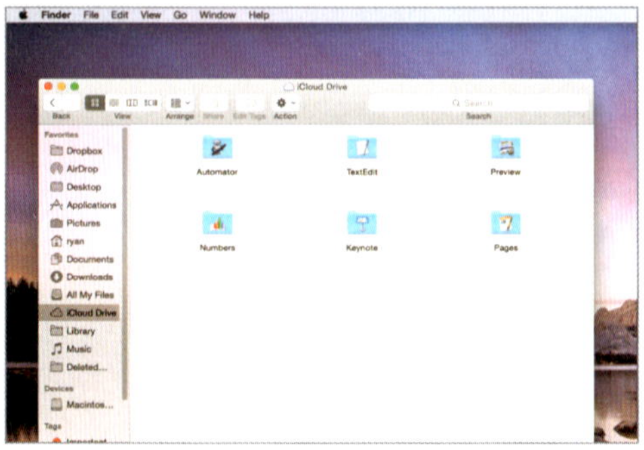

01: Documents and data

Store documents that you're working on in iCloud – access and edit them from any Apple device (iWork must be installed for editing).

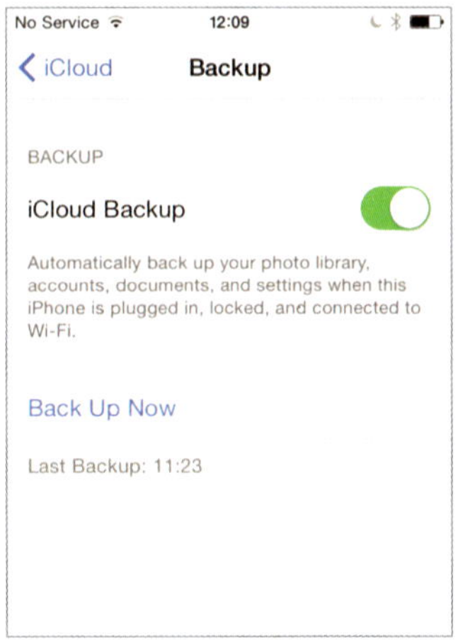

02: iOS device backup

iCloud offers a backup service for your iOS devices. iCloud will automatically back up your device when it's connected to the mains, a known Wi-Fi network and is asleep.

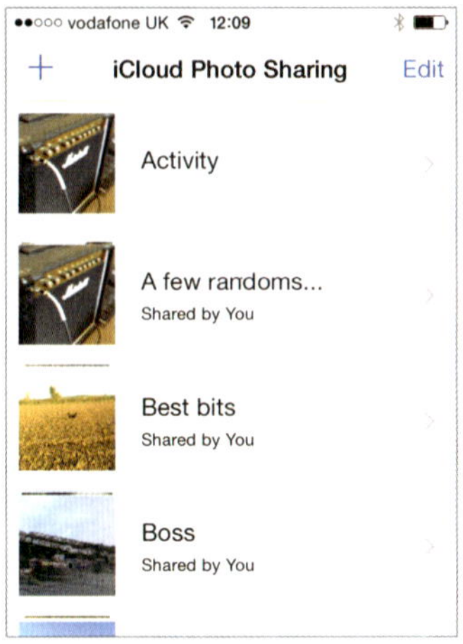

03: Photo Stream

Photo Stream automatically syncs photos taken on your iOS devices to your iCloud, syncing the most recent 1,000 photos you havzze taken with your iOS device.

OS X Yosemite's expanded iCloud

Discover some awesome new iCloud features

With the release of iOS 8 and Mac OS X Yosemite, Apple has ramped up its iCloud offering with some handy new features, which will make the storage and sharing of your files and folders across all your Apple devices a much more seamless and pleasant experience. We're going to take a quick look below at what you can expect from some of the new iCloud features when you upgrde to iOS 8 and OS X Yosemite. Transferring files to your iCloud Drive on Mac is as easy as dragging files to the iCloud Drive folder (open a new window and you'll see the iCloud Drive folder listed under Favourites in the side-bar. These files will then be accessible from any mobile iOS device, Mac or PC (using a web browser). It really couldn't be easier.

Photo backup

All of your photos on your Mac and iOS devices will back up to iCloud automatically. You can also upload your entire Photo Library to iCloud Drive.

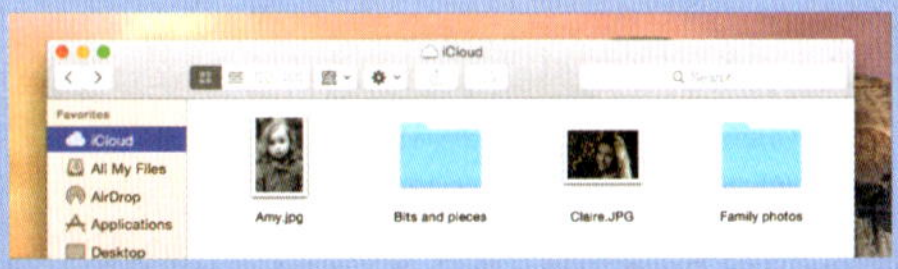

iCloud Drive

Upload, sync and edit important files and folders on any Apple device using iCloud Drive. iCloud offers 5GB of free storage, with extra starting from $0.99 per month.

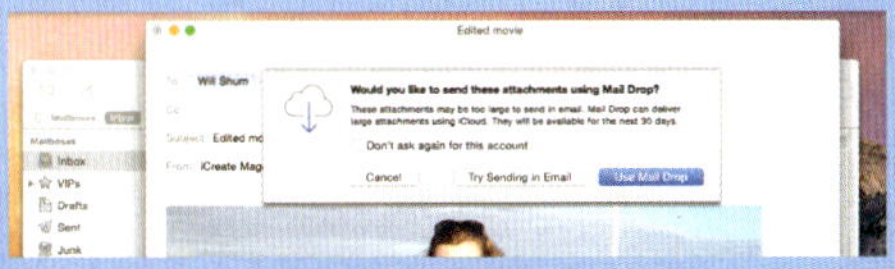

Mail Drop

In a feature named Mail Drop, Apple has increased the size limit of email attachments for iCloud users. You'll be able to email files of up to 5GB in size.

Getting started

All the basics are covered right here to get you in control of your Mac

42 Tailor your desktop

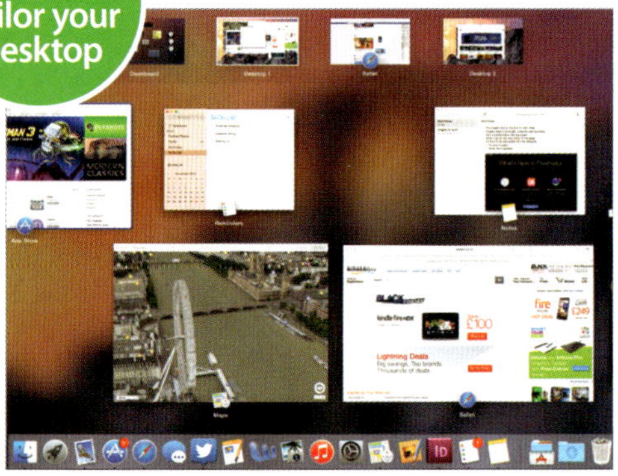

"Mac OS X helps you to customise your experience"

32
Connect to Wi-Fi

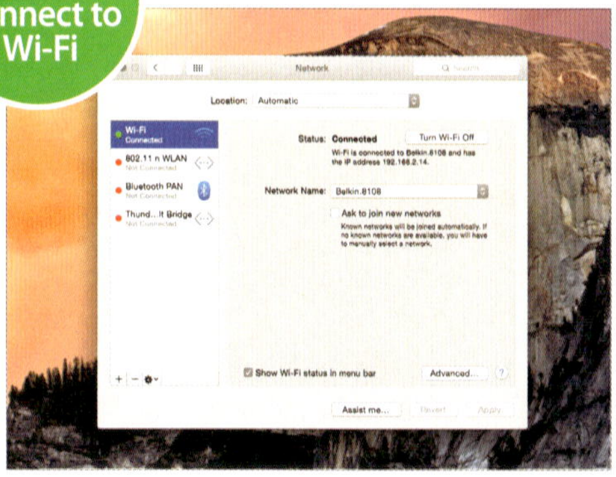

50
Change your settings

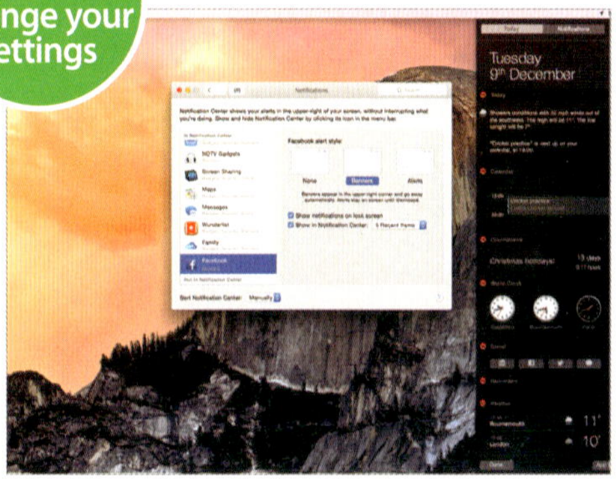

68
Share via the web

Connect to the internet

Gain access to the world wide web by hooking up your Mac to Wi-Fi

To get the most out of your new iMac or MacBook, you will want to connect it to the internet. Luckily, this is a simple process regardless of whether you choose to use either a wired or wireless connection to your router.

If you wish to connect your Mac to the internet with a wired connection, all you need to do is plug one end of an Ethernet cable into your Mac, and the other into your router. If you plan to go wireless, then you don't need any more equipment than your Mac and a wireless-enabled router.

Follow the four simple steps outlined below and you'll soon be able to access a whole host of content: you'll be able to browse the web with Safari, stay in touch with friends and family on Facebook, send emails in the Mail app, download tons of great new apps from the Mac App Store, share videos in iMovie, and much, much more. A whole world of entertainment awaits you!

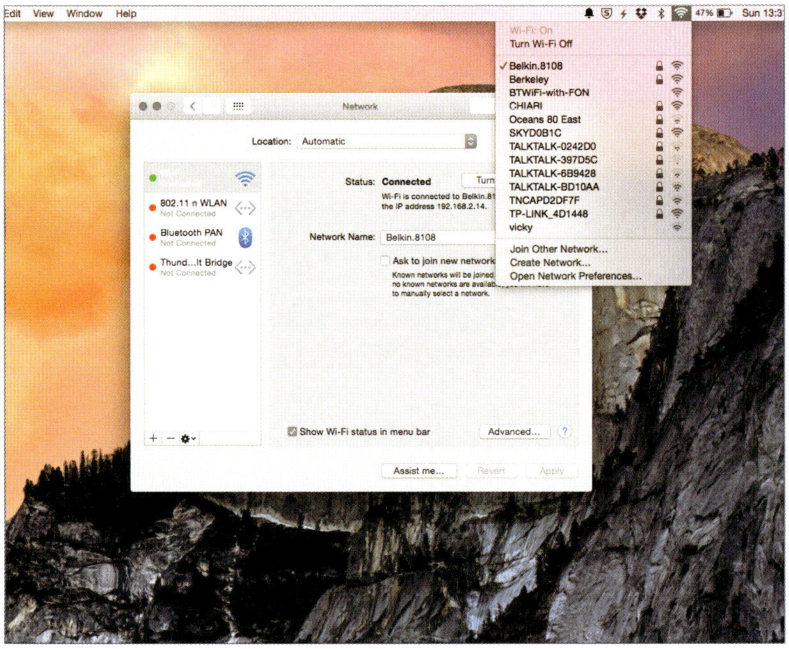

OS X Turn Wi-Fi on and go online

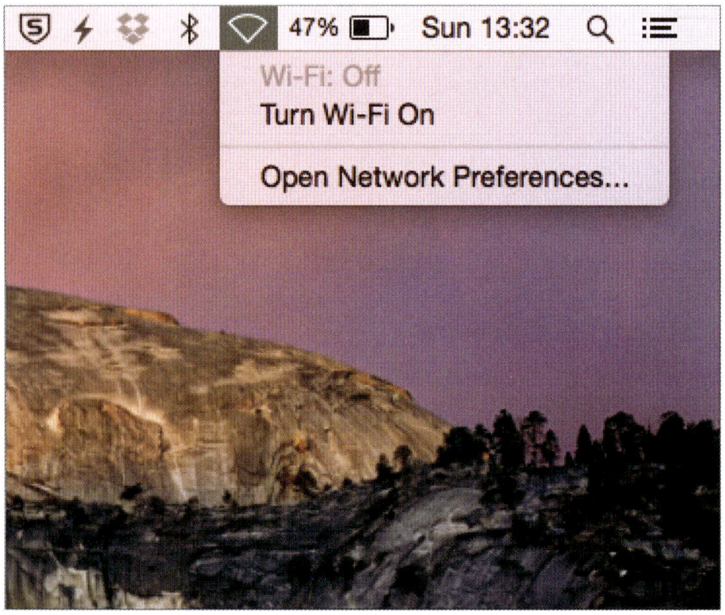

01: Turn it on

Although it should be on by default, your Mac's Wi-Fi may be turned off. If it's off, click on the icon to the left of the time and date in the top bar, then click turn Wi-Fi on.

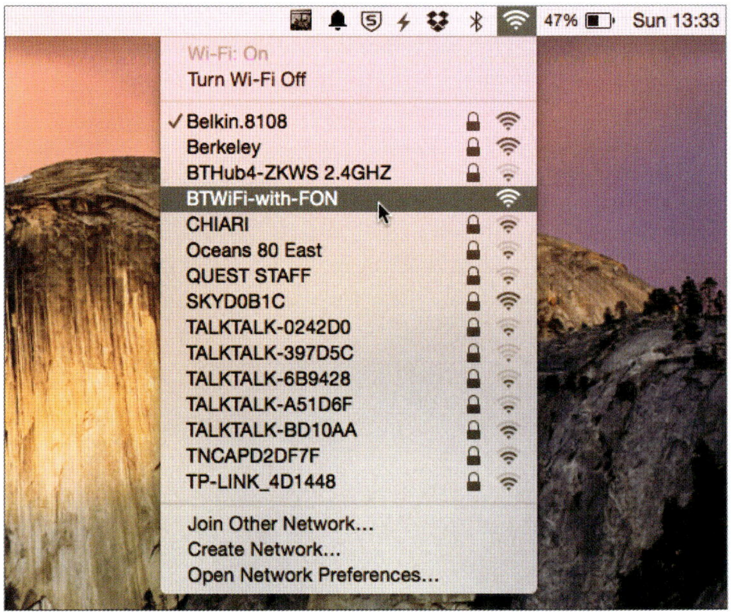

02: Look for networks

Once you've turned Wi-Fi on, the icon should turn into a greyed-out series of curved lines. Click on it, wait a couple of a seconds for a list of available networks to show, then click on your home network.

Network Preferences

How to control your Wi-Fi connection

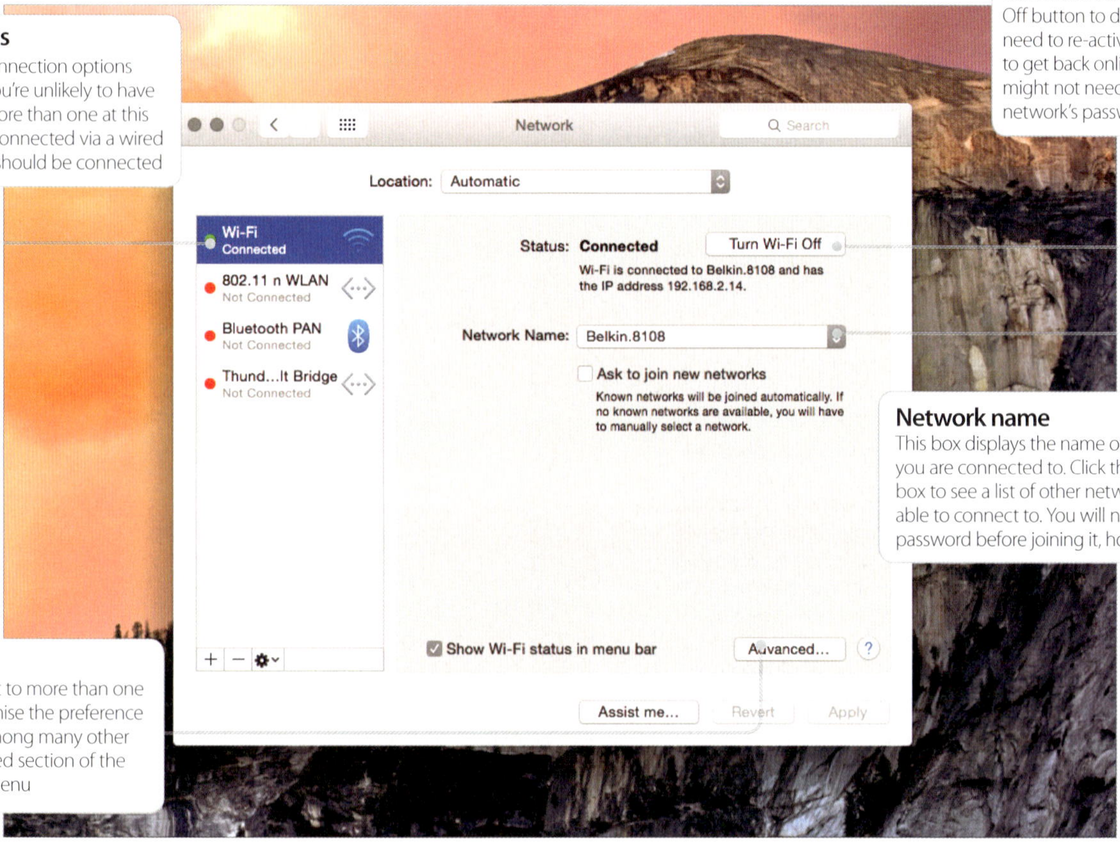

List of connections

Here are the various connection options that your Mac offers. You're unlikely to have a green light next to more than one at this point in time. If you're connected via a wired connection, 'Ethernet' should be connected

Status

When you're successfully on a Wi-Fi- network, this will always say 'Connected'. Click the Turn Wi-Fi Off button to do just that. You will need to re-activate it if you want to get back online; however, you might not need to enter your network's password again

Network name

This box displays the name of the network you are connected to. Click this drop-down box to see a list of other networks that you're able to connect to. You will need a network's password before joining it, however

Advanced

If you regularly connect to more than one network, you can organise the preference of these networks – among many other things – in the Advanced section of the Network Preferences menu

03: Connect to your network

For the first time you connect, you'll have to enter your network's passcode, which may be written on the back of your router. Once you've entered it, click 'Join' to connect to the internet.

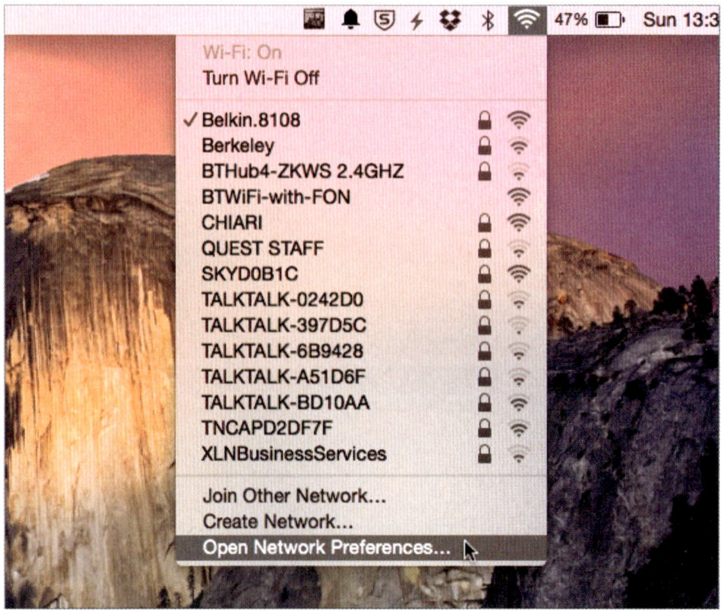

04: Edit preferences

Now you're connected, the greyed-out curved lines should be black. To edit your connection preferences, click on the icon, then click on 'Open Network Preferences'. You will then be taken to the System Preferences app.

Add a new user account

Share your Mac with the family by creating multiple user accounts

Your brand new Mac is packed with so many great features, both in its software and hardware, that it begs to be used by the whole family. However, you may not want each member changing the computer's settings or having access to your personal files every time they wish to use it. This is where multiple accounts come in.

Not only does having multiple accounts enable you to protect your private data, it also lets you protect children. It's simple to set up an account with Parental Controls, which enable you to limit access to apps and websites, as well as set usage time limits.

There's also a degree of customisation available. Not only can you set your own picture using the iSight camera (so you don't need to settle for stock imagery), you can also set which apps you would like to load as soon as you log in. Multiple user accounts are a great way to keep the whole family safe while still enabling them to enjoy your Mac.

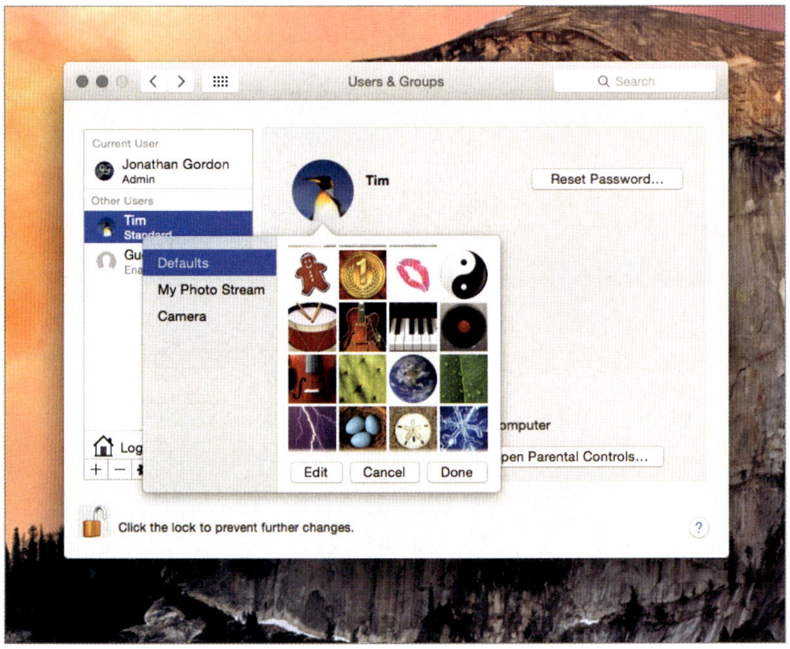

OS X Create and add a new user

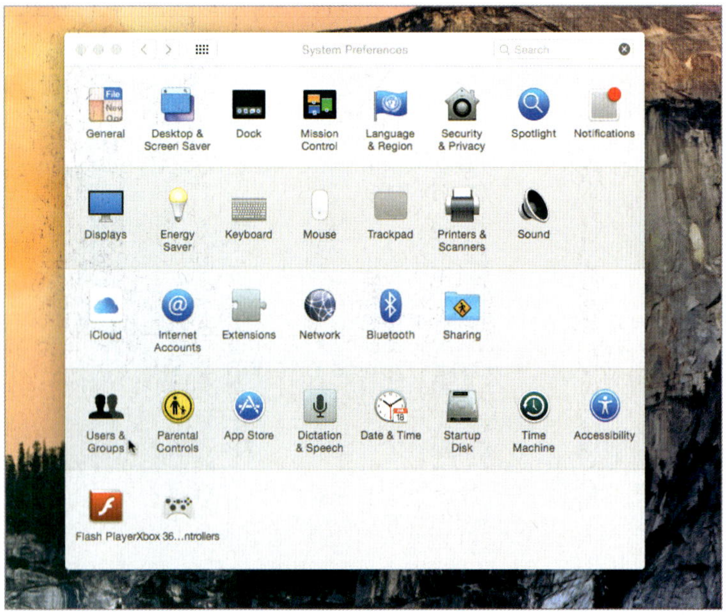

01: System Preferences

Click on the System Preferences app (three grey cogs) in the Dock to open it up, and another menu will appear. From this menu, click 'Users & Groups', which is in the fourth category down, 'System'.

02: Add new user

Click the padlock icon to enable changes, and click the + button to add a new user. If setting an account for a child, click the 'New Account' drop-down box and select 'Managed With Parental Controls'.

Parental Controls

Keep a child safe when they're using your Mac

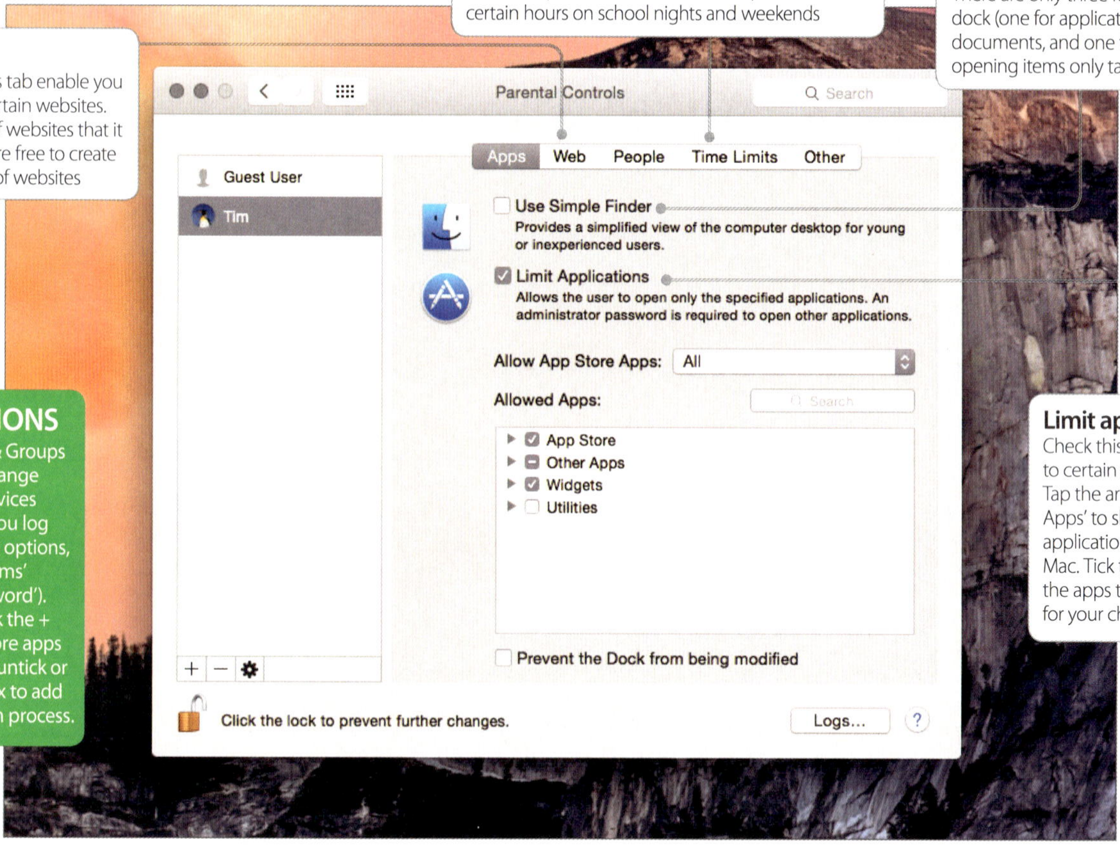

Web tab

The options under this tab enable you to restrict access to certain websites. Apple provides a list of websites that it deems safe, but you are free to create your own custom list of websites

Time Limits tab

This handy tab lets you limit time spent on the Mac. You can set Weekday time limits, Weekend time limits and prevent access to the computer between certain hours on school nights and weekends

Simple Finder

The Simple Finder is a stripped-down version of Apple's desktop environment. There are only three folders on the dock (one for applications, another for documents, and one for sharing), and opening items only takes one click

Limit apps

Check this box to limit access to certain apps on your Mac. Tap the arrow next to 'Other Apps' to show a list of all the applications installed on your Mac. Tick the boxes next to the apps that you are happy for your children to use

LOGIN OPTIONS

In the main User & Groups menu, you can change which apps or services open as soon as you log in. To access these options, click the 'Login Items' tab (next to 'Password'). Here, you can click the + symbol to add more apps and services, and untick or tick their checkbox to add them to your login process.

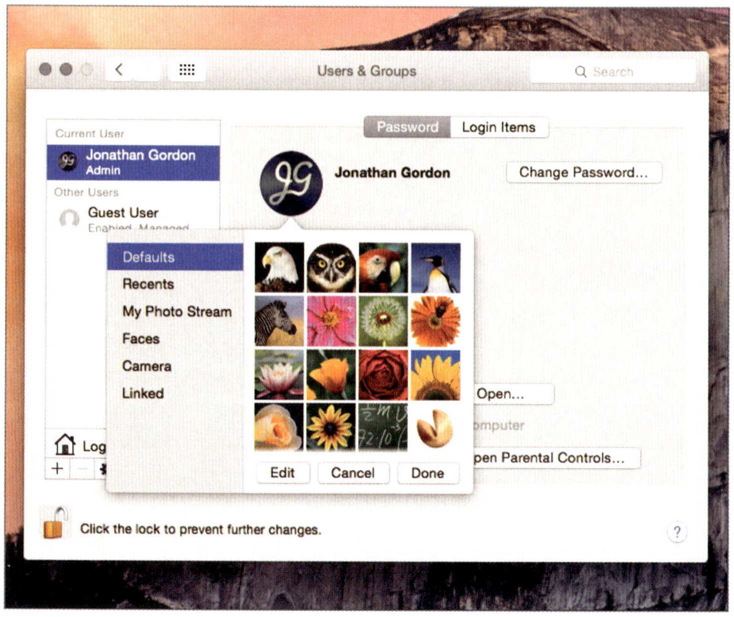

03: Set the picture

After entering a password and clicking 'Create User' you will have a new account on your Mac. To change the account's default picture, click the image next to 'Reset Password…'. To take a picture click the Camera tab, then the camera icon.

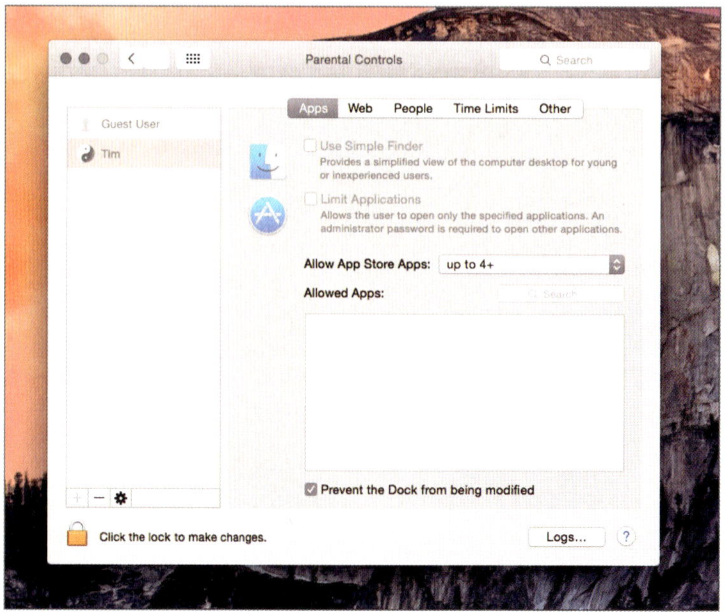

04: Parental Controls

After you've set your picture, click 'Open Parental Controls…' to access the parental controls. The tabs across the top grant access to several different ways to limit access to your Mac, including the ability to set time limits on usage.

Where is everything kept on your Mac?

A common problem is keeping track of your files and folders. Let's put an end to that

It happens to even the most experienced of us – you absent-mindedly put something somewhere and the next thing you know you're searching around wondering where you had it last. It happens to your car keys and it happens to the files and folders on your Mac. Luckily, your Mac makes it easy to save your stuff in the right place, quickly and often without having to think about it. The key to this is how your Mac handles Home folders, which are a special set of folders that are automatically created for each person that has a user account on your Mac. Know your way around here and you may never get lost on your Mac again.

Find the right folder

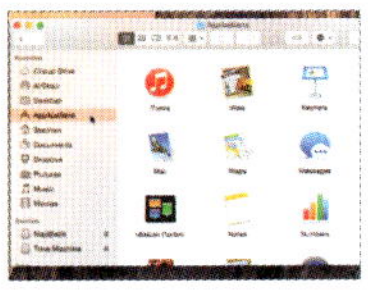

Finder sidebar

Every Finder window has shortcuts to the common folders in your Home folder. Click on one to head there.

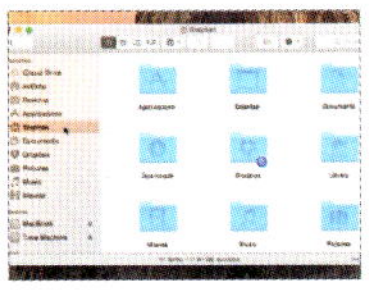

Head Home

Set new Finder windows to open your Home folder (see steps below) and you'll have common folders to hand.

Keyboard shortcuts

In the Go menu, there are a host of helpful keyboard and menu shortcuts to get you to your favourite folders.

OS X Tweak your Mac to get around quicker

01: A home in every window

To automatically show your Home folder when you open a new Finder window, choose Preferences from the Finder menu.

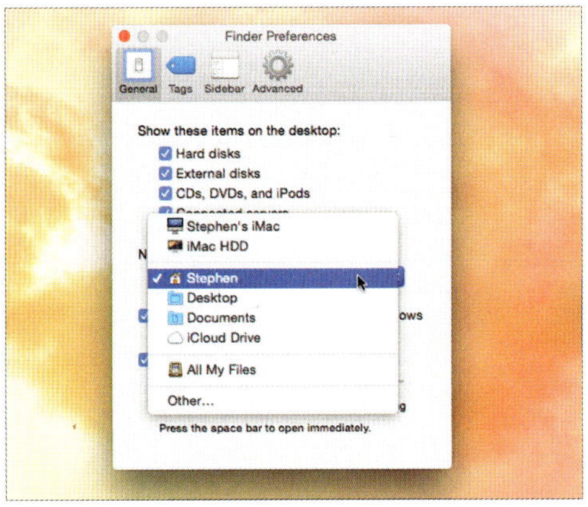

02: Home sweet home

While in the General tab, choose your personal Home from the 'New Finder windows open' menu to set your preference.

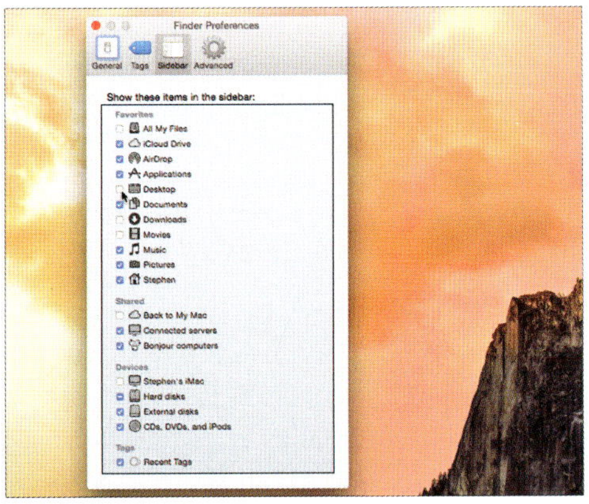

03: Trim Finder sidebars

Click the Sidebar tab and you can choose to turn off any Finder window sidebar shortcuts that you don't think you'll need.

04: Getting ticked off

Just click the checkboxes next to the options to remove them from every sidebar. You can always change your mind later if you wish.

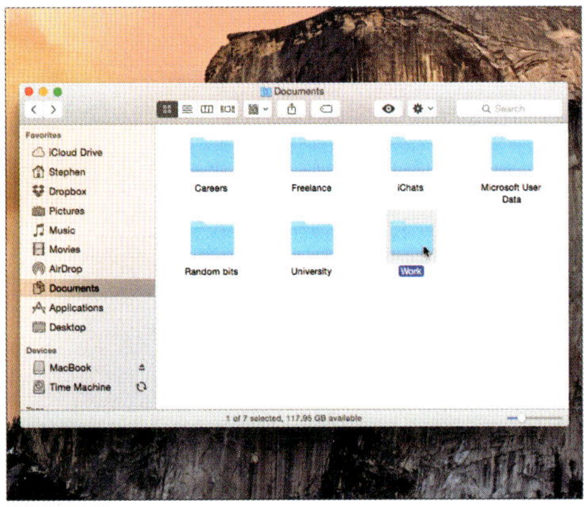

05: Set your own shortcuts

To get your own folder to appear in every Finder sidebar so you can get to it quickly, start by finding the folder on your Mac.

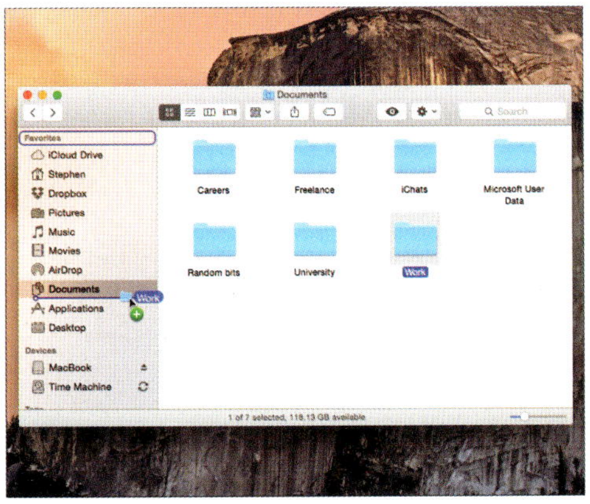

06: Drag it on, drag it off

Click on the folder and drag it into the sidebar and your Mac will pop in a shortcut. To get rid of it, just click on it and drag it back out again.

Folder by folder: what's where on your Mac…

Take a moment to snoop around your system and you may quickly become overwhelmed at the array of folders hidden away. Luckily, you only really need to know about just a few of the important ones

Macintosh HD

This is the first folder that contains everything else. It represents the physical storage device inside your Mac, called the Hard Drive.

Applications

Here's where you'll find all of the software that came with your Mac.

Utilities

This is where you'll find the programs you'll need for making tweaks.

The Library and System folders

With the innards that make your Mac tick exposed inside the Library and System folders, it's best to steer clear of these two!

Users

This folder contains the Home folders for every person that shares your Mac. This helps to give everyone the ability to have their own settings, music, bookmarks, photos, emails and documents. It doesn't have to all be separate though, and there's a shared folder in here too.

Your Home folder

This is where you'll find everything that makes your Mac yours – your files, folders, photos, settings and even your desktop. Luckily, it is easy to find, and so this is the starting point for finding or saving your documents. Learn the shortcuts (Cmd+Shift+H) to get here fast.

Shared

Any files stored in here will be accessible to all the users of the Mac – great for sharing documents.

Other people's Home folders

Even if it's your Mac, you won't be able to see what's inside the Home folders of the other users.

Desktop

Anything you dump on your desktop is really kept here inside this folder.

Used by: You, when you want to put a file somewhere quickly.

Documents

This is your general storage area for all your everyday, miscellaneous files and folders.

Used by: Most applications that don't use another folder.

Downloads

When you download a file from the internet and you haven't changed the default folder, it'll be saved to this folder.

Used by: Safari.

Library

The Mac's Library is used to save your preferences, settings and fonts – helping you to personalise your Mac.

Used by: Most applications.

Movies

This is where iMovie will save projects, and so it's where other iLife apps will look for your videos if you want to add them to other projects.

Used by: The iLife apps.

Music

iTunes will create a folder in here for its library, adding any tracks you rip as well as media you buy from the store.

Used by: iTunes.

Pictures

This is the default folder for your pictures, so it is used by iPhoto for its library. Photo Booth also uses it.

Used by: iPhoto and Photo Booth.

Navigate the folders in your Home folder

Your Home folder is your 'safe place' on your Mac – it's where you'll save your files, folders, photos, movies, music and more. Learn your way around it and you'll go a long way toward mastering Mac OS X and your Mac

Public

These last two folders are the only ones that other users can look inside. As the Shared folder does a better job, you'll probably never use them.

Used by: Hardly anyone.

Sites

If you're up for some tricky setting up, you can publish a website from your Mac. Most people won't though.

Used by: Fewer people than the Public folder!

Set up iCloud in OS X

Access your contacts, photos and documents everywhere

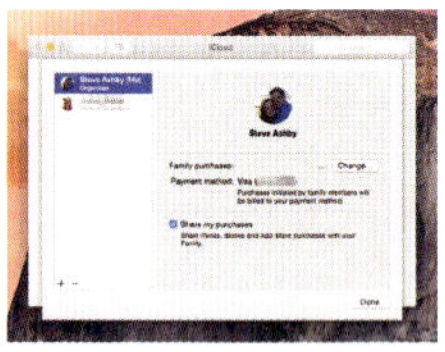

When you hear people talking about the cloud, what they mean is using the web to provide various services for computers and internet-connected devices, wherever you may be. iCloud is Apple's online hub for Macs, iPhones, iPads and iPod touch. Some companies provide general services that anyone can use, but iCloud has been optimised for Apple devices. It is primarily a syncing service, but it also provides an online storage facility for all of your files, apps and music.

The greatest benefit of using iCloud is that it enables email, contacts, calendar appointments, reminders, photos, notes and more to be synced across all your devices, and made available to you no matter where you are or which device you're currently using. You can create a document on your Mac and access it via an iPad, or add a contact on your iPhone and find it instantly appearing on your Mac.

iCloud is very easy to set up, even if you are new to the service, and in around five minutes it can be up and running. It's one of the first things you will see when you boot up a new Mac or if you log in to a Mac with a new user account; it's even easier if you already have an iCloud or iTunes account. And thanks to the new iCloud Drive service, you can use your iCloud storage like an online folder. Once set up, you can simply drag and drop any file you want into your iCloud Drive on the Mac to upload it, so you can access it anywhere.

iCloud provides 5GB of free online storage and this is more than sufficient for most. Extra space is available for purchase, which is great if you take hundreds of photos or want to store lots of files or music. You can buy 20GB, 200GB, 500GB or even 1TB of space. You can also access all your files even when you're away from your Mac; all you need is a computer with a web browser and you can log in at **www.icloud.com** to access them. Once you've used iCloud with OS X, you may very quickly wonder how you ever lived without it.

"Once you've used iCloud with OS X, you may very quickly wonder how you ever lived without it"

iCloud Get started with iCloud

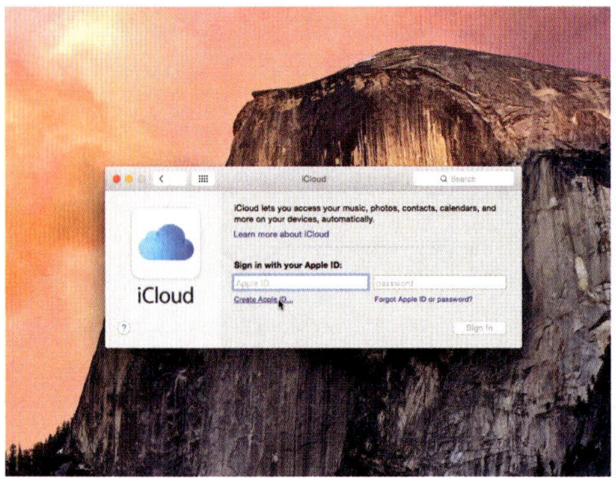

01: Sign in

You can open System Preferences and choose the iCloud section to log in. If you already have an Apple ID, use it here, or click to create a new account.

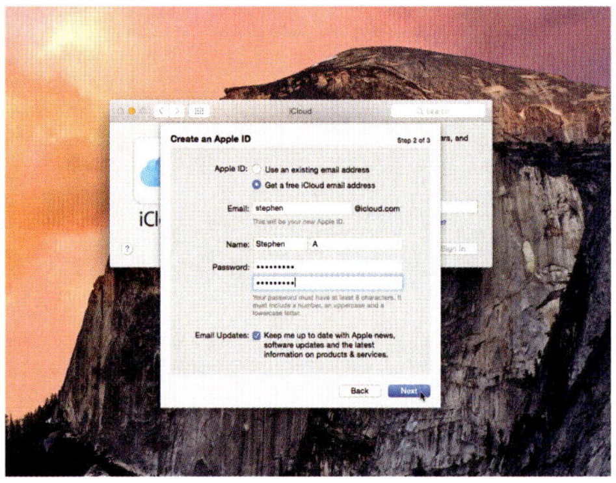

02: Free email accounts

After entering your birthday, you must add your name and email address. Even if you already have an email account, it's useful to get a free @icloud.com address.

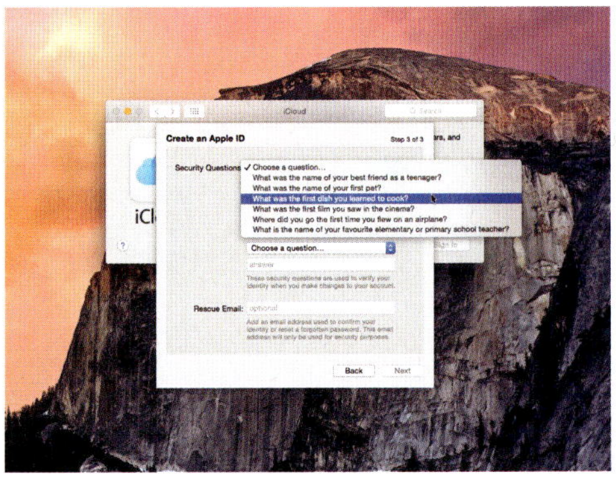

03: Call for security

As part of the signup process for iCloud, you will be asked to create three security questions. Make these memorable, as they're needed to reset your password.

Get connected to iCloud

Keep everything in sync with your Mac

Space evaders

Keep an eye on this bar at the bottom of the window. It gives you an overall view of the amount of storage space you're currently using – you get 5GB for free

Enable iCloud Drive

Check this box at the top of the list to activate iCloud Drive. This is like an online folder – drag and drop files into it to access them on any device

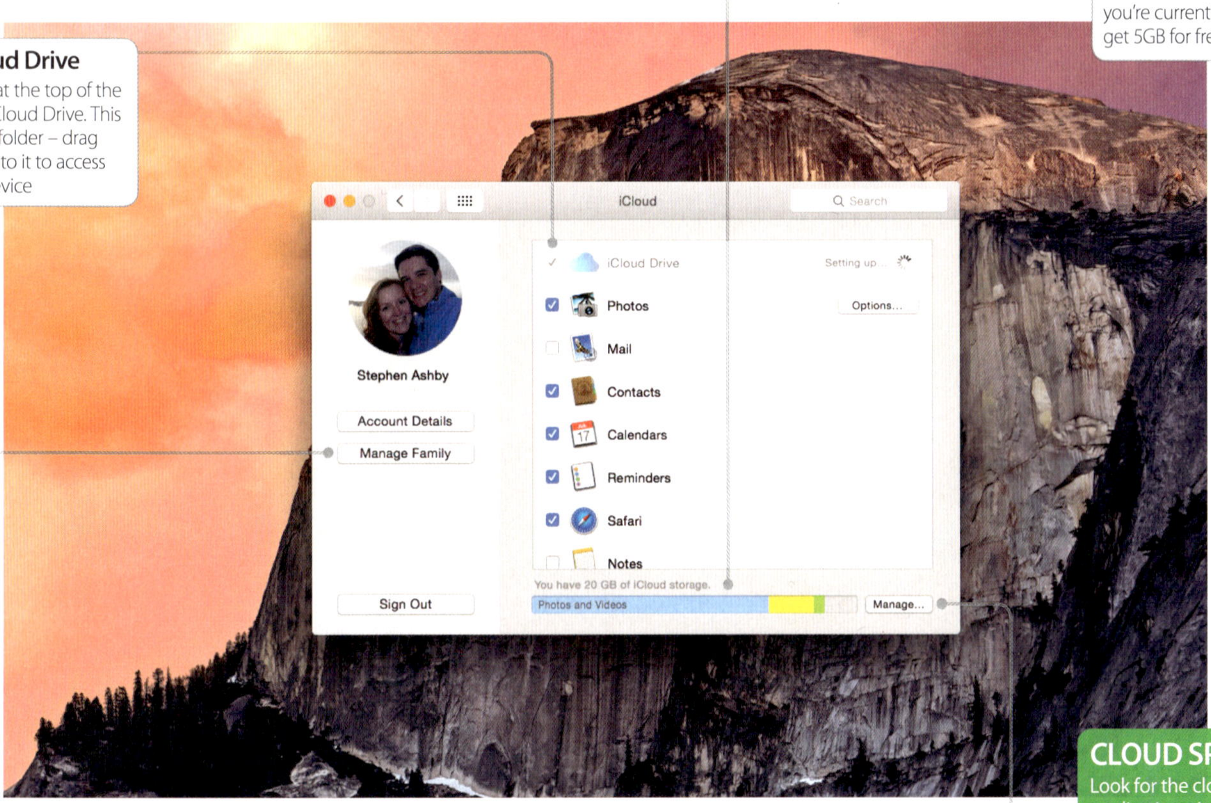

CLOUD SPOTTING

Look for the cloud icon in applications; it indicates that some feature or function uses iCloud. For example, if you start TextEdit, you'll see options to create documents on the Mac or in iCloud. Safari has a cloud button too, as do many other apps.

Manage Family

If several people in your family use iTunes accounts, you can link them all by clicking this button. This way, you can monitor and manage what your kids are buying

Manage your account

This button opens a window that shows which apps are using iCloud and the amount of space they are hogging. Click this if you are running short on storage

04: Set up iCloud

It couldn't be simpler and the final step is just to tick the iCloud features on for your apps and enable Find My Mac, then OS X will do the rest. In seconds.

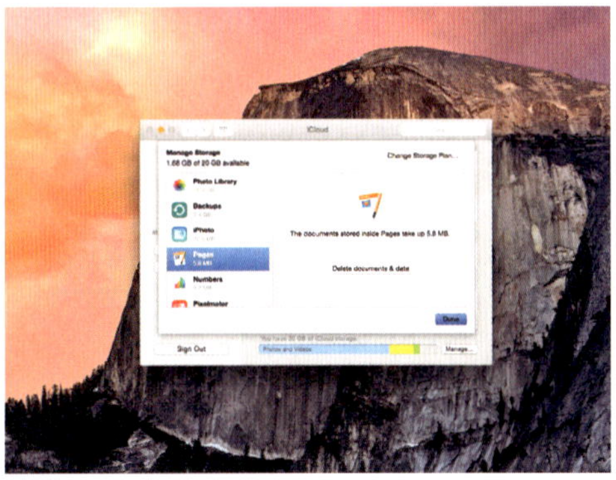

05: Manage storage

Click System Preferences in the Apple menu and hit the iCloud icon. Click Manage in the bottom right and you can see what accesses iCloud and the space it uses.

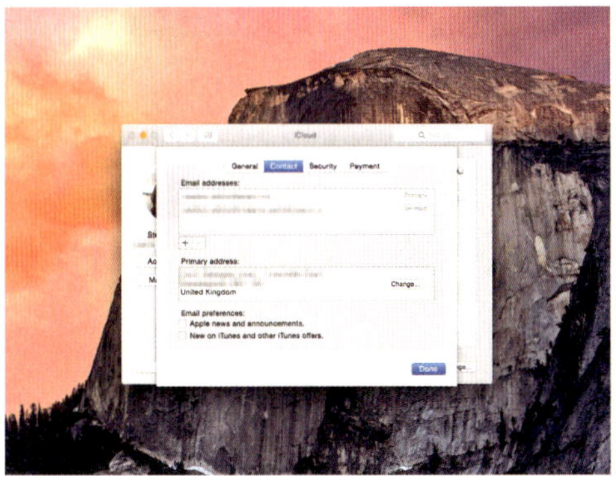

06: Update your account

Click Account Details to browse your details. You can change your name and photo, or add a credit card for iTunes, iCloud and other purchases too.

Work with applications

Without applications your Mac would just be a beautiful table decoration. Time to fire up some incredible creative tools…

It's easy to think of your Mac as a wonderfully creative toolbox, packed to the brim with inspirational tools to finely hone your projects. Those tools are the software saved on your hard drive, the applications. Software, for the most part, is kept in the Applications folder – a shared folder that any user of the Mac can see and open applications from. The beauty of Mac OS X is that each user's version of an application can behave differently and use different files, the same way that each user can have an individual iTunes library. Of course, before you start learning how to use specific applications, it's worth taking a moment to look at how you open, close and switch between them, which is just what we're going to do here.

Five ways you can start an application

You need to open an app before you can start playing with it

01: Launch it from the Dock

Apple places the most used icons in the Dock, where they require a single click to launch. You can add your favourite programs by dragging the app's icon down among the others.

02: In the applications folder

If there's an app you want to launch that's not in the Dock, click Applications in a Finder window sidebar, and scroll through the software list until you find it, then double-click its icon.

03: Double-click a file

Mac OS X is smart enough to launch the right application when you double-click a file that belongs to it. This is often the quickest method if you're working on a specific project.

04: Launch it using Spotlight

Click on the magnifying glass in the top-right corner of the screen, then start typing the name of the app you want to launch. When it appears, and it's highlighted, just hit Return.

05: Plug something in

There are some applications that are smart enough to launch automatically when you need them – iPhoto can launch when you plug in a digital camera, for instance.

The Application menu

Clicking an application's name in the menu bar gives you a few options for how you see (or don't see) it…

Hide The application's still running, but it will be hidden from view. Click its Dock icon to bring it back.

Hide others Want to focus on just one app? This option clears your screen of all other software.

Show All Brings back all the applications you've hidden.

Quit Closes down the application you're working in, giving you the option to save any unsaved work

The red button

The great thing about Apple is that there's a wonderful consistency to the products. Once you get used to the way something works you know it's going to work the same way for everything. Except on the very rare occasions it doesn't. For most apps, clicking the red button just closes that window, leaving the application running – go on, try it in iTunes. Now try the same thing in iPhoto and the app automatically quits when the window shuts. Now there is a rhyme and reason for this, and it has to do with how the application works with Windows, but for most people it's just plain confusing!

Five ways you can close an application

Finished playing? Close it down…

01: Application menu

Click on the application's name in the menu bar and choose Quit from the options.

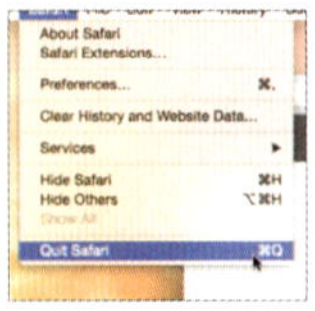

02: Learn the shortcut

Even quicker, press the Cmd key and Q together to gracefully exit the software.

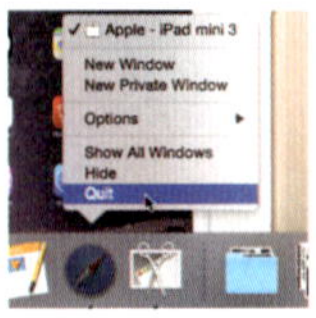

03: Click the Dock icon

Click the Dock icon, keep the mouse button held down, and a menu containing Quit appears.

04: Click the red button

Some apps, like App Store, quit when you close the window by clicking the Red button.

05: Application switcher

Press Cmd+Tab, release Tab, then press it repeatedly to get the app's icon. Then press Q.

Application windows

You can have more than one application open at once and most applications can have more than one window open, which can make for a lot of screen clutter if you're not careful! Luckily you can hide windows, minimise them down to the Dock (click the amber window widget) or use advanced features like Spaces or Exposé to manage your windows

Applications that just won't quit

Sometimes applications run into trouble, and when that happens they'll often just show you a spinning rainbow cursor and refuse to quit. Should that happen to you, just press Cmd+Alt+Esc to bring up the Force Quit window. Click the name of the problem application and then click the Force Quit button to shut it down

Organise your apps with Mission Control

Stay in control of all your apps and windows using this incredible organisational tool

Apple has always been innovative when it comes to organising windows and apps on a Mac. With the introduction of OS X Leopard in 2007, Spaces and Exposé gave users the ability to split their apps between four separate desktops and see all their active windows with just one keystroke. OS X Lion then brought these together to create Mission Control – a powerful desktop organisation utility that promises to bring greater efficiency to your computing.

Within Mission Control, now a feature of Yosemite, you can view all of your active application windows and assign them to different 'Desktops' (this is the terminology used for Spaces). You can also set up new Desktops, flick between them with a multi-touch gesture and then close them with ease.

Follow this step-by-step tutorial to see how to get the most out of one of the best features that was introduced by Lion. It really can help you keep your work and play spaces more organised.

Get to know Mission Control

The key aspects of the interface explained

Window grouping

In Mission Control, all open windows are grouped together by their related application. As well as a graphical display of each window, they also include the application's icon for easy identification and organisation

A space of its own

Dashboard occupies a space of its own in Yosemite, as opposed to Snow Leopard where widgets appeared on top of the desktop. You can revert Dashboard to the Snow Leopard style (step nine)

A clearer view

The best part of Mission Control is the clarity that it brings. Windows are displayed as large as possible and you can even move them around so you know exactly where everything is

MULTI-TOUCH GESTURES

Mission Control uses multi-touch gestures for best results. A three-finger swipe upwards on a trackpad will enter Mission Control and a three-finger swipe down will exit it. Swiping with three fingers to the left or the right will allow you to switch between different desktops, both in and out of Mission Control.

Add more Desktops

Roll your cursor up into the top-right of the screen and a faded window will appear with a '+' icon on it. Click this and a new, empty desktop will slide in from the right for you to open applications in

Mission Control

Customise and master Mission Control

01: A screen with a view

Launch Mission Control via the dock icon, the F3 key or through Launchpad. You'll see all of your active windows grouped by app.

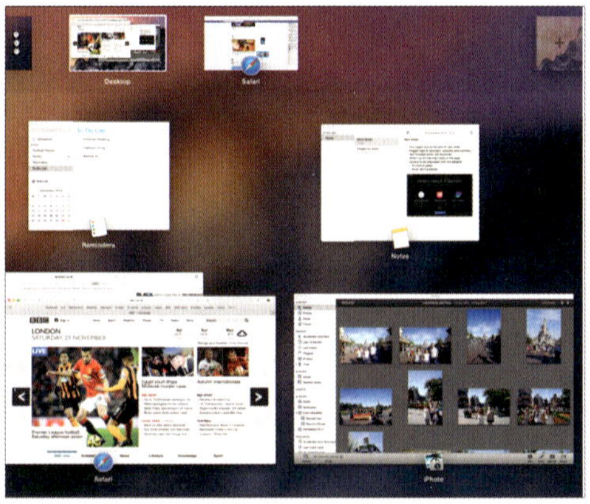

02: Double your desktops

To add a new desktop to the right of the rest, simply hover your mouse in the top right corner of the screen and click the plus icon.

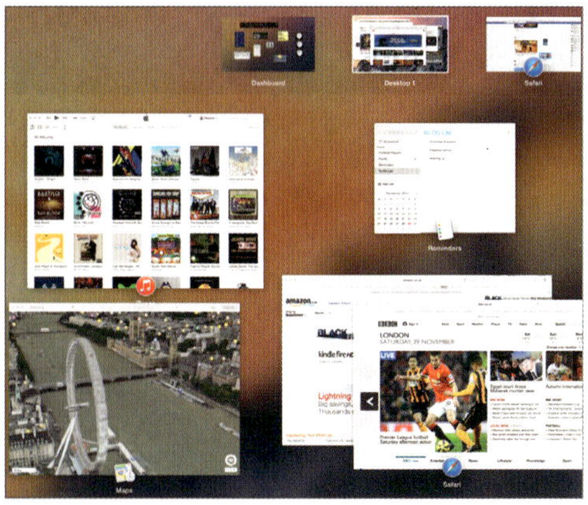

03: Organise your windows

Drag an active window onto any of the desktops at the top of Mission Control. You can have any number of apps or windows in each desktop.

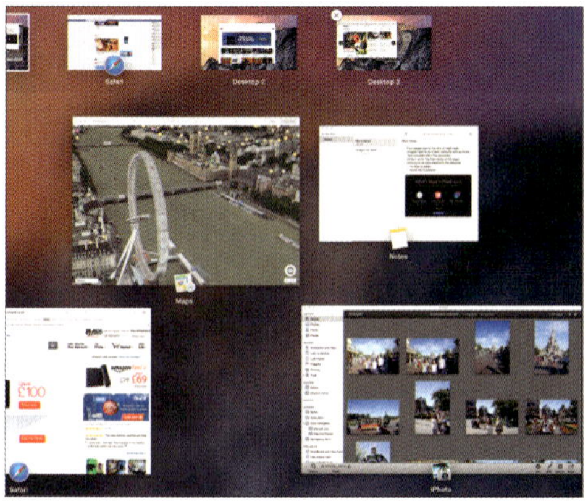

04: Desktops galore

Once a desktop is looking cluttered, simply add another. You can have up to sixteen in total, so there's plenty of room for all of your windows.

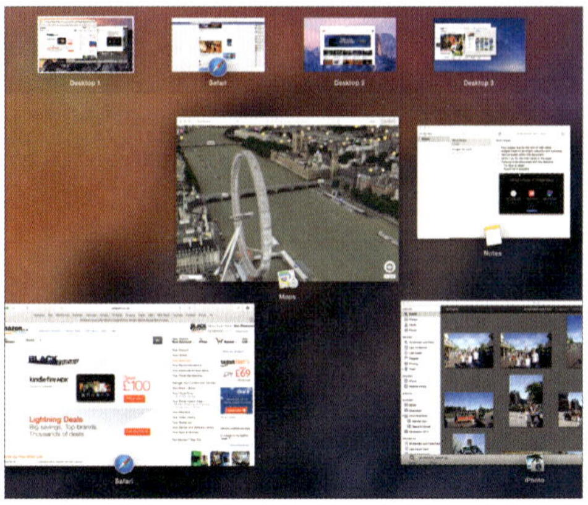

05: Background basics

You can change the background of desktops; this is useful for differentiating between projects, as well as personal and professional work.

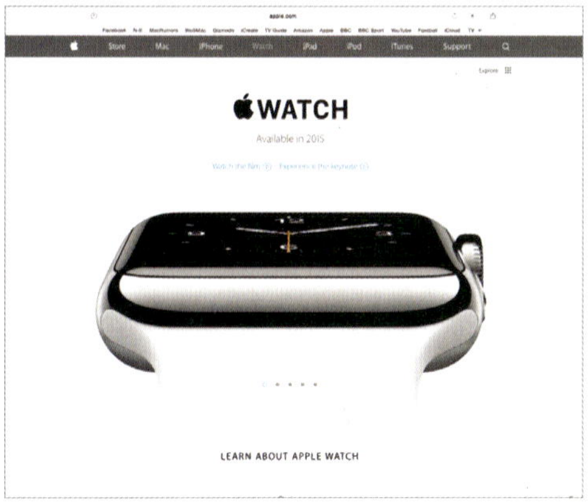

06: A space for full-screen

When you put an app into full-screen it will create its own space; you'll see this in Mission Control but you can't drop other windows into it.

07: Swipe through screens

Use a three-fingered swipe on a trackpad to switch between spaces. This allows your to quickly move windows between different desktops.

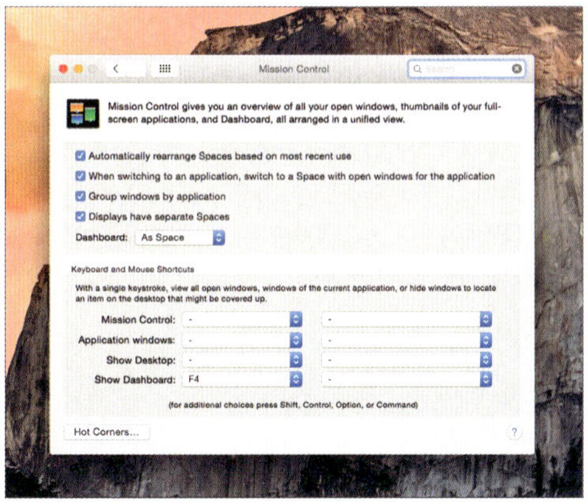

08: Customise preferences

Under the Mission Control pane in System Preferences you'll find ways to edit Mission Control keyboard shortcuts as well as Hot Corners.

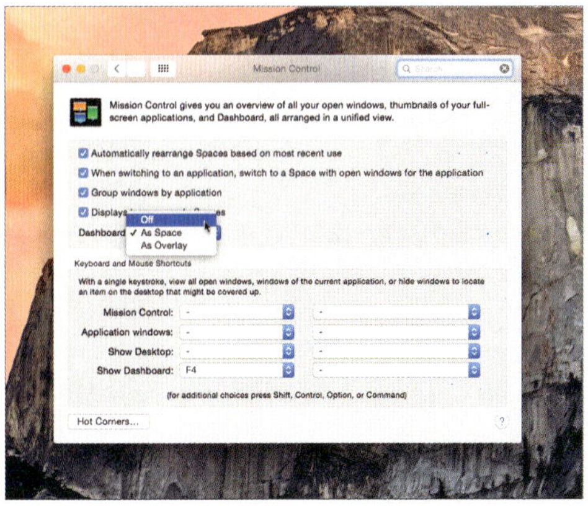

09: Decide on Dashboard

In Yosemite, the Dashboard occupies its own space by default. If you don't like this, you can add it as an Overlay, or switch it off entirely.

Organise Launchpad

Make Launchpad work for you with folders and Home screens

Launchpad is another great feature, introduced by Mac OS X Lion, mirroring the functionality of Springboard on iOS. Springboard is the app launcher that you'll find on your iPhone or iPad, which allows you to arrange icons for each of your apps across many Home screens and, if desired, nested into folders.

Every app you install appears automatically on your Home screen, and the same applies for apps installed on your Mac, with each finding its way onto your Launchpad. However, unlike the iPhone, the Mac App Store isn't the only means of getting apps onto your Mac, so how do you add, remove and control these non-App Store apps?

We've collected together a series of hints and tips to help you get the most out of Launchpad, including taking control of those apps you don't want to appear. We'll also show you how to spice up its appearance with custom icons, organise your apps and navigate around Launchpad quickly. Read on to find out how to tame your OS X Launchpad into submission.

Organise your apps

Control Launchpad to keep things in their rightful place

Gestures

Swipe with two fingers to slide between pages of apps, hold down Opt/Alt to automatically enter the organisation mode (where the apps quiver and allow you to move them around). Do a four-finger reverse pinch to exit Launchpad quickly, or tap Escape on your keyboard

Hide apps

Hide unwanted apps by installing the free System Preferences add-on, which is available from chaosspace.de/launchpad-control

Folders

Arrange your apps into folders by clicking and dragging one app onto another. This will create a folder that is automatically named for you. Rename the folder by clicking on its title and typing over the highlighted text

Pages

Each dot represents a different page of apps inside Launchpad. You can navigate between pages by swiping with two fingers, or quickly jump to a page by clicking on the relevant dot to save time

REMOVING NON-APP STORE APPS

One of the limitations of Launchpad is its reluctance to let you remove apps that didn't originate in the Mac App Store. Unless you're brand new to the Mac platform, it's very likely that you've got a reasonable collection of apps that didn't come from here, but when you enter quiver mode, these apps don't have a remove option, so how do you get rid of them? There are a couple of solutions: the easiest is to simply drag all your undesired apps into one folder and hide it on a screen all of its own at the end of the screens. The second is to install the preferences pane found at **http://chaosspace.de/launchpad-control**. This lets you untick apps you don't want to appear, removing the link from Launchpad, but not the app from your computer.

Launchpad Make Launchpad your own

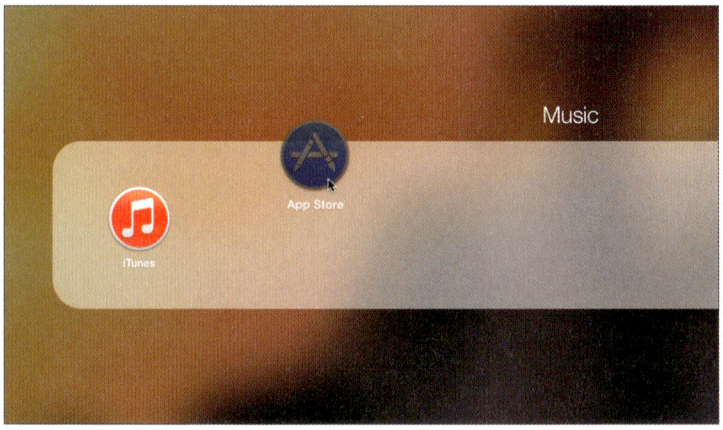

01: Create folders

Drag one app icon onto another. As you release your mouse, the two apps will form a folder, which will be named automatically for you.

02: Move your apps

You can easily re-order your apps within your Launchpad simply by clicking and holding on an app icon and then dragging it into position.

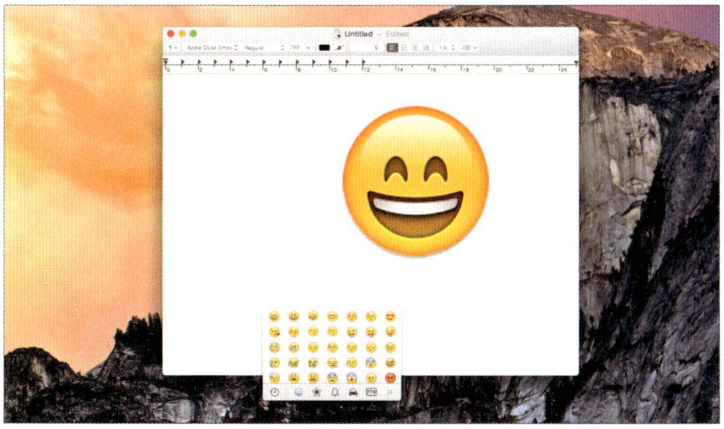

03: Liven it up

Use Emoji icons in your folder names by opening a new TextEdit document, choosing Edit>Special characters, and copying then pasting to the Launchpad.

04: Hide unwanted apps

Hide unwanted apps by installing the System Preferences add-on, which is available from **chaosspace.de/launchpad-control**.

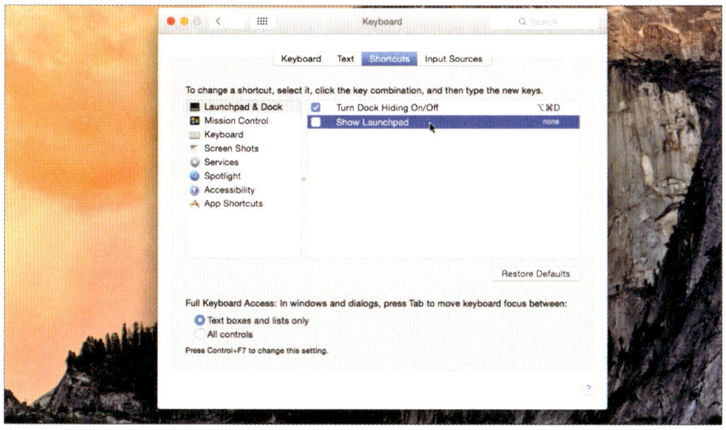

05: Set up a shortcut key

Choose System Preferences>Keyboard, and add a shortcut key into the Keyboard Shortcuts tab.

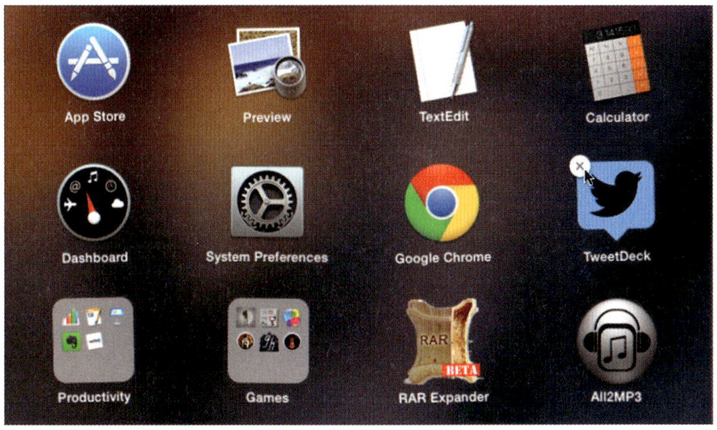

06: Delete apps

To remove apps from your Launchpad, click and hold on an app icon until all the icons quiver. Once they're shaking, click on the 'X' next to an app.

Get started with Dashboard

Learn everything you need to know about how Dashboard can make your life easier

The Dashboard has been present in Mac OS X for several years now, but with Lion it saw a lot of changes. At its most basic, the Dashboard is a place in which you can put widgets – which are small, always-on apps that can only be used when in the Dashboard.

Mac OS X has always included some useful widgets that you can use straight out of the box, but independent developers have spent hours creating hundreds more that you can easily install for free from Apple's website.

Since Lion, the Dashboard has changed from a screen that overlays your desktop (so that you can see parts of it underneath, but never use it) to a fully separate section to the left of the main Desktop screen. Swiping across the screen with your finger brings it up, and allowing you to play with widgets to your heart's content.

You can change your widget settings by clicking the 'i' that appears whenever you hover over them.

"At its most basic, the Dashboard is a place in which you can put widgets"

Discover Dashboard

Find out what each standard widget is for

World Clock
Displaying the time from anywhere in the world, adding a few of these lets you keep track of as many time zones as you want to

Safari Webclip
You can add a snapshot of your favourite blog or video by opening the page in the Safari browser and choosing 'Open' in Dashboard

Weather
This weather widget will tell you what it's like anywhere in the world. If you click it once, you can get a weekly forecast of your choice

Calendar
The calendar widget features three columns – today's date, a month view, and a column that displays your Calendar events for today

Translator
The translator widget lets you choose from a wide range of languages, translating text quickly and easily

Stickies
If you're always forgetting things, use Stickies to keep notes. Fonts and colours are changeable, making sure your notes will stand out

Unit Converter
Whatever you need to convert, the Unit Converter widget will do it for you in a pinch. Weight, time, pressure and energy are just a few of the many options for this powerful and useful widget

Tile Game
A simple game widget, the Tile Game is just the tip of the iceberg when it comes to widget-based games. Check out the Apple website to find more

Address Book
This widget allows you to quickly search your computer's contacts to find the person you need, without the need to open the Address Book app

Ski Report
If you're off on holiday to the mountains, and want to check the Ski Report, you can type a resort name in here and view the conditions of the snow

Dictionary
The Dictionary widget allows you to search for any word quickly, getting you a definition or synonym quickly

ESPN
If you're an American Sports junkie, the ESPN widget is made for you. Get news and scores for hockey, football, baseball and more

Calculator
Small, neat, and much quicker than Lion's app. Typing numbers and symbols is supported to increase productivity

Flight Tracker
Choose an airline, departure city and arrival city to view the status of flights. Incredibly useful if you travel with your Mac

Movies
If you live in the US, you can quickly check the latest times in your area, as well as buy tickets once you know what you want to see

Stocks
If you're financially minded and like to keep an eye on stocks, this will help do just that. Input your companies and away you go

Key features
Starting the Dashboard

Two ways to access Dashboard

Lion made it even easier to access your Dashboard. Since that version of OS X was released, Dashboard has become a space to the left of your main desktop that is there whenever you need it. Getting there is easy. You can swipe your fingers quickly to the right on your Trackpad or Magic Mouse and watch the Dashboard slide onto your screen. Alternatively, open Mission Control and click on the Dashboard thumbnail.

Adding new widgets

While there are only four widgets on the screen when you first open the Dashboard, there are a lot more available. Click on the '+' symbol in the bottom left corner of the screen and a screen will appear showing all of the available widgets. To add one, click on it and it will appear on your Dashboard and you can click and hold and drag it into position. See the opposite page to find out what each widget can do.

Arrange your widgets

When you first see your Dashboard, there should be four widgets in the middle of the screen; the Weather, World Clock, Calculator and Calendar. They certainly aren't stuck in those positions; if you want to move them around, you can click and drag them to a different area of the Dashboard. Unlike normal windows, there isn't a bar you have to click to move each widget – clicking and dragging from anywhere will work.

Manage your widgets

If you wish to remove widgets then the process is just as simple. Click on the '-' symbol and a 'X' will appear in the corner of every widget – click this to delete it. Once done, click on '-' again to return to normal. To download new widgets that aren't currently on your Mac, click the '+' symbol followed by the 'More Widgets' button at the bottom of the window, and choose from the hundreds of free choices on the Apple website.

Get to know Notification Center

A central place to view alerts, updates and more on your Mac

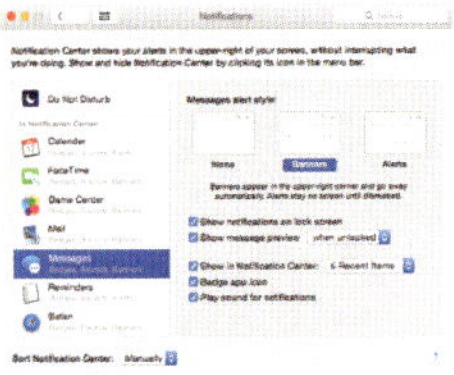

The Notification Center is a central focus for change on your Mac, recording new happenings and occurrences. It's a place where you can find information regarding updates for your apps and you can also see information on new mail that has arrived. Reminders are another area that the Notification Center handles, as well as information from the likes of FaceTime, Game Center, Calendar, plus messages from other third-party apps. The Notification Center can be configured by yourself, however, so it's not set in stone. You can tell the Mac just how you want to see your alerts, in what style and format and for how long you want these alerts to remain on the screen. This focuses on the visual end of the Center, but you can also include sounds in that suite of features too. Let's take a closer look at this useful facility.

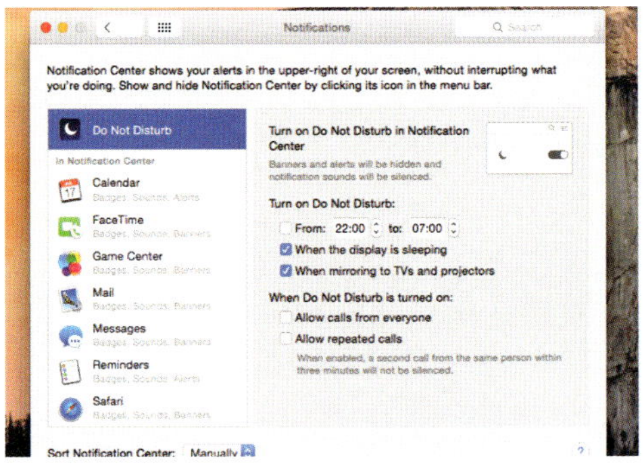

Explore the interface

Manage your alerts and updates

Notification Center

This main window is placed on the right of the screen and is normally hidden from view but can be triggered to open, revealing your alerts, updates and news

Timing

Next to each alert you will see a relative time/date to inform you when the alert arrived. On the desktop the notice badge alerts provide an alternative method of bringing change to your attention

DO NOT DISTURB

If you are busy or need to concentrate, then regular messages and alerts will not help. Swipe the Do Not Disturb switch to On, at the top of the Notification Center, to remove them all. Also, every time you get a notification an interactive bubble appears at the top-right-hand side of your screen. You can automatically reply to any message you get by hovering over the bubble and then pressing the Reply button.

Header

Each app provides a heading and icon, then the alerts, news or updates underneath. If you want to remove the information for that app, click the X next to the header

Notification Center Master the Notification Center in Yosemite

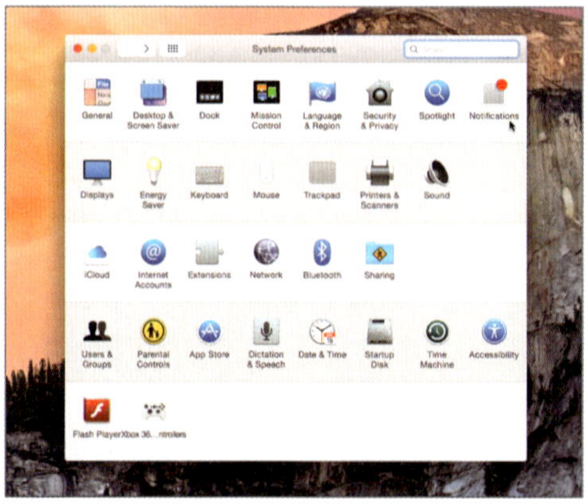

01: Open Notification Center

To open the Notification Center, click on System Preferences. On the first line, at the far right, is the Notification Center icon, so click it to open.

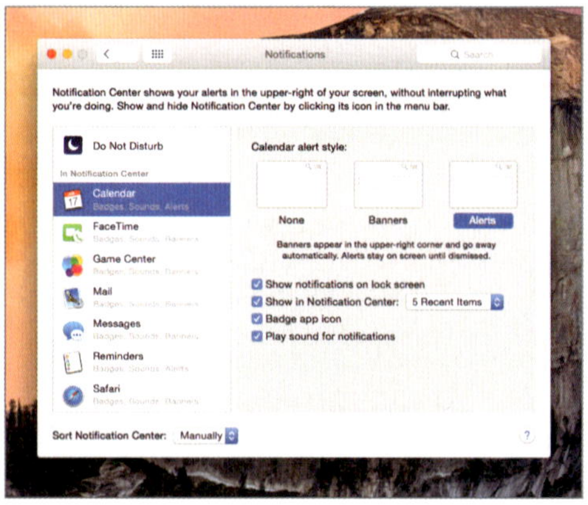

02: Choose an app

Pick which app you want to modify by looking in the left panel. Scroll the available list until you find your desired app and then click it.

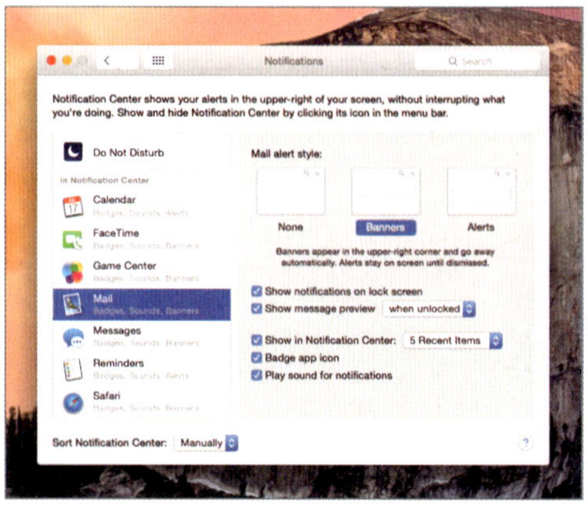

03: Choose style

You can choose from one of three possible styles: None; Banner (appears for a short time); and Alerts (stays until you remove them).

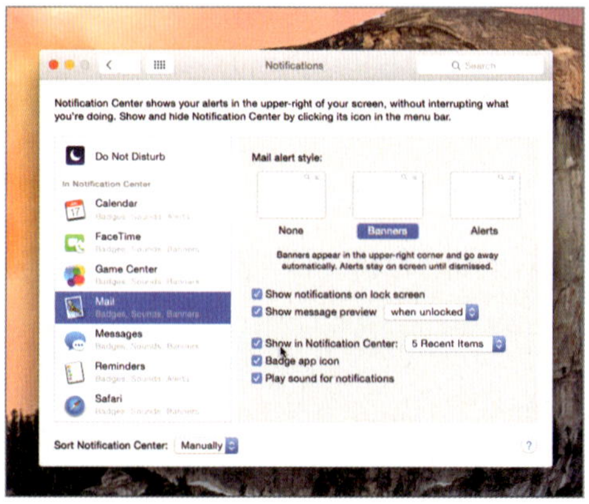

04: Show in Center

If you click on the Show in Notification Center option box then the alerts will always appear in the Notification Center on the right side of the screen.

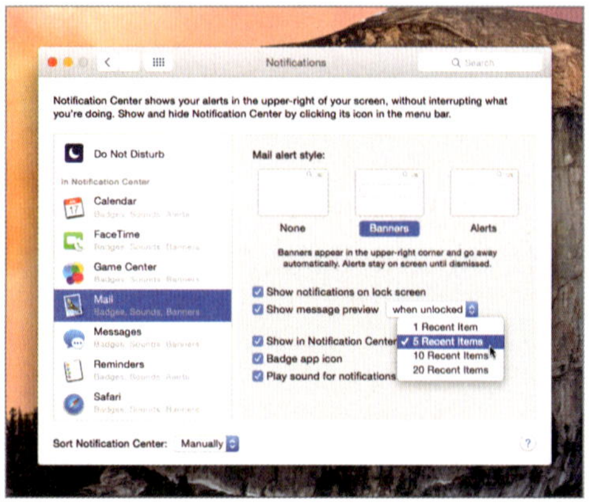

05: Recent items

Next to Show in Notification Center, click to see 1, 5, 10 or 20 Recent Items. This denotes how many older alerts will be retained in the Notification Center.

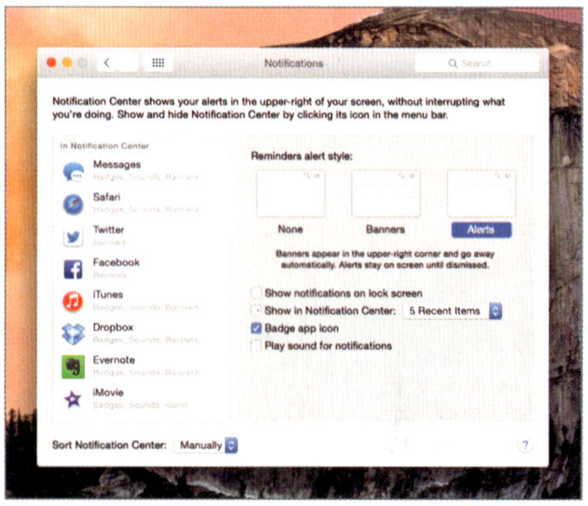

06: Badge icons

Click on the Badge app icon to enable alerts and/or updates to show badges on the icon of the app in the Dock. The red icon has a white alert number.

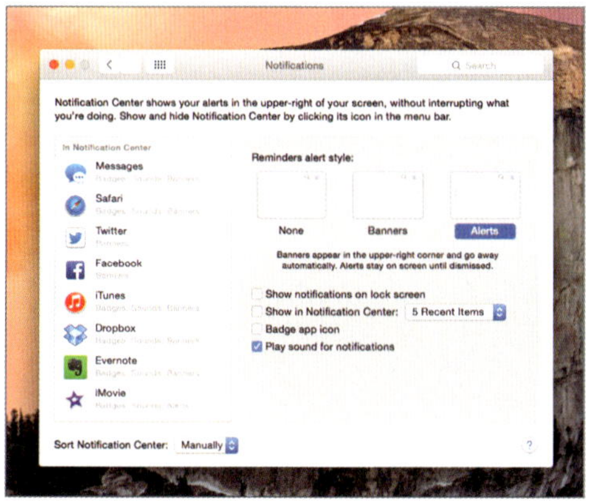

07: Play sound

Tick the Play Sound for Notifications box to ask the Mac to play its alert sound when you receive an alert, update or news item.

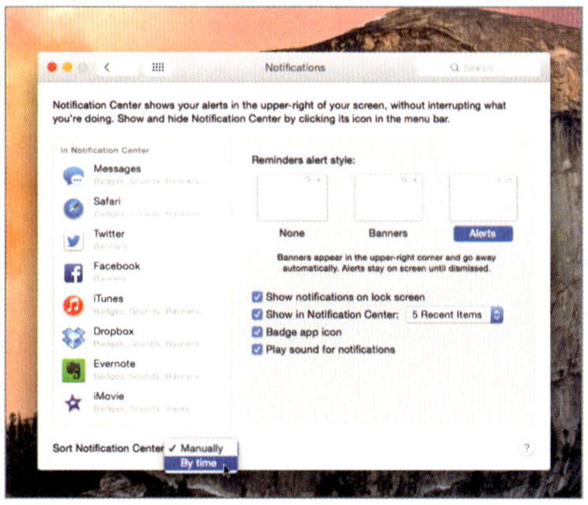

08: Sort notifications

Clicking Sort Notification Center will produce a pop-up menu with two options presented to sort Notification Center manually or by time.

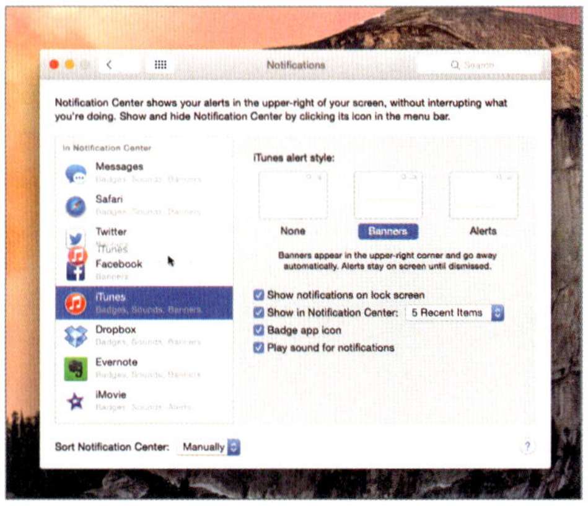

09: Order apps

If you aren't happy with the order of the apps offered in the Notification Center then you can click and drag an app to rearrange their order.

Set up widgets in Notification Centre

Extend Notification Centre's functionality through time-saving widgets

Notification Centre was introduced to Macs back in Mountain Lion and for the past couple of years has served as an at-a-glance method of viewing everything that's going on in your world. It gives you direct access to all your social interactions and business appointments. One major change in OS X Yosemite 10.10 was the introduction of the Today view, which – just like in iOS – gives you a run-down of your day's events from Calendar entries, Reminders, weather forecast and so on. Your entire day is laid out for you.

What's even better is that you can add widgets to your Today view by hitting Edit, for a fully customisable and personal Notification Centre. There are widgets to suit any interest or need, so you can modify the Notification Centre to your personal preferences. Essentially, Notification Centre's usefulness has been improved exponentially. We're going to guide you through setting up and using third-party widgets to Notification Centre, giving any new OS X user a time-saving method of checking vital information in no time at all.

Notification Centre: OS X 10.10 style

Up close with your pimped out Notification Centre

In-depth info
Most widgets are expandable and provide even more information with just a couple of clicks – just like the Weather widget shown here. Time to wrap up warm

Notifications
Don't forget the traditional Notifications tab, which lists all of your various unseen notifications and enables you to respond straight from Notification Centre

Do Not Disturb
Taking your Mac into an important meeting? Sleeping with it under the pillow? Just activate Do Not Disturb, set a time period for silence and tweak the settings as you wish

App Store
The ultimate place for an essential list of compatible apps can be found via this App Store shortcut in Edit mode under the Today view

THE END FOR DASHBOARD?

When widgets for Notification Centre were announced at WWDC, everyone shared the same thought: this is the end for Dashboard, Apple's home of the simple widget. Well, it still exists but its days are surely numbered. Using a widget in Notification Centre makes a lot of sense, is quick and easy, and is supported by a thriving community of third-party developers.

Notification Centre Customise the Today view

01: Basic setup

Access Notification Centre through a three-lines icon in the top-right corner of your menu bar. Your basic Today view is very useful but limited.

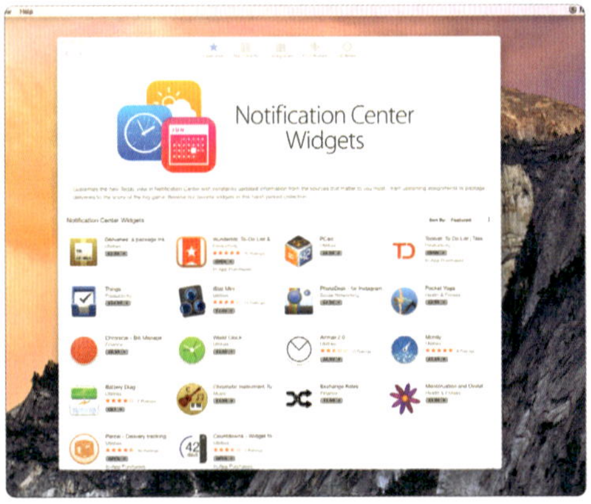

02: Mac App Store

A host of great apps already support the widget feature and there's a list on the Mac App Store's Featured page. Take a look and get downloading!

03: Edit tab

The Edit button at the bottom of the Today view powers up Notification Centre. Click it and you're presented with a new row of compatible widgets.

04: Click the plus

To add a widget click on the green plus sign next to its name. Click Done in the bottom-right and the widget is instantly added to your Today view.

05: Use a widget

Most widgets require a bit of personalising. The World Clock, for example. Hit the 'i' button and add a face by typing in a place and hit Done.

06: Add social accounts

Other widgets require you to add account details, like the Social widgets. Click Add Account and follow the steps to get your account running.

07: Time saver

Now you won't need the app or a browser. Send a Facebook update or tweet a post with all the usual additions, right from Notification Centre.

08: Reorder

Notification Centre lets you reorder the widgets on your Today view. Click and drag to reorder and banish widgets by hitting the red minus icon.

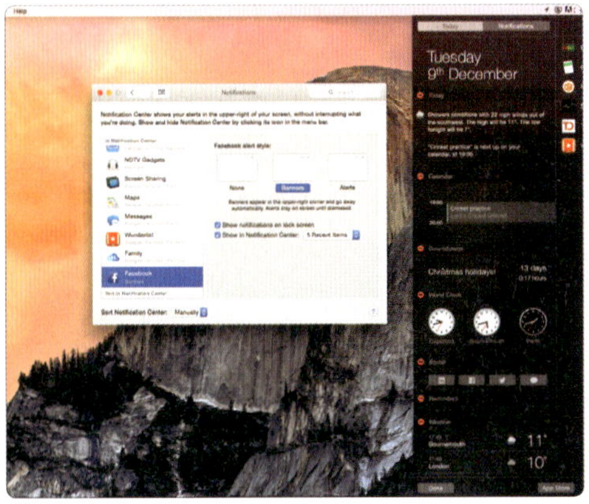

09: System Preferences

Edit mode leads you to System Preferences via the cog in the bottom-right. Customise how you receive notifications from your widgets here.

Inside System Preferences: Personal

Learn how to tune and tinker with the inner workings of your Mac by following this simple, four-part guide to System Preferences. First up: the Personal settings…

Many Mac users are happy to leave their Mac set up the same way it was the day they opened the box. That's fair enough – after all, why fix what isn't broken? However, if you're prepared to take a few minutes to delve into the wealth of settings at your fingertips, you may just find a few that could change the way you work, make your Mac a safer place or just spruce the ol' gal up a little. In the first of a four-part guide, we're going to take you, icon by icon, through the top row of the System Preferences window: the Personal settings…

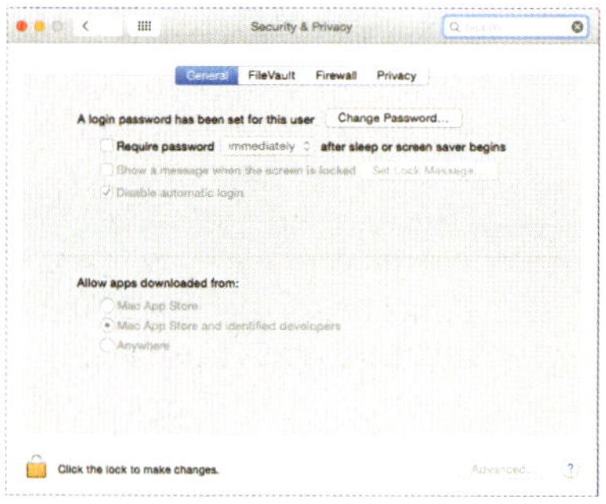

Security

Energy Saver

By setting your Mac to require a password when waking it from sleep or screen saver, your Mac will automatically lock while you're away. You can also set it to only respond to a certain remote control.

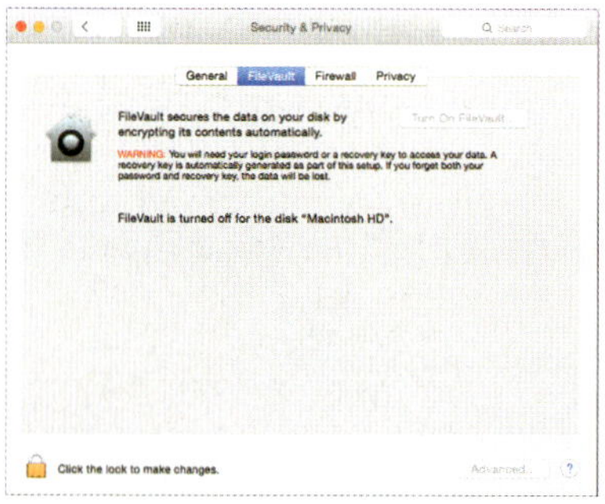

FileVault

By using FileVault, you can automatically encrypt every file on your Mac – great for security-conscious laptop users worried about losing their computer, and the sensitive data it contains.

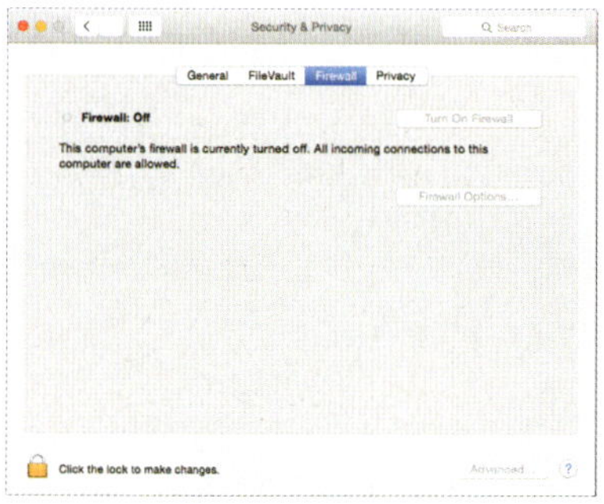

Firewall

It's no myth that Macs are safer on the internet than Windows-based computers, but if you'd rather be safe than sorry you can turn on the Firewall to monitor and block potentially dangerous connections from the net.

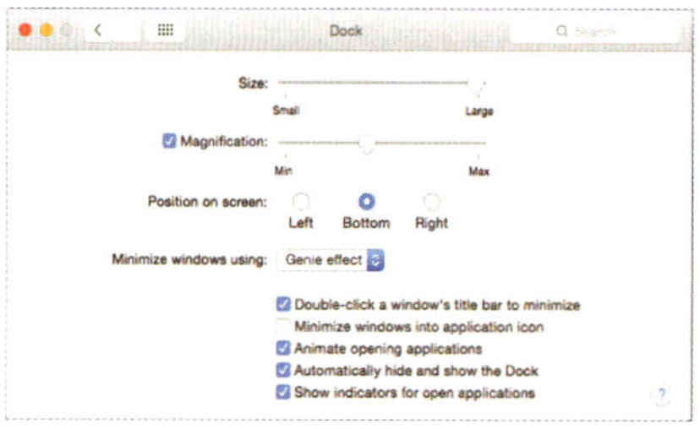

Dock

With these settings, you can easily control how the Dock (the bar of icons along the bottom of your screen) looks and behaves.

Finder File Edit View Go Window Help

Desktop & Screen Saver

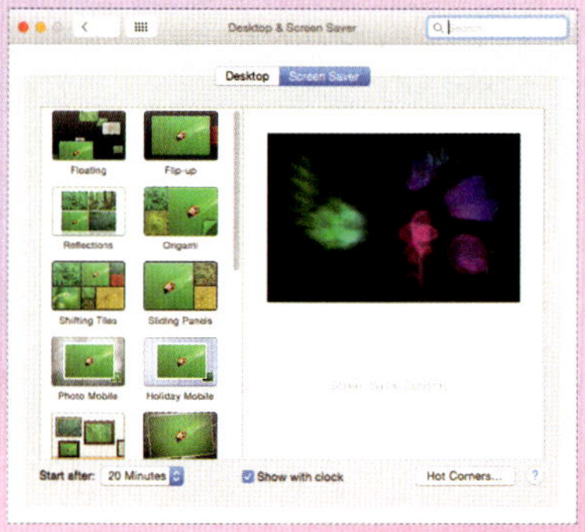

Desktop

Set the background picture on your desktop to one of the Apple-supplied images, one of your own photos from iPhoto or one you've downloaded from the internet.

Screen Saver

Set an animation that automatically starts when your Mac hasn't been used for a while. Choose from one of Apple's, or automatically create a slideshow from your iPhoto albums.

Mission Control

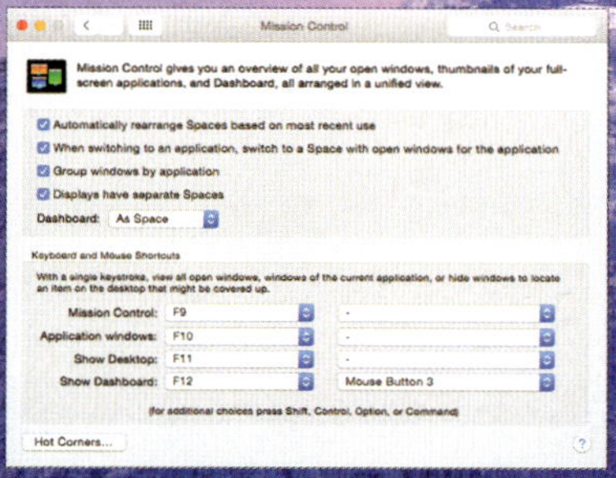

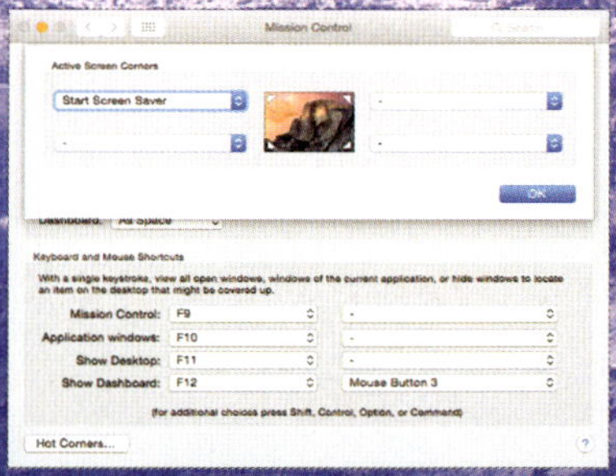

General

Sometimes you can't find the window you need among the many you have open. Mission Control provides a handy overview of all your open windows and applications all arranged in a unified view. You can tailor the views and shortcuts here.

Hot Corners

Accessible from the Mission Control pane is the 'Hot Corners' settings. You can move your cursor into a corner of your screen to trigger certain actions, such as screensavers and sleep mode. You can determine what corner performs which action here.

Scroll bar controls

With a scrolling mouse, you may never have used the scroll bars on the edge of every window, but there may still be settings here that you'll find extremely useful – such as the Jumping options

Text smoothing options

Without smoothing the words on your screen can appear harsh and jagged, but you might find text too fuzzy to read comfortably at smaller sizes. You can fine-tune the effect here

Search System Preferences

If you know there's an option you'd like to change but can't remember where it is, try entering its name into this search box to see matching icons dynamically highlighted

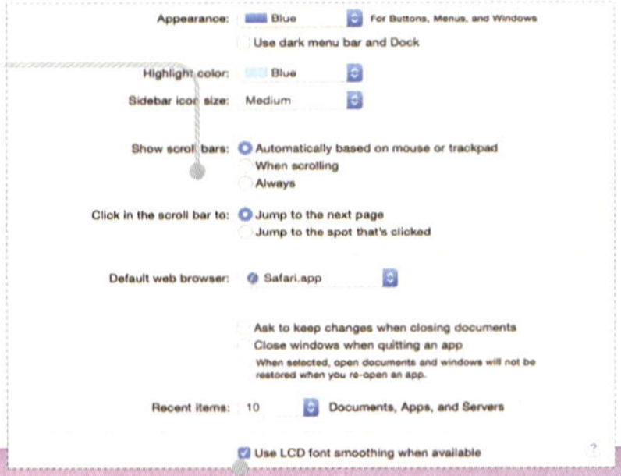

General

In this pane, you'll find the settings that affect how your windows and menus appear. You have the choice between the usual Blue theme, with shiny blue controls and red, amber and green window widgets, or – if you find all the colour distracting – you can switch to the Graphite theme where all the controls are grey instead.

Language & Region

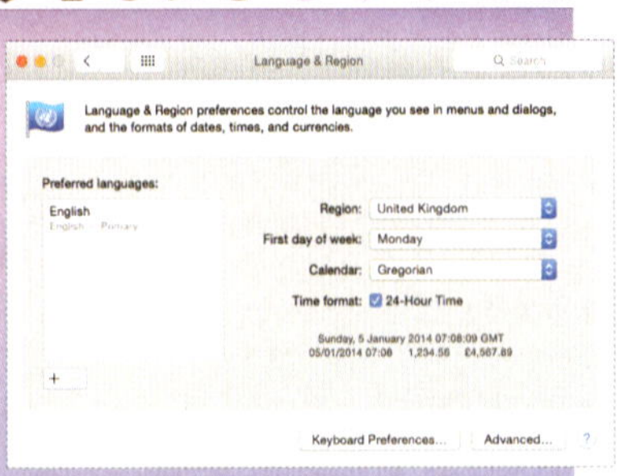

General

For most users, this will come preset, but you can quickly change the language of menus and controls in the left-hand pane of this screen.

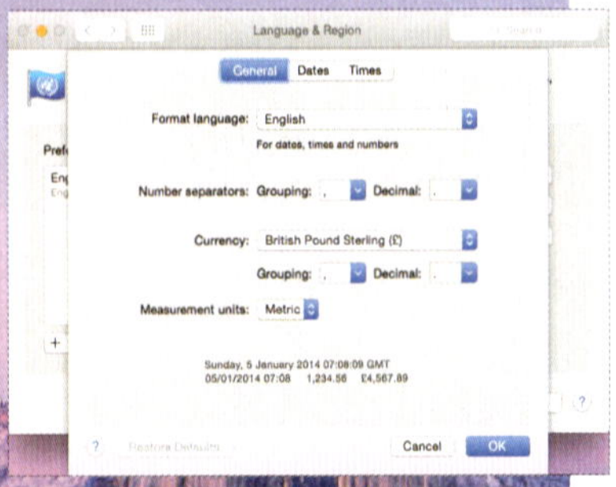

Advanced

Dates, prices or times not displaying the way that you would like? You can change how your Mac automatically formats numbers by clicking Advanced on the Language & Regions page. Presets for most regional variations are here.

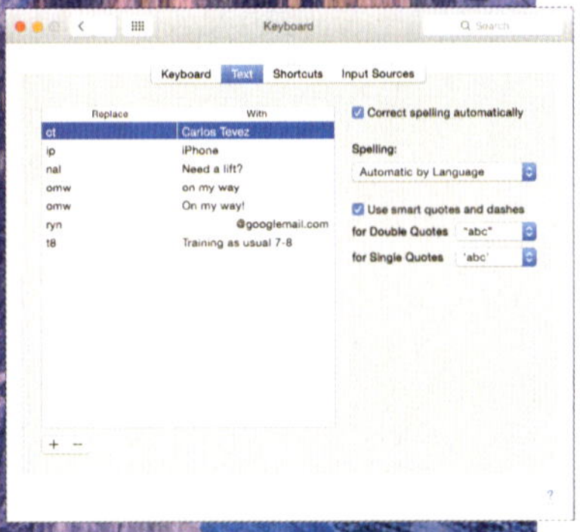

Text

Click Keyboard Preferences from the Language & Region panel to find the Text options. You can set your Spell Check options here, and also set your Mac to replace certain typed shortcuts with special symbols, like (c) for ©. This only works in supported applications.

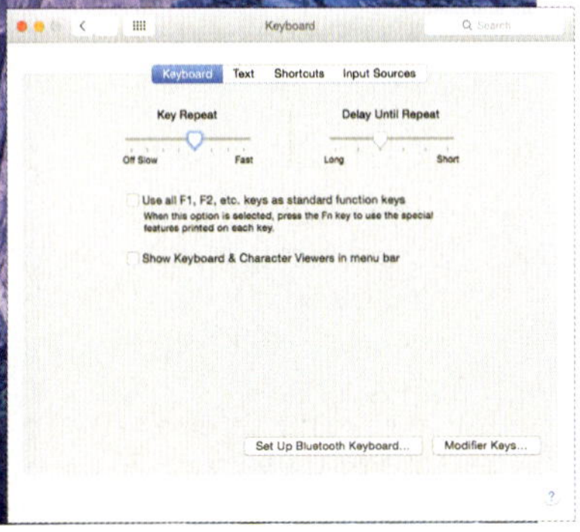

Keyboard

While you're here, click the Keyboard tab. The thing most users will find useful in this section of System Preferences is turning on the Keyboard and Character Viewer, which gives you a map of those hard-to-find symbols on your keyboard, like é, ü or °.

Notifications

In Notification Center

In this panel, you will be able to determine what apps alert you in your Notification Center and change the order by dragging the apps around.

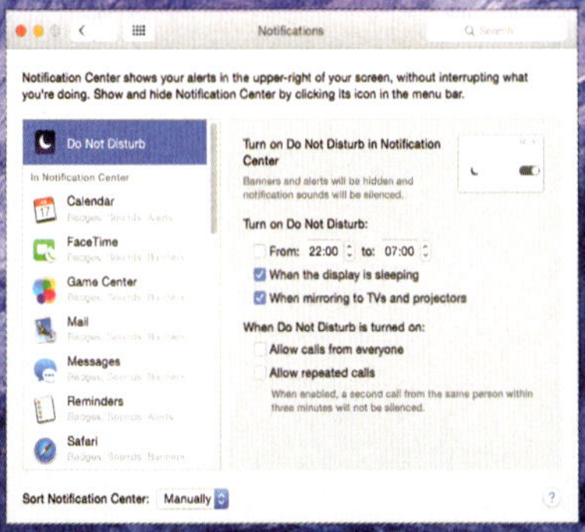

Alert style

Click on a listed app and then you will be able to determine how the alerts appear on screen, such as banners and alerts that pop-up on screen.

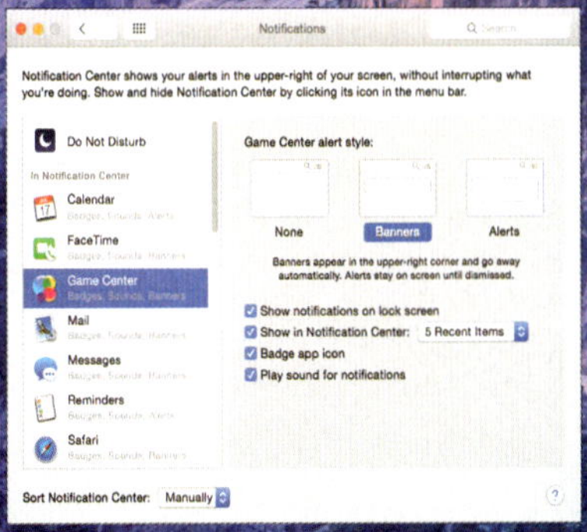

Inside System Preferences: Hardware

Get to grips with the technology inside your Mac by following this simple four-part guide to the System Preferences. Part two: get your hands dirty with the Hardware settings…

The simplicity of Mac OS X means that you don't have to become an expert on computer hardware to enjoy using your Mac. For most peripherals, you can just plug in and play; at the worst, you may have to install the occasional driver. However, with the improvements made in recent version of Mac OS X, even these installations are becoming fewer and farther between. This ease of use doesn't mean there aren't any settings to fiddle with, though – System Preferences has a whole row of icons dedicated to fine-tuning the hardware settings of your Mac, and a few well-chosen tweaks could vastly improve the way you work.

Displays

Make sure you're using the optimum viewing settings to get the most from your monitor

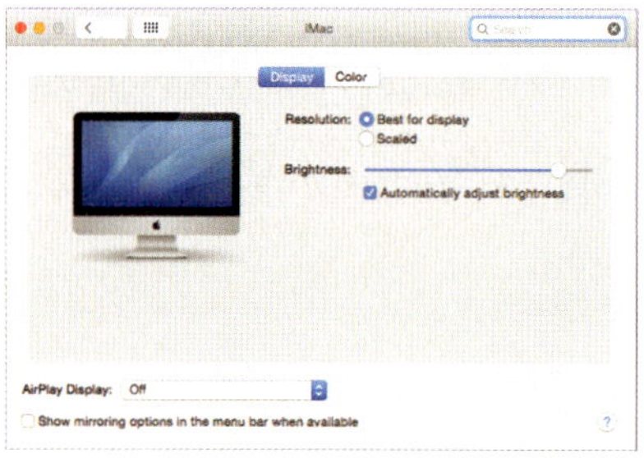

Display

Everything seem a little small on screen? The higher up the list you set the resolution, the more pixels and screen space you'll have, but everything looks a little smaller as a result.

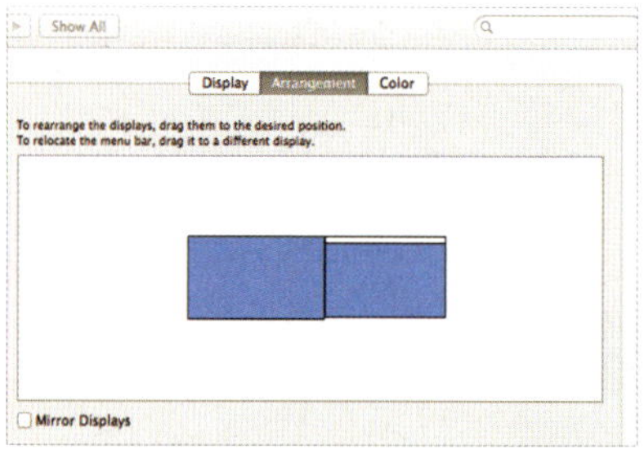

Arrangement

If you're sporting more than one monitor for your Mac, this panel lets you tell your computer how they are positioned and which one you want the Menu bar to appear on.

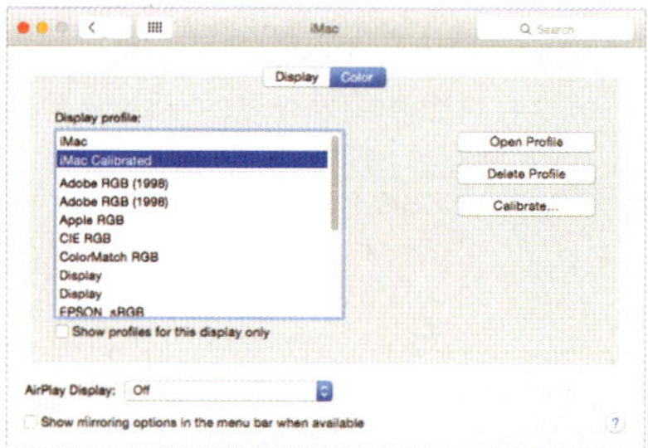

Colour

Ensure you're seeing the correct colours by either selecting the correct Display profile or, even better, by clicking the Calibrate button to create a bespoke setting.

Schedule

Want your Mac to be on when you wake up or get home from work? Use the Energy Saver schedule to set when your Mac turns on, turns off, goes to sleep or wakes up

Finder File Edit View Go Window Help

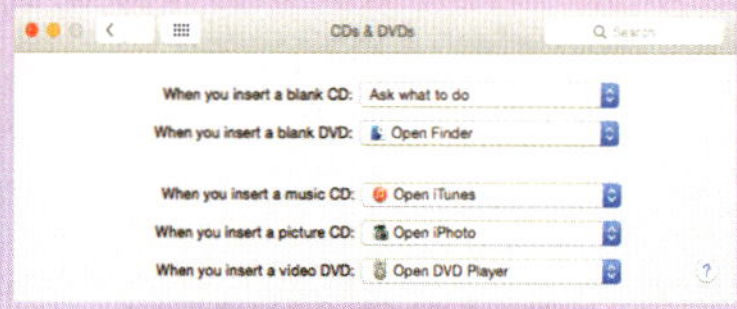

CDs & DVDs

It sounds a simple thing, but it makes a great deal of sense to set up how you'd like your Mac to behave when you slide a disc into the drive. Want blank CDs to appear on the desktop? Just set the blank CD action to 'Open Finder'. Don't want the DVD player to open when you pop in a movie disc? Just choose 'Ignore' from the video DVD menu, or set it to open in Front Row if that's how you prefer to watch your films.

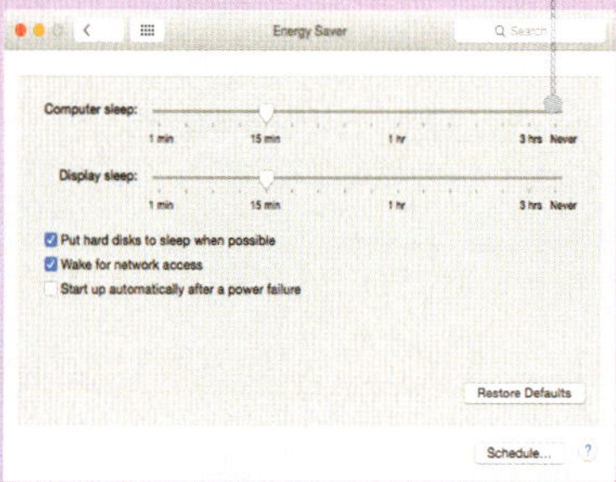

Energy Saver

Possibly the most useful of this row of preferences, the Energy Saver settings do much more than cut down your electricity bill. The Computer Sleep slider sets how long you'd like your Mac to stay on when you're not using it, while a second slider lets you set the same for just the Display.

Keyboard

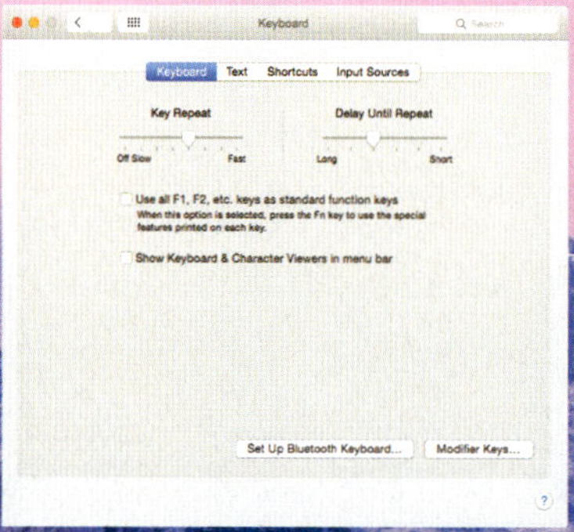

Keyboard

Considering how much of the time you spend sitting in front of your Mac, you also spend time tapping away at your keyboard, so it's good to make sure you've got it set up perfectly. If you're a slow typist then increasing the 'Delay Until Repeat' setting is an especially good idea if you often find yourself typing repeating letters.

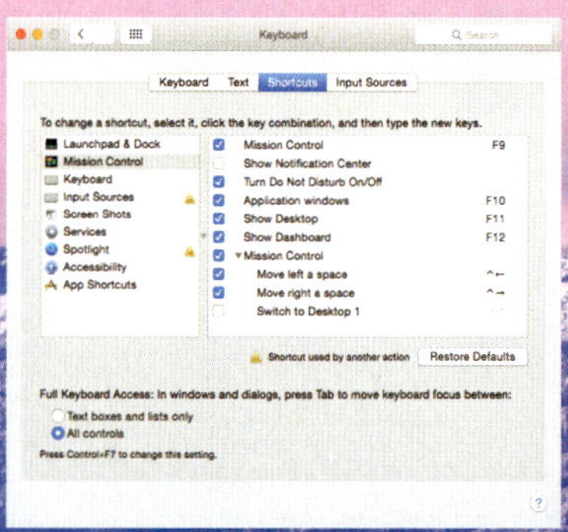

Keyboard Shortcuts

Mac OS X comes crammed with many keyboard shortcuts that can speed up how you work, saving your hand a trip to the mouse or Trackpad. Not only can you discover what they all are from this pane, you can also tweak and change them to better suit your fingertips – a great way to personalise your Mac for the way you work.

Share your printer

Although Wi-Fi printers are surprisingly cheap these days, if you have a non-networked model you can still share it across multiple Macs (and PCs) by ticking this checkbox

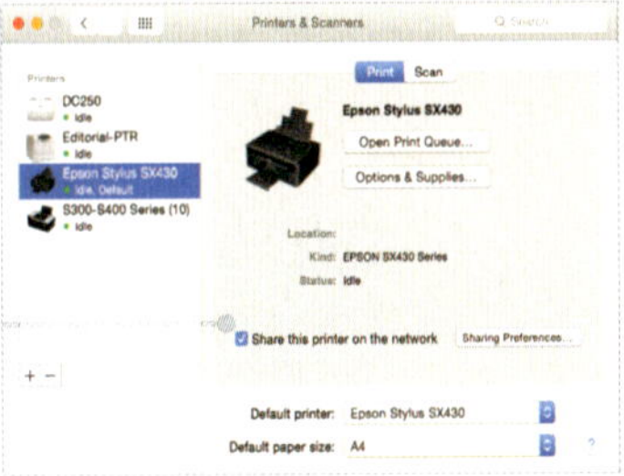

Printers & Scanners

With every new version of Mac OS X, Apple has significantly improved the printer installation experience. So much so that many users will never need to visit the Print & Scan preference pane – simply plug in your printer and most times it will just work. That said, it's still useful to set your default paper size or check the amount of ink in your printer by clicking the Options & Supplies button.

"If you're the arty type and use a graphics tablet, you might want to have a play with the handwriting recognition built into Mac OS X"

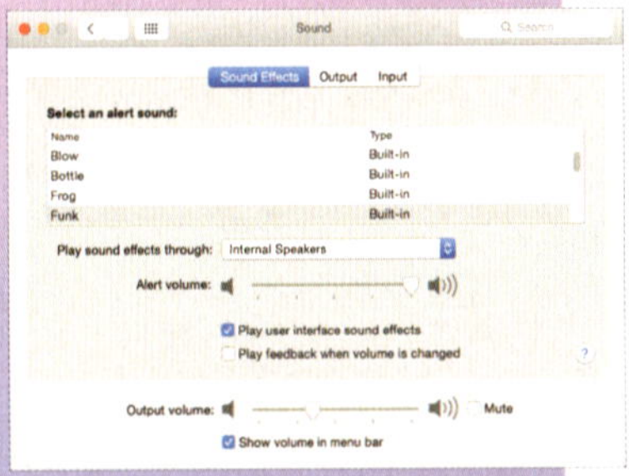

Sound

Sound Effects

Your Mac makes a number of small noises to give you feedback on certain events. Choose which ones you'd like to hear, and how loud you'd like them to be.

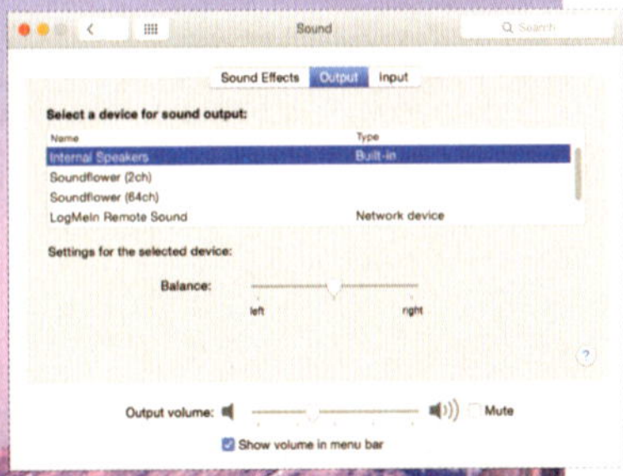

Output

On most Macs there are a number of ways to pipe the audio out – through headphones, the built-in speakers or through a digital optical cable, for example. You can choose which one to use from this pane.

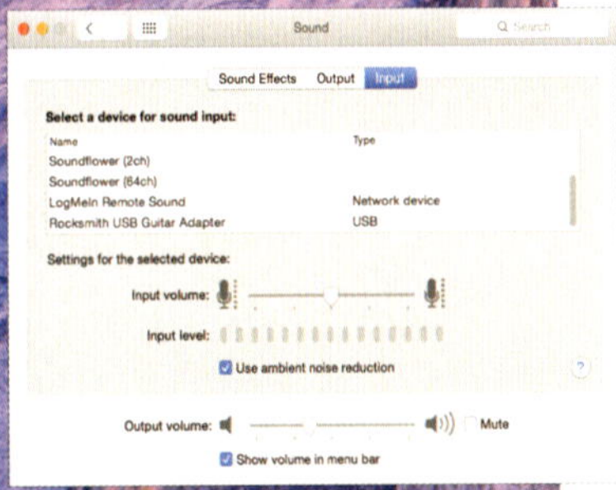

Input

The audio input options are less useful to most users, until you decide to try Skype, record a movie voiceover or experiment with GarageBand. Choosing the right input device will depend on the equipment you use, but it is vital for a great result.

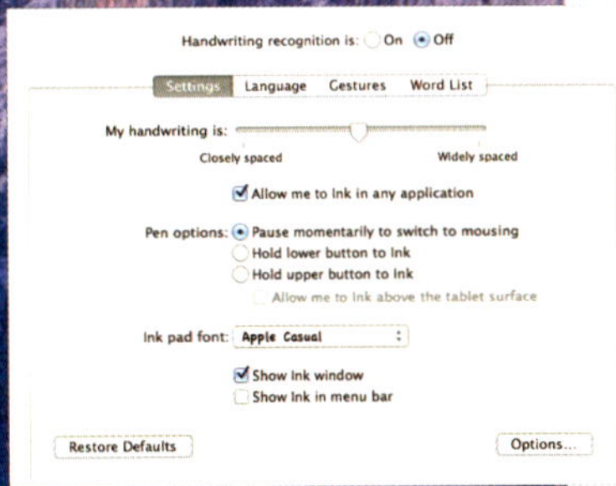

Ink

If you're the arty type and use a graphics tablet, then you might want to have a play with the handwriting recognition that's built into Mac OS X. Ink allows you to enter text using your pen and tablet instead of the keyboard, and it can be great for taking notes. You can also set up gestures to control your Mac with the pen.

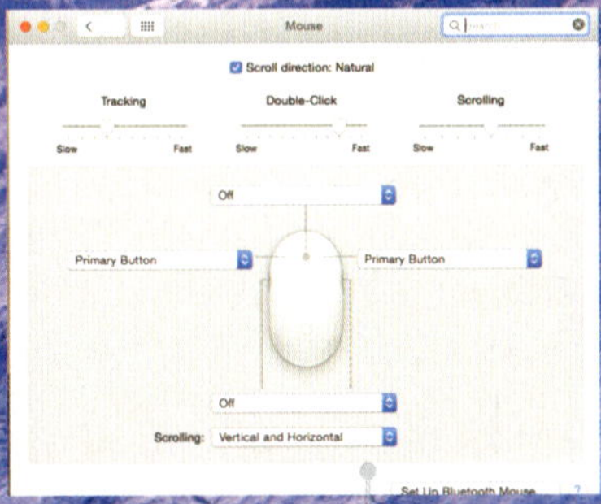

Mouse & Trackpad

The pane that you see here will depend on whether you use a laptop with a Trackpad, a Magic Mouse, Mighty Mouse or a third-party mouse. As with the keyboard settings, considering how much time you spend controlling a cursor, it's important to get these settings perfect – especially the tracking and double-click speeds.

Learn your gestures

As multi-touch devices, like the Magic Mouse or the Trackpad on your laptop, improve the way you get around your Mac, you'll find yourself faced with more and more gestures and actions. You can customise them so the different buttons suit you

Inside System Preferences: Internet & Wireless

Get to grips with the technology inside your Mac by following this simple, four-part guide to the System Preferences. Part three: networking and syncing

There's one aspect that sets the computers of today far apart from those we were using just ten years ago: networks. Back in 2000, the internet was only just starting to become commonplace, and if you did have it then you probably only had it on one computer in the house (which wasn't really a problem, as most houses only had one computer). Now, with the advent of easy Wi-Fi and cheaper computers (plus iPods and iPhones), many houses have a handful of connected devices sharing the airwaves and, with a little setup, sharing their connections, files and data too. The Internet & Wireless row of icons in System Preferences is all about your Networks – local and worldwide – how you interact with them and how you choose to share across them, be it sharing your files, screen, printer or even disc drive.

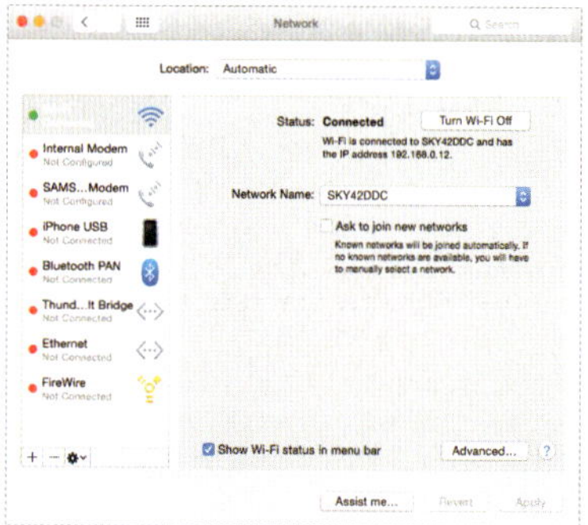

Network

For most users, this should hopefully be one of those 'set it and forget it' preference panes, if you ever need to set it at all. With most modern networks, you should find your Mac just connects and configures itself. Bliss.

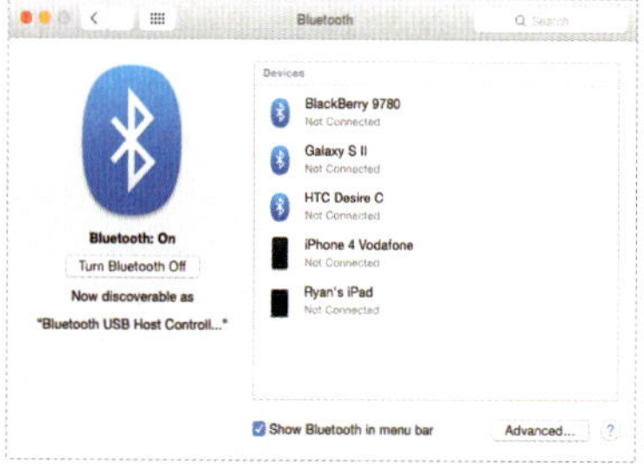

Bluetooth

Check out the status of the Bluetooth peripherals you have connected to your Mac. To add a new Bluetooth device, like a mouse, keyboard or phone, click the '+' button.

> "You should find your Mac just connects and configures itself"

Sharing

DVD or CD Sharing

Share your DVD drive with a Mac that either has a broken drive or doesn't have one at all, like the MacBook Air or the Mac mini server.

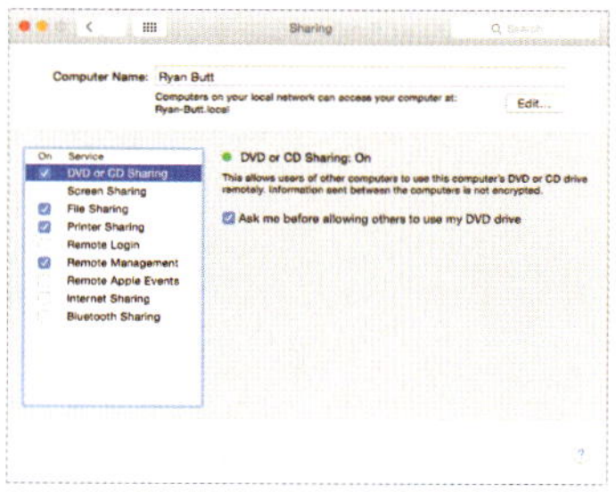

Finder File Edit View Go Window Help

Screen Sharing

Allow another computer (or iPhone) on your network to see your screen, and even control your Mac remotely.

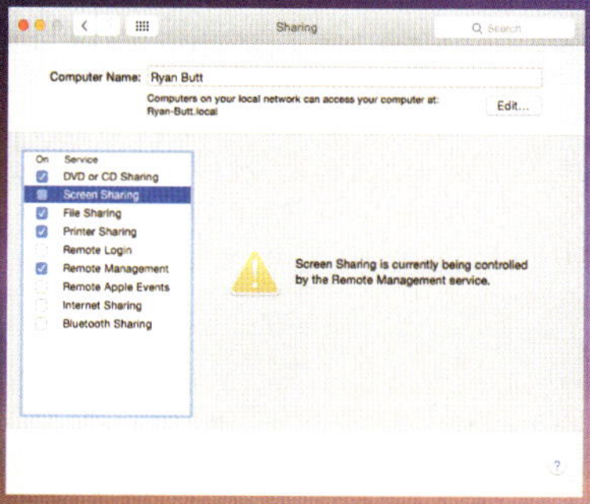

File Sharing

Make files in certain folders available to other computers on your network. You can control who sees what.

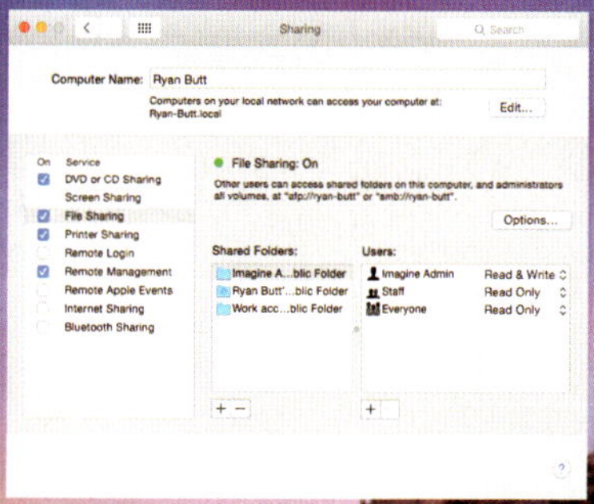

Printer Sharing

With the tick of a box, you can share any printer connected to your Mac with any other local computer.

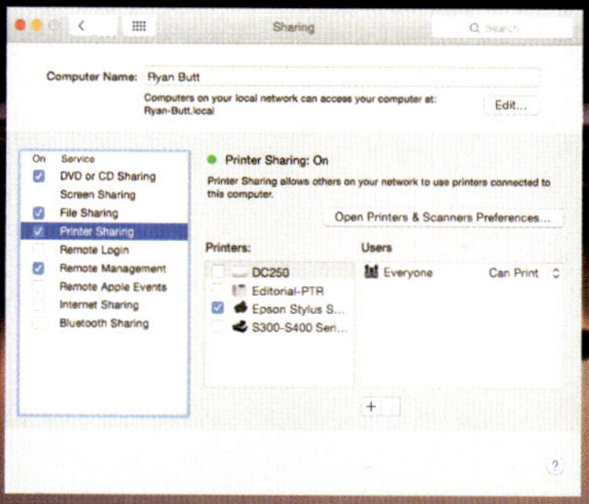

Scanner Sharing

With Mac OS X Yosemite, this feature has now been incorporated into the Printer sharing settings.

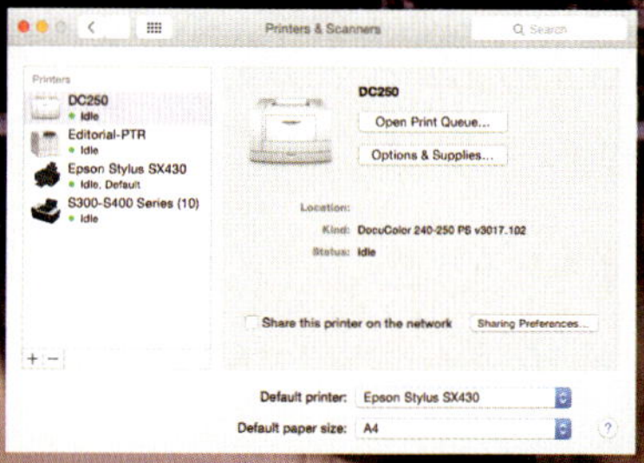

Internet Sharing

Share your internet connection with another computer by ticking the box and selecting the correct ports.

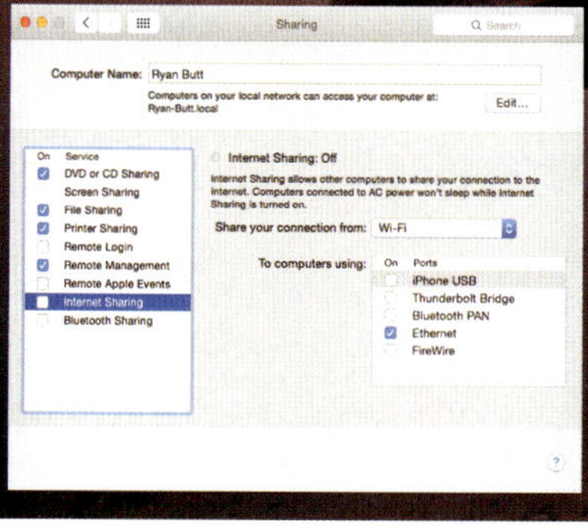

Remote Login

For those users happy typing commands into Terminal, this setting allows remote login to the Mac.

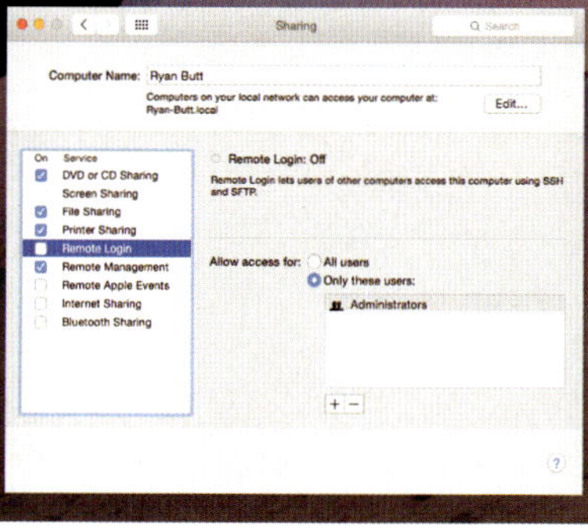

iCloud
Account Details

Sign in with your iCloud details to be able to sync details, files, music and movies across all of your devices.

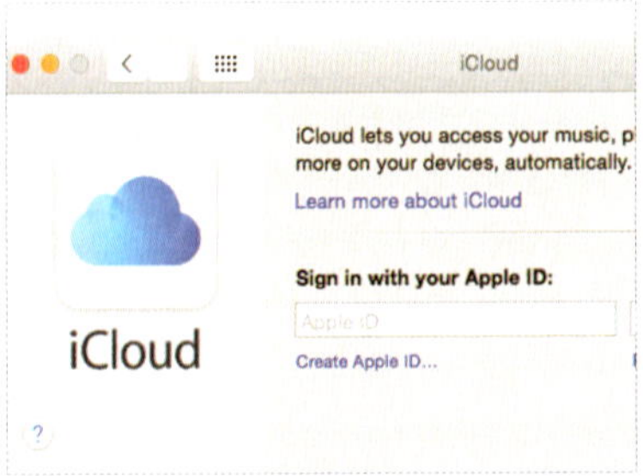

Sync

Syncing across iCloud allows multiple Macs and iPhones, even those in different locations, to share the same bookmarks, address books, calendars and more.

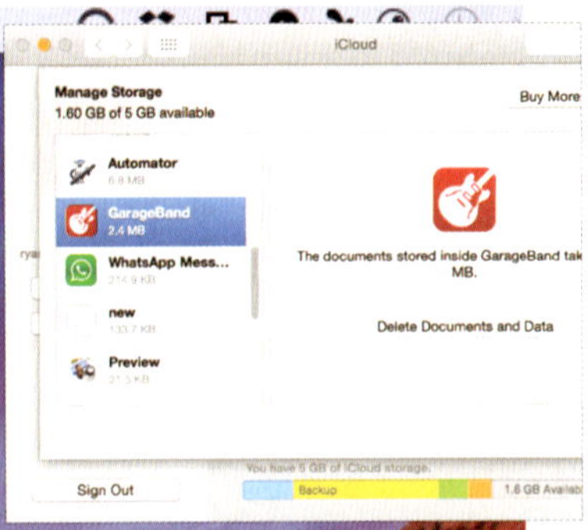

Manage

The iCloud is your virtual hard drive on the internet. You can use it to store photos, movies and files. This preference pane lets you check your space – you are provided with 5GB as standard but can purchase more if you need it.

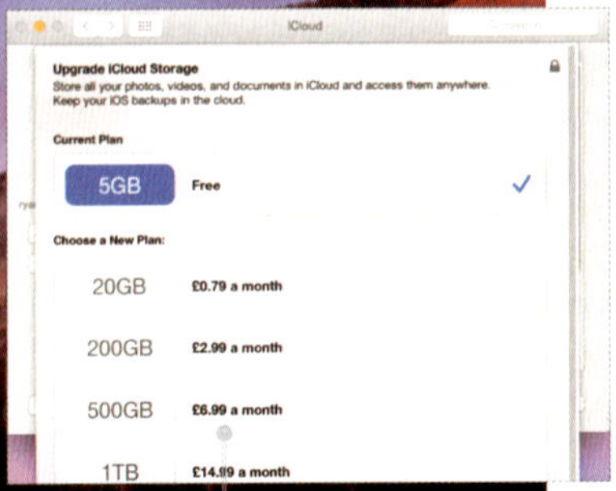

View Account

You can use this option to check that your existing account details are correct or edit them to reflect any changes in your address or credit card information. You can also upgrade your iCloud account with more storage.

Remote Management

A step-up from Screen Sharing, Remote Management allows system-level control of your Mac from afar.

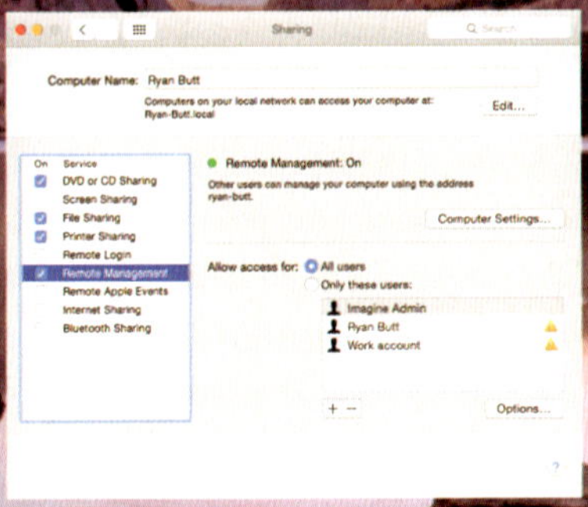

Remote Apple Events

For the real power users, Remote Apple Events allows your Mac to be automated by other computers.

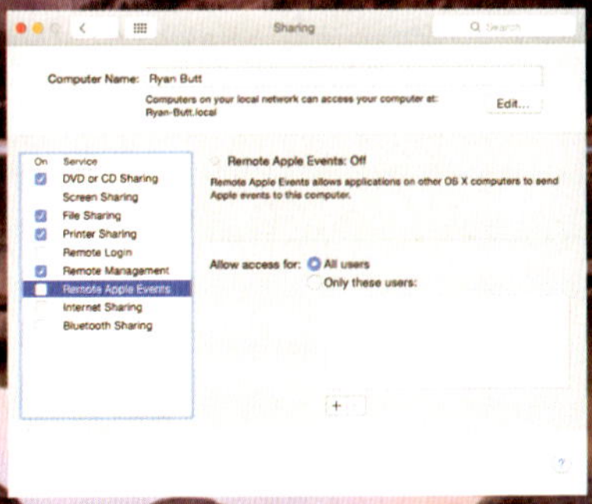

Purchase more space

Your iCloud account comes with 5GB of free space as standard, but if you come to realise that you require more, then click on 'Manage Account' and then click 'Change' next to the Storage option and purchase anything up to 50GB in storage space

Stay safe

You don't want to let just anyone send your files over Bluetooth, especially if you use a laptop in crowded areas like airports. To be safe, tick both 'Require pairing' boxes and leave the 'When' options as 'Ask What to Do'

Bluetooth Sharing

Share photos, ringtones and more with a mobile phone using Bluetooth Sharing to create a short range network to pass files across.

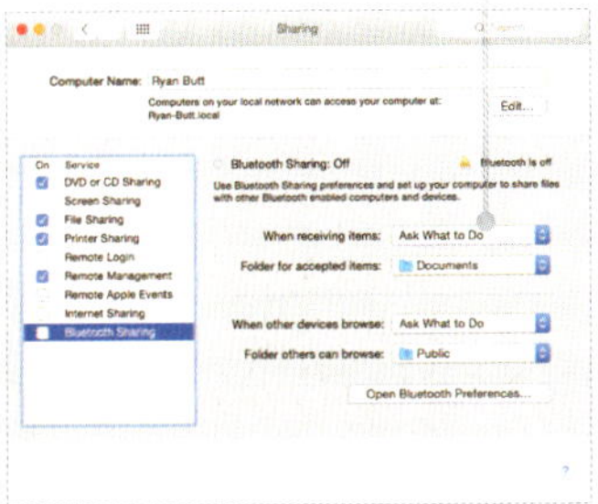

Inside System Preferences: System

Get to grips with the technology inside your Mac by following this final part of our guide to System Preferences. In this section: delve into the final row – the System settings

The System settings, like the Network settings above them, get deep down and dirty into the depths of OS X. Many of the changes affect all users of the Mac, and it's here where you'll discover the tools you need to control which users can do what. It's also where you'll find Accessibility, the first place you should go if you have physical difficulties that make it hard for you to enjoy using your Mac.

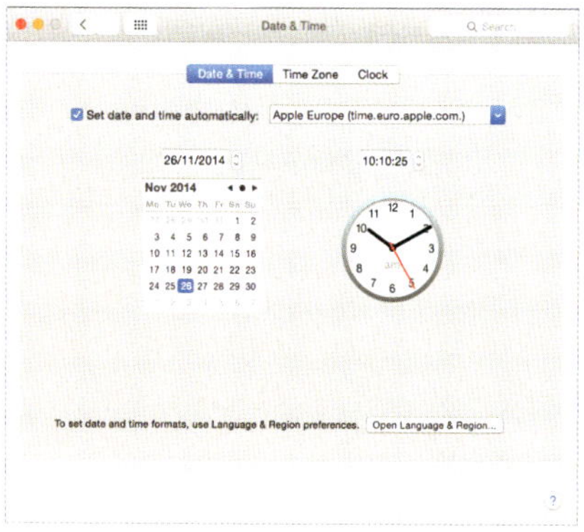

Date & Time

Always be sure that your Mac's clock is bang on time by setting it to automatically stay synchronised with Apple's time servers over the internet.

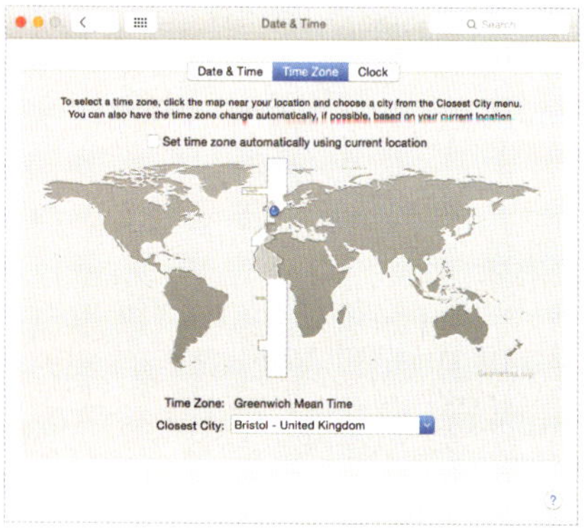

Time Zone

Let your Mac know where you are in the world by clicking the map near where you are, then choosing the closest city to you from the pop-up menu at the bottom of the screen.

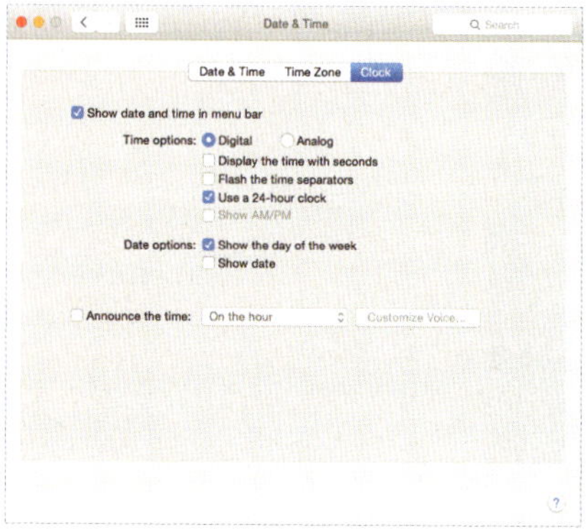

Clock

Set how your Menu bar displays the date and time. If Menu bar space is at a premium then you can choose to see a tiny analogue clock, or even get rid of it completely and have your Mac announce the time on the hour, every hour.

Finder File Edit View Go Window Help

Users & Groups

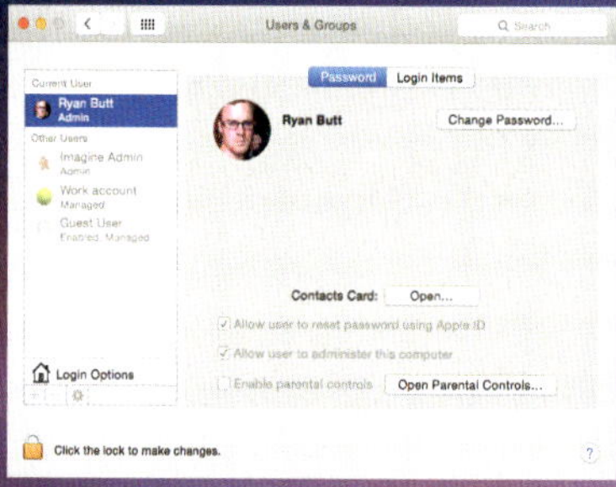

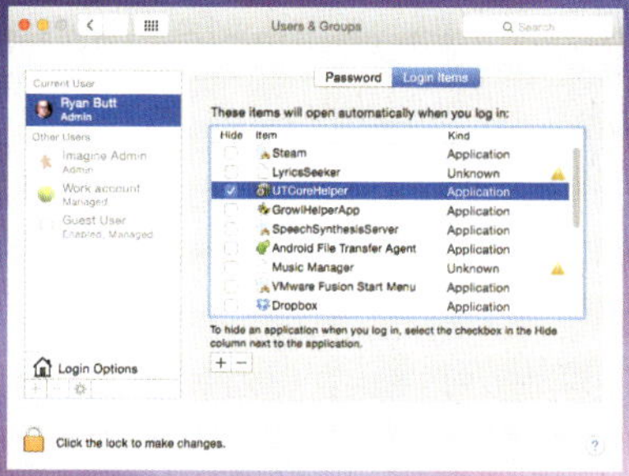

Password

The left panel of the Accounts screen allows you to create new user accounts, or select the account you wish to edit (only if you're an Admin user though). The settings on the right enable you to change your password and name (but not your short name that's used elsewhere on the system).

Login Items

Adding an application, by clicking the '+' button, sets it to automatically launch when you log in to your Mac. You're not limited to just applications though, as you can also set your regularly used documents to automatically open by adding them in the same way.

Dictation & Speech

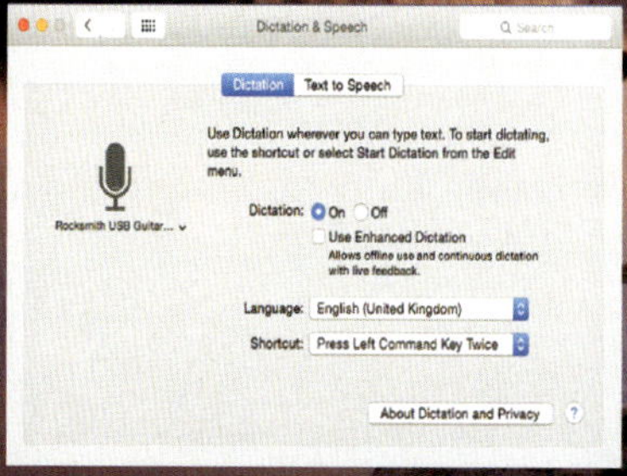

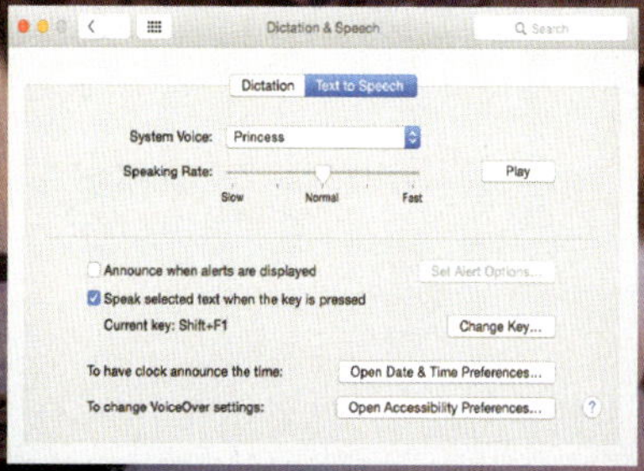

Dictation

Wherever you can type text on your Mac, you can now speak it instead. By activating this feature and using your Mac's built-in microphone, you can dictate to your machine and then the recording will be digitally sent to Apple and converted into text. Read more about it in the pane itself.

Text to speech

Not only can you talk to your Mac, it can talk straight back at you. Text to Speech can give you valuable audio feedback when your Mac requires your attention, speaking alert boxes and more. You can also choose your Mac's voice from a wide range of styles and speeds.

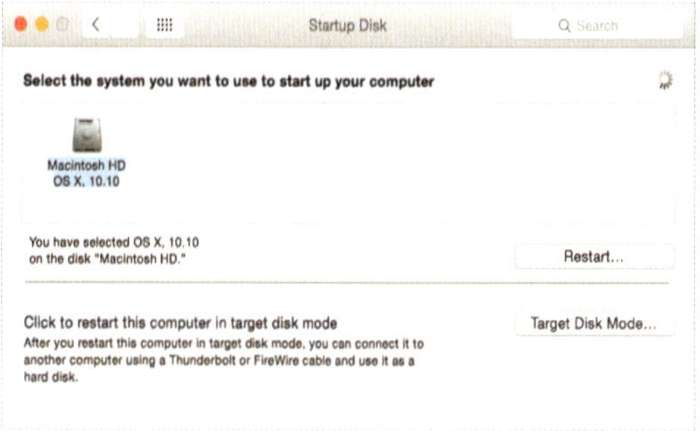

Startup Disk

For power users with different versions of Mac OS X installed across multiple hard drives, this pane enables you to pick the drive you'd like to start from.

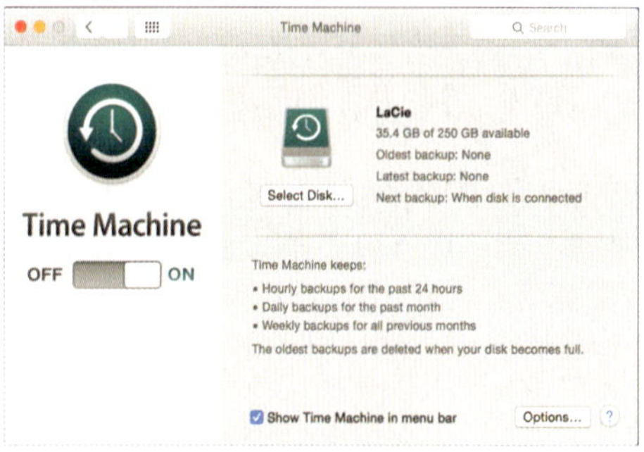

Time Machine

Mac OS X comes with what is arguably the best 'set it and forget it' backup utility: Time Machine. Turn it on, select a disk and then rest assured that your data is safe.

"You can choose how often you would like it to check for updates or run a manual check yourself"

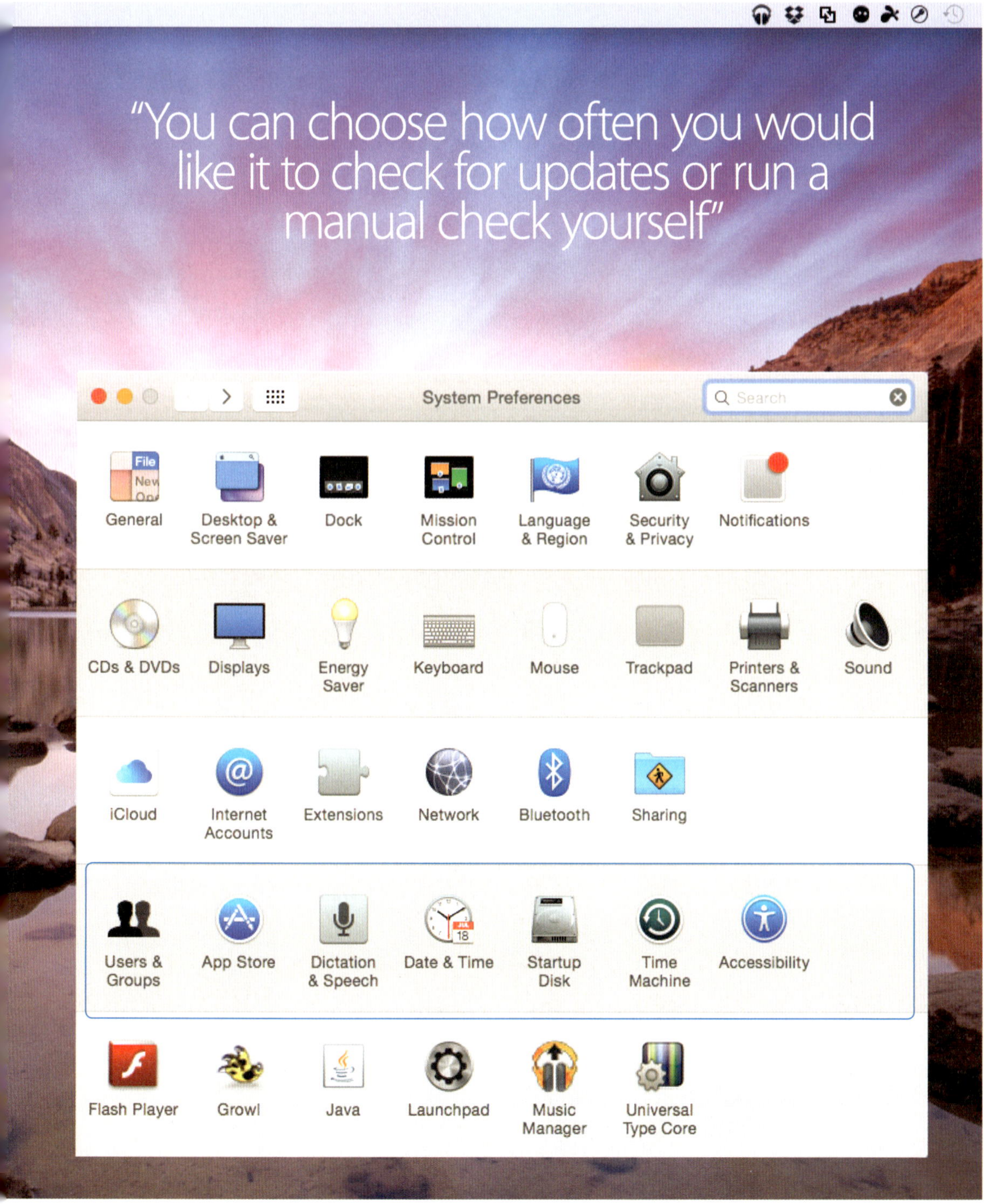

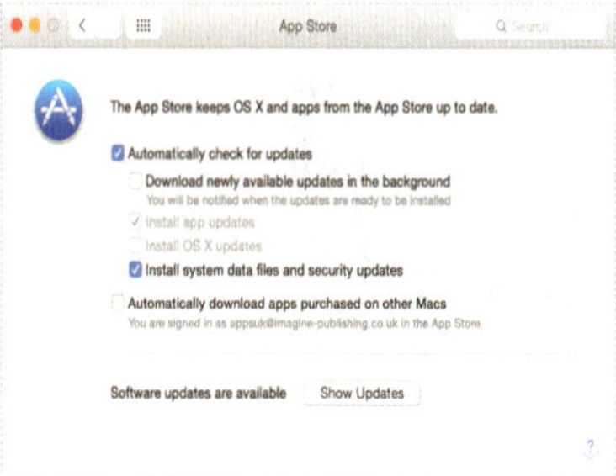

Software Update

Software Update runs automatically to ensure your Mac is always running the most up-to-date version of any Apple software you have installed, including OS X, iPhoto, iMovie, Pages and more. It lives inside the App Store app, but you can access Software Update via the App Store tab in System Preferences.

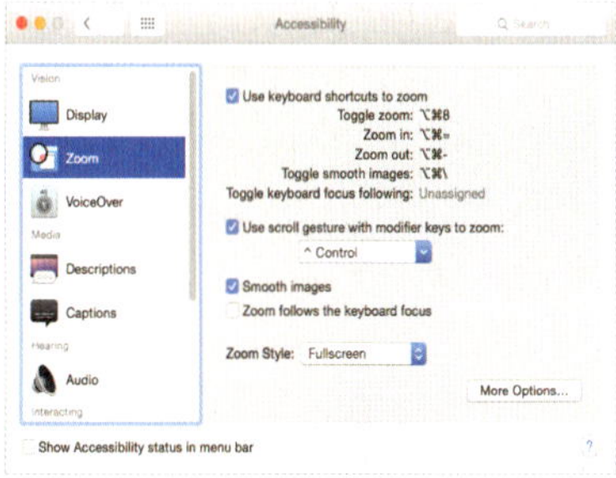

Accessibility

This pane houses all of the options to make the Mac much easier to use if you are visually impaired, hard of hearing or find it difficult to hold down multiple keys simultaneously. Here, you will find options relating to the display, keyboard, mouse and more, to tailor your Mac to your needs.

Tweak your trackpad settings in System Preferences

Learn how to change the settings in System Preferences to master multi-touch gestures

If multi-touch gestures, introduced with Snow Leopard, are the cornerstone of the OS X experience, then the trackpad can certainly be seen as the bricks and mortar that holds it all together. Without the built-in multi-touch trackpad on the MacBook Pro or MacBook Air, or the amazing wireless Magic Trackpad, OS X and its myriad new features wouldn't run half as smoothly.

The trackpad settings pane in System Preferences helps to make that experience even better by allowing you to decide which gestures perform what action, as well as playing you a handy video of exactly how to perform them. It means you can make the trackpad work exactly how you want it to and tailor it to your needs. In this tutorial, we'll show you how to get the best out of this little-known feature in order to make the most of your OS X experience. It's an easy process that will soon have you finding your way around your Mac with smooth moves that suit you.

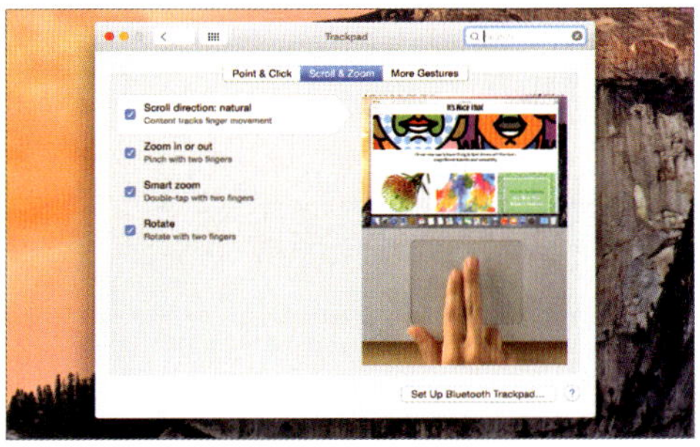

Using the preferences

Make the trackpad settings suit your needs with this window

MASTERING GESTURES

In order to get the most out of OS X, it's a good idea to get used to the gestures that will save you time. For example, pinching with your thumb and three fingers with a claw-like movement will bring up Launchpad, while pushing three fingers upwards will bring up Mission Control. Both gestures allow you to speed up things like organising your desktop and launching apps.

Tabs

Different trackpad settings are grouped under three different tabs – this makes finding exactly what you want to adjust a lot easier and quicker. It also helps to de-clutter what can often be confusing preference panes

Making settings simple

Recent versions of OS X have improved the UI of its trackpad settings by spacing out different settings and making it clear which ones relate to which gesture with the use of highlights, arrows and videos

Tracking problems?

If your Magic Trackpad is slow or unresponsive, your first port of call should be the tracking speed slider in the trackpad settings. If that doesn't make any difference, try replacing the batteries in your trackpad and reconnecting

Video previews

Even if you don't want to change any of your trackpad settings, the video previews in System Preferences can really help you master some of the more tricky multi-touch gestures. They're time-savers and worth learning

System Preferences Tweak your trackpad settings

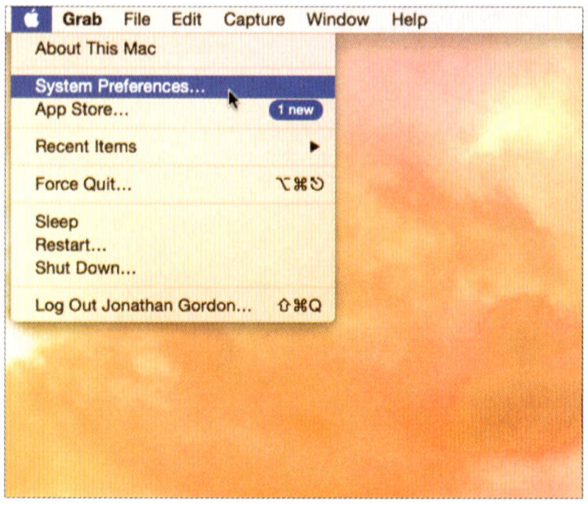

01: System Preferences

Click on the Apple logo in the menu bar, then click on System Preferences. Here you'll find all the settings for your Mac.

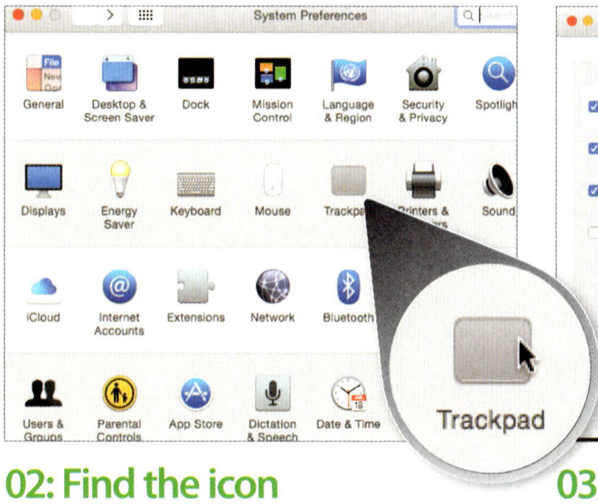

02: Find the icon

Click on the Trackpad icon in System Preferences – this is known as a preferences pane. When you install apps, they'll create preference panes here.

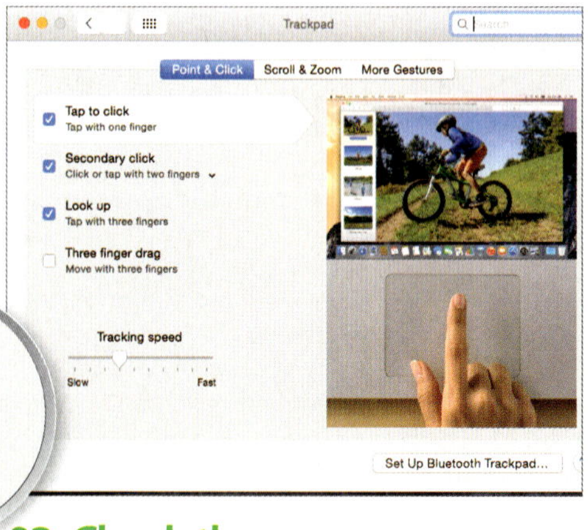

03: Check them

Trackpad settings are displayed as checkboxes; check or uncheck them to activate or deactivate the settings. A video description is included to help you.

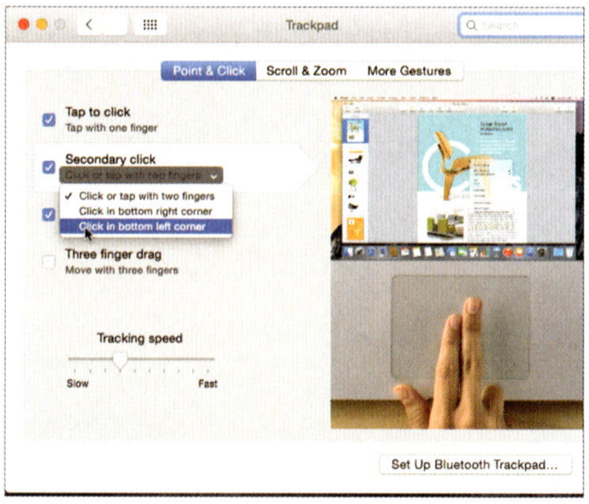

04: Change the gesture

Under some settings, you can change the gesture that controls them. Click on the drop-down menu and choose the gesture that best suits you.

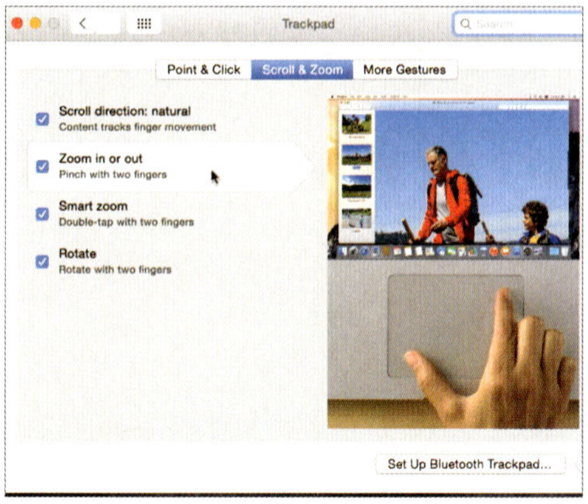

05: Hover and preview

A short video animation is displayed to help you understand how to perform different gestures. Simply hover over the gesture's name to preview.

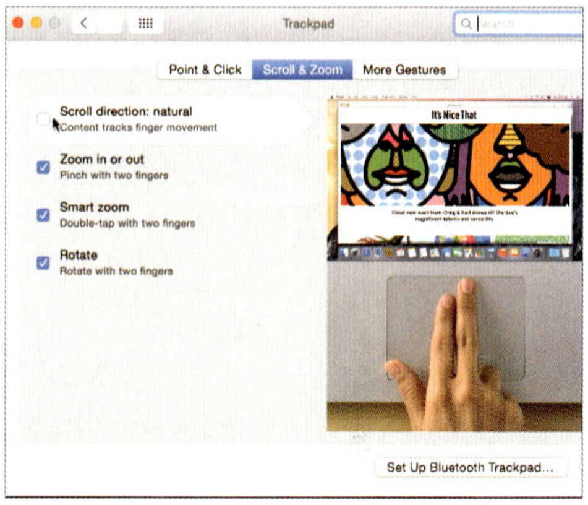

06: Different directions

Uncheck 'Scroll direction: natural' to revert two-finger scrolling to pre-Lion behaviour. Since then, content follows your finger movement.

07: More Gestures

Under the More Gestures tab you'll find some of the more complex gestures. Make use of the videos to master these new features.

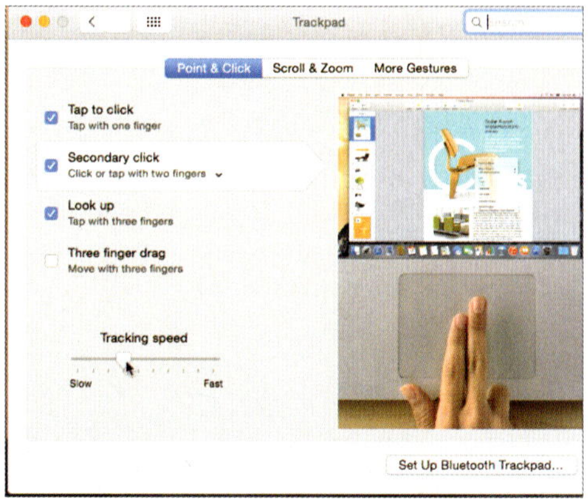

08: Tracking Speed

Drag the Tracking Speed slider to adjust the sensitivity to your finger movement. The faster on the slider, the more responsive it will be.

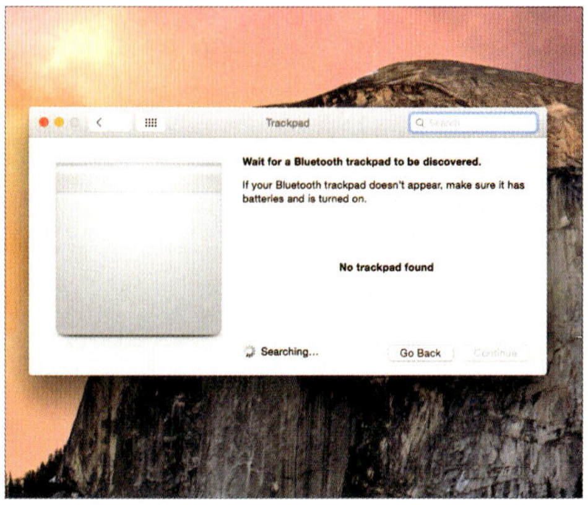

09: Magic Trackpads

If you own a Magic Trackpad, set it up by clicking 'Set Up Bluetooth Trackpad' in the bottom corner of the Trackpad settings window.

Recover files with Time Machine

Your guide to restoring lost and changed files with Apple's built-in backup app

A lot of the files on your Mac will no doubt be quite valuable. There are videos, music, photos, personal and work-related documents, and much more on the disk drive. How would you cope if you lost them? Fortunately, Time Machine aims to solve the problem by making backups – copies – of files, and storing them elsewhere in a safe place. If you lose a file for whatever reason, be it an accidental deletion or a disk fault, then Time Machine lets you recover it.

It is called 'Time Machine' because that's what it is. For all intents and purposes, it effectively allows you to go back in time, and if a folder contained a file last week that you can no longer find, then you simply turn back the clock and retrieve it. It's a brilliant feature, and not just for lost files; you can retrieve earlier versions of files that have changed, too. The latest Time Machine is the best yet, and you no longer need to have a second disk drive in order to use it.

> "You don't need a second disk drive to use Time Machine"

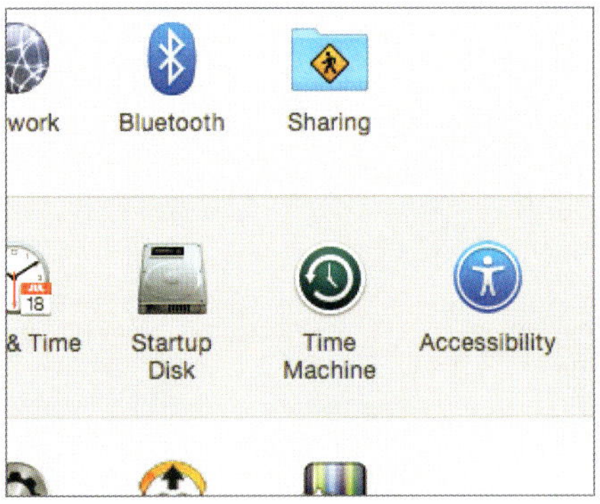

Work with Time Machine

The key parts of Time Machine you need to know

OS X'S LOCAL BACKUP

Suppose your MacBook at home or work is connected to a USB disk drive in order to enable Time Machine to back up the whole hard disk drive. When you go out with your MacBook, that Time Machine disk is no longer available. Don't worry; since Lion, Time Machine continues to back up files by using spare space on the local internal disk.

Browse the disk

Time Machine opens the current Finder window or the desktop. You can then navigate the disk, and change to any folder using the usual Finder features. The Sidebar shows Favourite locations

The timeline

On the right is a timeline that stretches from the present back to the distant past. Dates where backups were made to the Mac's disk are in grey, and purple shows backups to a USB disk drive

Restore the file

You can select a single file or a whole folder of files in the Finder window, and click the big 'Restore' button. Ctrl/right-clicking a file reveals other options, such as 'Get Info'

Back and forth

Guess when your lost file is located by clicking a title bar in the stack, or by clicking the timeline. Then use the forward and back buttons to move one step at a time and find the file

Time Machine Find and restore lost files

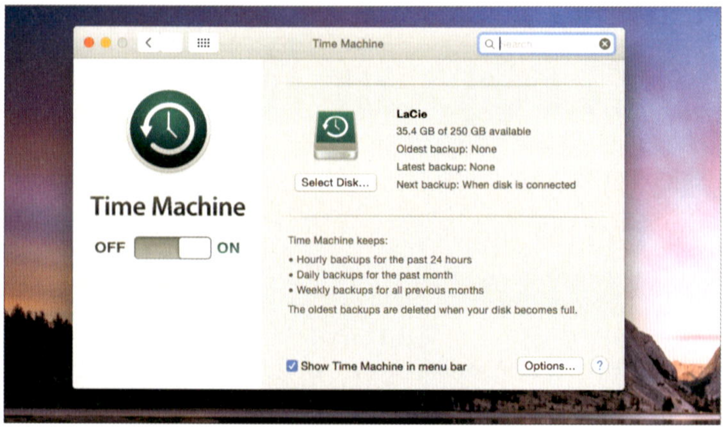

01: Turn it on

Go to System Preferences on the Apple menu, and click 'Time Machine'. There is a useful option to show the status in the menu.

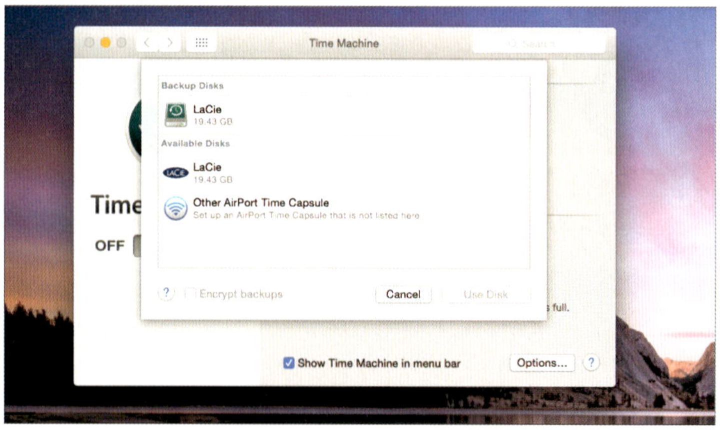

02: Choose a disk

Click the 'Select Disk' button, and the disk drives connected to the Mac are displayed. Time Machine works best if you select a large empty disk.

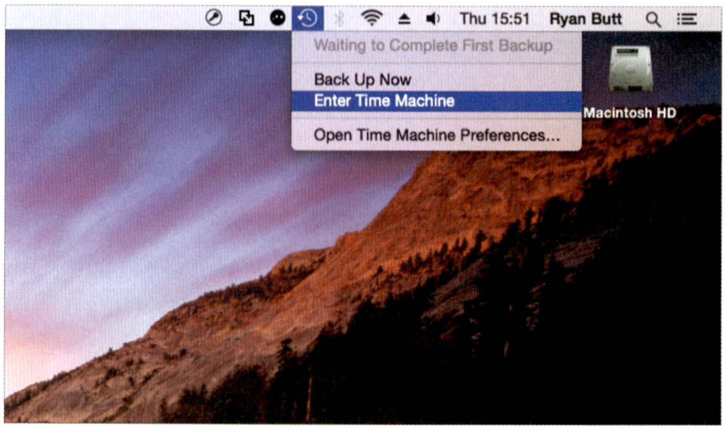

03: Enter Time Machine

Once set up, you won't notice it. Click the menu bar icon, and there are options to start a backup immediately, or enter Time Machine. Let's enter it.

04: Browse the backups

A stack of Finder windows are displayed, and you can navigate the disk to any folder. Move back in time using the arrows or timeline on the right.

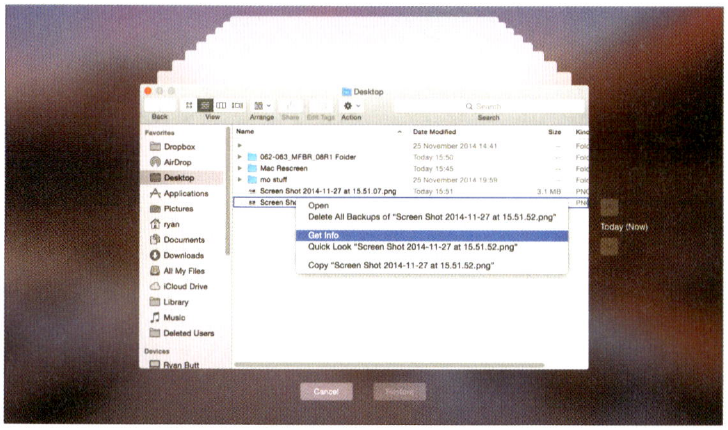

05: Select and restore

A file can be selected in the Finder window, but there are more options available by Ctrl/right-clicking. Alternatively, click on Restore.

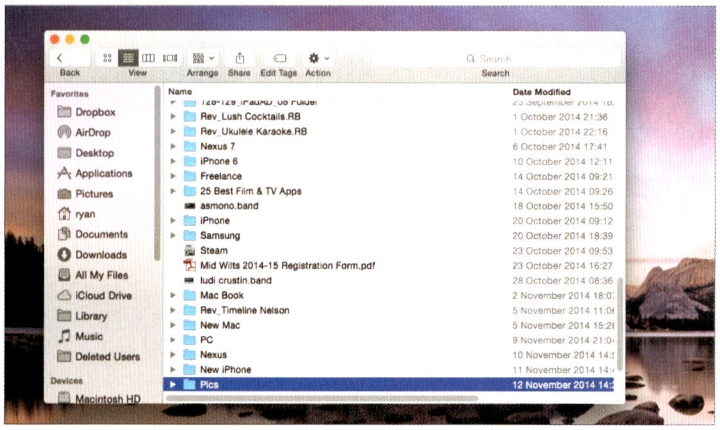

06: Save the file

Time Machine asks you to select a folder in which to put the file. It can be put back in the folder it went missing from, or stored in a different one.

Use Disk Utility to check the health of your hard drive and repair it

Checking and improving the health of your hard drive is easier than you think. With a couple of clicks you can set your mind at rest…

It can become pretty scary when your Mac starts to show tell-tale signs of wear and tear. As well built as they are, like everything else on the planet, they are susceptible to the pitfalls of ageing. Prolonged use and writing and rewriting of data can cause things to slow down, and in some cases cause errors.

Luckily, Apple has made it very easy for you to check on the health of your hard drive. Using an application called Disk Utility, users can very easily check disks, repair damage and even erase free space to keep the volume healthy and happy. If used on a regular basis you can quite easily keep your hard drive from slowing down and retain that great snappy feeling you had when you first bought your Mac. You will also, with regular use, be able to spot any serious problems before they cause any devastating loss of data.

"Luckily, Apple has made it easy to check on the health of your hard drive"

Get a snappier drive with Disk Utility

Clearing free space on your drive can have a marked improvement on performance

Erase options
Here you can choose the level of erasing you wish to use. The 35 step is the best, but it will take an incredibly long time. Pick whichever method suits you best

Tab it up
Clicking here will take you to the Erase section. Be extra careful before you click anything here as you could wipe important files

Double check
Be sure that you are making changes to the correct disk. Check and double check before starting actions in Disk Utility

Erase Free Space
This will only erase space that isn't being actively used; so if you've done some house keeping and cleared a lot of files out then this is a good way to get some performance back as a result of the change

SERIOUS PROBLEMS
Disk Utility may not be able to repair serious problems, but it will definitely let you know if it spots anything untoward. Any serious problems will be highlighted in red and often there will be advice on the best course of action. In serious cases, this will be to contact Apple or a reseller.

Disk Utility Use Disk Utility to repair your hard drive

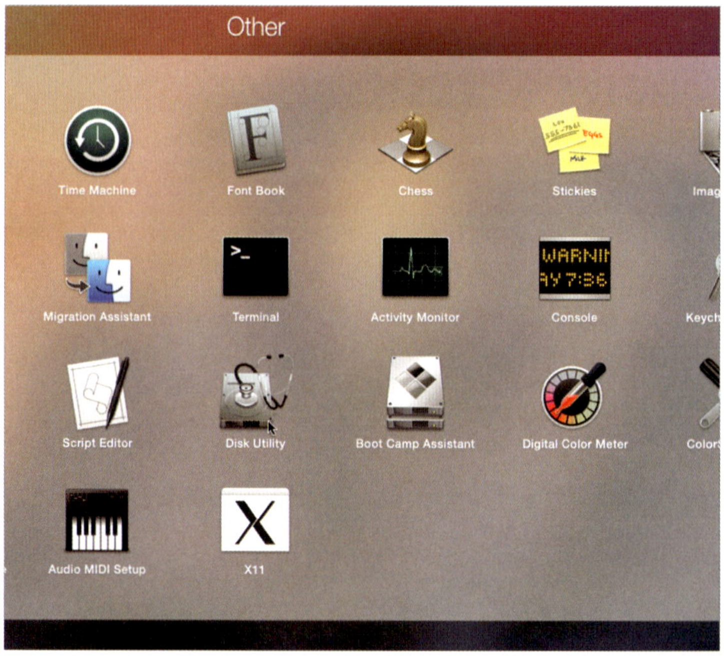

01: Load it

You can find Disk Utility by going to your Applications folder. Once you have navigated here, choose the Utilities folder and double-click on the Disk Utility app. Alternatively, use Launchpad from your Dock and navigate to the folder called 'Other'. You will find Disk Utility in here.

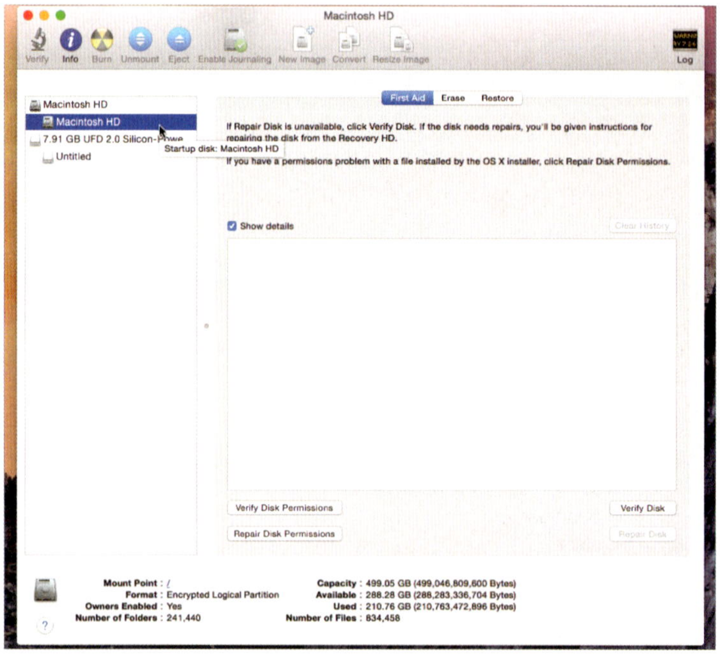

02: Pick a drive

The utility will work on any connected drive, including your startup disk. These will be shown down the left hand side. You just need to remember to click on the disk that you want to check before you start carrying out any specific actions.

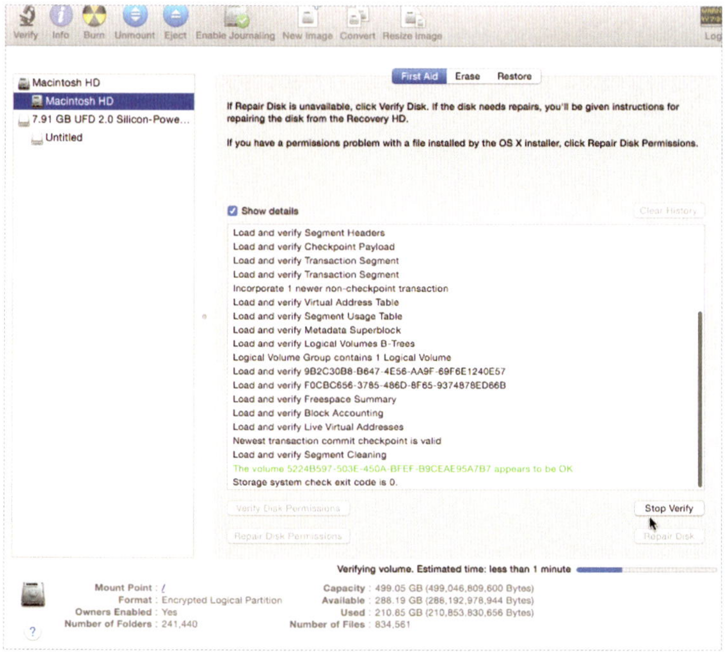

03: Verify Permissions

Click the Verify Permissions button and the utility will begin checking the disk for any errors. Depending on the size of the drive and the speed of your processor, this could take some time so why not go and make yourself a cup of tea while you wait?

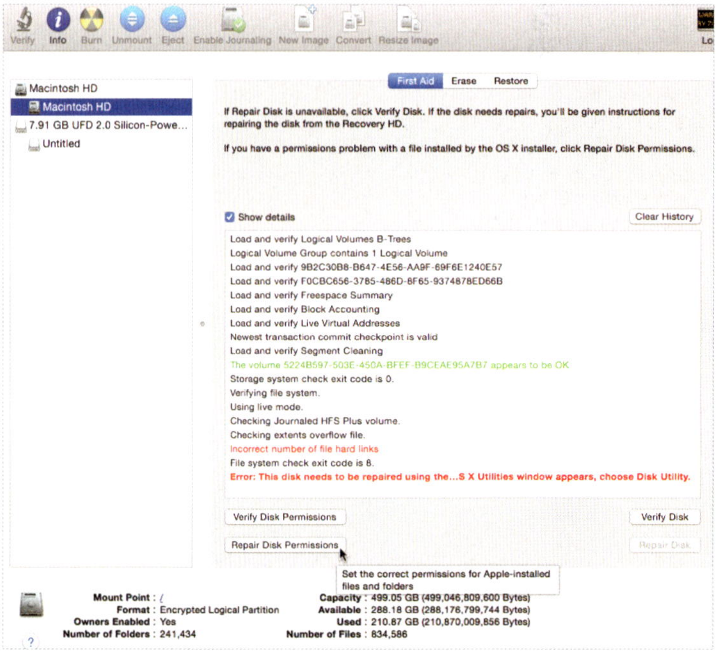

04: Repair Permissions

When the disk has been verified you should get a report detailing what it has found. If there are any warnings in there then you will need to click the Repair Permissions button. Again, this could take a while, so be patient. After that you're all done.

Discover the Activity Monitor utility

A lot of your computer functions take place behind the scenes. Activity Monitor helps you check and control these activities

Quietly tucked away in your Utilities folder, Activity Monitor is one of those simple yet useful applications that is a crucial part of what makes a Mac great to use. First of all, it can give you a great deal of information about what is happening inside your computer and, secondly, this very convivial software consists not only of an instructive tool for the beginner but also a troubleshooting powerhouse for the more experienced user to monitor activity with when things are hard to explain.

Activity Monitor principally provides a flexible list of all the system and user processes taking place at any given moment inside your Mac. Additionally, it allows a quick look at your Mac's resource allocation and system performances. Let's see how to use this tool with our step-by-step guide to Activity Monitor's main functions.

"It can give you a great deal of information on what is happening"

Understand processes

The inner workings of your Mac explained

View menu

Activity Monitor's View menu controls many aspects of the information displayed, from the type of Dock icon to the nature and number of columns in the main window, including the update frequency of the readings

WHAT ARE PROCESSES?

Processes are software running in your computer's memory and CPU that take part in the running of applications; some software consists of several processes running together. For instance, Mac OS X is made up of a large number of System processes launched during your computer boot sequence. In contrast, the Finder consists of one single User process initiated at login time.

Terminate a process

When stalled processes or the remains of a crashed piece of software are found, they can be terminated by selecting them in the list and clicking the red hexagonal Quit Process icon in the application toolbar

Application icon

The default Activity Monitor Dock icon can be replaced with a number of alternative ones showing live information about your system. These can display CPU workload, disk activity and network activity as well as memory usage

CPU AND MEMORY MEANINGS

The Central Processing Unit (CPU), also known as the processor, is the brain of your Mac. It works closely with RAM (Random Access Memory) and Virtual memory, also known as swap file. RAM and Virtual memory are kinds of data storage; the latter is located on your hard disk and the former in the electronic chips inside your computer.

Process sorting or filtering

Since column information can be sorted with a click on a header, the list can also be filtered by either typing a keyword in the toolbar search field or choosing a process from the drop-down list

Activity Monitor Inside the Activity Monitor utility

01: Locate and launch

Select Launchpad from the Dock, then click on the 'Other' folder and click on Activity Monitor to open up the app.

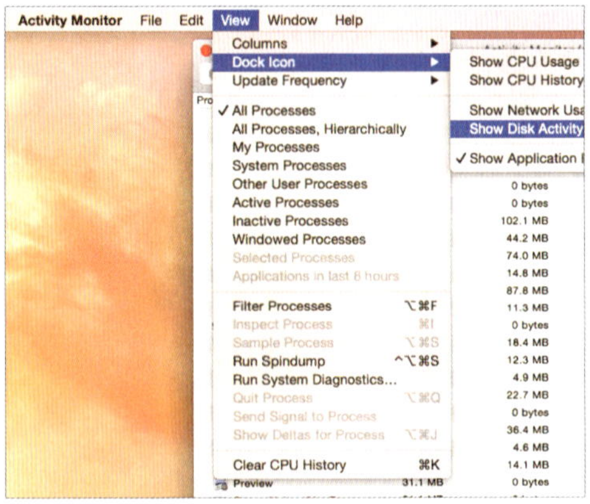

02: Activity Monitor's menus

The Activity Monitor menu has no Preferences menu item – its most relevant functionalities are located in the View and Window menus.

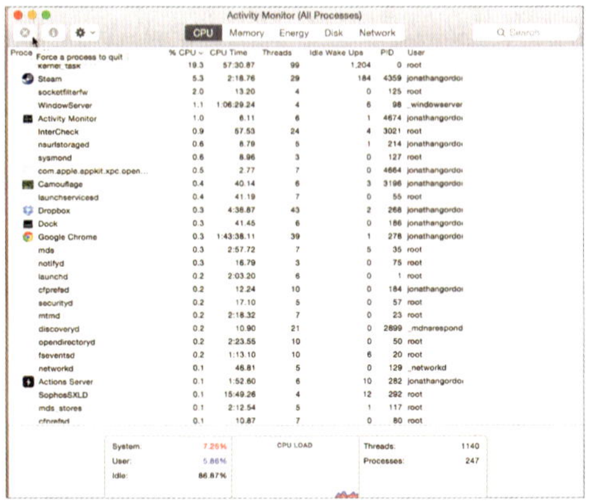

03: Toolbar

Many of AM's functions are accessible from its toolbar: terminating or inspecting processes and allowing the filtering and sorting of process data.

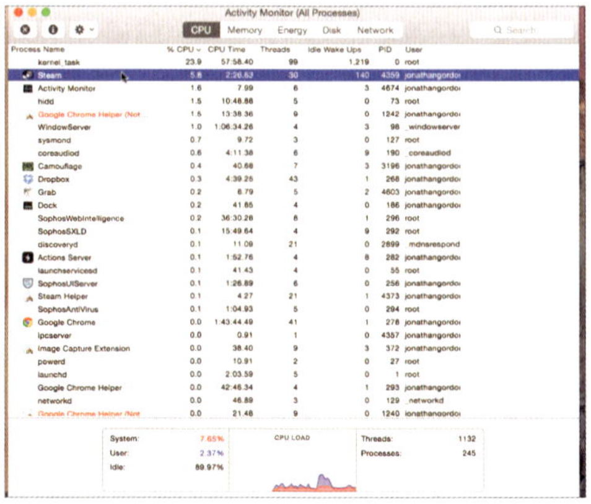

04: Process list

The main window is devoted to listing all the processes taking place on your computer. It's configurable and displays process information.

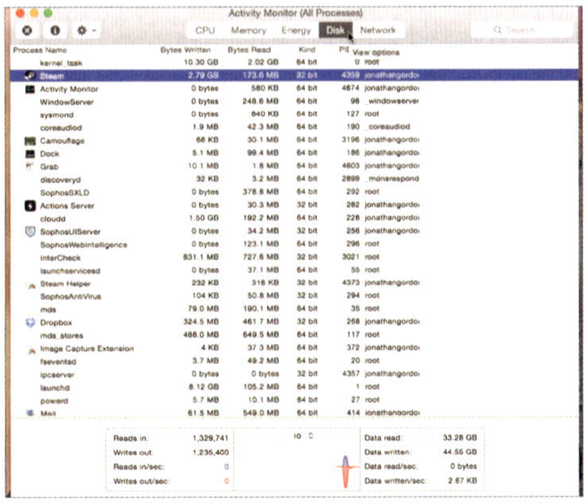

05: Monitor tabs

Above the process list a row of monitoring tabs present info on CPU, System Memory, Disk and Network activity as well as performances.

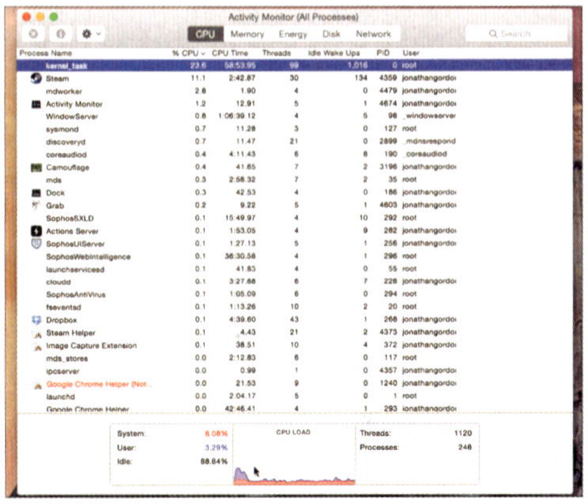

06: Monitor CPU power

Using a live display, this permits the monitoring of processor activity. It shows the amount of power used by User System and idle processes.

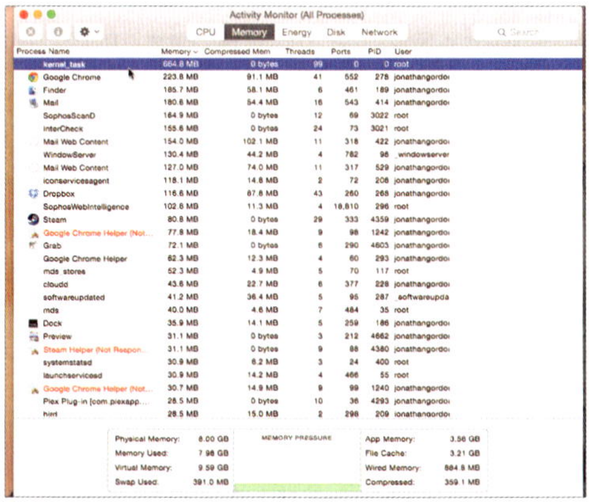

07: Monitor System Memory

The System Memory tab interface is very detailed – the colour scheme used to list the amount of memory allocated can also be used in a pie chart.

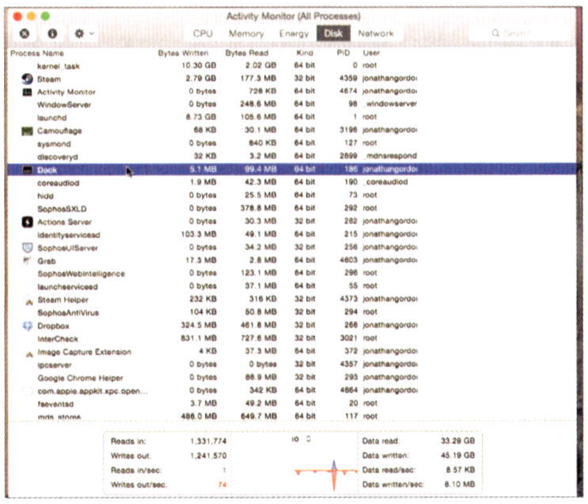

08: Disk Activity & Usage tabs

The Disk Activity and Usage tabs allow you to assess free and used space. They also give control of the amount of read/write operations occurring.

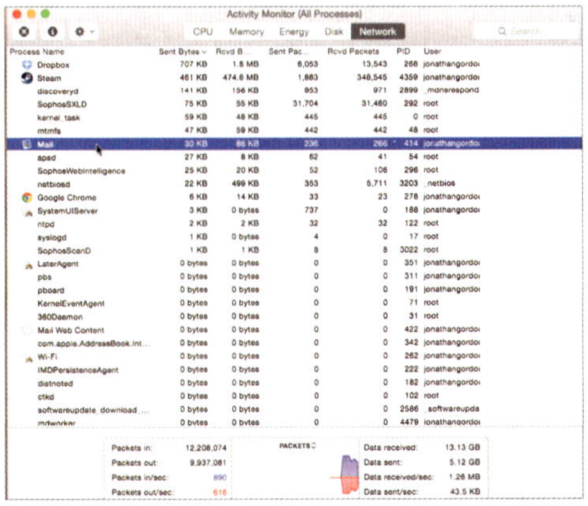

09: Network monitoring tab

The protocol-level, network tab shows the number of sent and received data packets over your connection and a live view of traffic.

Use AirDrop to share files

Get to know AirDrop, one of OS X's most useful features for transferring files fast

Transferring files had, for a long time, been an incredibly tedious process. Before Wi-Fi was commonplace, users were forced to save their files to floppy disks and USB Flash drives, unplug them, plug into another device, then drag the files onto their desktops. Even now, for many users the process involves creating an email and sending it to themselves, a process that not only takes time, but also inbox space.

Since Lion, there's been a much simpler solution to this problem, and it's called AirDrop. When you open up the finder, you'll notice that there are a number of icons in the sidebar on the left hand side. One of these is the AirDrop icon, which is in the shape of a radar mast. Clicking this icon will start AirDrop, and any other users who have also opened the AirDrop section will appear in the finder window. From here, you can drag and drop documents, images, movies and more onto the icon and send them through the air quickly and simply in seconds.

> "Drag and drop files and send them through the air"

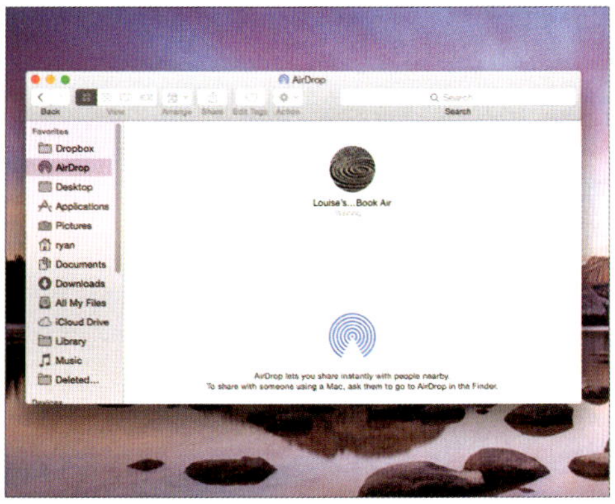

The AirDrop interface

Find your way around the key parts of this sharing service

Multi-user
If there are a number of computers in the area with a recent edition of OS X installed, you will be able to view them all at once in the same window and drop your files into any one of them instantly

Get Info
If you Ctrl/right-click and select 'Get Info', this window will open. For most applications there is a lot of information, but for AirDrop, all you can really do is copy the icon from the top left corner

Scanning
The spinning radar icon shows that AirDrop is constantly scanning for other users while this window is open. They will need to open the AirDrop tab as well if you want to find them locally

WIRELESS NETWORK
Unlike applications like Dropbox and DropCopy, you don't actually need to be connected to a network to use AirDrop and share your files. When you open AirDrop, your computer will start sending out a wireless signal, and when other users do the same, the machines can detect each other. Even if there is no wireless network around you, you can still send files, as your Mac will create a temporary, secure network specifically for the transfer.

Limited options
Again, because AirDrop is a system-level application, you are severely limited by the view options. For most folders you could change almost everything, but this is strictly limited

AirDrop Transfer your files wirelessly

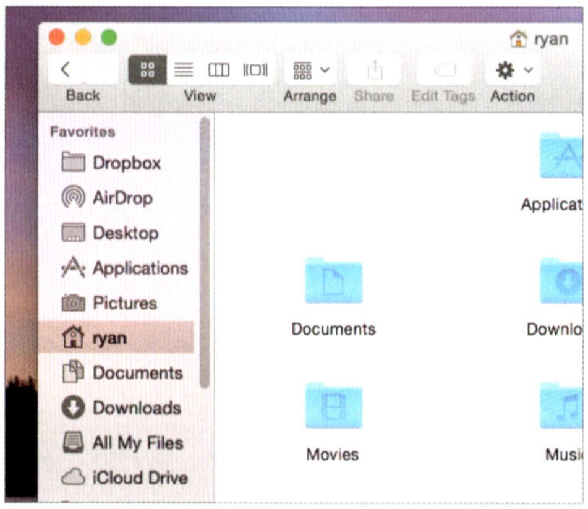

01: Find AirDrop

All you need to do to activate the system is open a Finder window and look in the sidebar. AirDrop is the circular icon with radio mast.

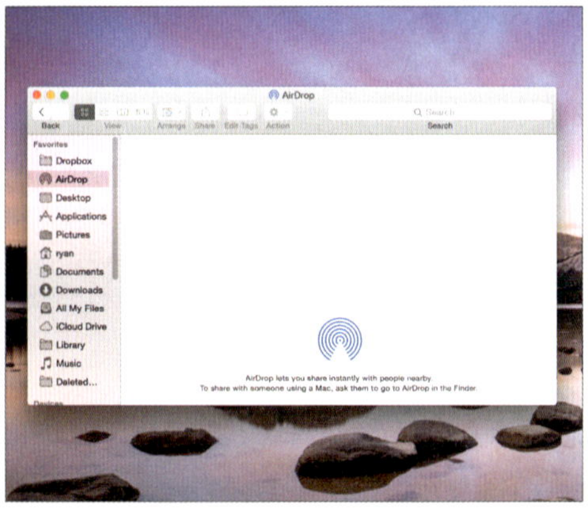

02: Radar on

When you click the AirDrop icon, it will display a radar-style display with a line rotating around the main AirDrop icon.

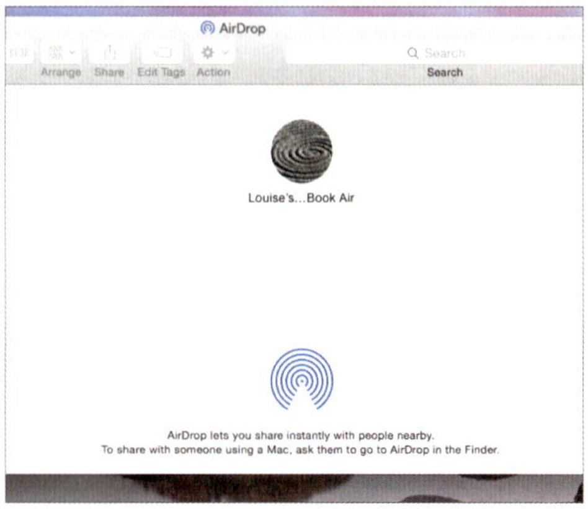

03: View other users

When another OS X user clicks on AirDrop, they will become visible in your AirDrop window. You can have more than two people at once.

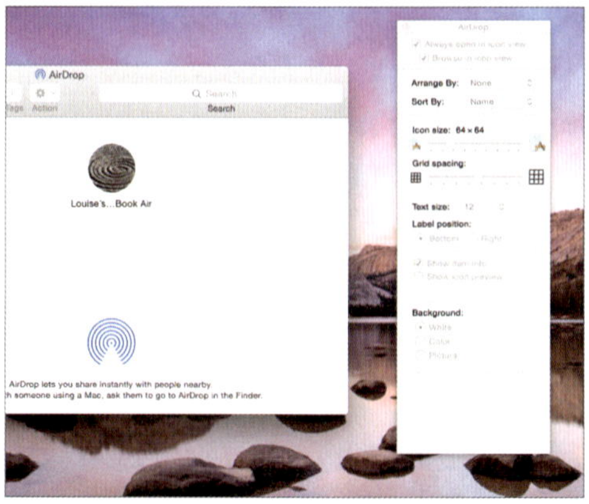

04: View options

If you Ctrl-click in AirDrop and choose 'Show View Options', you'll see a grey Menu. AirDrop is a system app, so you can't change view options.

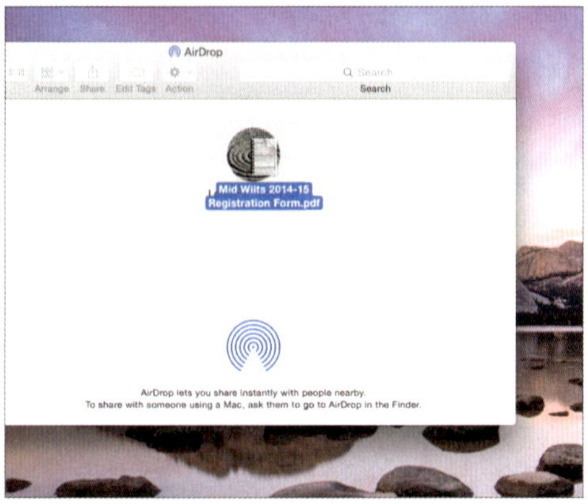

05: AirDrop

When you have found the file you want to transfer, simply drag and drop it onto the icon of the person who has connected to you.

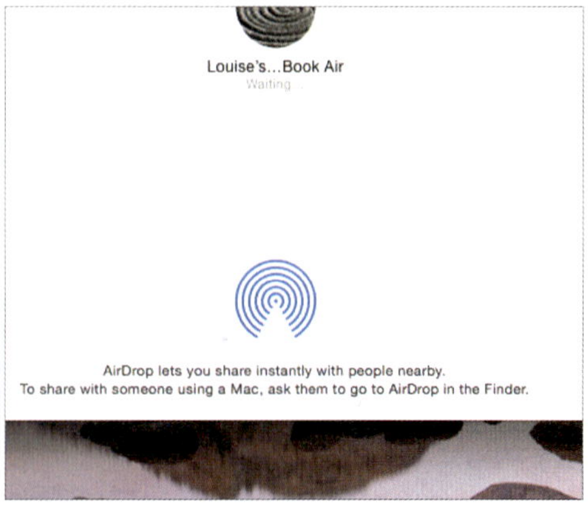

06: Prompted

Before it is sent, you'll be prompted to ensure this is the file you want to send. It will give you the full rundown of what you are transferring, and where.

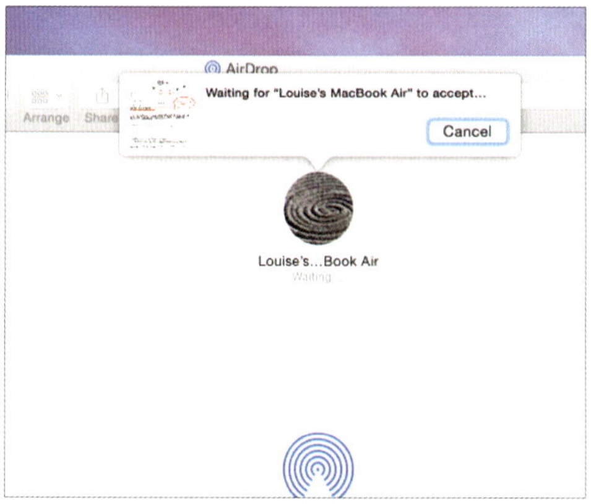

07: Receiving the file

On the other machine, a prompt will let you know someone is transferring a file. You have to choose an option before the transfer can begin.

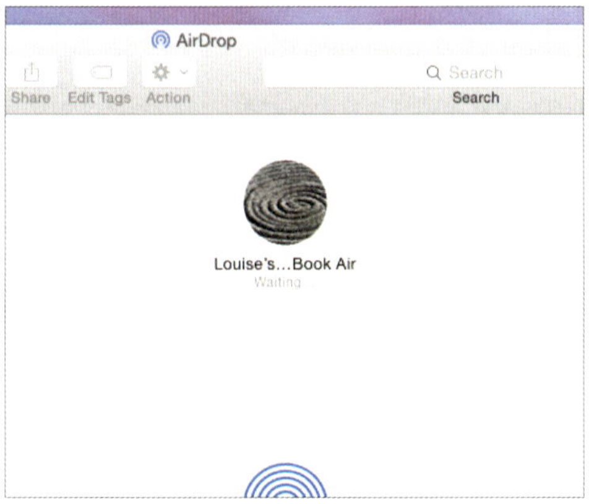

08: Awaiting transfer

As the file is transferring, you will see a progress bar that circles the icon of the sender. It will meet itself at the top when the transfer is complete.

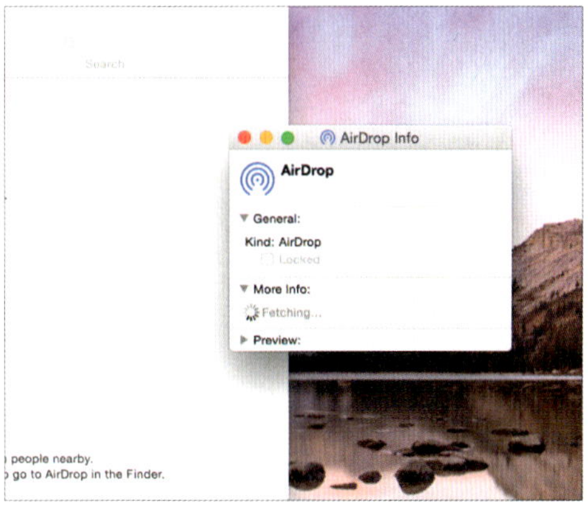

09: Find out more

If you want the AirDrop icon, click in the window and choose 'Get Info' to see this menu. Nothing can be changed about the file, as it's locked.

Set up and explore iCloud Drive

Access your files instantly – anywhere and at any time with one of Yosemite's coolest features

iDisk was Apple's previous virtual disk drive, but with iOS 8 came a reinvention and a new name – iCloud Drive – and a whole host of new features to boot. Not only does iCloud Drive enable you to store any type of file up to 15GB in size, it syncs the documents created in your favourite Apple apps such as Pages and Keynote so they're ready for editing on all of your other Apple devices – just like the Documents in the Cloud functionality.

In this tutorial we're going to walk you through the process of getting iCloud Drive set up and ready to use (don't worry, it's really easy). All you need to do is upgrade your Mac's OS to OS X Yosemite, which is available from the Mac App Store, totally free of charge.

> "iCloud Drive syncs your favourite apps"

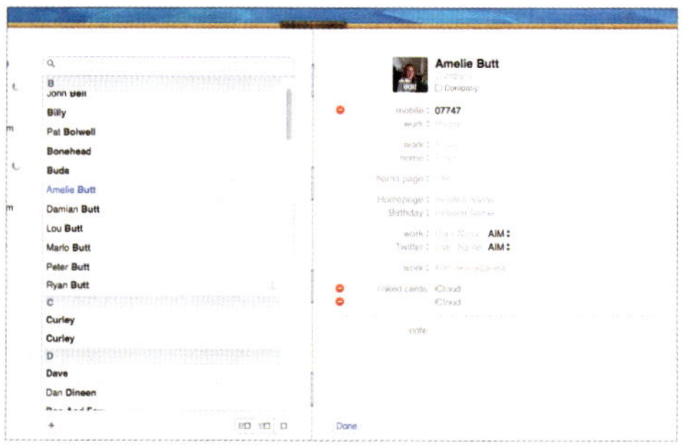

iCloud Drive Set up and use Apple's newest storage solution

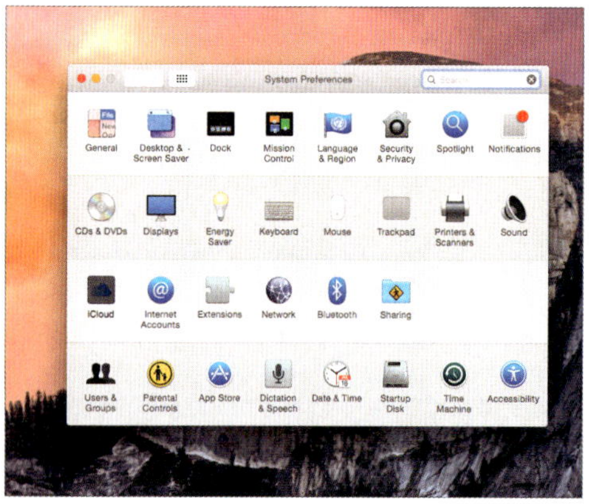

01: Launch iCloud Preferences

Click the Apple logo (top-left). Select System Preferences from the drop-down menu, then click the iCloud icon.

02: Sign in to iCloud

To sign in to iCloud, enter your credentials. If you are signed in, ensure there is a tick in the box next to the iCloud Drive option.

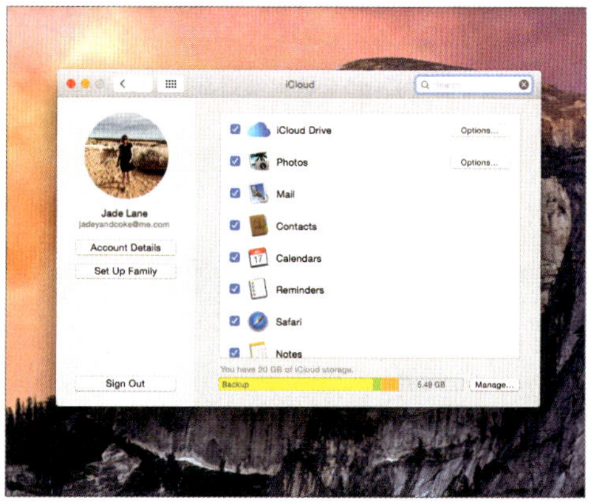

03: Activate iCloud Drive

Place a tick inside the iCloud Drive box. This will activate iCloud Drive for your iCloud account and move existing iCloud documents to the service.

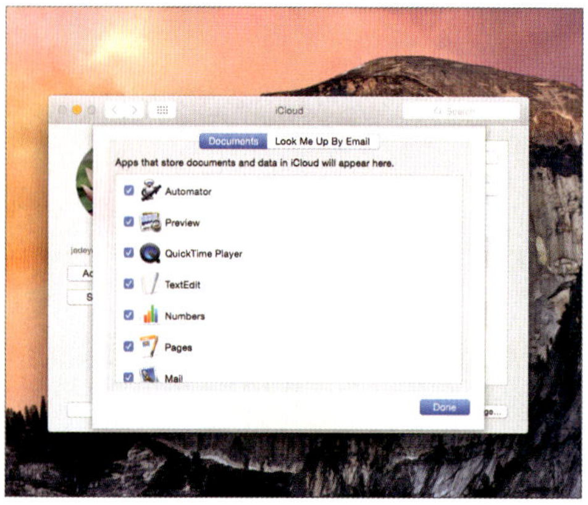

04: Documents in the Cloud

Click 'Options'. Ensure that the apps you were using previously with Documents in the Cloud are ticked. This will move your documents over to iCloud Drive.

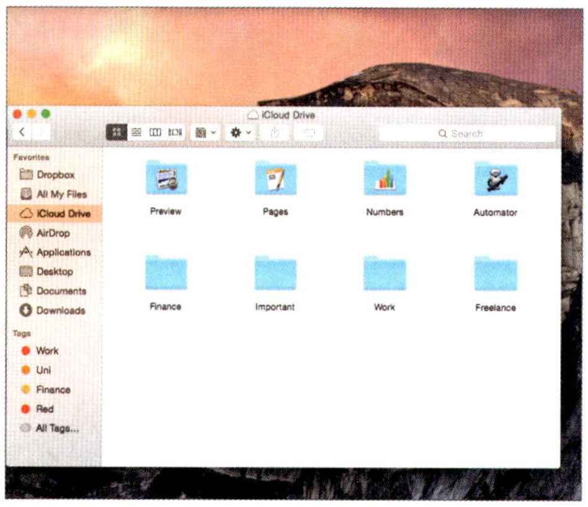

05: Access iCloud Drive

Access by launching Finder and selecting iCloud Drive. Create new folders or drag documents from your Mac's hard drive to iCloud for instant access.

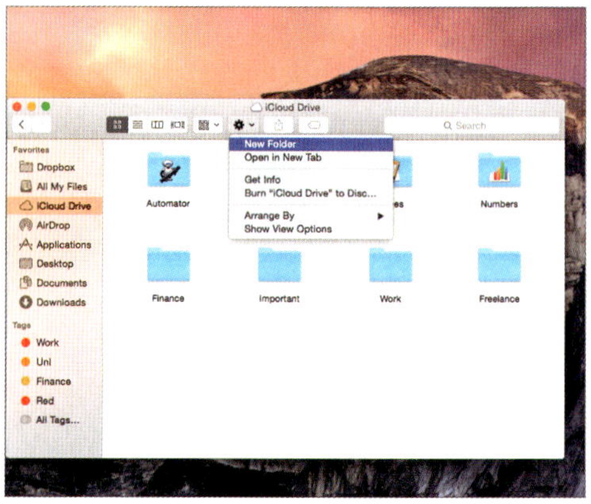

06: Create new folders

To create a new folder, right-click in iCloud Drive and select New Folder from the drop-down. Or, click on the cog icon and choose New Folder.

Create a document

A quick overview of creating and saving straight to iCloud Drive

Launch Pages, Numbers or Keynote

Launch the Pages, Numbers or Keynote app from your Applications folder in Finder. If you don't have them installed on your Mac already, you can purchase or re-download them from the Mac App Store

View document in iCloud

To confirm that your document is being saved in iCloud, select the File menu and hold down the Cmd key. Click on the Save As option – the save location should be listed as iCloud Drive

Set save location

Select iCloud Drive from the left-hand column; alternatively, choose it from the Location drop-down menu in the top centre of the interface. This will be the save location for your new document

Create new document

To create the document, click the New Document button in the bottom-left corner of the interface. Choose a template for your new document and begin working on it in the app as you would usually

ICLOUD DRIVE SYSTEM REQUIREMENTS

iCloud Drive is only available on Macs running OS X Yosemite and iOS devices running iOS 8. If your Mac is running Yosemite but your devices are running iOS 7 or earlier, your documents will not sync to all devices. OS X Yosemite is available for free from the Mac App Store, while iOS 8 is free to download on your iOS device.

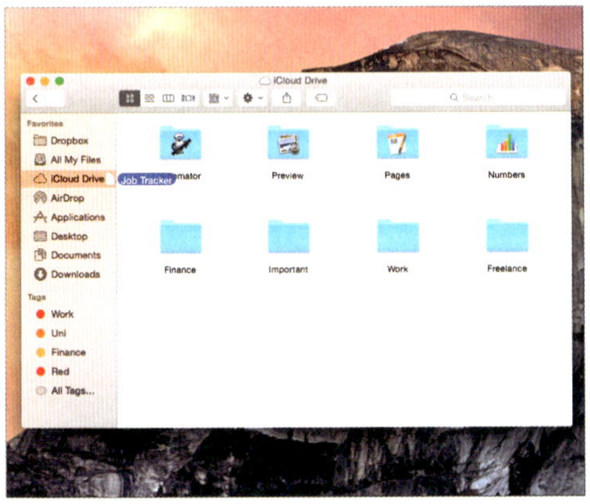

07: Add items to iCloud

To add items, drag and drop files from your Mac to the folder and they will sync to iCloud Drive – there are no restrictions on the file types you can add.

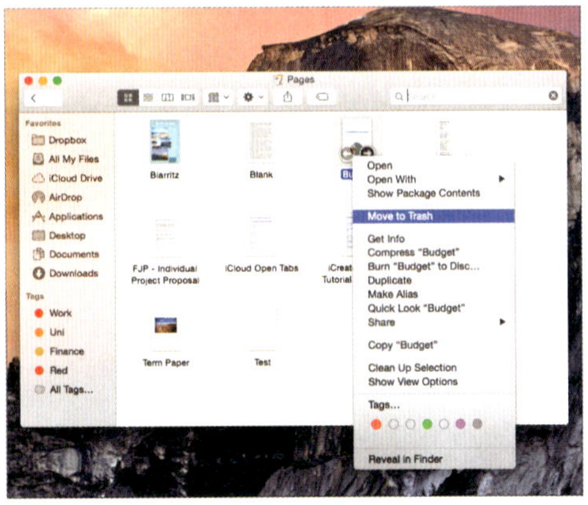

08: Delete unwanted files

You can delete files from any folder in iCloud Drive – including those for apps such as Pages. To do this, trash the file in the same way you would normally.

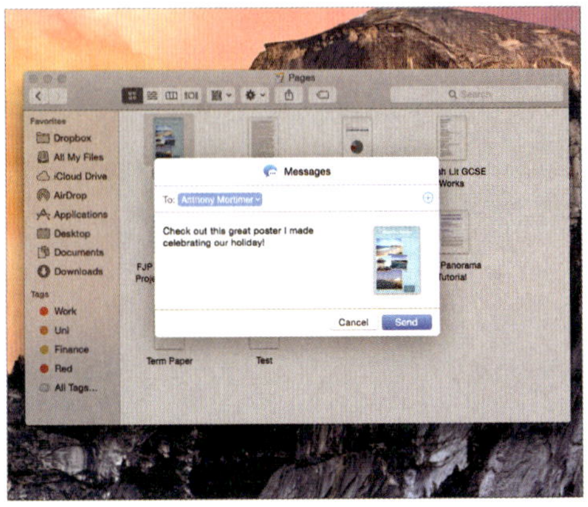

09: Share iCloud Drive files

You can share iCloud files and folders by clicking the item and selecting the Share icon. Choose your sharing method, then enter the recipient's details.

Get to grips with Family Sharing

Get to know AirDrop, one of OS X's most useful features for transferring files fast

Does your household have more than one Mac? One for you, of course, but also others for partners, children, grandfathers and parents? With Apple's new Family Sharing option integrated into OS X Yosemite, you are able to link these accounts to one credit or debit card. So when an app is bought on one Mac, it will become available on another and the same goes for iTunes and iBooks purchases. That way, individual Family members don't have to splash out more than once.

You can add up to five family members to your Family Sharing account. Children under 13 can have their own Apple IDs and they can make purchases using it as long as they have your approval (or not – you can decide on this). You can also allow other adults to give permission to children in the Family group. What's more, all members have the option of instantly discovering each other's location. Of course, Family Sharing doesn't purely have to be about real-life families. You could easily set up work or hobby families too.

"Link your accounts to one credit card"

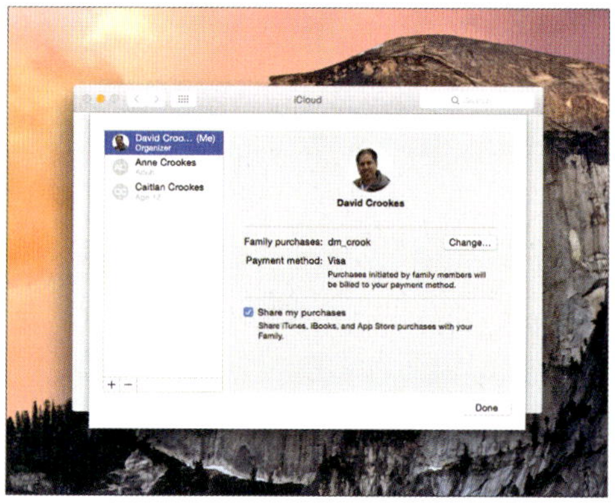

Set up sharing for a child

Have a child under 13? They can have Apple IDs too

Create an Apple ID

A child can have his or her own Apple ID and this will be usable across Macs and iOS devices. As part of the process, you will be asked to use the CVV number on your credit card to grant parental consent

Sharing your child's location

Want to keep an eye on your child when they are out and about? By sharing the child's location with your Family, their location can be obtained via Messages and Find My Friends

Add the Date of Birth

The Date of Birth is the most important part of the process because it will determine the services that will available to the child and it will also help from retrieving forgotten passwords

WHICH APPS CAN YOU SHARE?

Not all apps can be shared but you can clearly see which can and cannot by heading over to the Mac Store and looking under the Information section on the description page of each app. If it says no next to Family Sharing, the app cannot be shared.

Adding a child

Without an Apple ID, a child will be unable to participate in Family Sharing. You will need to click this + icon and then select 'Create an Apple ID for a child who doesn't have an account'

Family Sharing Setting up Family Sharing

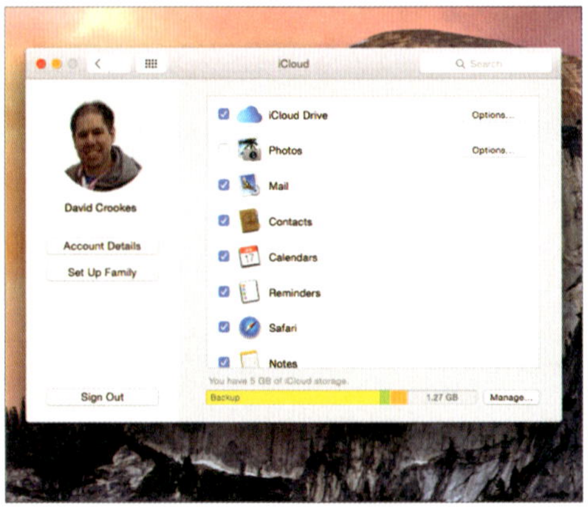

01: Open System Preferences

First of all, go to System Preferences and click on the icon for iCloud. To the left of the iCloud window is an option which states Set Up Family. Click on this.

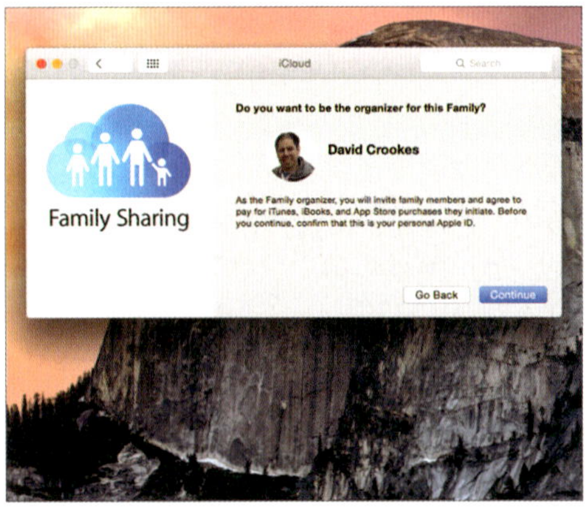

02: Choose an organiser

One person can become the Family organiser. If you want to be the organiser, your credit or debit card will be used by default and you can invite others.

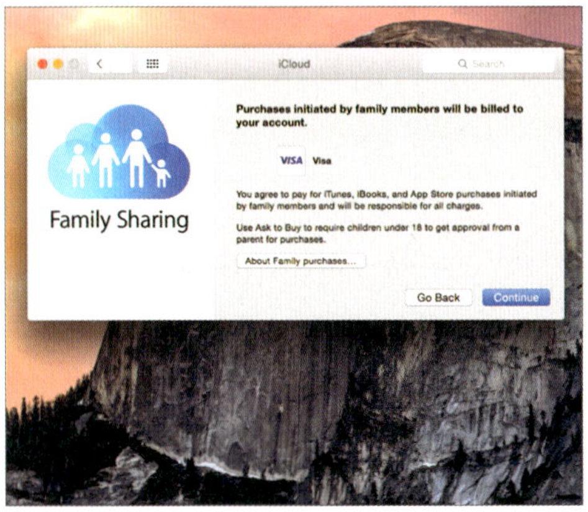

03: Select an account

Verify here to share purchases made with your Apple ID with your Family or select Use a Different Account. Confirm that your payment card is correct.

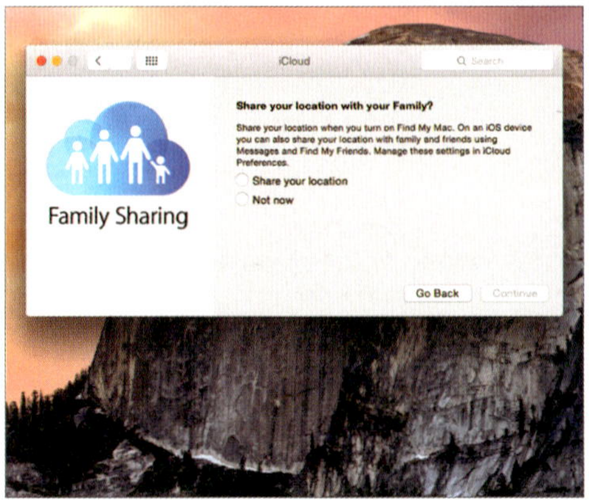

04: Share your location

A benefit of Family Sharing is allowing other Family members to see your location via Messages and Find My Friends. Just click Share your location.

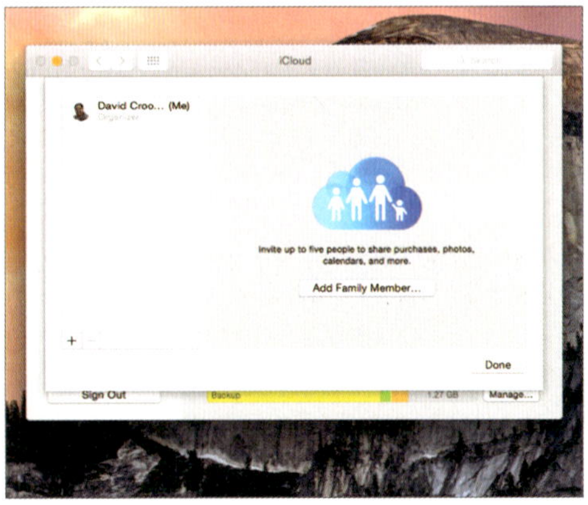

05: Add Family members

Now you are set up as the Organiser of your family, you can invite up to five people. To do this, click Add Family Member or select the + icon.

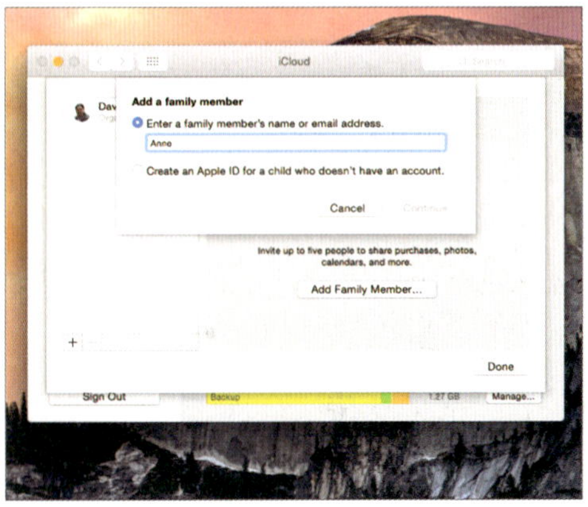

06: Input a member's details

Enter a family member's name or email or create a new Apple ID for them. The member can enter their password immediately or receive an invitation.

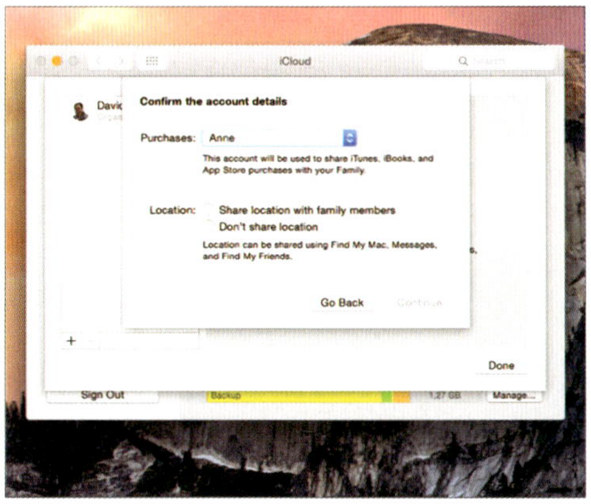

07: Confirm the account

Purchases made by the new Family member will be shareable with other members. The new member can choose whether to share locations or not, too.

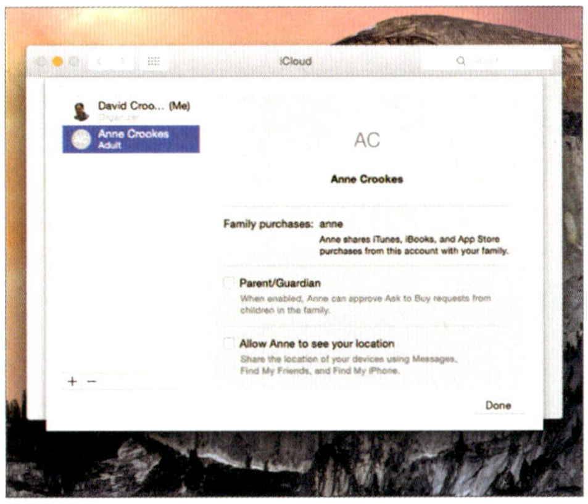

08: Toggle the settings

You can make more amends, like whether individual members can view your location and setting people up with parent and/or guardian status.

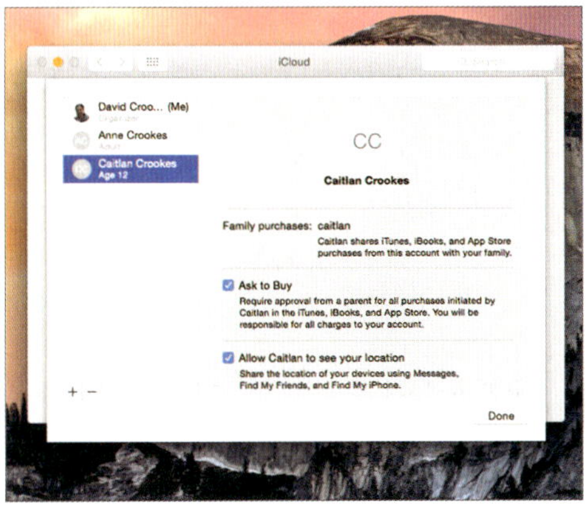

09: Settings for children

If you have a child under 13, you can ensure that their purchases in iTunes, iBooks and the App Store need your approval. Tick Ask to Buy on their profile.

Share to Facebook and Twitter

The latest versions of OS X have social networking options built into their core

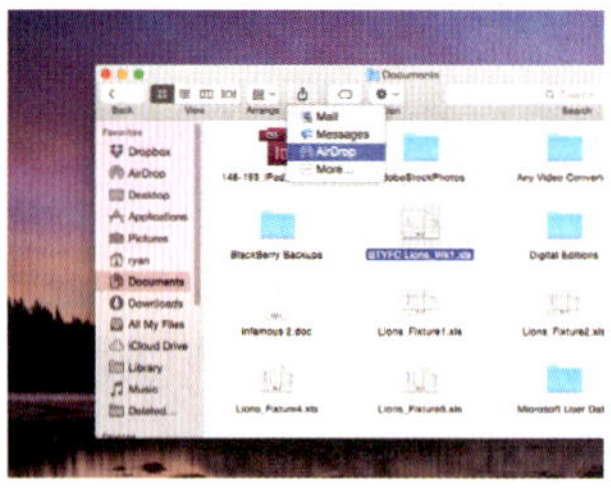

The sharing facilities built into Yosemite are more extensive than in previous versions of OS X. In fact, the features that have been added are more like those available on iOS devices like the iPad and iPhone, so you may well be familiar with some of them already. However, while the sharing system is similar to the one used by iOS, it also offers more features than the latter.

One feature with which iOS users will be familiar is the instant sharing of web pages. When you are browsing the web and you come across a page that has something funny, interesting or useful, you might want to share it with your friends. On an iPhone, you'd just click the Share button, and now there is a similar button in the Safari browser on the Mac. Simply click the button in the toolbar and you can share the page in an email, a tweet or via Messages. The Notes app is a handy place to store all manner of content, such as text, images, web links and more.

It is all synced to your iPhone and iPad, but you might want to share a note's contents with others. A note could contain the outline for a work project or meeting, for instance, and clicking the Share button would enable you to send it to work colleagues. You could share it using Messages if the intended recipients have Macs or

"One feature with which iOS users will be familiar is the instant sharing of web pages"

Spreading the word

Simple sharing options

Sharing options

The options available depend on what you are sharing. For example, a photo can be shared through Flickr and Twitter or by using AirDrop

SHARING IN YOSEMITE

With Yosemite, OS X is now more geared towards sharing than ever. Social media sharing is fully integrated into Maps, iBooks and, of course, Safari, which has a new Shared Links sidebar displaying URLs tweeted by friends and contacts.

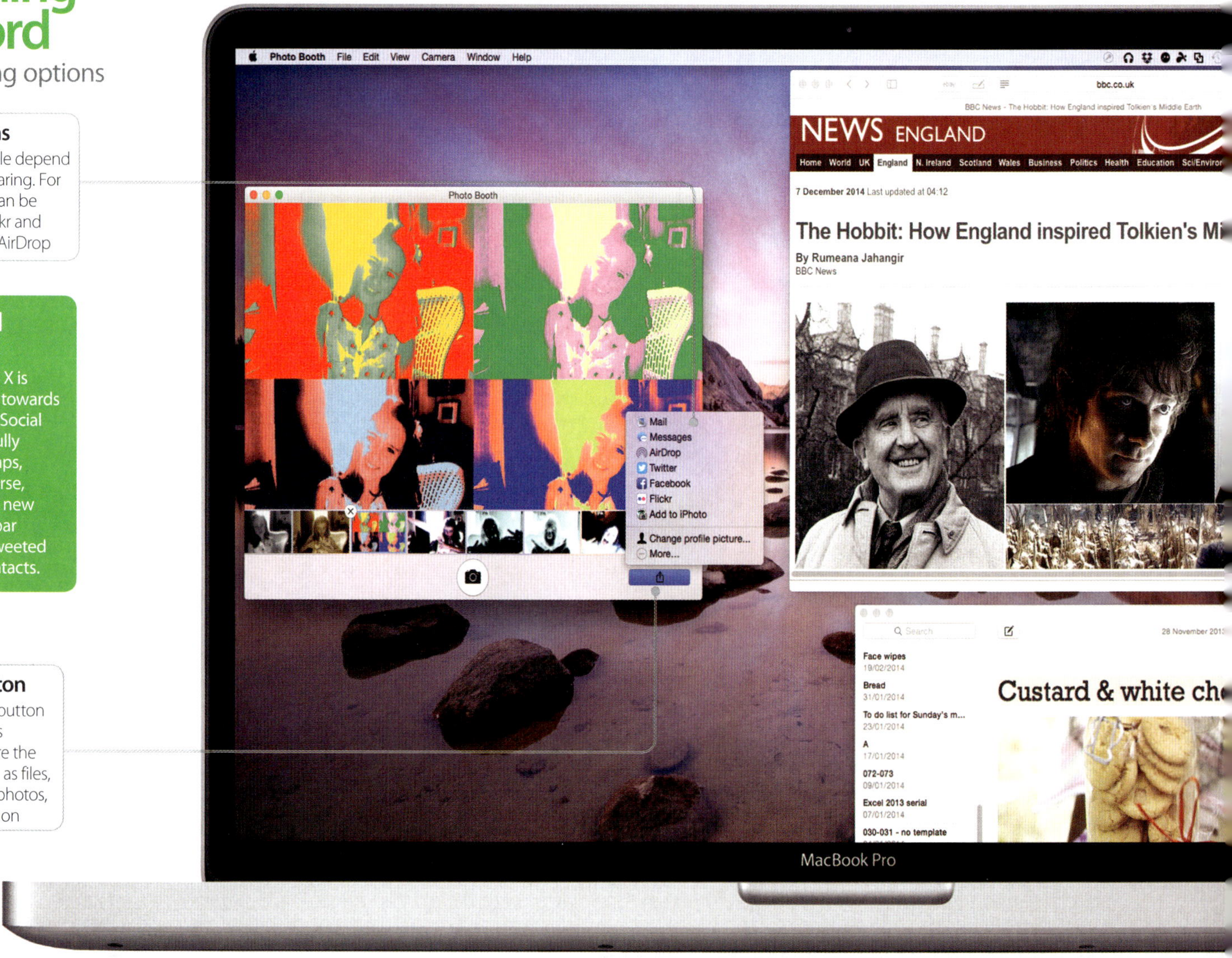

The Share button

Look for the Share button or icon in apps. This enables you to share the selected item, such as files, web pages, notes, photos, documents and so on

send it by email if they don't. Either way, all the files are included.

The Photo Booth application previously only had the option to email photos and, while this was useful, now there is a Share button that lists lots of great sharing facilities. These include email, Twitter, Messages, Flickr and AirDrop. You can even set your Twitter account picture directly from Photo Booth. It simply makes it more fun to use when you have all these sharing options.

Files can be shared from within Finder and Ctrl/right-clicking any file or folder displays the options available. The menu changes for different file types, so you can share a picture via Flickr but not a document. Finder provides access to AirDrop, which was introduced in Lion and is continued in Mavericks and Yosemite. It is an easy way to discover other Mac users nearby and to send and receive files directly via Wi-Fi (without the need to be on the same local network). You just drag and drop to exchange files, so it's super-simple to use.

Share websites
When you are browsing the web and find an interesting page, share it with everyone by clicking this button and posting it to Twitter, Messages or sending it via email

Share your notes
Notes are synced to all iCloud devices, but to share them with another person you can click the Share button and email the note, or use Messages

Finder, Safari, Notes Share files with friends

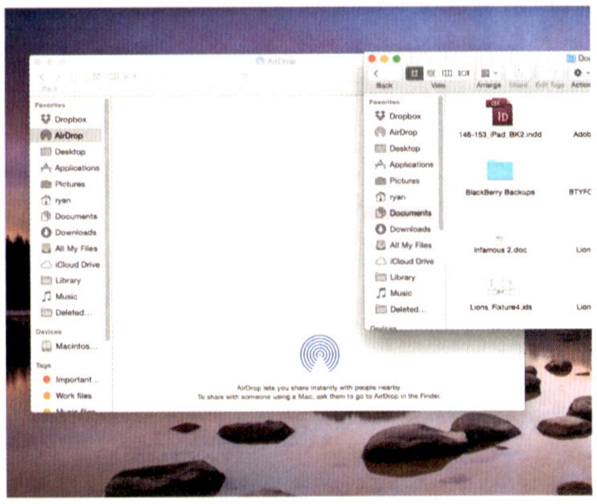

01: Share with AirDrop
Click Finder in the Dock to open a window and then select AirDrop in the left panel. Do the same on another Mac and you will see each other's computers.

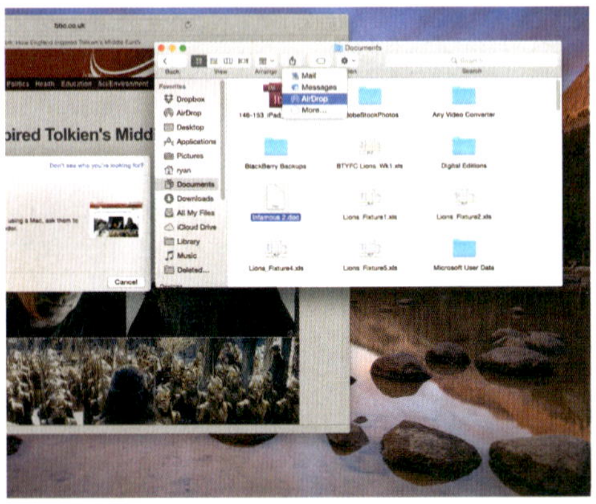

02: Drag and drop
To share via AirDrop, simply drag the file to the other computer in the AirDrop window. Alternatively, click on the share button and choose AirDrop.

03: Share a page
The Share button in the Safari toolbar provides access to Twitter, Messages and email. Let's post a message on Twitter about this story on the web.

04: Compose a tweet
A small Twitter window opens with the web page attached to a paperclip. Click in the box, enter the text and click Send. The character count is also visible.

05: Share a note
Start Notes and select one of your notes. At the top of the note display is a Share button that enables you to email it, share it using Messages and more.

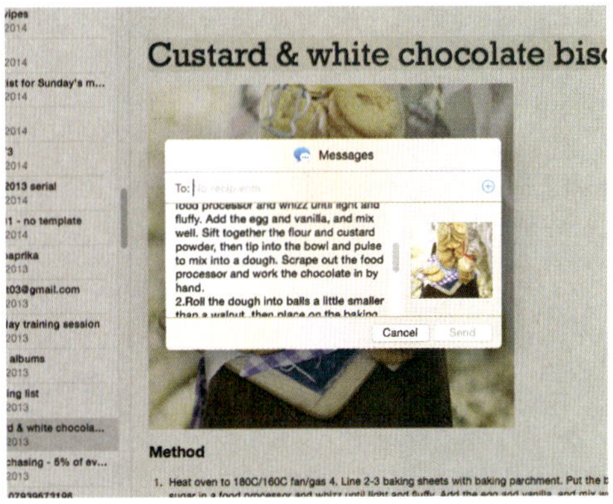

06: Send a message
Select Messages and the note is displayed in a new window. Click the To box and type in a name. Click in the list of suggestions if there are several matches.

Perform a deep clean of your Mac

Use CleanMyMac 2 to give your Mac a spring clean to speed it up and save storage space

As we move more and more information onto our computers, the need to account for every spare megabyte on our Macs has become more important. CleanMyMac 2 is a useful tool to ensure that your hard drive has all the space you need for your files.

CleanMyMac 2 does exactly as its name suggests: it cleans your Mac, removing unneeded system files, duplicated files and unused applications so you can maximise the amount of free space. With CleanMyMac 2, you can save space quickly by performing an Automatic Cleanup. But our focus in this tutorial takes a little more time and attention. We're going to show you the different tools you can use in order to perform a really good spring clean of your Mac's hard drive.

> "CleanMyMac 2 does exactly as its name suggests"

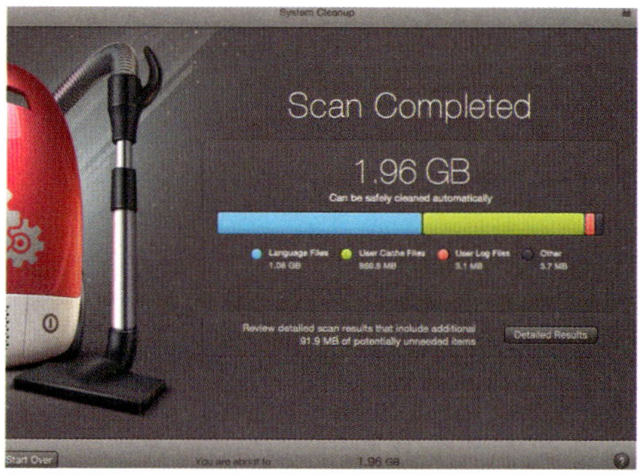

CleanMyMac… even more

Take a deeper look at some of CleanMyMac 2's hidden features

View

Customise the look of the CleanMyMac 2 interface using the View menu option from the top of your screen. Add and remove tools from the interface according to how much you use them

Scheduler

In the Preferences pane, click on the Scheduler tab. Here you can schedule regular reminders to scan your hard drive and keep it spick and span – choose from periods between one week and one year

Preferences

Get down to the nitty gritty of CleanMyMac 2 and customise the app's advanced settings such as managing files to include in a scan, the ability to regularly monitor the Trash size and schedule frequent scan reminders

Ignore List

If there are files, applications or folders that you don't wish to scan or remove information from, add them to the Ignore List. This isolates them from any scans that the CleanMyMac 2 app performs

IPHOTO CLEANUP

Whenever you edit a photo in iPhoto, the app makes a copy of it. CleanMyMac 2 offers a tool which searches your iPhoto Library and displays edited photos and groups them according to the edits made. The app will display the original and the modified photo so you can choose which one from each pair it is that you want to remove.

CleanMyMac 2 Give your Mac a good clean

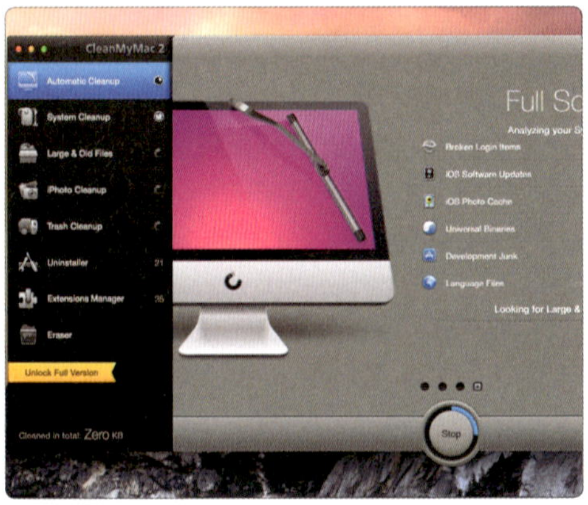

01: Automatic Cleanup

The quickest option an Automatic scan. Select Automatic Cleanup and press Scan. When it's complete, click the Clean button to remove the files.

02: Start the detailed cleanup

For more control of the files removed, select System Cleanup and click Detailed Results. The files you can remove are in categories in the middle column.

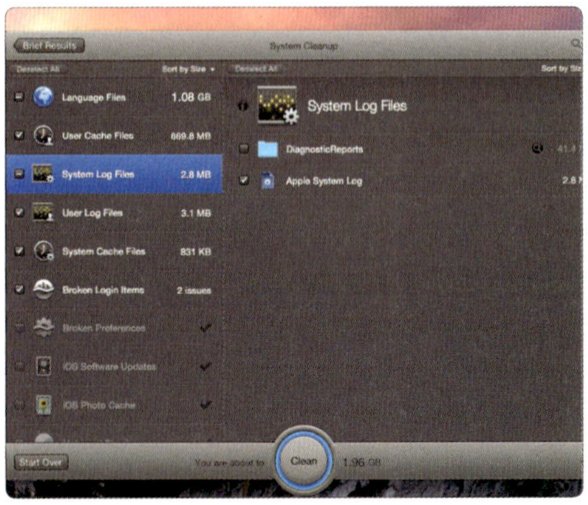

03: Remove large files

The categories are arranged by size, largest first. Click on a category to view a list of applications and folders that the files will be removed from.

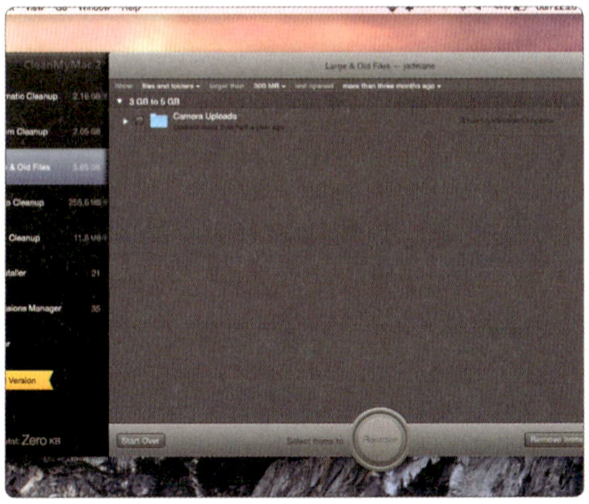

04: Large & Old Files

View large files and folders which haven't been used in a while with Large & Old Files. A selection of drop-down menus are shown at the top.

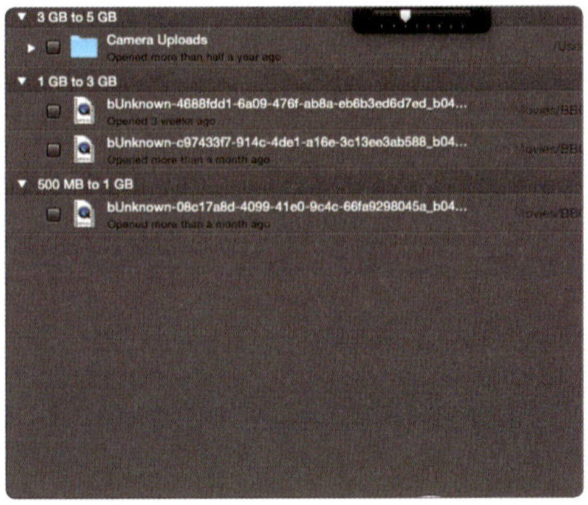

05: Remove old files

Using the menus, display and remove files that haven't been opened for a certain time; files over a specified size; or choose just to view files or folders.

06: Empty the trash

If you use apps with in-app Trash cans, select Trash Cleanup. CleanMyMac 2 displays all of these Trash cans and enables you to empty them in one place.

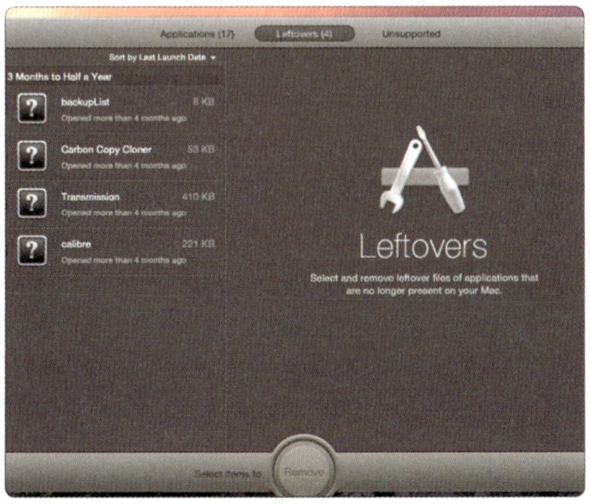

07: Deal with leftovers

Uninstaller lets you completely uninstall apps. Click the Leftovers tab to also remove leftover files from apps you've previously removed from your Mac.

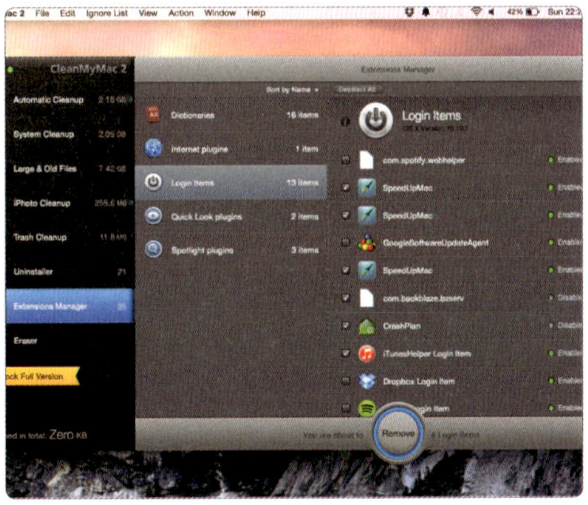

08: Speed up your Mac

Click on Extensions Manager to manage files that are taking up space or slowing down your Mac, eg files that open when you log into your Mac.

09: Securely remove files

The Eraser tool securely deletes files. When you normally trash a file, it leaves a trace in the hard drive. Eraser securely removes them without a trace.

Learning Apple apps

From Mail and iTunes to Safari and Game Center, discover how to use these essential Apple applications

"Mac's most popular apps, from Maps to Mail and Safari to iTunes, will cover all the things you want and need to do with your computer, and much, much more"

80 Start using Mail

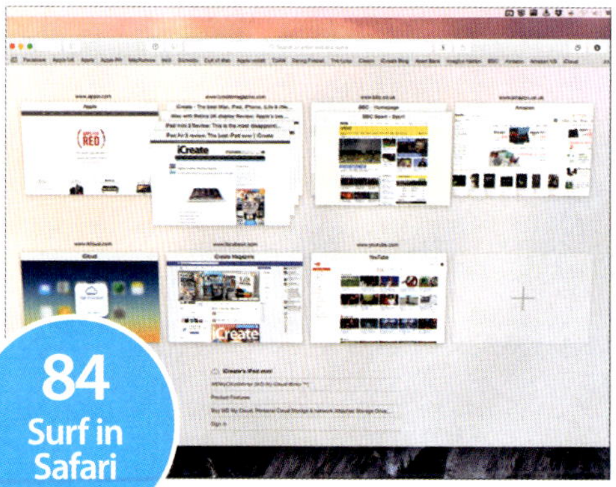

84 Surf in Safari

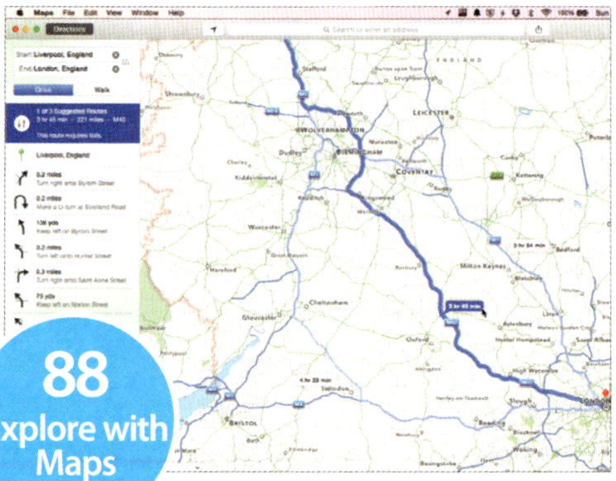

88 Explore with Maps

100 Discover iTunes

108 Create a book

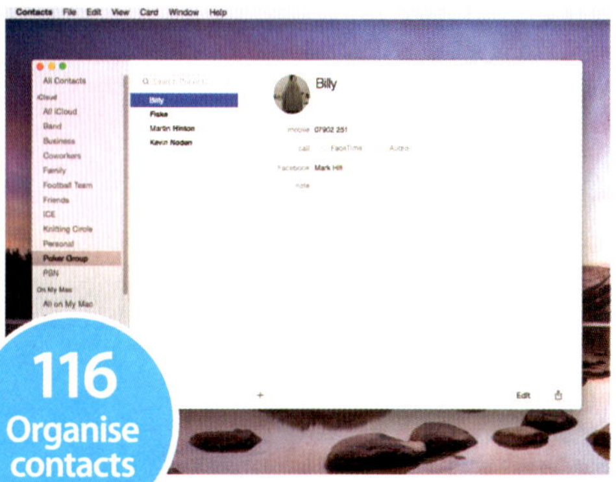

116 Organise contacts

Set up email on your Mac

The Mail app on the Mac is as painless as an application can get. Follow these steps to get started and send and receive your emails with ease

It's easy to overlook Mail on the Mac when we're accustomed to browsing emails on the web. And with social networking becoming ever more popular, many people will communicate solely through the likes of Facebook and Twitter. However, if we're lucky enough to own an iMac or MacBook, we really should make use of our sophisticated machines and allow them to do what they do best: make life a whole lot easier! Mail on the Mac is a smart way to manage your emails as you work and play.

Now, the beauty of your Mac is of course its simplicity. But when that simplicity is a new application staring at you expectantly, it can feel a little intimidating. Pushing buttons at random in the hope you will eventually work it out is never going to be the best approach, so with this helpful little guide to setting up Mail on the Mac, we'll have you sending and receiving emails to and from your favourite people in no time. We'll also show you how to customise your messages to give them that personal feel, and explain how to attach documents and keep the Mail interface clean and tidy so you know where all your messages are.

"Mail on the Mac is a smart way to manage your emails as you work and play"

Mail Get your mail up and running

01: Run Mail

Click on the Mail icon in your Dock to kick it into motion. After a quick bounce, you should be prompted by a Welcome to Mail pop-up window.

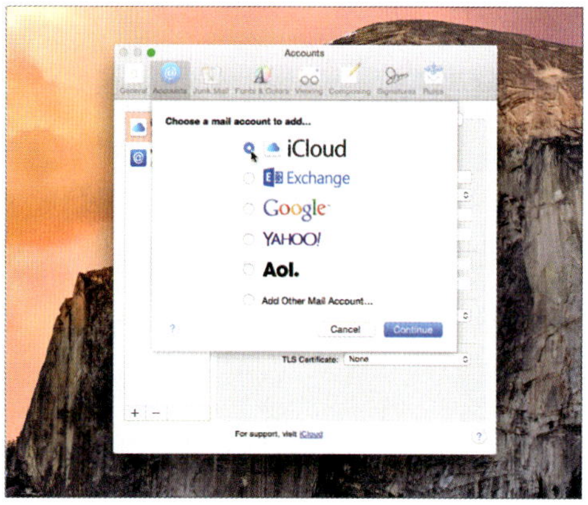

02: Mail's Setup Assistant

This wizard can configure accounts that use the most popular email services, including Gmail and Yahoo. Choose your favourite.

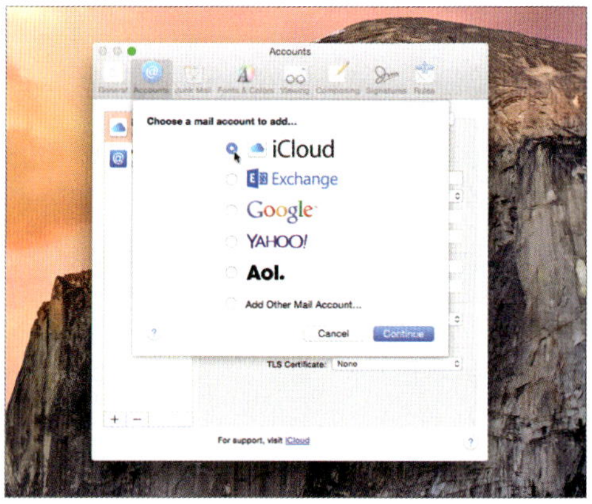

03: Enter your details

Enter the full name, email address and password for your existing email account the same as you would in the browser of your service provider.

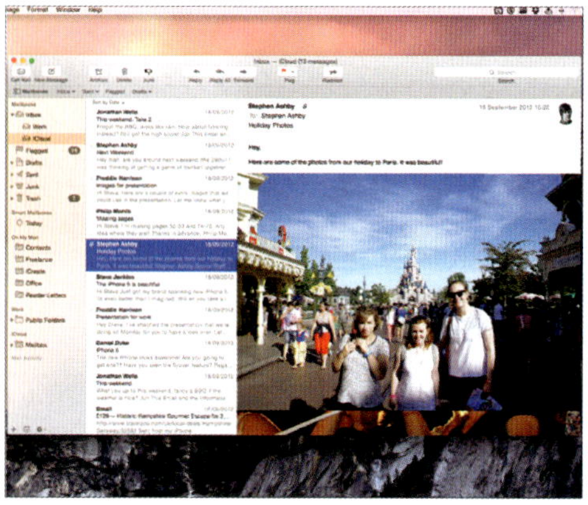

04: Create and enjoy

Click on Create in the Mail Setup Assistant and be taken to your new Mail Inbox. You'll have the same mailboxes as in your web browsing version.

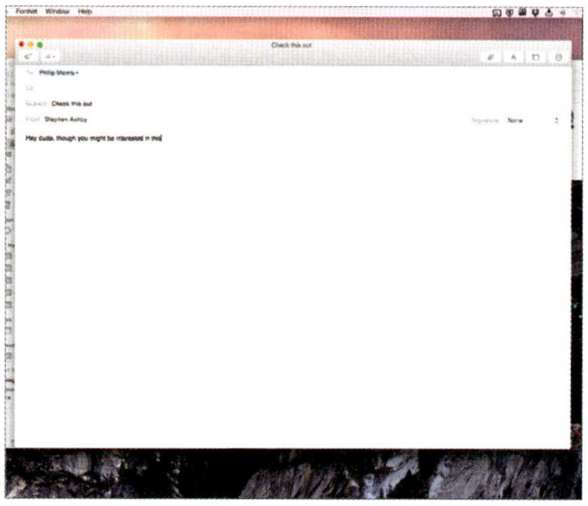

05: Compose a message

Hit New Message to summon an email draft. Enter the address of your recipient in the To field and fill in your Subject and message accordingly.

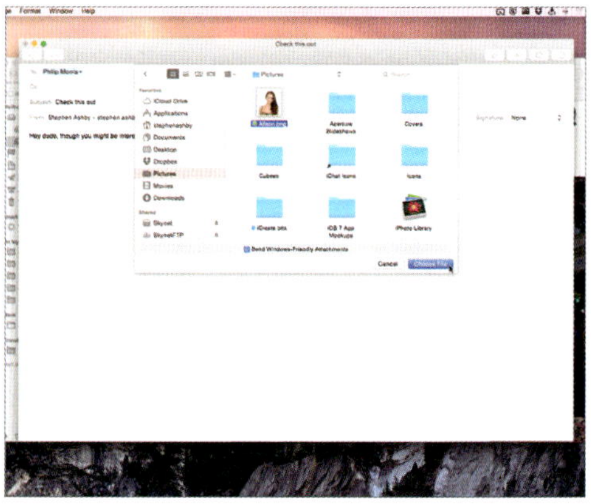

06: Attach a file

To send your recipient a file, click on Attach and pick one. Set up iCloud on your Mac and you can attach files up to 5GB thanks to the MailDrop feature.

Master Mail on your Mac

Everything you need to send and receive emails

Happiness is shortcuts

As Mac users, we love our shortcuts. Ctrl and click on the emails in your Inbox to bring up various time-saving options: Reply, Forward, Mark As Unread, Delete, and Move To folders of your choice

The Mail toolbar

You'll find handy buttons for all the most-used functions right at the top of your Mail interface. Delete, send mail to the Junk folder, Reply, Forward and create New Messages to your heart's content

ADD NOTES WITH MARKUP

If you are sending a photo or PDF document to someone through Mail, you can use Markup to add notes and annotations to them. Click the arrow in the top-right of the file and choose Markup. You can then draw on the photo or document, make notes, and even add your signature to a letter or other file type

Keep it tidy

Creating folders to store your emails for quick reference is a great way to prevent oversized Inboxes. Go to Mailbox>New Mailbox and set the Location and enter a Name for your new folder

Sort and search

It's there but it's hiding. Sort by From, Subject or Date Received, and use the Search field in the top right to track messages with specific words in the Entire Message, From, To or Subject

07: Add some style

If you're feeling adventurous, you can change your fonts and add colour by clicking on the appropriate Fonts and Colors buttons.

08: Save or send

If you're not yet ready to send, click Save As Draft and it'll wait in your Drafts folder. When happy, hit Send to start your message on its journey.

09: You've got mail

Click Get Mail in the top left to download emails. Unread messages are highlighted by blue dots – the icon in your dock also shows new messages.

Master preferences in the Mail app

Increase productivity with a Mail app that's tailored to suit you

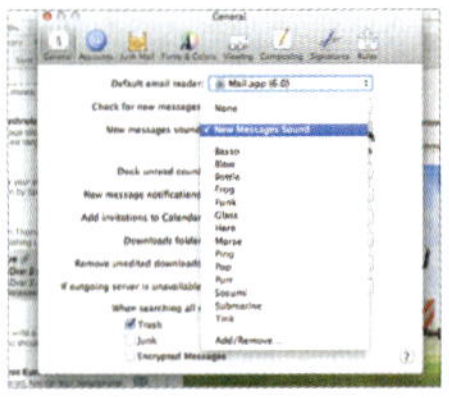

Mail is a typically Apple product – sleek and uncluttered, but full of functionality. The latest version borrows from the Mail application found in iOS, and particularly on the iPad. To get the most out of Mail, it's important to understand how to set up and customise it, since this will let you add important things like mail signatures and formatting, control junk mail filtering, and apply rules – which are really useful when you're managing multiple accounts.

The General tab holds a lot of the really important stuff, including how often Mail should automatically check for messages. Accounts lets you control and edit all the different email accounts you own. The Junk Mail option lets you control how Mail filters any mail it suspects to be spam. Check out the preferences to take control.

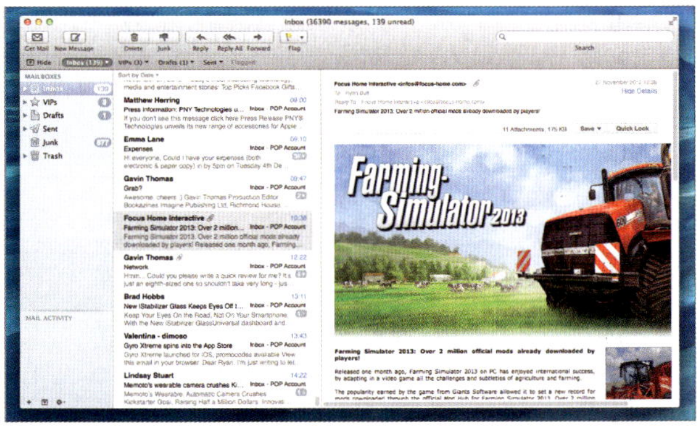

The Mail interface

Learn your way around the Mail app

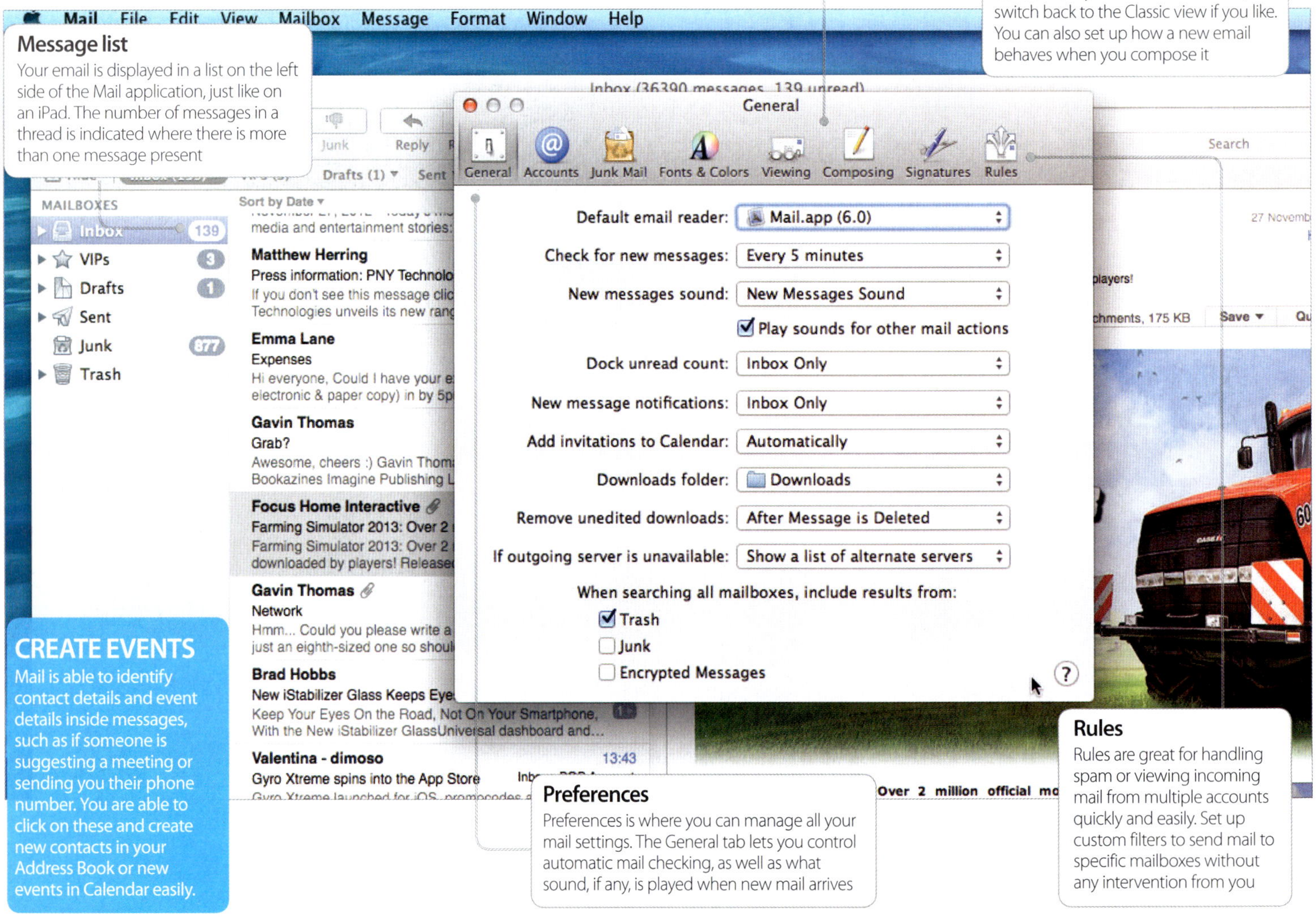

Message list

Your email is displayed in a list on the left side of the Mail application, just like on an iPad. The number of messages in a thread is indicated where there is more than one message present

Viewing and composing

Control how your emails are viewed, and switch back to the Classic view if you like. You can also set up how a new email behaves when you compose it

CREATE EVENTS

Mail is able to identify contact details and event details inside messages, such as if someone is suggesting a meeting or sending you their phone number. You are able to click on these and create new contacts in your Address Book or new events in Calendar easily.

Preferences

Preferences is where you can manage all your mail settings. The General tab lets you control automatic mail checking, as well as what sound, if any, is played when new mail arrives

Rules

Rules are great for handling spam or viewing incoming mail from multiple accounts quickly and easily. Set up custom filters to send mail to specific mailboxes without any intervention from you

Mail Master Mail's preferences

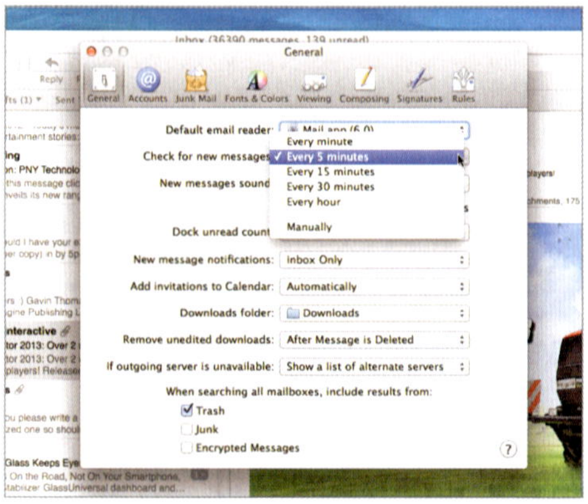

01: The General tab

Open Preferences, and set an interval for Mail to check the server for new messages. Alternatively, you can choose to turn off automatic checking.

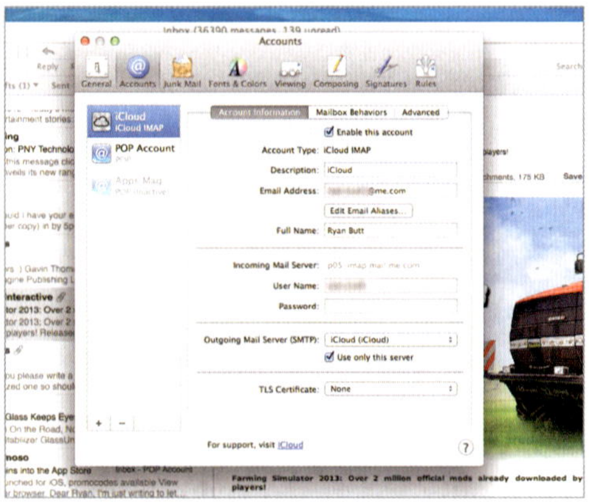

02: Manage accounts

In the Accounts tab, you can see all of your email accounts. To manage how each one behaves, click on the Mailbox Behaviors tab.

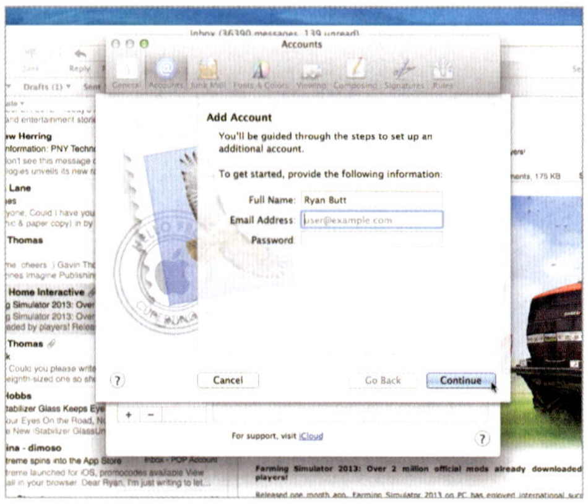

03: Add an account

To add a new account, go to the accounts list and click on the '+' button. Choose the type of account from the list, or select Other if necessary.

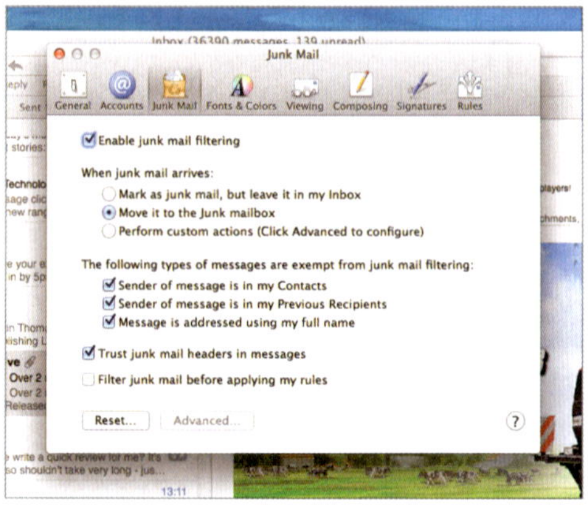

04: Junk mail

Go to the Junk Mail section, where filtering should be enabled. Click Advanced and tell Mail what you want done with any spam mail.

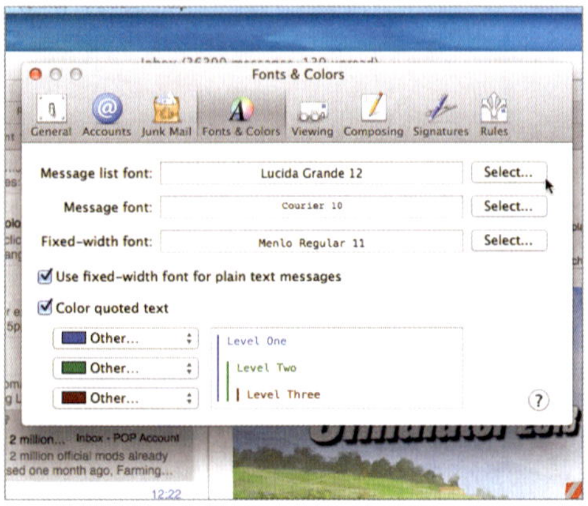

05: Fonts & Colors

In the Fonts & Colors section, you can specify the fonts and type sizes that you want to use. This is handy if you need to increase the size of email text.

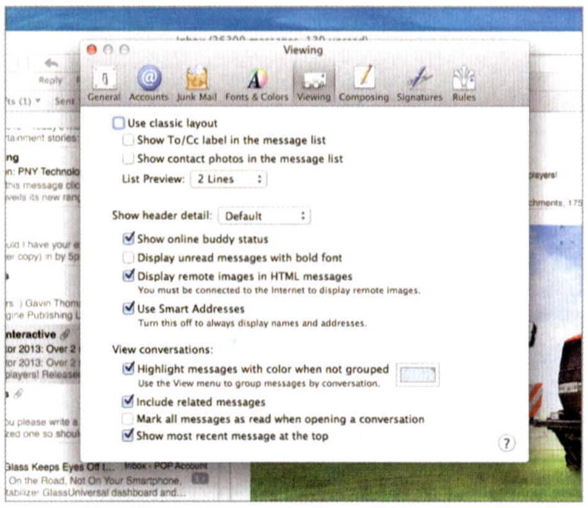

06: Viewing options

In the Viewing section, you can switch between the old and new viewing system. The default settings are good, but you can edit them to taste.

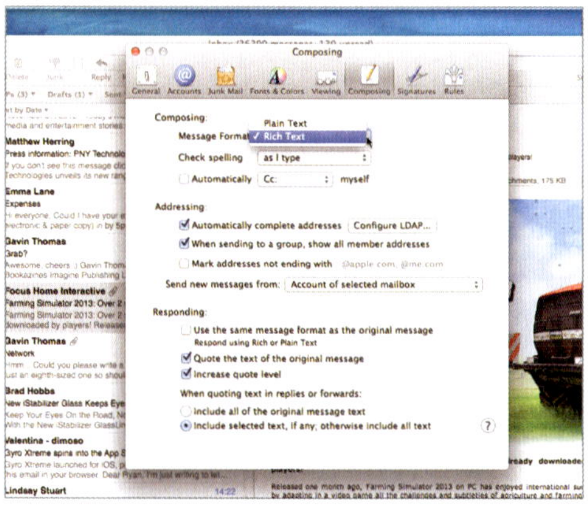

07: Composition options

Here, you can change the format of emails to plain text, as well as disabling spell-checking. You can also set up how replies are formatted.

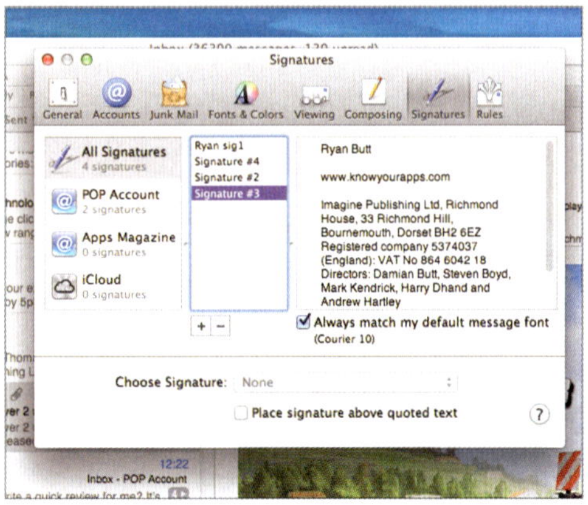

08: Signatures

In the Signatures section, you can add signatures to appear at the end of your emails and choose which ones should be associated with which accounts.

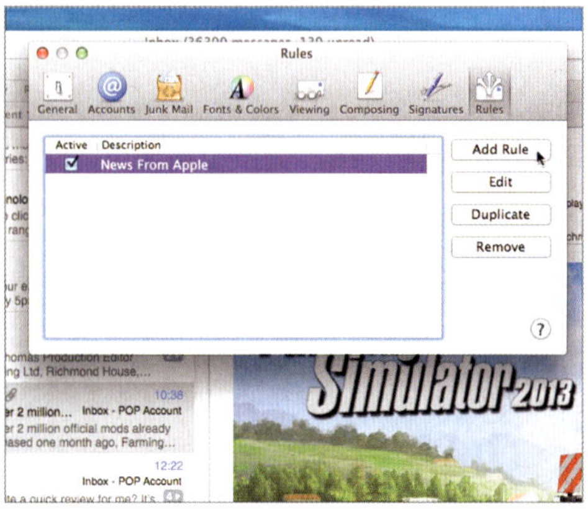

09: Rules

Rules are really useful and can essentially help you to sort mail as soon as it arrives. Use multiple criteria to create advanced rules.

Browse the internet

Apple's Safari web browser makes it easy to surf the web

Safari is Apple's own web browser and it's tightly integrated into the operating system. Although for most of its previous life it was much more stripped-down than other browsers, largely for the sake of speed, it has more recently taken on more features such as Extensions that will enable you to customise it, in addition to a range of things you can change in its preferences.

Perhaps unsurprisingly it is the most Mac-like of any browser – it's sleek, polished and easy to use. Most of its options are accessed through the Preferences section and it is here that you can, for example, change the default search engine and the location for downloaded files.

There are also some great security applications, such as the ability to block the annoying pop-up windows and warnings you get when visiting a website that might be fraudulent. All in all, you'll discover it's a great way to safely browse the web.

> "Safari is sleek and easy to use"

Sidebar
By toggling on the Sidebar you can view bookmarks, Reading List items and see all the shared links from your various social networks

Homepage
Set the default page that Safari will display when you open a new page or tab

Handy placement
The handy download manager buttons are both located at the top right hand corner of the window

Sort extensions
The Extensions tab lets you switch Extensions on and off as well as changing their behaviour

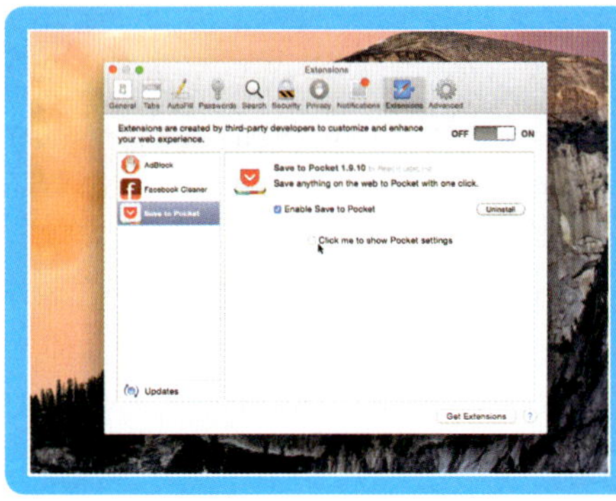

Extensions

Add to Safari's functionality with Extensions…

Extensions are small snippets of code that use HTML5, CSS3 and JavaScript technologies to incorporate quick links to other web services or tools (such as ad blocking) into the browser. The idea is that you only download and install the ones you want and that suit your needs. There are none installed by default. Best of all, Extensions are digitally signed, which means you can't accidentally install malicious ones that might do your Mac harm. They are also sandboxed, which means that even if one crashes it won't take Safari or the Mac OS down with it. They even install easily without the need for you to restart your Mac.

If you head to **extensions.apple.com** you will find a list of all the Extensions available. Some of the most popular include Twitter and eBay, the ability to add items to an Amazon wishlist and the all-important ad blocker that gets rid of embedded ads. There are some really useful ones here.

Key features

What does Safari do that's really cool?

Full-screen toolbar access

Mac OS X Yosemite supports full-screen applications, so when you enter full-screen mode, everything else on your monitor is hidden. It's a good way to focus only on the task at hand. In Safari, move the mouse to the very top right hand corner of the window and click on the dual arrows icon. When in full-screen, move the mouse to the same location to reveal the reverse icon, which will return you to windowed mode.

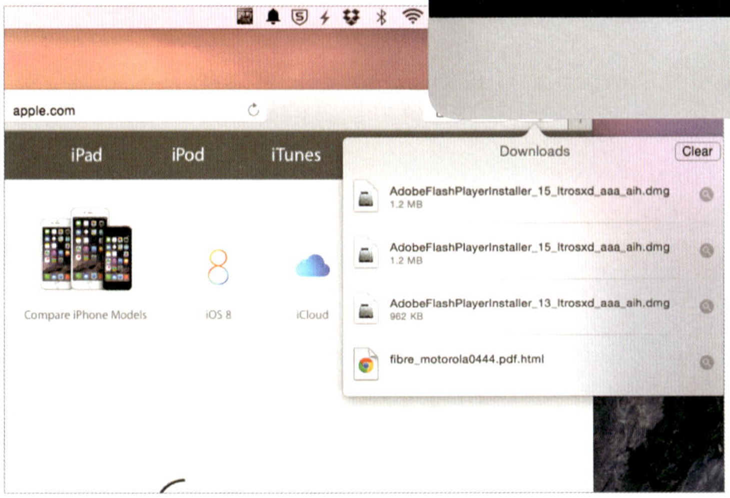

The download section

In OS X Yosemite you can track your downloads thanks to a small, integrated window. At the top right of the Safari interface you will see a small icon with a downward pointing arrow and when you download a file, clicking on this will reveal the progress of the download. Even after it has completed you can click on the same icon to reveal recent downloads, and click on the magnifying glass icon to reveal them in the Finder.

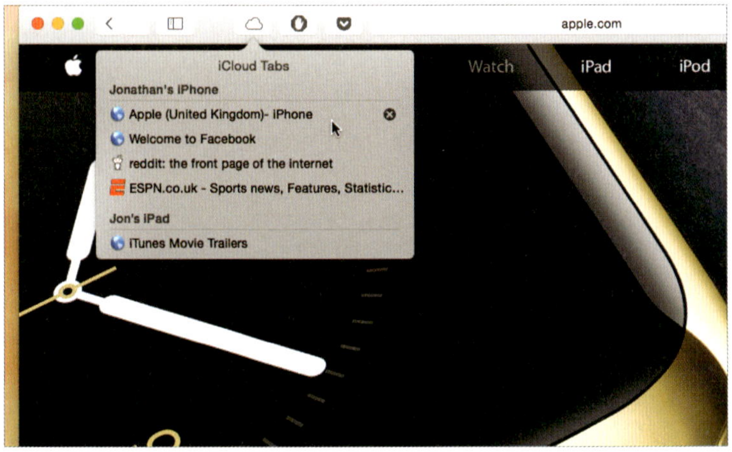

iCloud tabs

One of the best recent additions to Safari is iCloud tabs. Since OS X Mavericks and Apple's last mobile operating system, iOS 8, work together, as long as you are logged into the same iCloud account on your Mac and on your iOS device then all of the Safari tabs that you have open on one device will be accessible on the other by clicking on the 'iCloud Tabs' button. Essentially, you can pick up your iPad when you leave behind your Mac to catch a train and keep on surfing.

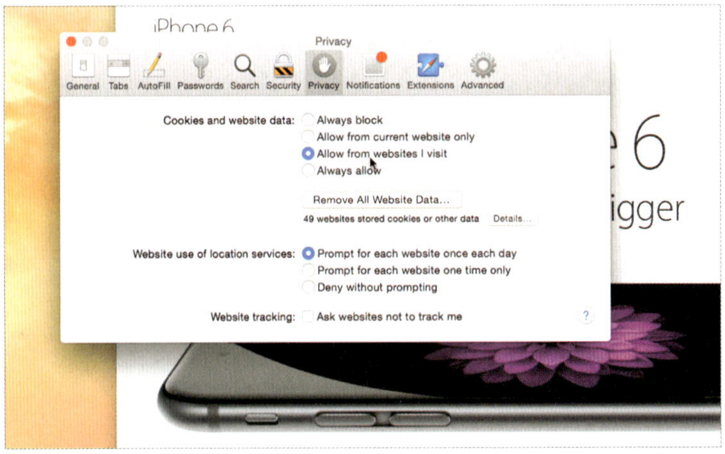

Privacy settings

Online security is very important, and in Safari's Privacy tab there are some handy options available. The 'Remove All' button lets you delete all stored data from websites as well as view this data prior to deletion, and you can also choose to block cookies from certain types of website so that advertisers can't track your browsing habits. There's also the option to control whether websites can use information about your location or not.

Surf with Tab View in Safari

Handling multiple websites is easy using OS X Yosemite's new tab feature

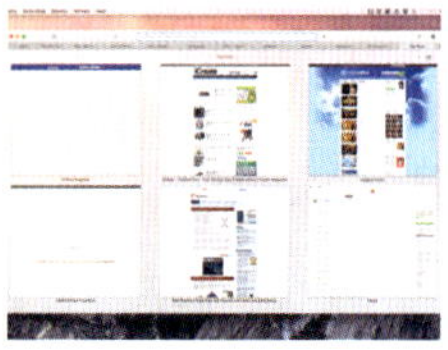

Yosemite brings many new features to OS X on the Mac and there are some welcome enhancements to Safari that make browsing easier, more convenient and enjoyable. Along with new sharing options and a brilliant new Search bar that offers results from places like the App Store and iTunes, there is also an all-new tab view that offers you an overview of all your open tabs on one screen.

Tabs are one of the most useful features of modern web browsers. When you are browsing websites and searching for information, instead of going back and forth between sites and pages, or managing multiple windows, you can open them in a new tab. This makes it easier to return if you need to refer to information on them and it enables you to open a group of pages and then read them more easily.

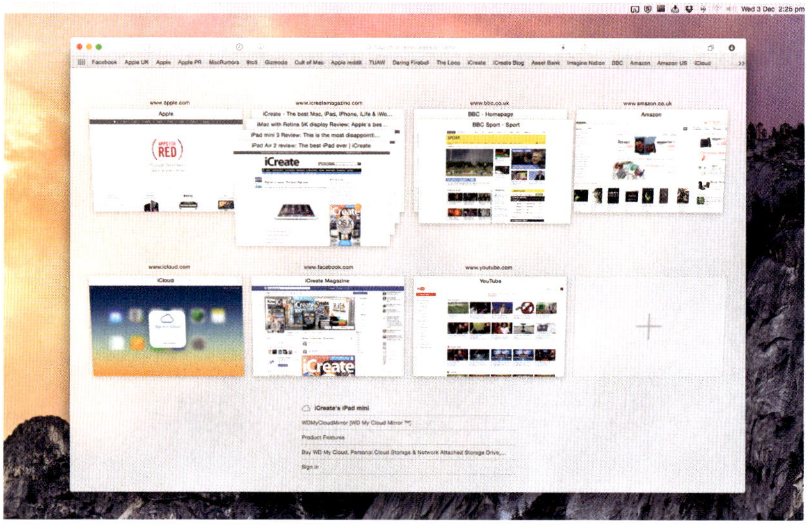

The new Tab View can be accessed using a mouse and keyboard, by simply clicking the small icon in the top-right of the screen. Click it and your current page will zoom out, revealing all your tabs in a 3D grid. Tabs are even better when they are used with a Trackpad on a MacBook, or an iMac with a Magic Trackpad. Safari enables you to pinch your fingers together to see the overview with a single gesture. If you own and iPad, you may recognise the tab layout – it's clear that Safari has taken inspiration from iOS 8 in OS X Yosemite

There are several useful actions you can perform with tabs, and if you have an iPhone or iPad you will be able to start browsing the web on one of those devices and then continue on your Mac in Safari. This is because tabs are synchronised across all your computers running Yosemite and devices running iOS 8 through iCloud. This means that you can browse the web anywhere at any time, continuing exactly where you left off if you ever change devices. Even better, iCloud tabs provides live updates between each of your devices. So if you're surfing the web on your iPad, for example, the web page you have open on your iPad will also be displayed on your desktop Mac. Simply scroll down in the tab view to see iCloud tabs.

For now though, fire up Safari, open up a few tabs and grab an input device capable of accepting multii-touch gestures (you'll want one to make the whole experience even better), then we'll take you through the very best of Tab View in Safari.

> "Safari enables you to pinch your fingers together to enter the tab viewer in a single gesture"

Safari Browse tabs in Safari

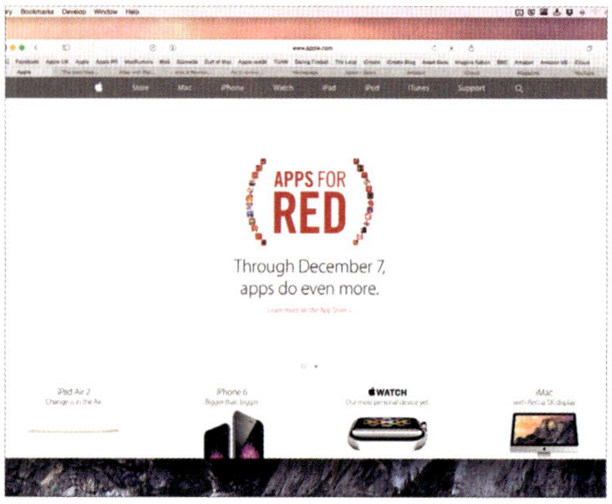

01: Start Safari

When you are browsing the web and you want to open a new page without leaving the current one, press Cmd+T, or click the '+' icon on the right.

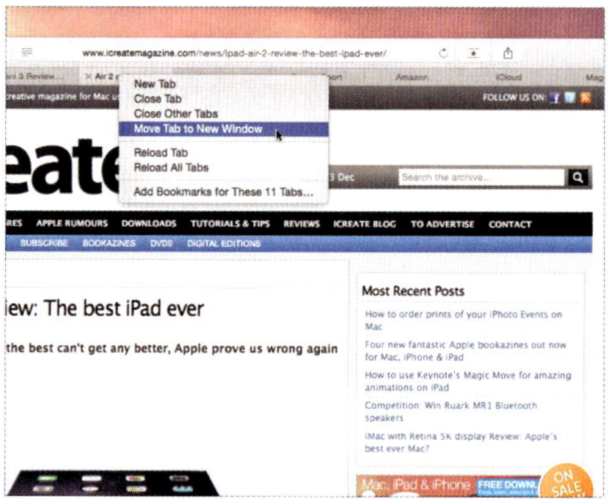

02: Handy tab functions

When two or more tabs are open you can drag them left or right to rearrange their order, while Ctrl/right-clicking a tab displays a menu with useful functions.

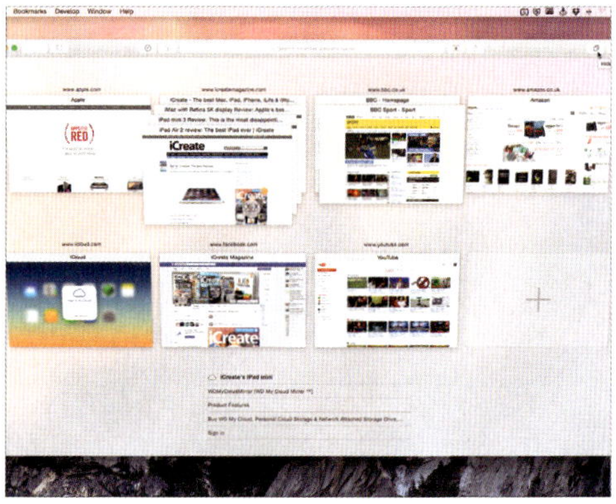

03: Browse tabs

Click the button in the top-right of the window, or use a pinch gesture on a trackpad and your tab will zoom out to reveal all your open tabs in a 3D grid.

Surf better with Safari

A close look at Safari's Tab View

Fingers or keyboard

You can use two fingers on a trackpad to pinch together and enter the tab view on your Mac. Alternatively, click this button in the top-right of the window

Live tabs

The tabs are live and you can see this icon when browsing tabs that are showing video clips. The video continues to play and page updates can be seen

iCloud tabs

Down at the bottom of the tab view you'll see all the tabs that you have open on your other devices. Click one and it will open instantly

Close iCloud Tabs

Hover over an iCloud Tab and you will see a small 'x' icon appear next to its title. You can click this to close the tab on the relevant device, without even touching it

BOOKMARK YOUR TABS

If you have a favourite set of websites or pages you regularly visit, you can save them all as a single bookmark. Open all the sites on separate tabs and then go to the Bookmarks menu and select Add Bookmarks For These Tabs.

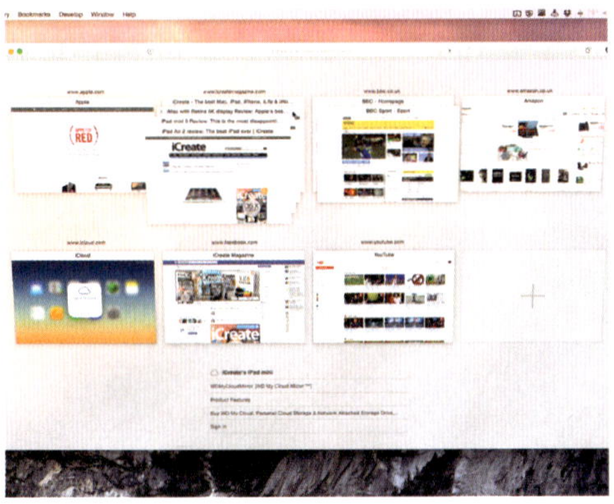

04: Stacking up

If you open multiple tabs from a single root page, the tabs will stack up to save space. You can click any of the tabs in the stack to view it in full-screen.

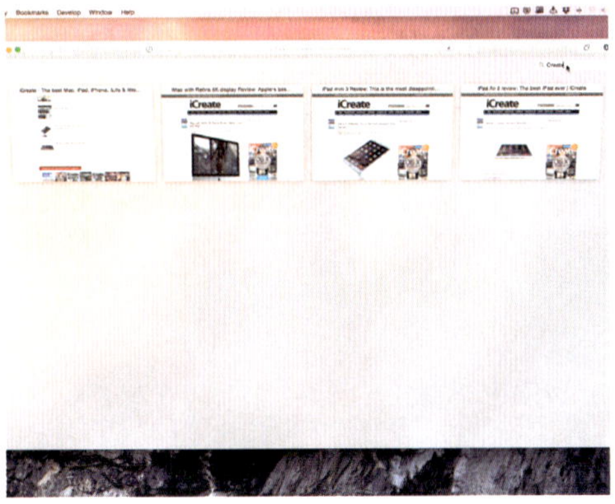

05: Search tabs

When you're in the tab view, simple start typing and a search bar will appear in the top-right.Safari will search the tabs for the word and show those that match.

06: Tabs on iOS

Scroll down in Safari's new tab view and you'll see all the tabs that are open on iOS devices like the iPhone and iPad, as long as they're running iOS 8 with iCloud.

Start using Apple Maps

Explore the world, get directions, find attractions, businesses and more

Maps has been on iOS devices for over a year and now it's available on Macs too. iPhone and iPad users will find many familiar features, but there are also new ones and there's lots to discover in this fantastic app. From a large map of the country, you can smoothly zoom in right to your street, or whichever location you are interested in. There are three different views to select from and you can opt to view a standard map, a satellite photo image or a hybrid of the two.

All three are useful and switching from one to the other is very easy and intuitive.

You can find businesses around you or look up the attractions at a place you plan to visit. The information, reviews and collections of photos provided are very useful. If you aren't sure how to get somewhere, Maps can display a list of directions for travel by car or walking. It even displays traffic information and roadworks. There are also stunning 3D views, which are great for exploring cities.

> "There are also stunning 3D views, which are great for exploring cities"

Two views
These two buttons select different views for the map: standard, or satellite

Get directions
Use Maps to get driving or walking directions between two locations

Map icons
Icons on the map show places of interest such as museums, hotels, parks, restaurants and so on

Map pins
Search for places and Maps will put pins on the map. Click one for more information

Shortcuts and gestures

Learn all the tips to better control Maps and get more out of this powerful app

It's true that Maps' basic features are easy to use, but there are advanced features that aren't quite so obvious. For example, Cmd+L positions the map over your current location and zooms in. You can move around either by clicking and dragging with the mouse or using two fingers on the trackpad. Although there is a zoom in/out control, you can also double-click the mouse to zoom in and Opt-double-click to zoom out. Pinch and spread on a trackpad works too. In fact, there are other useful trackpad features such as using two fingers to rotate the view.

Zoom right in using satellite view, click the 3D button, then click and hold the mouse over the compass as you push up and down. This tilts the map and as it flattens, real buildings are displayed in 3D. Many large cities and attractions have 3D views, meaning you can explore London, Paris, New York and other places. Pull down with two fingers on the trackpad to fly over a city in 3D.

Key features

Use 3D views, find businesses, bookmark places and more

Explore in 3D

The 3D views are the most entertaining features of the Maps app, offering a way to explore the world from your desk. Go to San Francisco and see the Golden Gate Bridge, look around the London Eye and Tower Bridge, fly low over Manhattan in New York, explore the skyscrapers from every angle and so on. You'll see world-famous buildings and attractions as if you were really there. There are some amazing views, so enter your destination in the Search box.

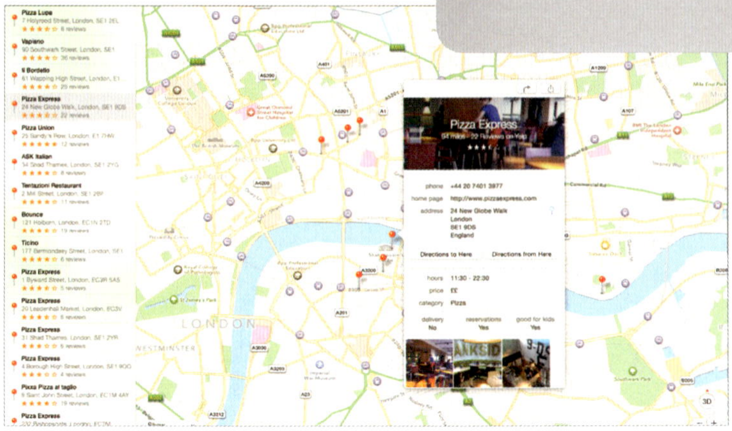

Find local businesses

The Search box in the top middle of the window isn't just for finding cities and streets, it can also track down businesses such as restaurants, plumbers, garages and so on. If you fancy a pizza, for example, just enter 'pizza' into the Search box and pins are automatically placed on the map to show the locations. Clicking a pin displays more information, such as the address and phone number. Sometimes there are reviews and you can even get directions.

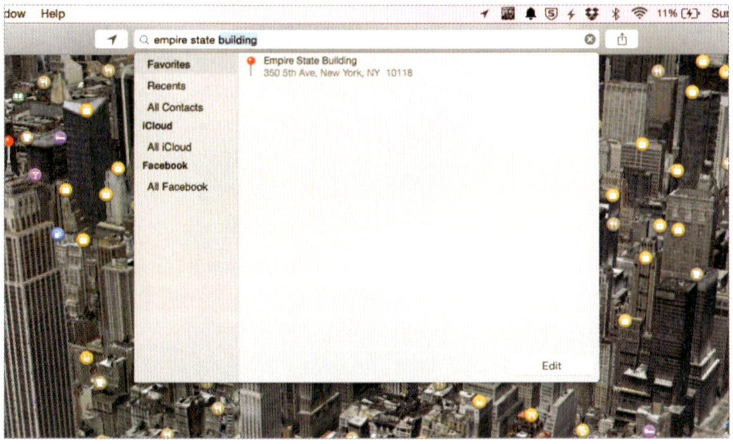

Bookmark favourite locations

Places of interest or places you regularly visit can be bookmarked, which enables you to quickly return to a location without having to search for it in Maps. There are a couple of ways to add a bookmark. For instance, after searching for some place, click the pin in the map and then click the Add Bookmark button. You can also place a pin in anywhere using the Drop Pin option on the View menu. Simply click this to add a bookmark.

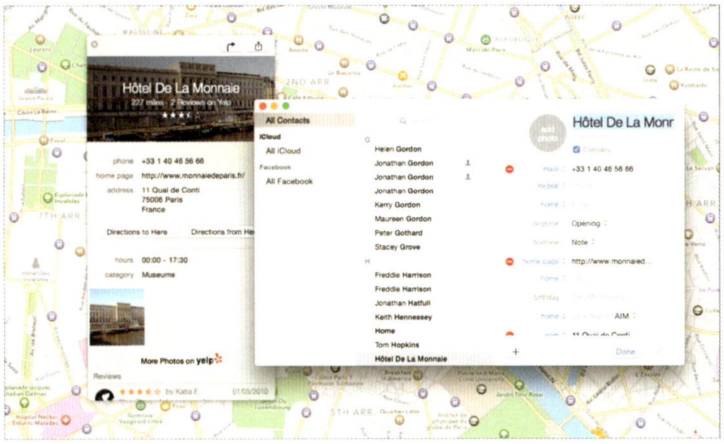

Build up your contacts

Maps is integrated into other apps and when viewing an address in an email, for example, you can click it to open Maps and view the location. When using Maps and viewing a business or attraction, you can click Add to Contacts to store the name, phone number and address. It's useful to build up your contacts with useful local businesses, particularly when you are planning a trip. You might not have your Mac, but the information is synced to iPhones and iPads.

Find your way with Apple Maps

Maps makes a great route-planner and shows turn-by-turn directions

When you need to plan a long journey and you aren't sure which route to take, the Maps app will provide all the answers you could possibly need. It can work out your current location, which means you only need to enter the destination and click the Directions button to see a complete turn-by-turn breakdown of the route to take. You can also manually enter start points, so you could plan several trips before even setting off on holiday, for example.

A nice feature is the ability to zoom into every turn and see it in detail on the map. Another handy trick is the live traffic information and notifications of road works, closed roads and other problems. You won't always have your Mac with you when travelling, so a great idea is the Send to iOS Device on the Share button. Work out the route on your Mac and then just send it to your iPhone.

Key route features

Select and explore all the routes

Start and end

After displaying a route, you might want to see the directions to return home. Just click this button to switch the route's start and end locations to find your way

Alternate routes

There are three different routes on this map and each one is indicated by the time in the bubble. Simply select one to see where the route takes you and try the alternatives

Walking or driving?

With short routes there is the option of walking, of course. Clicking this button rewrites the route with walking in mind, often taking shortcuts

Route directions

The route directions are displayed with symbols, but if you aren't sure about a turn, click it to zoom into the map. This way you can step through each turn

READING THE TRAFFIC

When live traffic information is showing on the map, you will see roads with orange dots and some with red dots. Orange means that there is heavy traffic, but it's moving slowly. Red dots mean stop-and-start traffic.

Maps Get instant travel directions

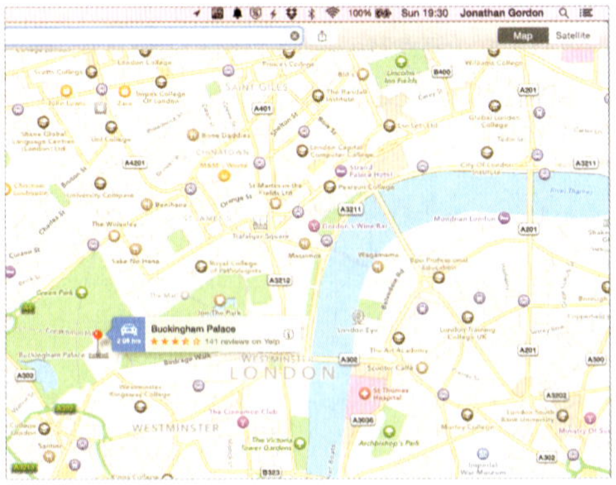

01: Enter your destination

Where do you want to go to? Enter the destination into the Search box and Maps will find it and place a pin to show where it is.

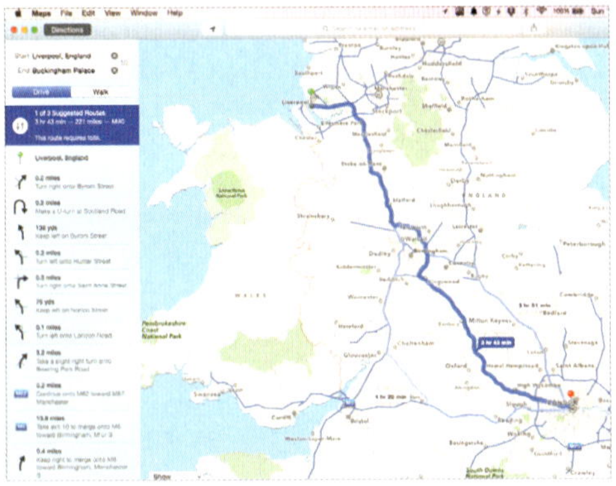

02: Get directions

Click the Directions button to open the panel on the right. Click Directions in it to see the route on the map and turn-by-turn instructions.

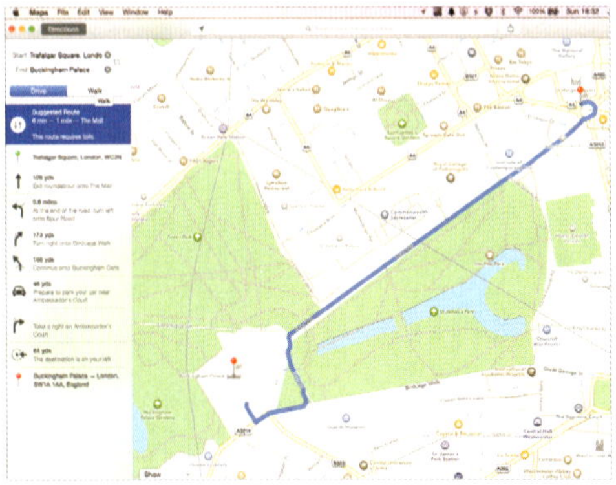

03: A new start

Suppose you want to start from somewhere else. Click Delete Current Locataion in the Start box and replace it with a new location to see the route.

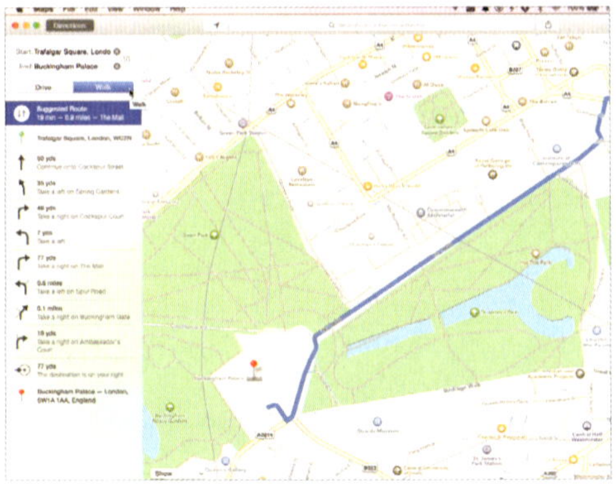

04: Driving vs walking

This route is a short one and it would be possible to travel on foot. Click the walking icon in the Directions panel on the right to see the path.

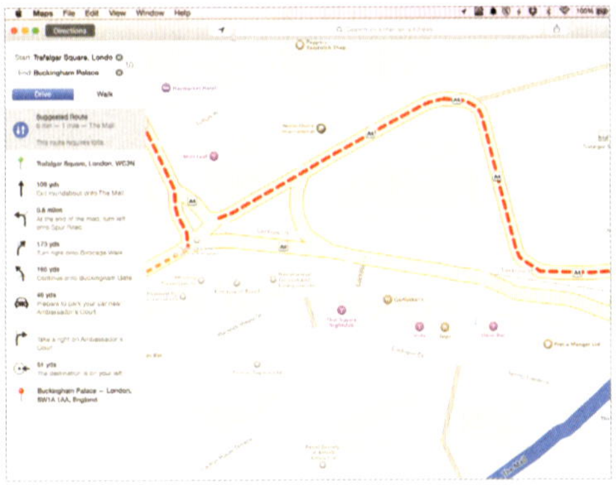

05: Avoid traffic jams

If you are travelling by car, you can see whether there is any traffic by clicking Show in the bottom left of the window. The red roads are the busiest.

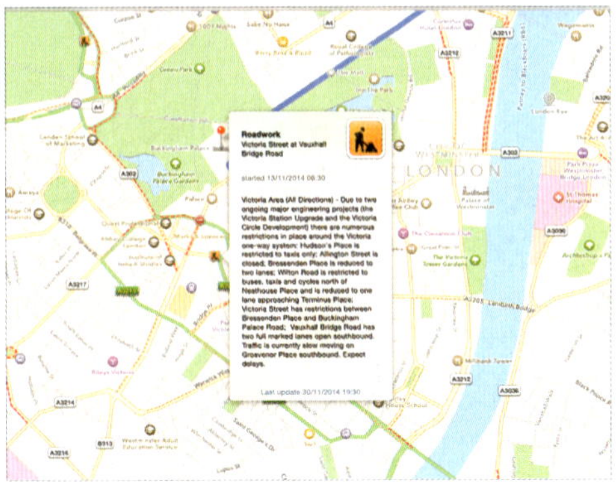

06: View road warnings

When the traffic status is displayed, there are symbols on the road and clicking them displays information such as road works and closed roads.

07: Use your iPhone

Travelling with a Mac isn't ideal and iPhones and iPads fit your pocket or bag. Click the Share button and send the route to your iPhone.

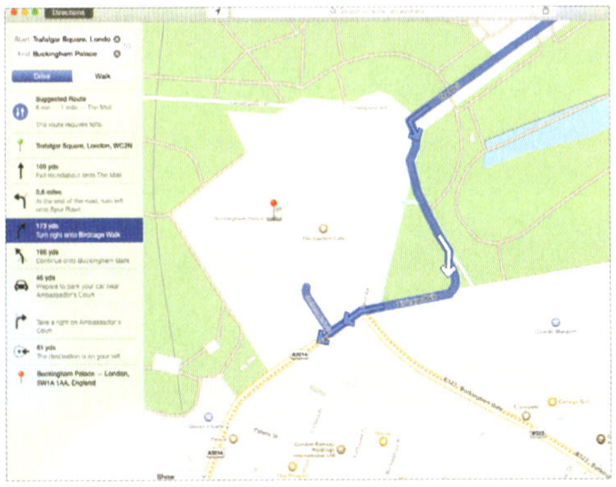

08: Zoom into turns

If you aren't sure about a change in direction, click it in the Directions list on the right and the map will zoom into that location.

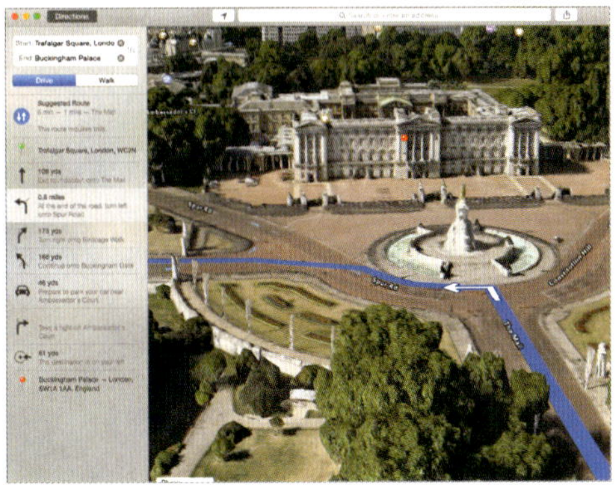

09: Switch to 3D

Still not sure about which way to go? Switch to 3D with the second toolbar button to get a better street-level view of the route.

Get to know the Mac App Store

The Mac App Store guarantees easy access to a wide range of free and paid apps. Find out what it's all about right here…

The Mac App Store first appeared in Mac OS X 10.6.6 and is home to a diverse range of apps aimed at enhancing the functionality of a Mac computer. As a bonus, the majority of apps are either reasonably priced or free.

As we have come to expect from Apple, the interface is intuitive, and finding and acquiring apps is a breeze. This is largely because the store has adopted a very similar look, feel and process to shopping to that used by the iTunes App Store. When you want to buy an app, simply enter your iTunes ID and password, and it's purchased. It really is as simple as that. The app is automatically downloaded and installed in the Applications folder, and can be accessed via Launchpad when required. You can even search for apps by title, developer/publisher, category or description. All apps are organised into convenient categories and this makes the process of navigating the store an effortless experience. Here we show you how to explore the virtual aisles…

Log in to the Mac App Store

Start downloading apps immediately

If you're new to the Mac App Store, there are two ways to launch the service; either click the App Store icon in the Dock, or click the Apple menu and select 'App Store'. Do this, and you are free to browse the store using the 'Featured', 'Categories' or 'Top Charts' windows.

If you've ever used the iTunes App Store then you'll already have an Apple ID so click 'Sign In' from the 'Quick Links' tab to the right of the window, or Store>Sign In from the Mac App Store menu. When the 'Sign In' screen appears, all you have to do is enter your Apple ID and password, and click 'Sign In'.

If you don't have an Apple ID, click the 'Create Apple ID' button on the 'Sign In' screen, and you'll see a window welcoming you to the App Store. Click 'Continue', agree to the terms and conditions and follow the online instructions to create an Apple ID. Once you've completed the process, you can start downloading apps immediately.

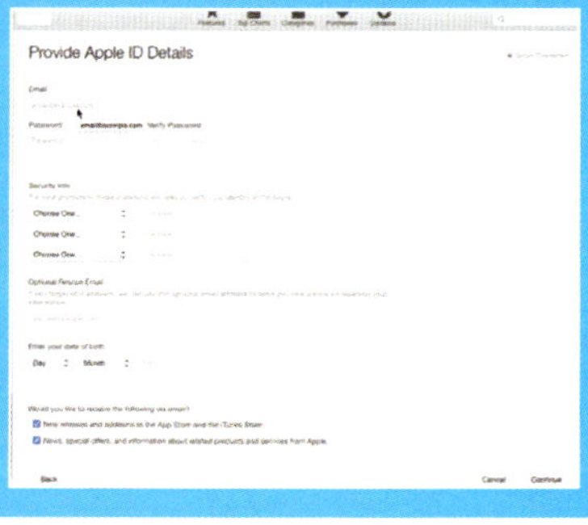

Key features

How to navigate the Mac App Store

Featured

Take a look at the Mac App Store's main storefront window. It's well organised, and you'll see five buttons at the top. Select the 'Featured' view, and you can browse apps that Apple has deemed 'New & Noteworthy', which is handy if you want to see the latest apps Apple deems worthy of your time. If you're more interested in apps with favourable user reviews, however, then scroll to the 'What's Hot' section to see all of the top rated apps.

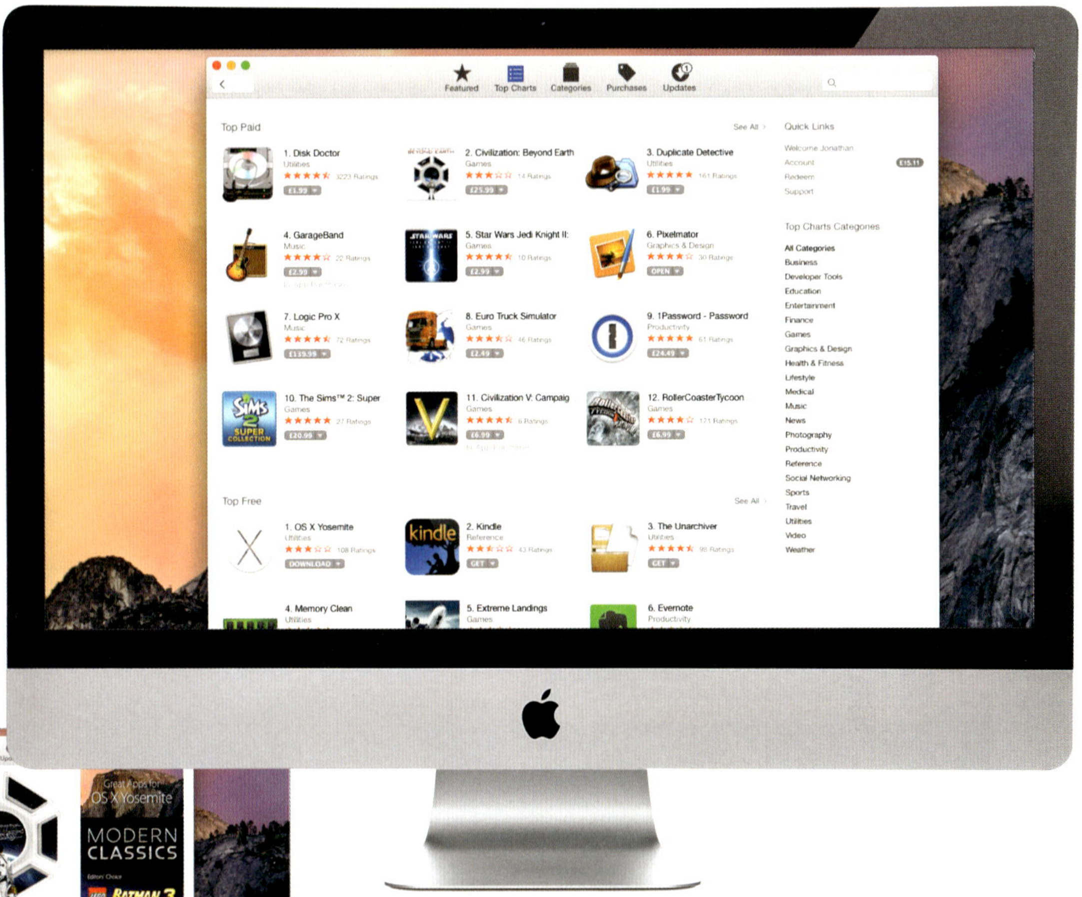

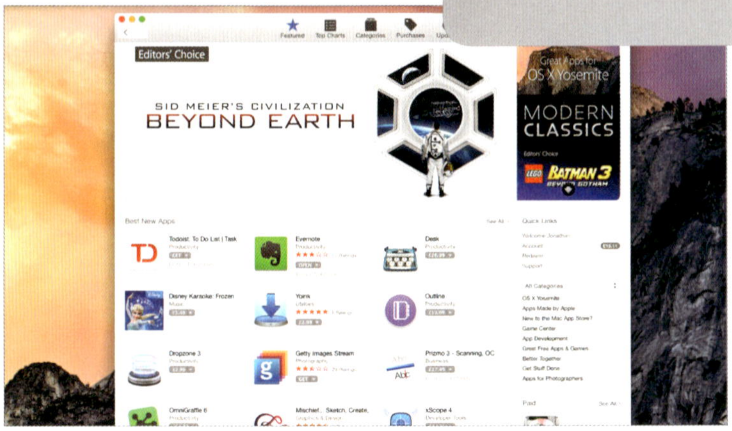

Top Charts

If you're interested in the most popular apps that people have purchased, click the 'Top Charts' button at the top of the main window, and get instant access to the top apps. Here, you can download OS X Yosemite, if you're not already running it, and apps that include Pages, Numbers and Keynote. To the right of the window are links to the categories. Click one, and you'll see a range of popular apps. Each device will have a similar menu available.

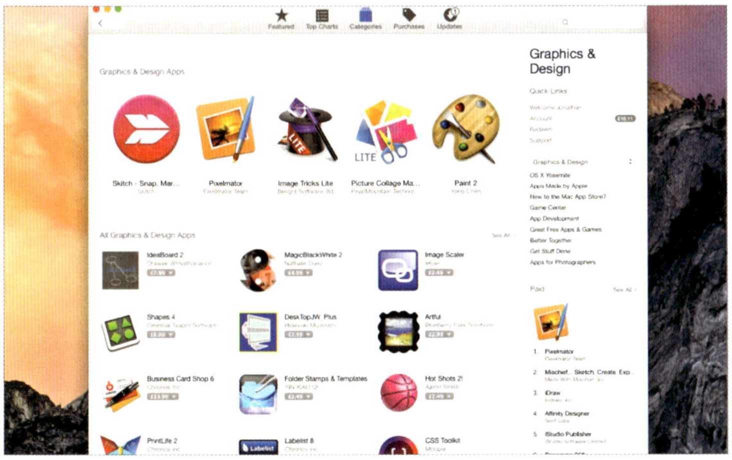

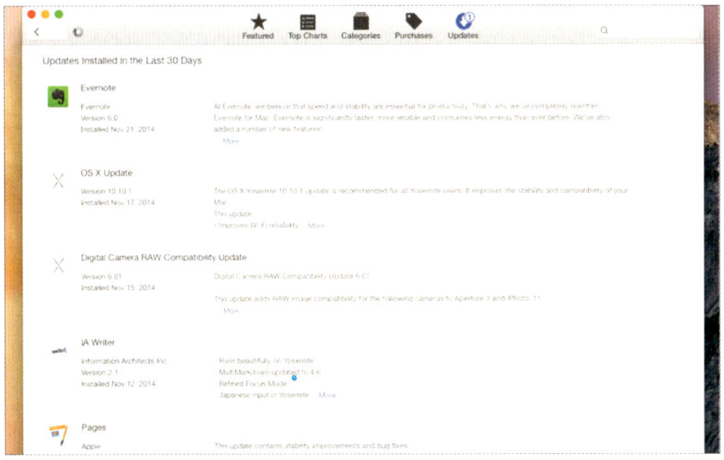

Categories

If you know the type of app that you are looking for, then try using the 'Categories' view. All apps in the Mac App Store are organised into one of 21 categories, ranging from 'Business' and 'Weather', to 'Developer Tools' and 'Video'. Click the category title to see all the apps in that specific category. You can now browse the apps. If you see one you'd like to know more about, then simply click on the thumbnail image.

Updates

The Mac App Store offers similar functionality to the iTunes App Store. If you use an iPhone, you'll know that you are notified of app updates as and when they become available. It's no different with the Mac App Store; click the 'Updates' button, and you'll see all available updates for apps you've downloaded. You are then given the option to install them. These updates may iron out any glitches or add extra features to your apps.

Create a Mac App Store account

Follow our tutorial to create an Apple ID and start downloading apps from the Mac App Store

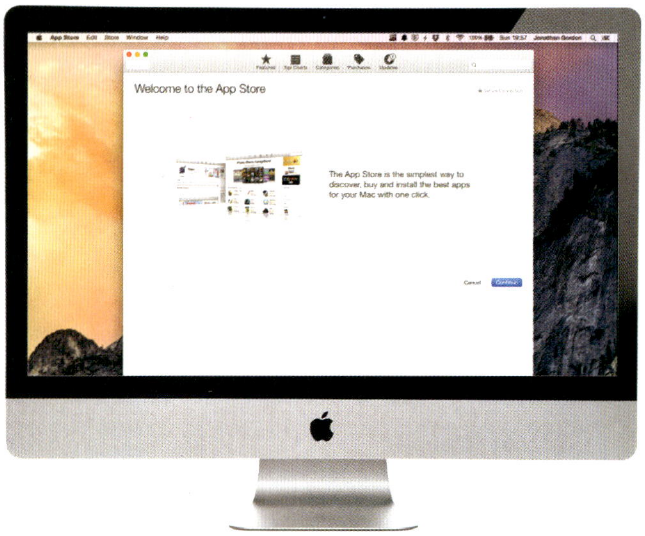

An Apple ID lets you personalise your Apple experience. Once you've created one, you can use it to access Apple resources that require you to identify yourself and make purchases from the Apple Online Store, the iTunes Store and the App Store. If you have held a MobileMe account, or use an iPhone, iPad or iPod touch to access the iTunes store, you will already have an Apple ID, and this can be used to sign in to the App Store.

But what if you don't have an Apple ID? Well, you can still browse the Mac App Store, but you cannot download either free or paid apps. Creating an Apple ID is a very straightforward process and, although the majority of people use iTunes to set up their account, you'll be pleased to learn that you can also create an Apple ID via the Mac App Store. Read on, and we'll guide you through the process of creating a new Apple ID for either yourself or a member of your family.

"An Apple ID lets you personalise your Apple experience and access Apple's resources"

Access the App Store

How to use your Apple ID to browse the Mac App Store

Password
Your email address will be your new Apple ID. Type this, and choose a mixed case password of at least eight characters when prompted during the setup process. Use this information to sign in

Sign in
There are two ways to sign in with your new Apple ID. The quickest is to click 'Sign in' under the Quick Links tab. Alternatively, select Store>Sign In from the main App Store menu

Create Apple ID
Enter an Apple ID and password, and you can download and purchase apps. If you haven't got an Apple ID, click the 'Create Apple ID' button to create a new account and personalise your Apple experience

Browse apps
There is a diverse range of apps available for download and purchase from the Mac App Store, but unless you sign in using an Apple ID, all you can do is browse

REDEEM A CODE
Create an Apple ID via the App Store and you are then required to either enter a payment method or redeem a voucher. If you are creating an Apple ID for a younger member of the family, then you may redeem a voucher code. This way, you won't be surprised by any unexpected credit card bills!

Mac App Store Create an Apple ID

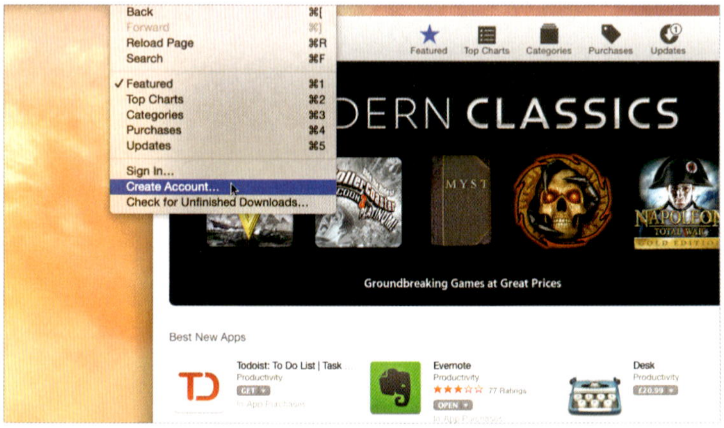

01: Create Account

Launch the App Store. From the main Mac App Store menu, choose Store> Create Account. You will now see the 'Welcome to the App Store' window.

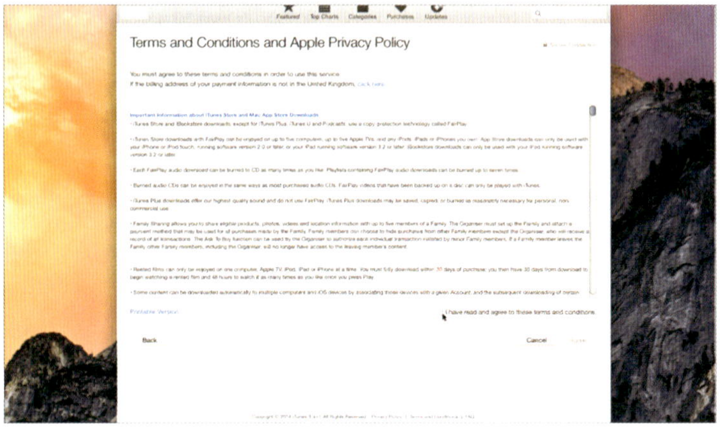

02: Terms and conditions

Click 'Continue', and read the terms and conditions. Confirm that you have read and agree to them, and click the 'Agree' button.

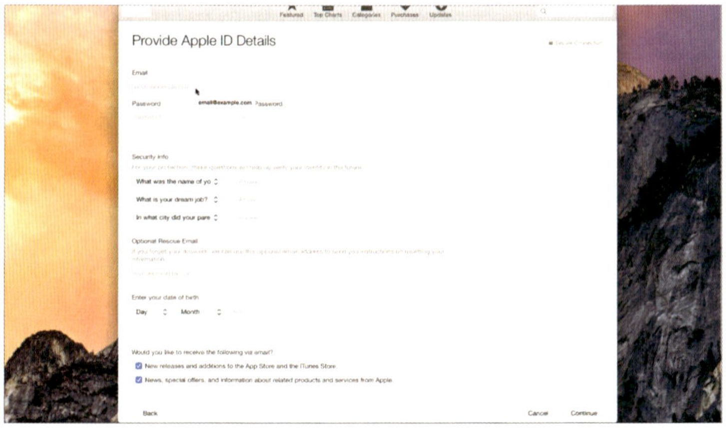

03: Apple ID details

Enter your Apple ID details. Type your email address, a mixed case password of at least eight characters, and the other details requested.

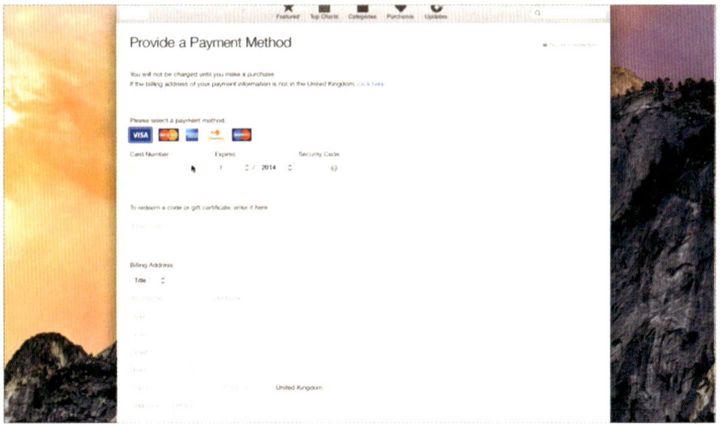

04: Payment method

Click 'Continue', and provide a payment method on the window that appears, or opt to redeem a gift certificate or prepaid iTunes Gift Card.

05: Create Apple ID

Enter your name, address and telephone number, then click 'Create Apple ID'. A verification email will now be sent to the email address you provided.

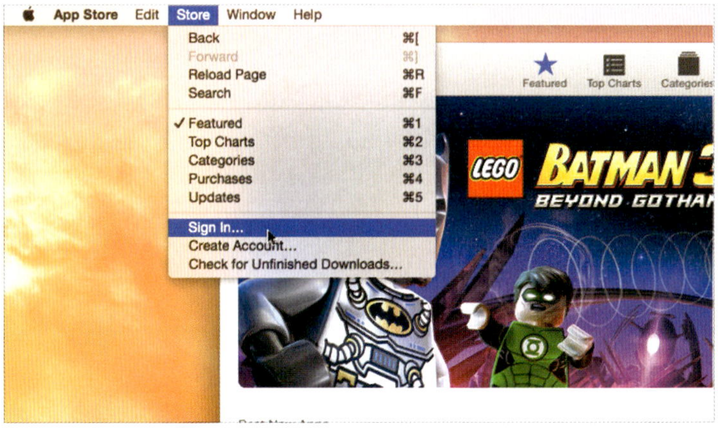

06: Verify email address

Check your inbox, and click the link to verify your email address. You can now use your new Apple ID and password to sign in to the App Store.

Download apps from the Mac Store

The Mac App Store is your hub for new software. Here's how to get your hands on amazing apps

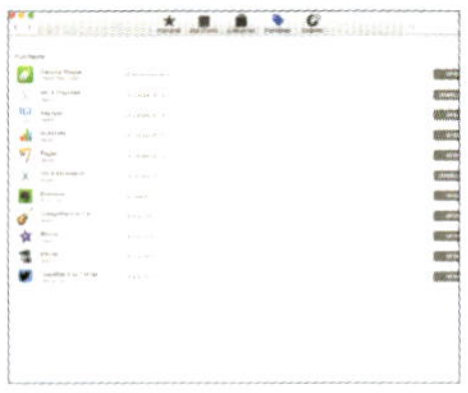

When it launched at the beginning of 2011, the Mac App Store offered Mac users an entirely new way to browse and download apps that had never been seen before. There was widespread shock at Apple's decision to do this because it was a move based on the success of the iPhone App Store, and one not guaranteed to work on the Mac platform. As has been the case for many a year now, Apple was right and the Mac App Store became an instant success.

These days, a lot of people take the Store for granted, while others don't even know it exists and have never even opened it up. If this is you, you're missing out on a huge amount of incredible content. In this tutorial, we'll start you at the basic level. If you have an Apple ID, which you would use to buy iPhone and iPad apps as well as songs and movies in the iTunes Store, you can use that to log in. If not, check out the tutorial on the previous two pages.

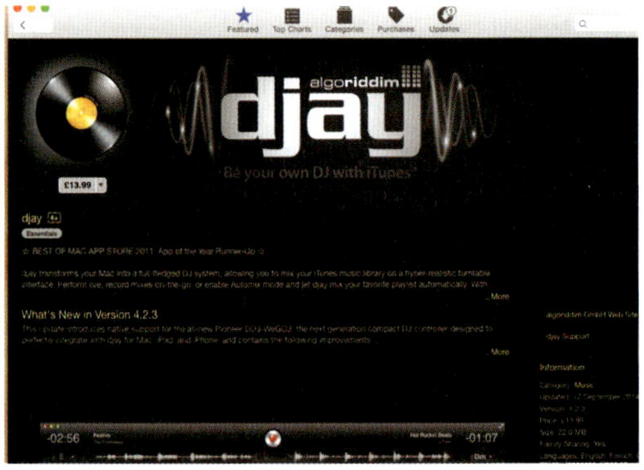

Mac App Store Start downloading now

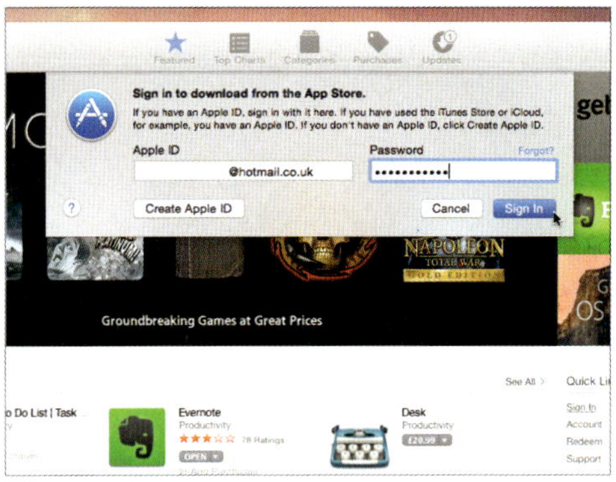

01: Apple ID

Open the Mac App Store and look at the Quick Links on the right. Click Sign In. Input your Apple ID and password, or create one if you don't have one.

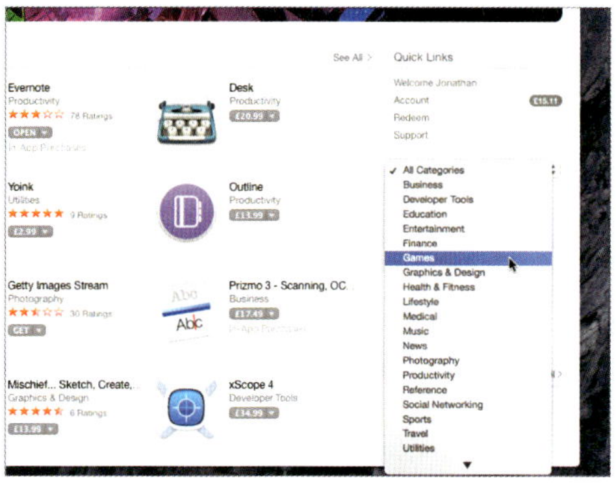

02: Categories

Below the Sign In button you will see a drop-down box that says All Categories. Click it and you can quickly navigate between categories in the Store.

03: Chart topping

Along the top of the Store are five options. The second one is Top Charts; select this and you can see what is being downloaded the most.

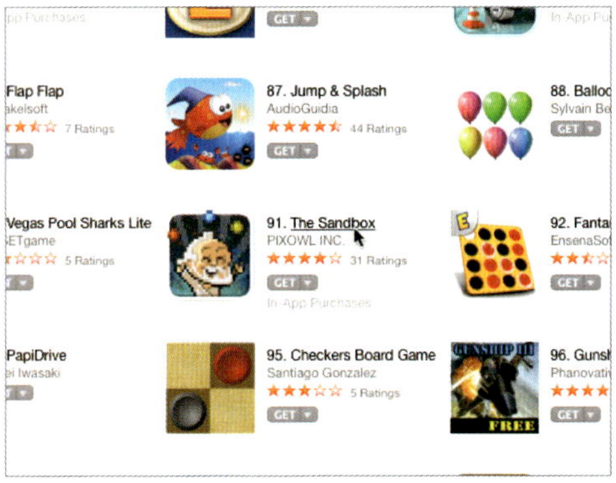

04: Well paid

The opening page of the Top Charts section shows you the most downloaded apps. When you find an app you're interested in, click its name or icon.

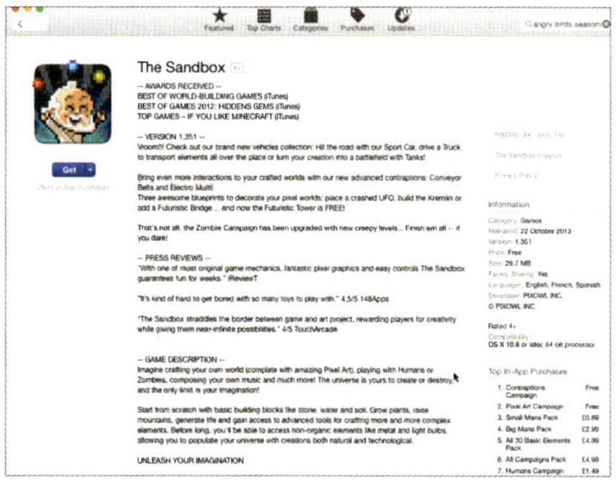

05: App details

Clicking on an app's name will take you to its page. You can read a description here. Click on More to reveal all the information about the app.

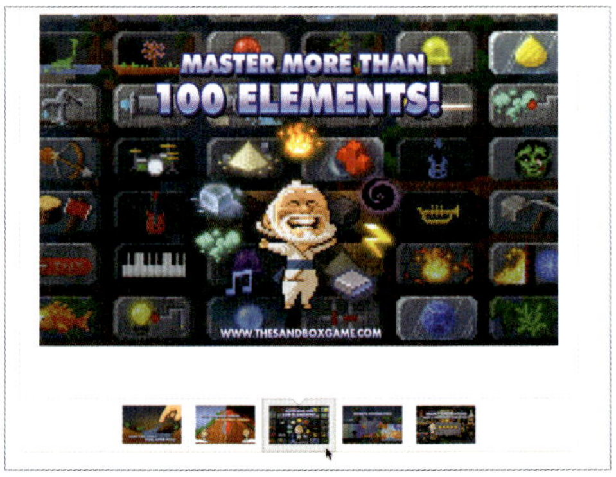

06: Screenshots

Scroll down and you can flick through screenshots of the app, just like on the iOS App Store. This gives you a better idea of how the app will work.

Mac App Store interface explained

Discover a world of great software

Quick buy

If you know you want an app, you don't have to view the app's page before you download. These grey buttons act as 'Buy' buttons, so you can click these and download apps straight from this page

Past purchases

The Mac App Store recognises when you buy something with an Apple ID. You can click the Purchases tab at the top to view all of your previously downloaded apps

DON'T HAVE THE STORE?

It might be that you don't see the Mac App Store anywhere on your machine. If you are running a version of OS X from Lion onwards, the Store will be included automatically. However, before Lion, the Store was only available on OS X 10.6.6 – Snow Leopard. Earlier systems don't support the Store, and Leopard users will need to download it from Apple's website.

Up to date

When one of your apps needs updating to a newer version, the Mac App Store will show an alert in your Dock. Click it and choose Updates from the top of the window to download the latest version of the app

Search and download

If you know exactly what you're looking for and need to find it fast, you can use the Search bar in the top right of the window. This will offer suggestions of apps as you type, so you can find things instantly

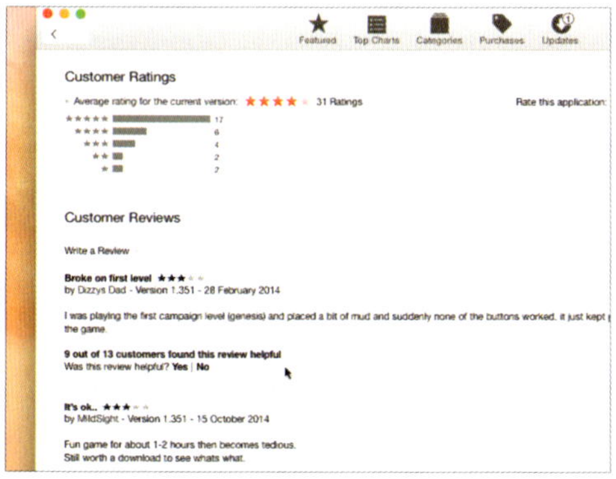

07: Tough crowd

Move further down and you can read reviews from other users. These offer brilliant and real opinions on the app, away from the marketing blurb.

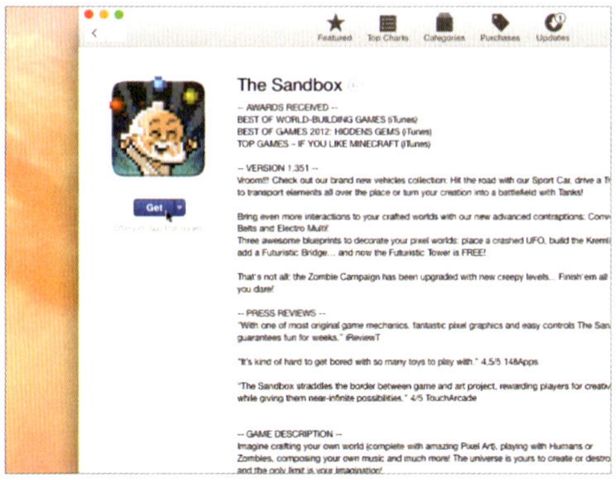

08: Ready to buy

If you want the app, go to the top of the page and click the Buy App button. It will turn green. Click it again, then input your Apple ID and password.

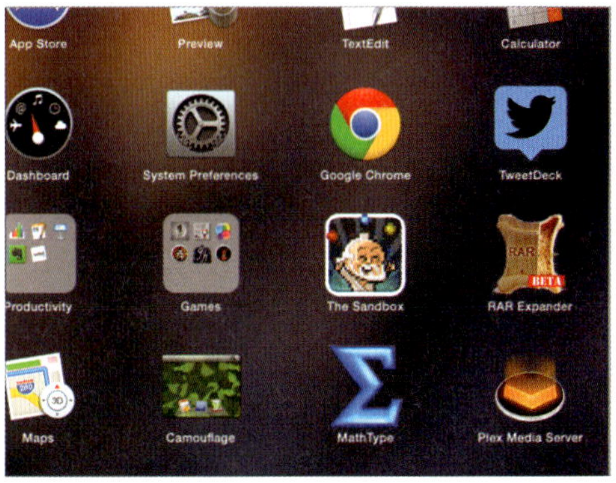

09: Installed

Once you've clicked Buy App, the Mac's Launchpad will open automatically and your app will appear on the grid. You can now click on it to launch it.

Delete and reinstall apps on your Mac

Deleting apps downloaded from the Mac App Store is a breeze

Uninstalling apps has always been a whole lot easier on a Mac than on a Windows PC, and you'll be pleased to learn that the most recent versions of OS X make the process even easier. Don't go looking for an 'Uninstall Programs' setting, as you won't find one! The latest versions of the OS have adopted the automated click-and-hold method used by devices such as the iPhone and iPad. This means that deleting any apps downloaded from the Mac App Store is an absolute breeze. In fact, if you've ever used an iOS device such as an iPhone to remove apps downloaded from the iTunes App Store, then you'll instantly feel familiar with the process.

Read on and we'll show you how to use Launchpad to delete an app that has been downloaded from the Mac App Store. We'll then show you how to reinstall the app should you ever require it again in the future. As a bonus, you don't even need to empty the Trash, as Launchpad handles everything for you. It's an extremely simple process and we show you how to do it.

Delete with ease

A quick look at the app deleting process

Navigate Launchpad

All apps (paid and free) that you download from the Mac App Store can be viewed on Launchpad. If there is more than one page of shortcut icons, use your mouse to swipe through the screens

Confirm deletion

Removing an app that is no longer required is a breeze; simply click on the black 'X' badge, and then 'Delete' when asked to confirm that you want to delete the app. The whole process is automated

Reinstall apps

You can reinstall apps downloaded from the Mac App Store using the Purchased view. Click 'Install', and the app will be reinstalled, and appear in the first available space on the Launchpad screen

Click and hold

Click and hold on an app that you wish to delete, and all the app icons will start wiggling. Apps that can be deleted (that is, those downloaded from the Mac App Store) will sport a circular black 'X' badge

DELETE FROM FINDER

Experienced Mac OS X users may have noted that apps downloaded from the Mac App Store cannot be moved to Trash from the Applications folder. Although the easiest way to delete apps is via Launchpad, there is an alternative method. Open Finder, click Go>Applications, and select an app. Press Command+Delete, enter your password when prompted, and the app will be moved to the Trash.

Mac App Store Uninstall and reinstall apps

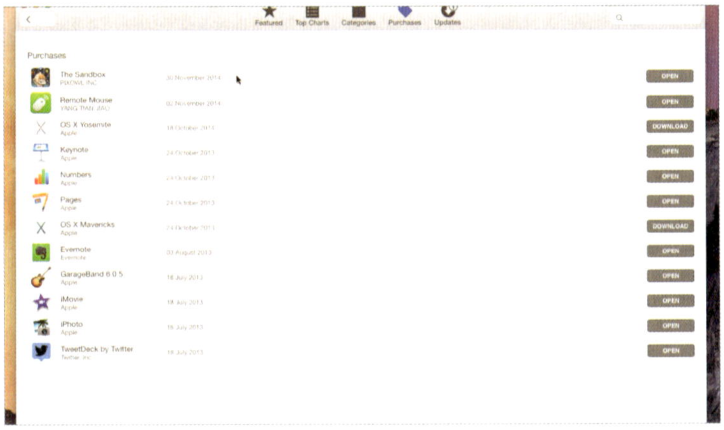

01: Purchased apps

The first step is to check which apps you have downloaded. To do this, launch the App Store, and click the 'Purchases' button at the top.

02: Click and hold

Browse the apps installed, find one you no longer need, and click the Launchpad icon. Click and hold on the app's icon until it starts wiggling.

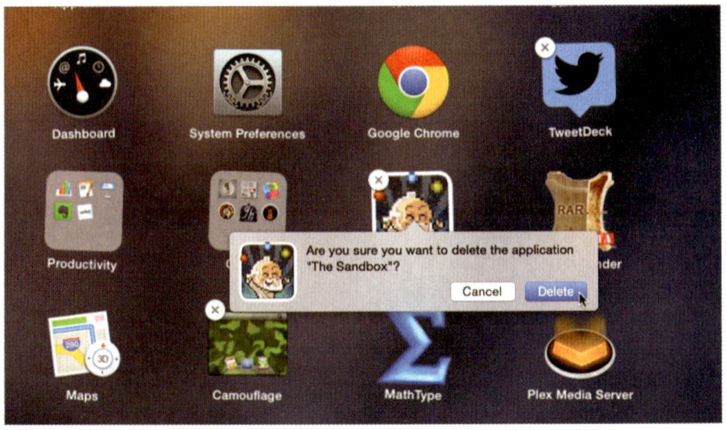

03: Confirm deletion

All downloaded apps will now sport an 'X' icon. Click the relevant 'X' icon, and when asked to confirm that you want to delete the app, click 'Delete'.

04: Familiar process

The app will now be removed. The process will be familiar to anyone who has used an iDevice, as the tap and hold method is used by all iOS devices.

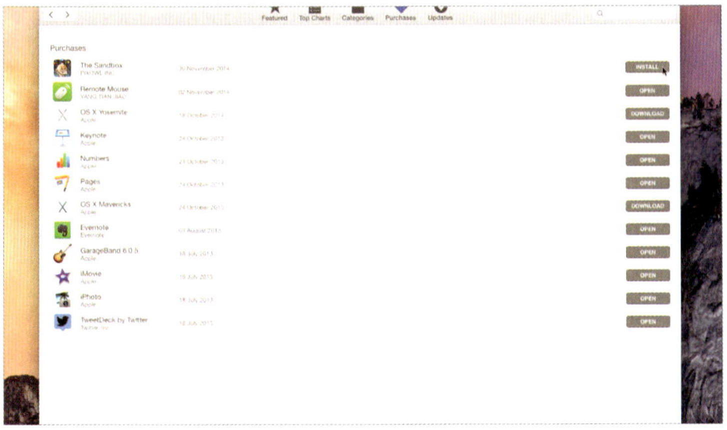

05: Reinstall the app

If you want to reinstall the app, launch the App Store, and navigate to the 'Purchased' view. When the store recalls your purchases, click 'Install'.

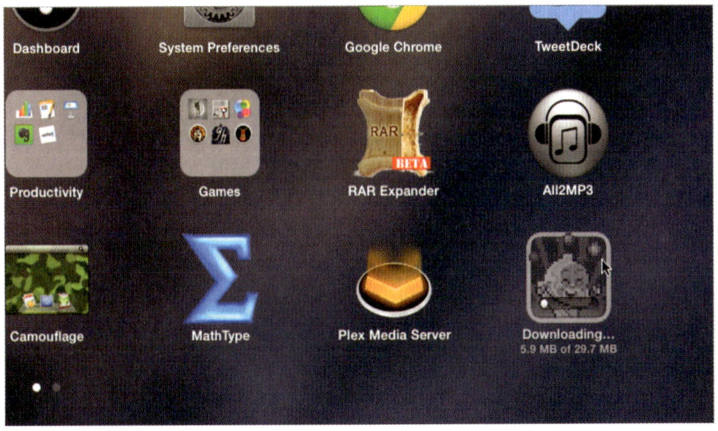

06: Track progress

Launchpad will appear. You can track the progress of the app download and reinstallation. The process is automated, with no user input required.

Get started with iTunes

Learn to find your way around the iTunes app and discover all the amazing content on offer

iTunes is the place you go to for entertainment on your Mac, whatever it is you fancy doing. Movies and TV series, new songs and albums, smart playlists that are based on tracks you like, books that you can start reading on your Mac and carry on reading on your iPad, even a digital store full of educational courses, plus podcasts and apps for your iOS devices; iTunes has it all. While the App Store (with its own blue and white icon in your Applications folder) is the place you go to find apps like iPhoto, Pages and Numbers. iTunes is for everything else.

The app comes in two, very big, halves: the Library and the iTunes Store. The front page of the Store has a carousel that you can browse, featuring new and noteworthy apps, albums, films and deals. All you need to do to get going is sign in with your iTunes account.

Once you've loaded iTunes up with your favourites content, you can use the Library, and the iTunes Player, to enjoy your media. Stream through AirPlay devices and sync everything with your iPhone and iPad so you can enjoy it on those too. There's a lot to see, so we'll show you around first.

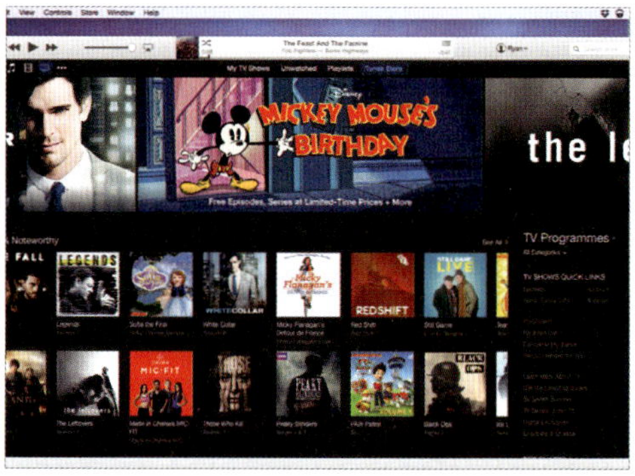

Using iTunes to play media

Listen to songs without even leaving the Store

Access a device
When your iOS device is plugged in, you will be able to access its page of options, including syncing, or eject the device by clicking this button

Visit the Store
This contains a link to the iTunes Store, where you can rent or purchase more content, and you can also have links to things such as your Purchased apps

Find your content
All the music, movies, TV shows, podcasts, audiobooks and apps you own can be accessed via the buttons here. Click on the three-dot icon to access more of your content

Playing files
Once you've selected and played a track or playlist from the main area below, use these playback controls so you can pause and skip tracks while browsing iTunes

STORE, LIBRARY AND PLAYER
iTunes comes in two halves: a Store, where you can buy and rent films and TV episodes, apps, music and more, and then a Library and media player where you can enjoy all this content. While in each, you can use the tabs at the top of the screen to access other places.

iTunes Find your feet in iTunes

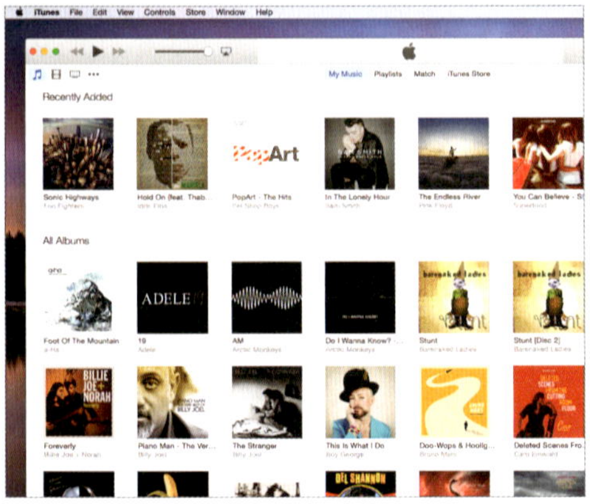

01: Find your music

Open up iTunes and use the icons in the top-left corner to switch between Music, Movies, TV Shows and more. Start off by selecting Music.

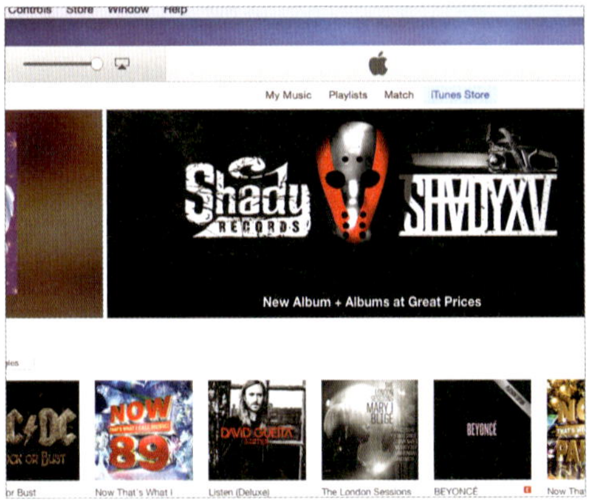

02: Browse the tabs

Use the tabs in the middle of the bar along the top of the main window to switch between My Music, Playlists, Match and the iTunes Store.

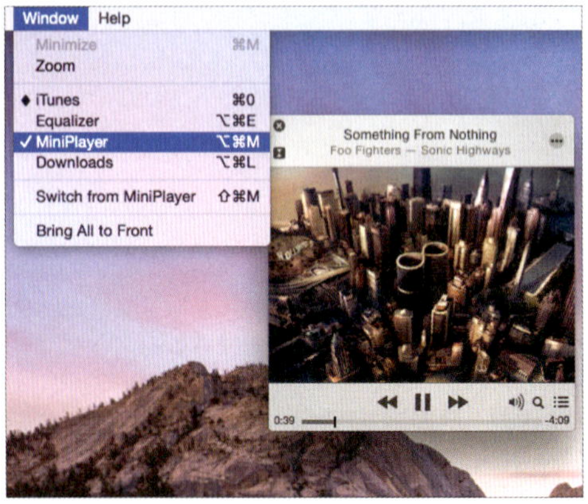

03: Use the MiniPlayer

You can create a smaller version of the iTunes player by selecting MiniPlayer from the Window menu at the top. It's more powerful than you think.

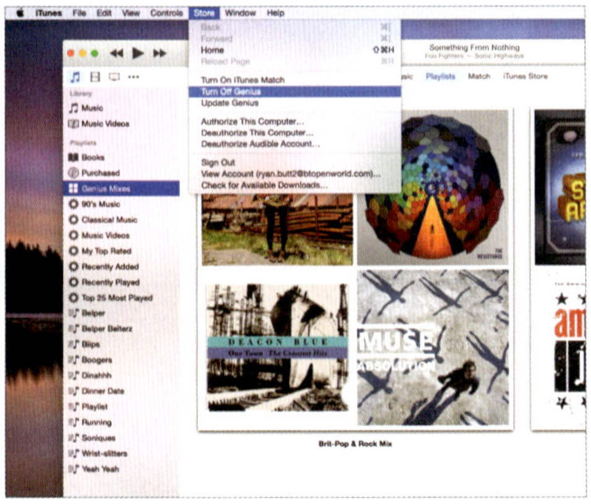

04: Switch on Genius

Choose Genius from the Store menu to get instant recommendations and playlists depending on the tracks you choose.

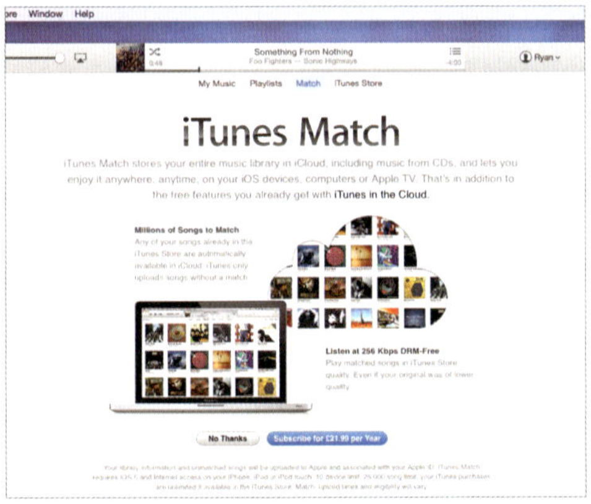

05: Match your collection

If you sign up for an iTunes Match subscription, you can upload all your music to the cloud and enjoy it on all your devices.

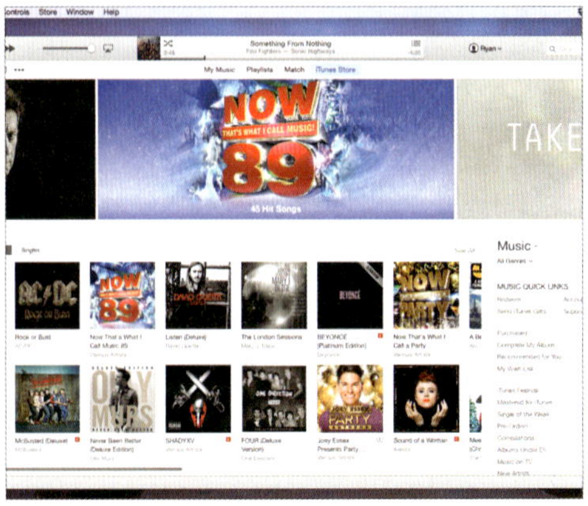

06: Go to the Store

Click the iTunes Store button at the top. Find new apps, music, videos, books and more. Featured content is on the carousel on the main page.

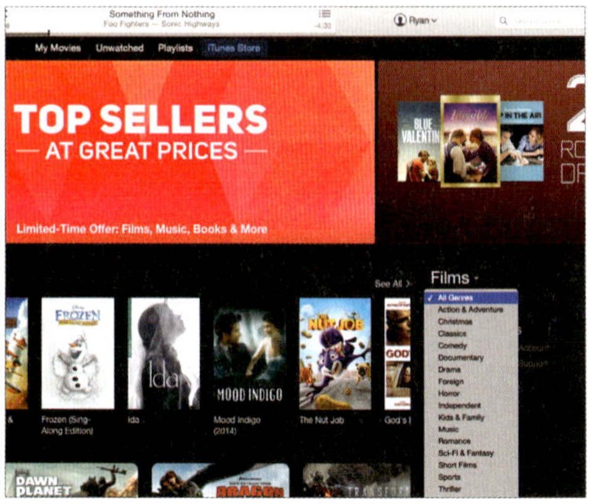

07: Find a movie

Choose Movies from the menu to the right of the main window. As well as featured content, there are further categories. Pick a film you want to see.

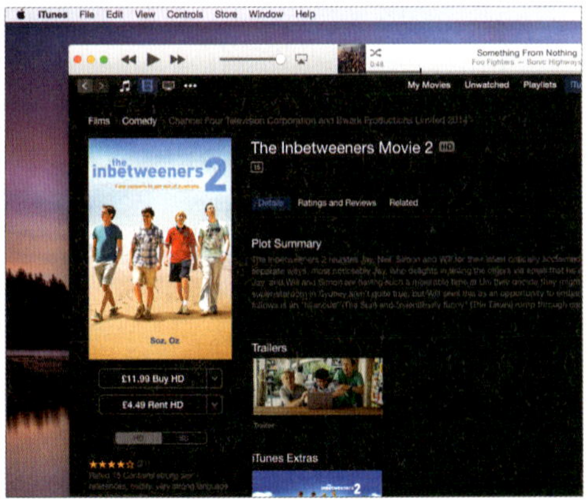

08: Rent or buy

On the film's info page, depending on availability, you can buy or rent in standard or HD. With albums you can buy songs or whole albums.

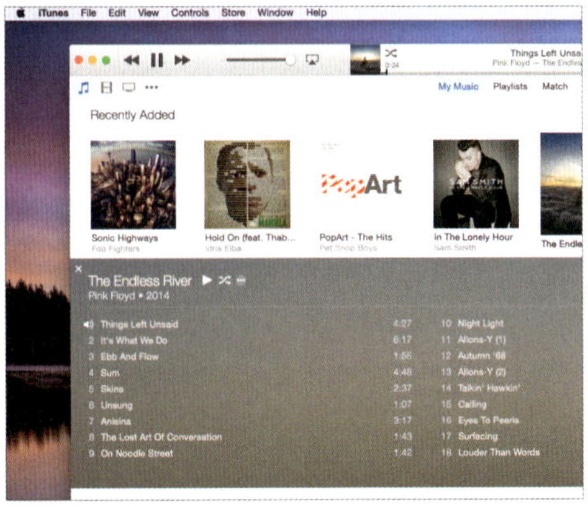

09: Hit play

Once you've downloaded something, it'll turn up in your Library view. Hit play and enjoy it on your Mac, or go and see what else is in the Store.

Download music from the iTunes store

Music is still one of the most important features within iTunes, so make the most of it

iTunes was born to help people manage their digital music, and over time it has grown to offer all of the entertainment you could possibly want to carry with you. However, music is still a very important part of the service, and being able to download new songs or albums is extremely handy when you want a quick music fix. The library is huge, and all of the major new releases are available as quickly as they are on competing services, and it has reached the point where almost every artist you like will have a large selection of content on offer.

You can quickly search for individual songs, albums and tracks via the search bar, and also dig down deeper within an artist's catalogue to find the music you're looking for. There are multiple ways to browse music, and once you have an account set up with a valid credit card or gift card code, the process is as simple as choosing what you want and then letting the software do the work for you.

In this tutorial, we will explain how to download and purchase music from iTunes and then move it to your iPod. Indeed, there are settings you can choose to make the process almost fully automated and with so many options open to you, it is unlikely that you will need to use any other service to get the music you want. Your only problems will be finding the music you require within such a large library and making sure you have enough space to install it all.

> "Almost every artist you like will have a large selection of content on offer on iTunes"

iTunes purchasing options

Many purchasing choices are available

Buy an album
Clicking this button will prompt an immediate purchase of an album. You will need to enter your password, and the process only takes a few seconds. The tracks will then download

Check the popularity
The popularity indicators will give you an idea of how popular a particular track is, which can be useful when making individual track choices

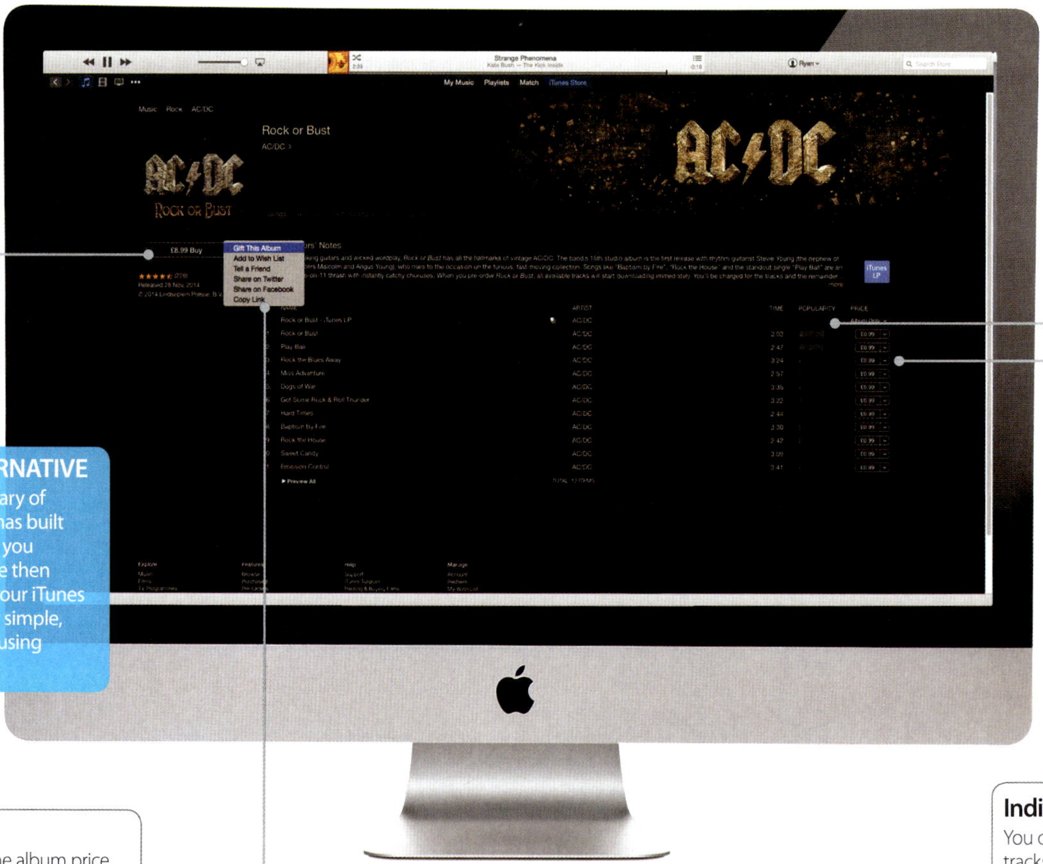

THE AMAZON ALTERNATIVE
Amazon offers a huge library of digital music as well, and has built installer software that lets you make purchases, which are then automatically pushed to your iTunes library. The process is very simple, and almost as efficient as using iTunes directly.

Send a gift
Clicking the arrow next to the album price lets you send the album as a gift or add it to a wish list for purchasing later. You can also share the album details with others

Individual tracks
You can purchase individual tracks as well, but if you buy a lot of them it will work out more expensive than buying a whole album in one go

iTunes Purchase albums and tracks from iTunes

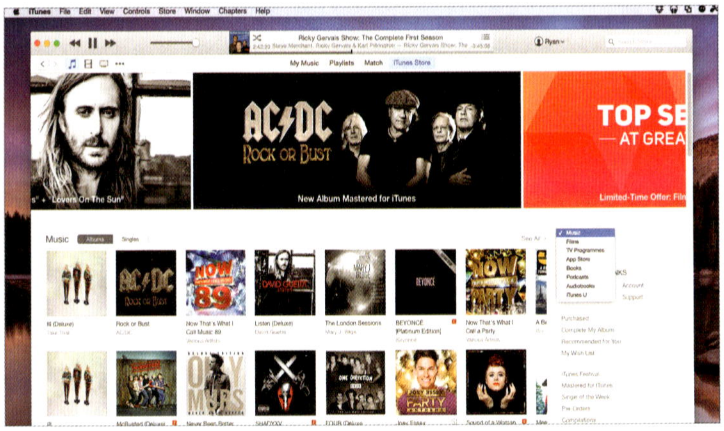

01: The music section

To access the iTunes Store, click on the iTunes Store button at the top of the screen. Now use the side column to the right to ensure Music is selected.

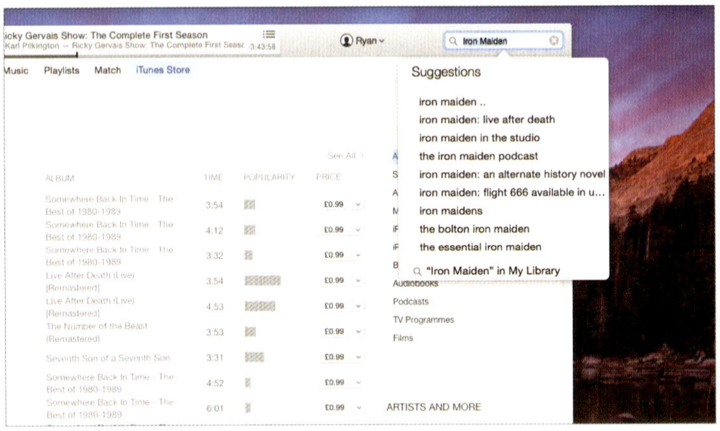

02: Search for music

In the top right you will search a search box. Enter the name of the artist you are looking for and hit Return. A selection of songs, albums and videos will appear.

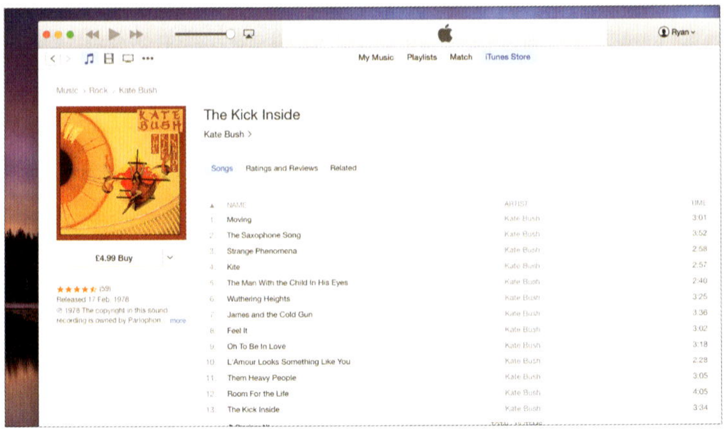

03: Choose an album

Once you've checked the offerings and decided what to buy, you can click the price button to make your purchase. Individual track prices will be available too.

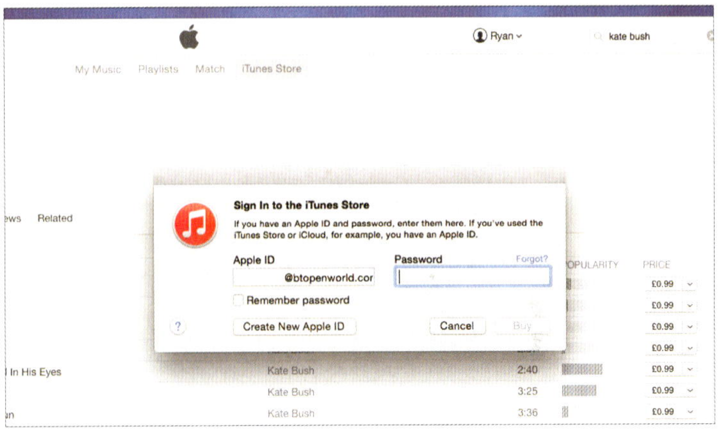

04: Enter your details

You'll need to enter your password. Once you have done this, a confirmation box will appear. Select 'Buy', and your tracks will download in the background.

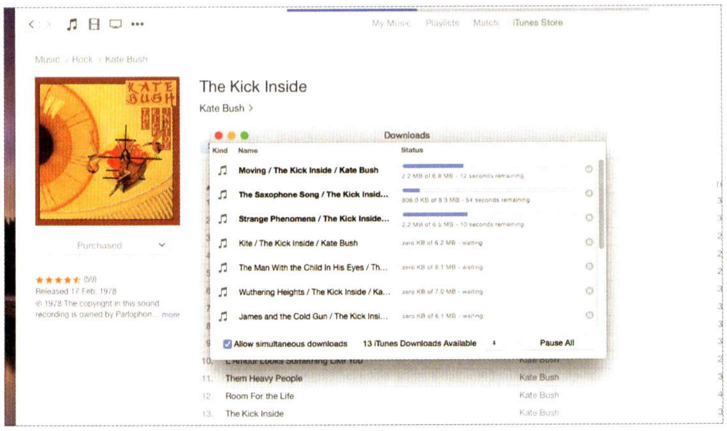

05: Check the progress

You can select the arrow icon in the top right to display the downloads as they progress. They usually download in minutes, depending on your connection.

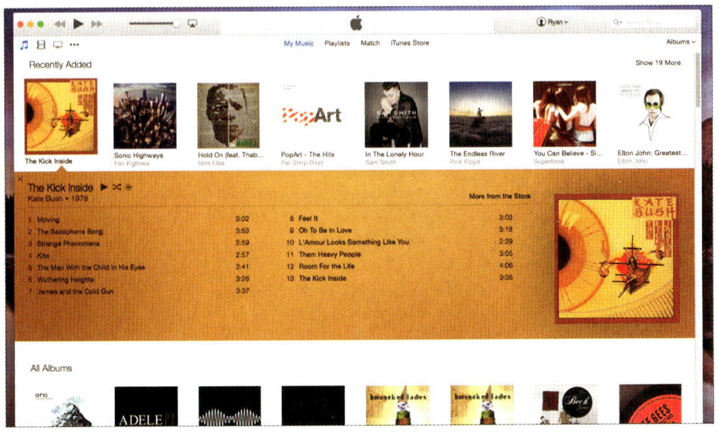

06: Use your purchase

Tap the 'My Music' option at the top of the screen, and you will see your recent purchases. You can now play it or move it to your iPhone/iPod/iPad.

Rent and buy movies on iTunes

Get the best new movies on your desktop with iTunes 12

As well as being one of the world's largest digital music hubs, the iTunes Store is also home to great movies and TV programmes from all over the world. To access this incredible selection of brand new and classic films, you can either scroll down on the iTunes Store home page or select 'Films' from the tabs at the top of the screen instead.

As well as being loaded with content, the Film marketplace is an easy place to navigate. In addition to searching through the Store with the search bar, you can also use the drop arrow in the right column to search by genres, like comedy, drama or sci-fi & fantasy. For some films, there's also the option of iTunes Extras. Not entirely unlike bonus features on a DVD or Blu-ray, Extras gives you the option to check out exclusive behind-the-scenes footage, deleted scenes and much more.

Once you've found the content you're after, you can either buy or rent it. Buying will, of course, be more expensive, but you can watch your film as many times as you wish. Renting, on the other hand, is usually far cheaper, but you only have 30 days in which to start watching it, and then only 48 hours to finish the video from the moment you hit 'Play'.

Thanks to the power of iCloud, you can watch your downloaded film on any device. If you start watching your movie on your desktop computer through iTunes 12, but then have to hop on the bus, you can download it on your iOS device and it'll resume playing from exactly where you left off.

> "The marketplace is an easy place to navigate"

The movie page

Find out about your chosen film

TV PROGRAMMES

It's not just films that the iTunes Store offers – you can also download entire TV series or individual episodes. They're not exactly cheap, but you can watch them on any Apple devices you own, including iPod touch and selected iPod nano generations. Most feature both SD and HD options. You can download episodes in the same way you download movies.

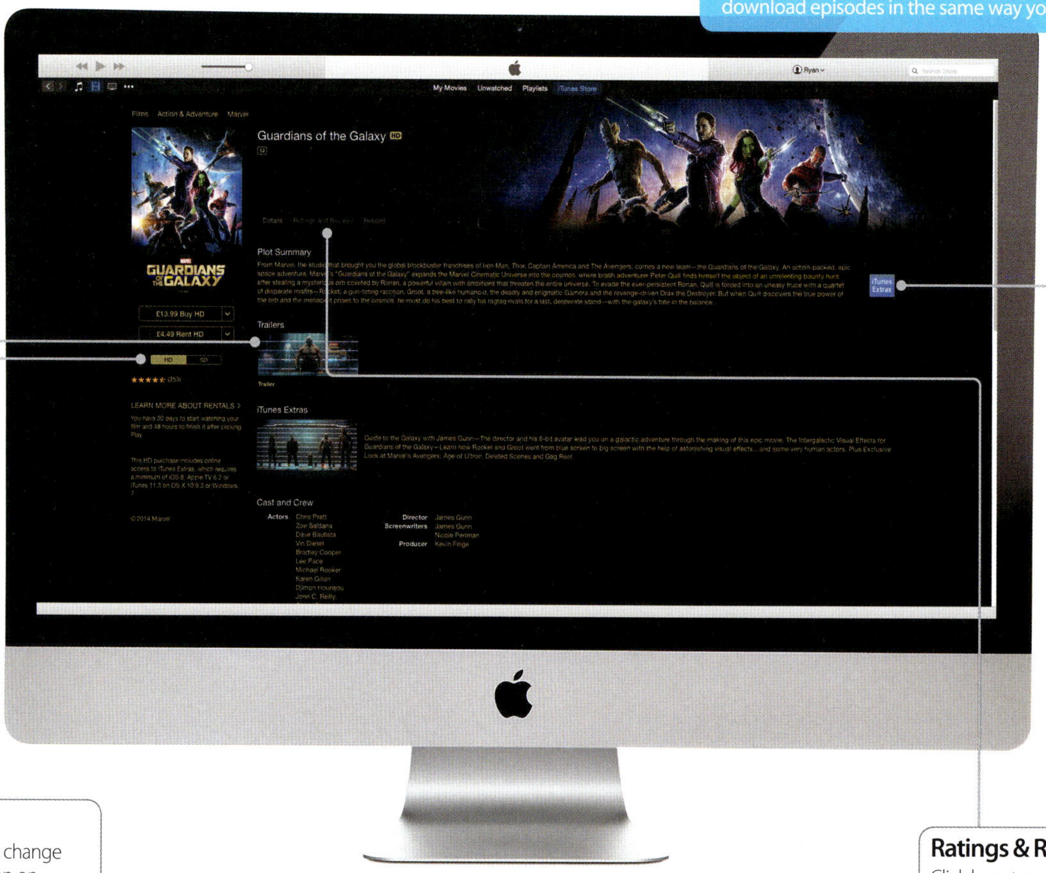

Trailer
If you want to see a sample of your film, click on a trailer. You can't download it from iTunes 11, but you will start streaming it when you click it

iTunes Extras
If your film has any bonus footage or deleted scenes, it will carry an iTunes Extras badge. You will not have to pay any more for this added privilege

HD or SD?
Click the HD/SD buttons to change between formats. If you plan on watching on your iPod, it's best to go for SD. On your desktop, we would recommend HD

Ratings & Reviews
Click here to see what other people thought about your chosen film. After you've seen it, you can leave your own review and rate it out of five stars

iTunes Download a film from iTunes

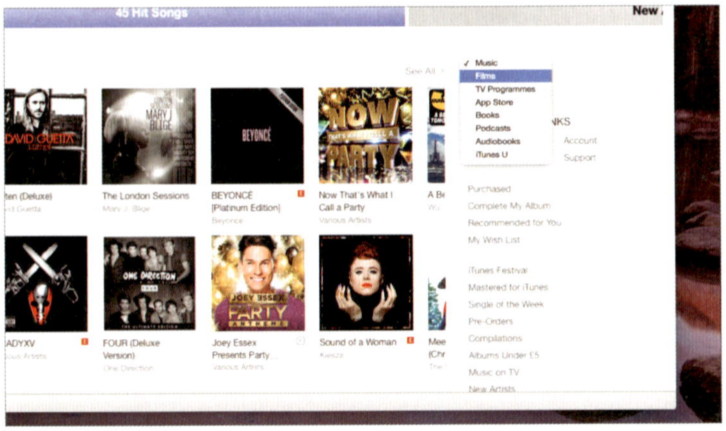

01: Open the store

Open up iTunes on your computer and click the arrow next to the Music option in the right-hand column. Now select Films from the dropdown menu.

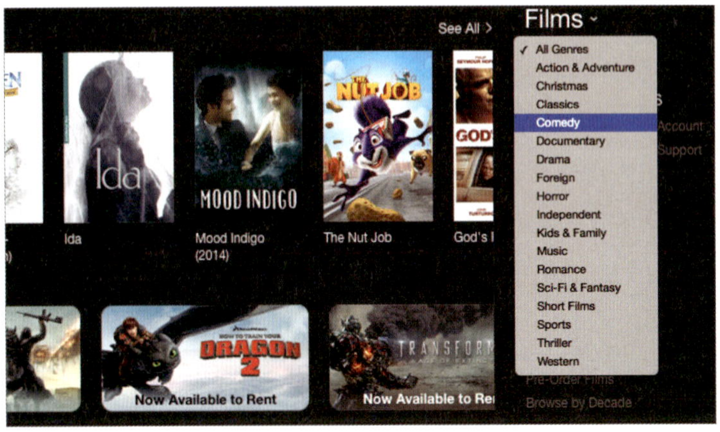

02: Find your genre

Click the drop-down arrow next to the 'All Genres' menu option and then pick a genre that appeals to you from the extensive list of options.

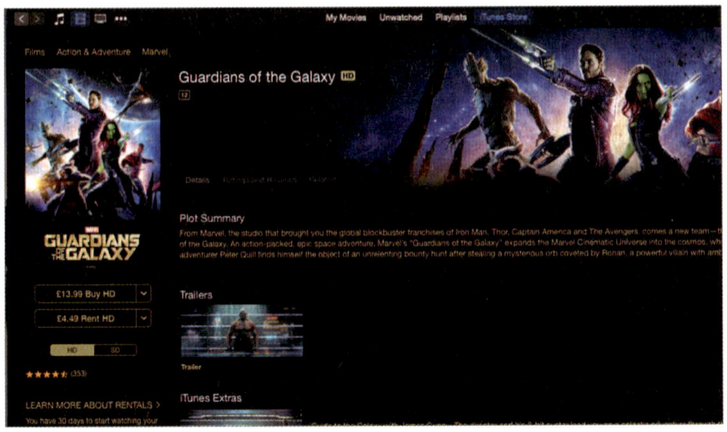

03: Choose your title

Once you've chosen your genre, select the film you want by clicking on it. This will open up the film's iTunes page, which will feature details, ratings and more.

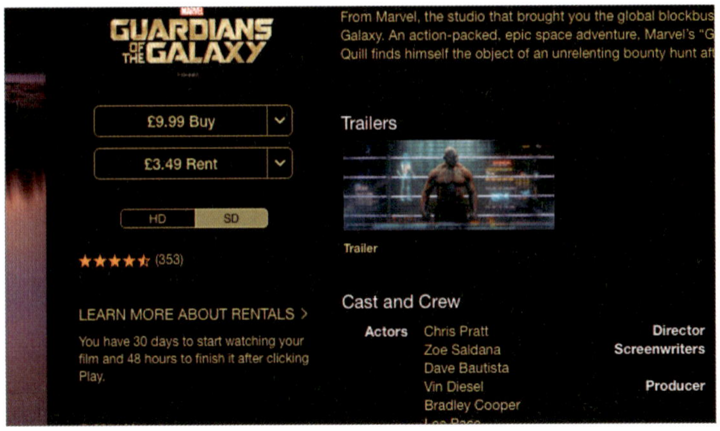

04: HD or SD?

You may have be able to choose a high definition version (HD) or a standard definition version (SD). SD's cheaper, but won't look as good.

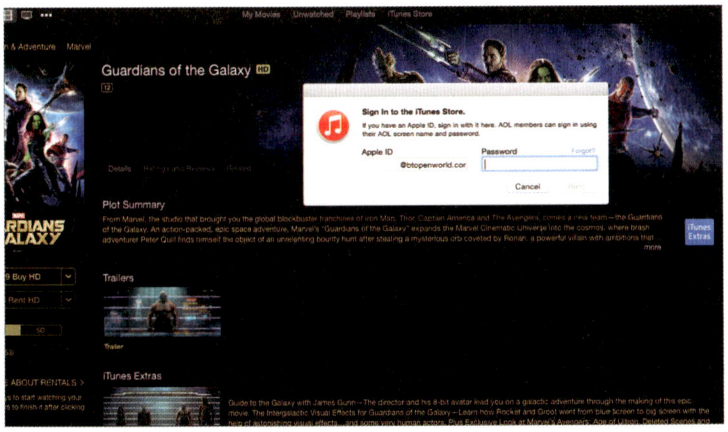

05: Download it

Click either 'Buy' or 'Rent', and you will start downloading the movie. Progress will be shown in the main media bar.

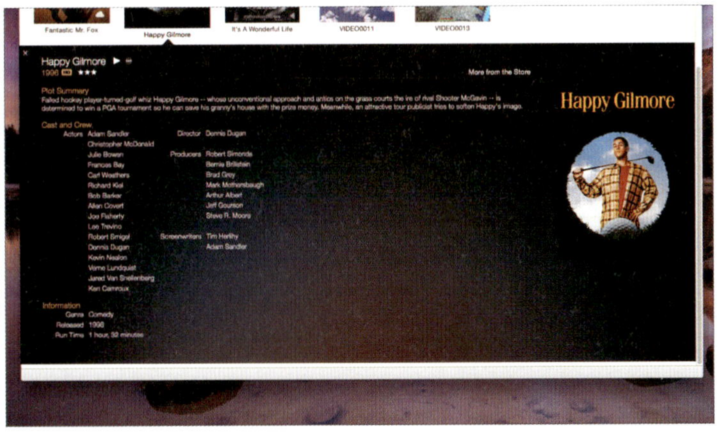

06: Watch it

If you have a fast connection, you will be able to stream it after a few minutes. When it's done you will find it in the 'Movies' section of your iTunes library.

Navigate the new iBooks

Use the iBooks app in OS X Yosemite to read, manage, purchase and take notes with more than 1.8 million books

iBooks has been around since 2010, first appearing as an app on the iPad. Since then its popularity has kept on growing. iBooks connects to the iBooks Store, which functions just as iTunes does – giving users the ability to have access to a digital library of literature that has made iBooks so successful. Now, with the introduction of Yosemite OS X, iBooks has been made available on the Mac. iBooks syncs perfectly with all your devices, letting you access your books in any format. If you start reading a book on your iPad then come back to it on your Mac, iBooks will let you pick up right where you left off. Although iBooks is much more tablet-friendly than on a desktop, (since you might not be used to reading from your computer) there are a series of functions such as note-taking, highlighting and searching within a book that are so much more simple to execute from a Mac. Follow these six simple steps to getting set up and reading in no time with Yosemite's iBooks app for Mac.

> "iBooks syncs perfectly with all your devices, letting you access your books in any format"

iBooks reading interface

Navigating the reading interface and tools of iBooks in OS X Yosemite

Formatting options

To format a book's settings, click here to access the Appearance window. Here you can change the size of the book's text, choose from a selection of different fonts or change the text colour

Navigation

Here you can search through the entirety of a book with key phrases and words. The toolbar also offers a table of contents and a bookmarking tool to make browsing easier

Managing Notes

Notes can be accessed here by clicking on the page number to be taken to the page where a note was added. Right-click on a note to share it via Facebook, Twitter, Messages or Email

Creating Notes

Select a body of text to open the Notes window where you can highlight text and add notes. From the More menu you can search for the text online have the text spoken

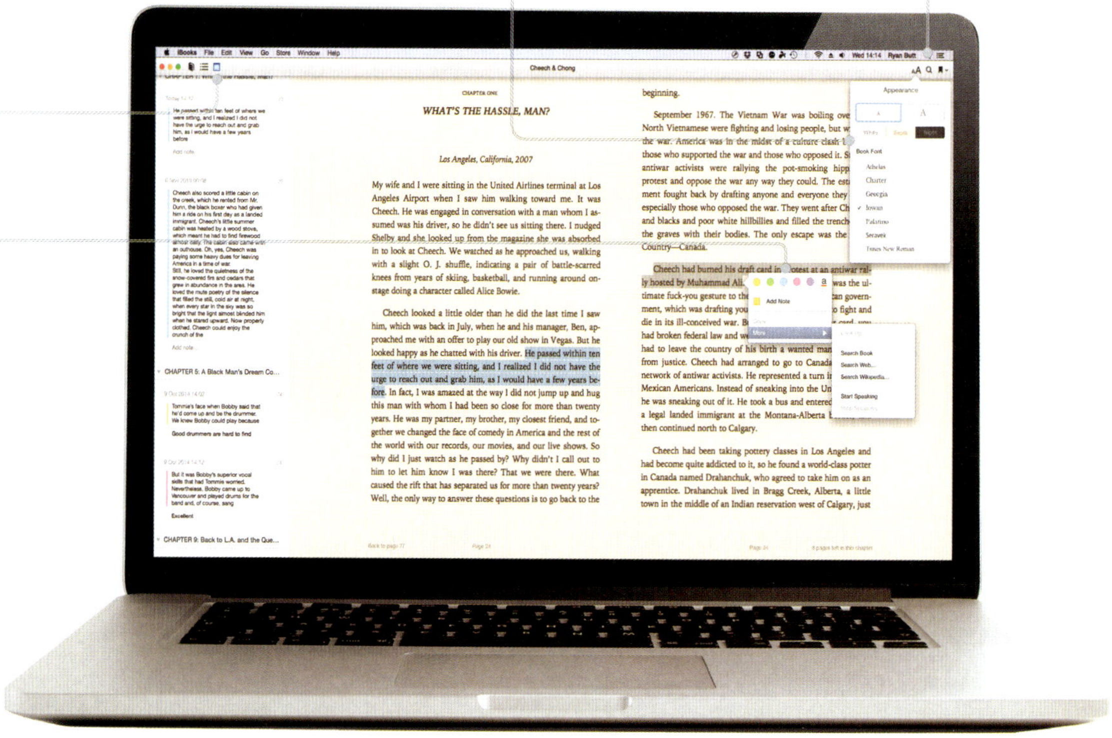

iBOOKS AUTHOR

If reading via iBooks is getting you inspired to write your own novel, then why not download the free iBooks Author software from Apple. This tool lets you create and publish your very own book from scratch or by using templates including images, interactive options and videos – all built to work with iBooks.

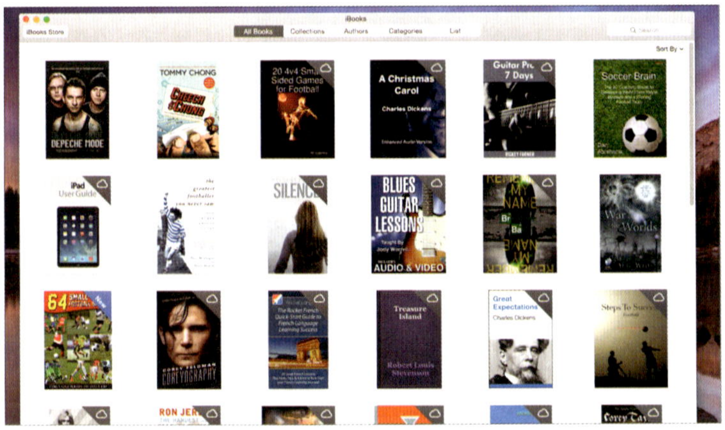

01: Launch iBooks

If you're starting iBooks for the first time on your mac, log in via your iTunes account to sync iBooks with your iPad or iPhone app.

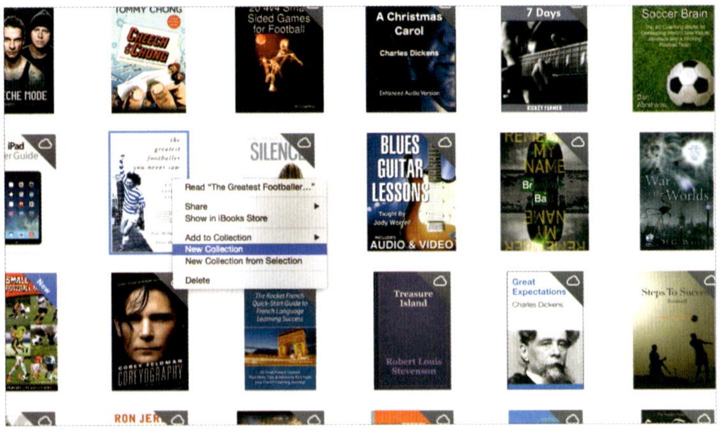

02: Build a collection

All previous purchases will sync with the app, placing them in the All Books window. Right-click on a book, then click on New Collection.

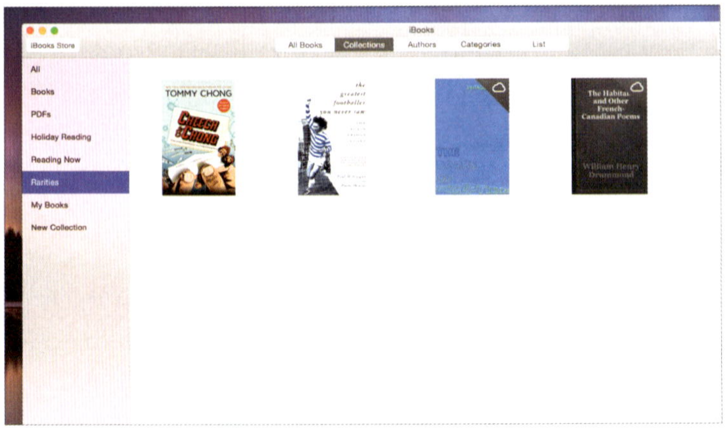

03: Manage your collection

Double-click on New Collection 1 to rename it. Right-click on a book, then select Add to Collection to include it in your new collection.

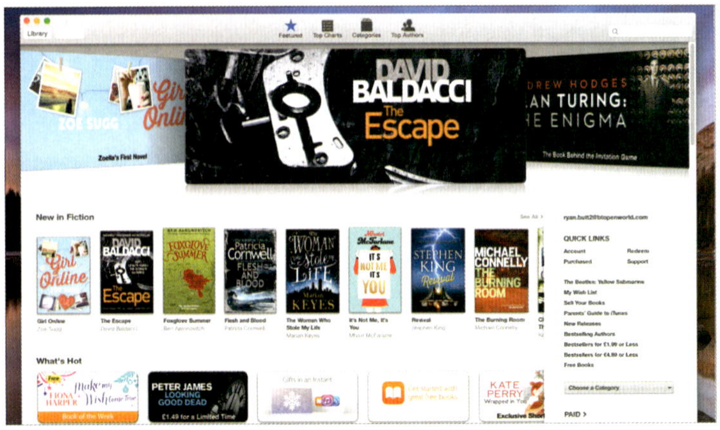

04: iBooks Store

Click on iBooks Store in the top-right-hand corner. Search by Category, author or keyword as you would in iTunes to find a book.

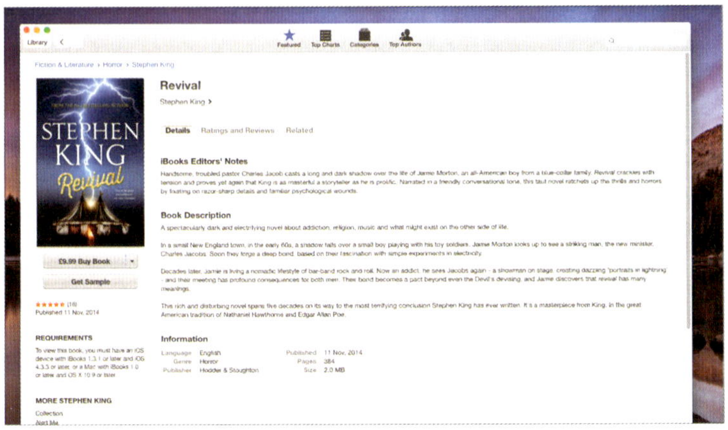

05: Samples and purchasing

Select a book, then click Get Sample to add the first few pages of the book to your library or purchase it using your iTunes account.

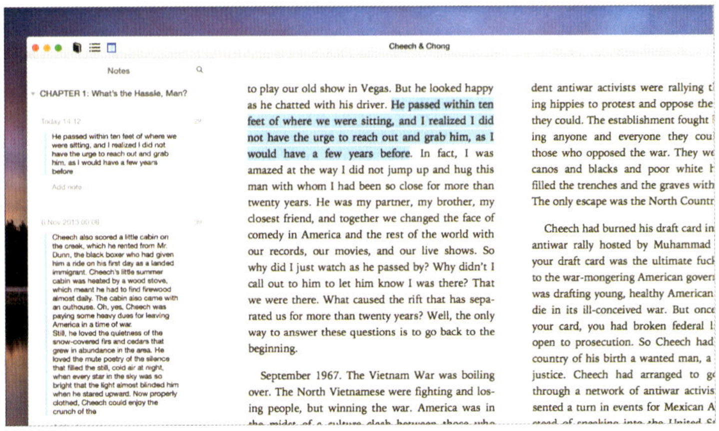

06: iBooks' reading interface

Double-click on a book in your collection to read it. Using the toolbar you can adjust Font Size, add notes, bookmark and search.

Create a stunning digital book with iBooks Author

Every fancied getting involved in the digital publishing revolution for free? Here's your chance

You've probably figured out how powerful your Mac is by reading this book. Apple makes it beautifully simple to get creative, whether you're working with photos, video or other media. Apple's digital publishing app, iBooks Author, is no different. Combining an intuitive interface with serious power, the app gives you the chance to have a go at digital publishing – for free.

In this tutorial we're going to take you through a whistle-stop tour of the app. Want to show off all those family recipes into a cookbook? No problem. Want to publish an interactive children's book? No worries. Need a platform to create a textbook for educational purposes? You get the idea.

Best of all, iBooks Author gives you a head start by supplying a host of templates. Adding pages, images, video and all sorts of media is done with a press of your mouse. You can drop in interactive widgets and exploding diagrams – again with the touch of a button. So what are you waiting for? Get creating!

Inside iBooks Author

Up close with Apple's brilliant digital publishing tool

DEVELOPER ACCOUNT

If you want to publish to one of Apple's stores, you'll need to sign up for a Free or Paid Books Account, depending if your intention is to sell the book for money. Both are free to sign up to and just require an Apple ID to get started. If you choose to sell for money, Apple will take a cut of all your profits.

Creative options

These five tabs at the top are crucial when it comes to building your book. They give you plenty of options for adding eye-catching elements. Have a play around to discover which one suits your particular iBook

Inspector calls

Customisation is key to making your book stand out, and iBooks Author's Inspector is the most important panel in the app. It holds the key to all manner of edits, and changes depending on what you have selected at the time

Book contents

As you add pages to your book it's nice to be able to catch a quick glimpse in this section. Pages, chapters and sections are all in play here; simply click on one to move to that part of your book

Orientation

This may seem like a straightforward step, but it's surprising how many will get it wrong. Choosing the correct orientation means you're building your book for the right device. Landscape will be the most common option

iBooks Author Your very own digital publishing platform

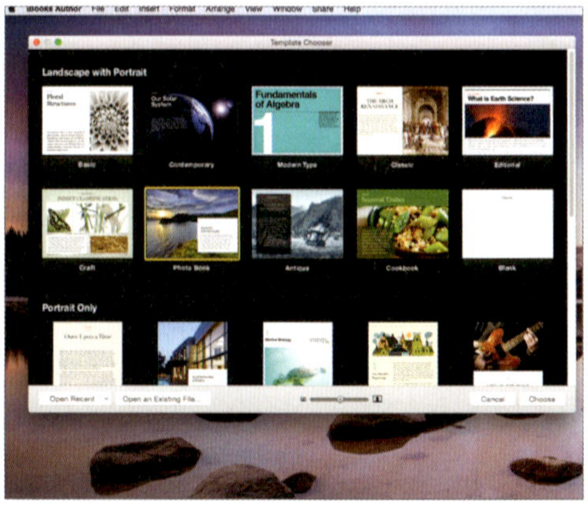

01: Templates

iBooks Author provides a selection of built-in templates that cover most bases. Flick through them, find one you think suits and hit Choose.

02: Placeholders

We've chosen to make a photo book. Everything in the chosen template can be customised. It's currently made up of placeholder images and text.

03: Edit text

Click over a text box and type to enter text. You can get more specific with styles by heading to the Inspector in the top-right and its Text tab.

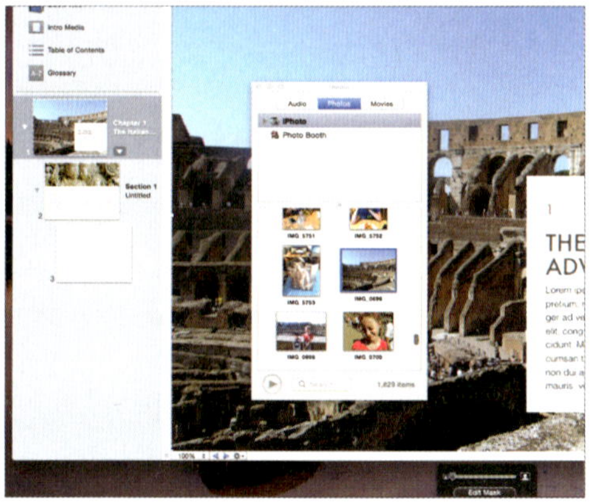

04: Add images

The Media tab up in the top-right is your best friend when it comes to adding images. It'll load up a tab where you can select an image from your device.

05: Add pages/chapters

Head to the Add Pages + sign up in the top-left corner and select how your new page will be set up by choosing from the different options.

06: Widgets

It's possible to add interactivity to your books. By heading to the Widget menu you get see what's on offer – we're going to add an Interactive Image.

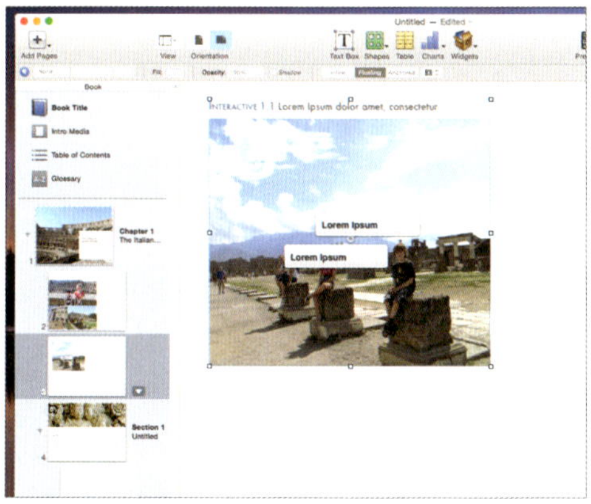

07: Interactive Image

Your widget will be dropped onto the selected page. Add an image and have a play around with the placement of the exploding annotations.

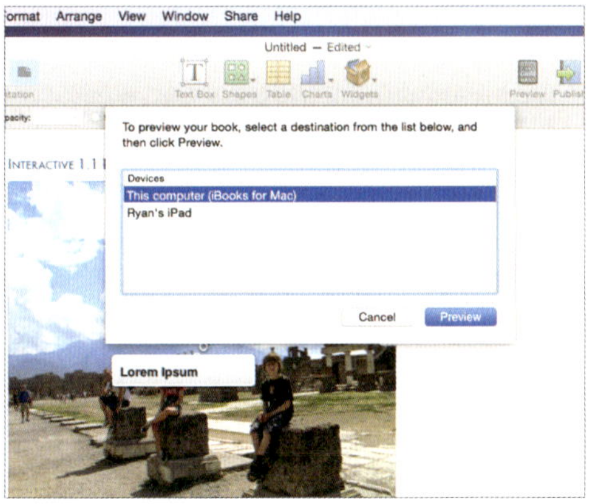

08: Share as a PDF

To test how your iBook works, select the Preview option to share to a connected iPad or even open your project on your Mac in the iBooks app.

09: Publish

Once you are happy, head up to the Publish icon in the main toolbar to start the process of publishing it to the iBooks Store.

Get organised with Calendar

It's an incredibly important app that can help get you organised

Calendar (formerly known as iCal) is one of the unsung heroes of OS X and iOS. It is the Mac-based predecessor to Calendar on your iPhone or iPad. This application has the ability to really help you organise your life and – with the ability to share your calendars – the lives of others.

As you would expect, Apple has made the app simple yet effective, with an incredibly user-friendly interface. You can colour code certain calendars, for example, so that you can set up different ones for work, social events, sport matches and more. You can set any events that you create to a certain time or to 'all-day', and there are plenty of other options that will suit your needs.

In this introduction to the application, we'll show you how to create a new calendar and add an event, as well as how best to view your busy schedule. Armed with this information, you can keep track of important meetings, birthdays, social events and much more with ease.

> "This app can really help you to organise your life"

Calendar Get to grips with your calendar app

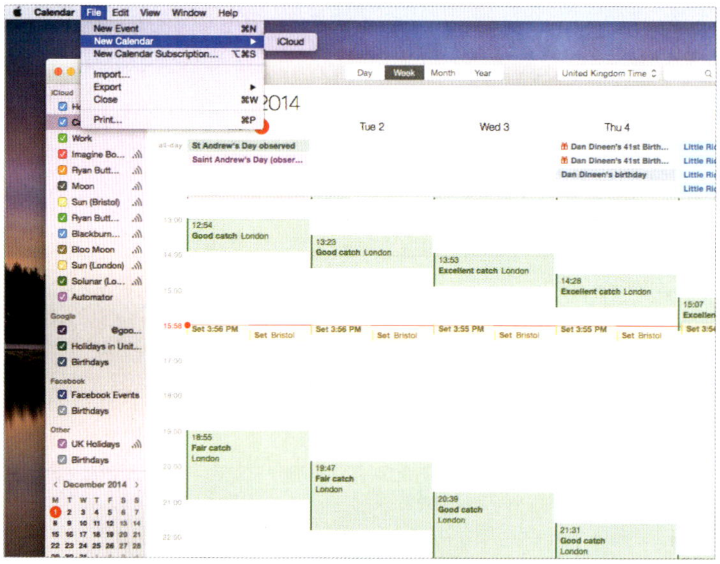

01: Add a calendar

The very first step will be to open up Calendar (or iCal) on your Mac. Use the '+' button in the top left corner of the Calendar interface to add a new quick event. Alternatively, you can click on the File menu and click 'New Calendar' to create a brand new calendar.

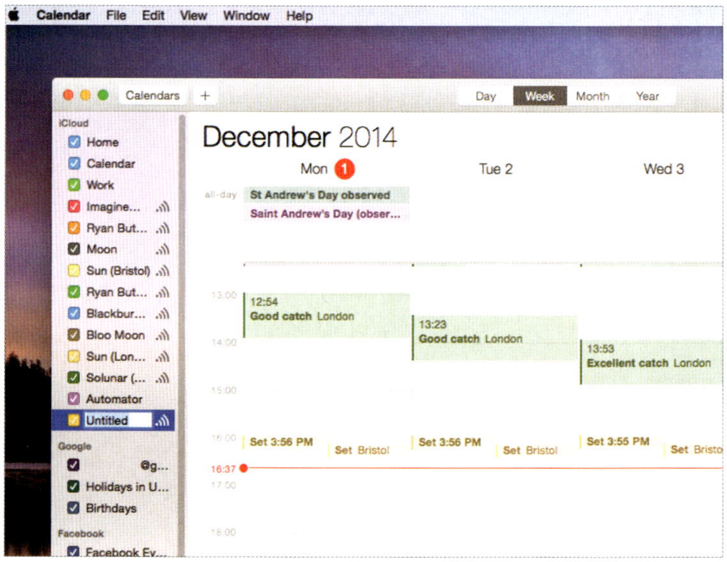

02: Name it

Naming your calendar is important, as this will specify the kind of events that you add and help you divide the kinds of tasks you complete in your everyday life, which is important if you have separate calendars for work and home. You can, once your calendar is made, tick and untick it to reveal and hide events.

Grasp the interface

View your calendar however you want to

Day view

If you're a really busy bee, this is where you'll need to be to organise every moment of your life. Click on an event to view all of the details to the right

Month view

Use this to view the weeks ahead and to get a feel for how busy you are. You can easily skim through months at a time, which makes it the best place to plan holidays and larger projects

Week view

This is our favourite view, as it offers you enough detail to see entire days well-planned-out, but it also offers a quick overview of the entire week ahead. We live in this view

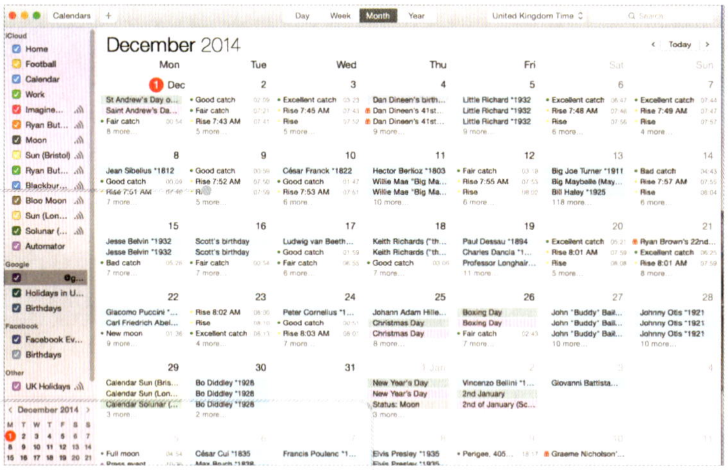

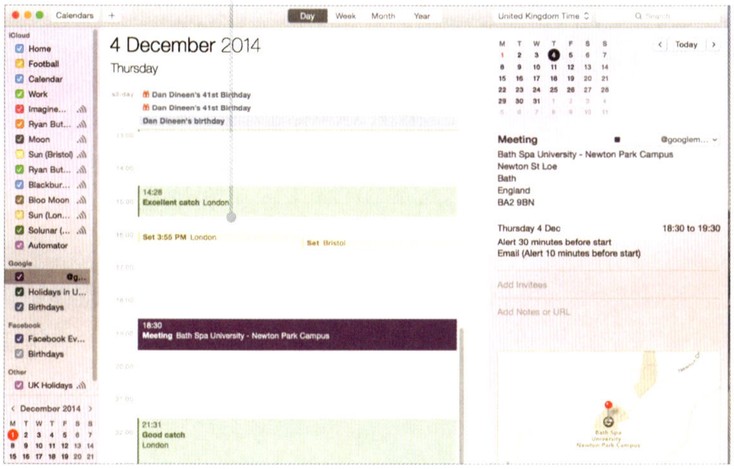

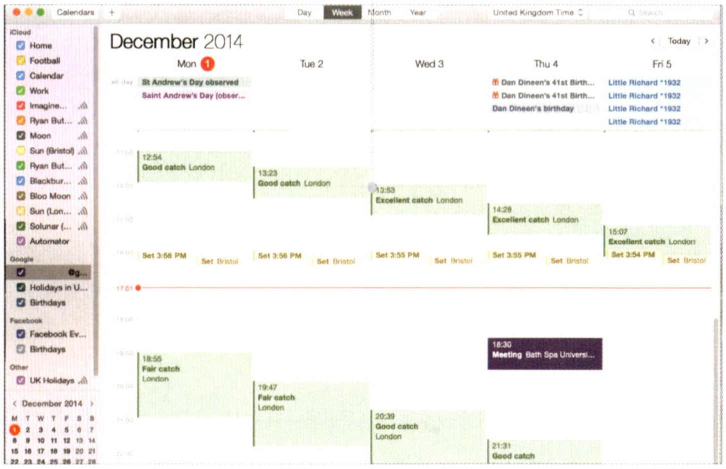

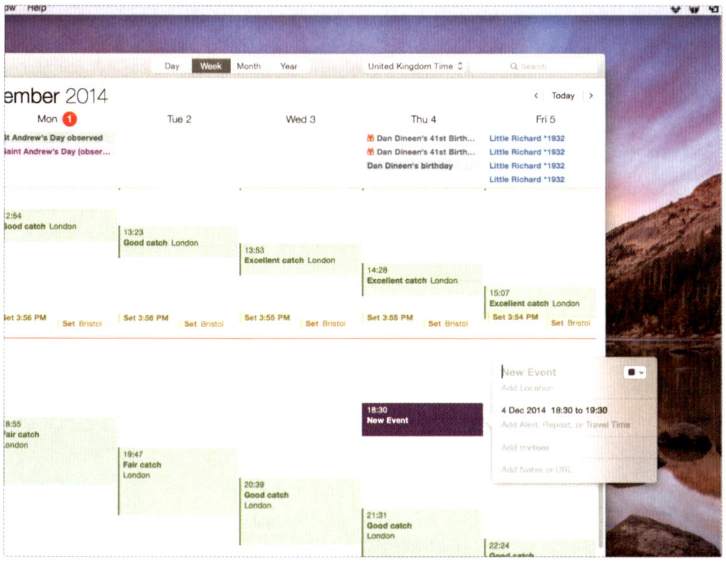

03: Double-click

Double-click on a day and time to add a new event to your calendar. A pop-up window will appear, allowing you to add all the pertinent information you want to the new event. Be as detailed as you can, as this will help you recall the event when the time comes.

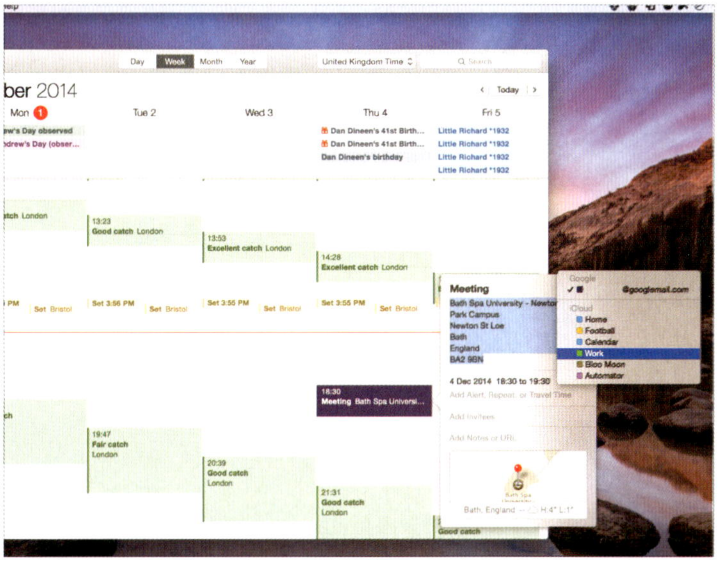

04: Assign to a calendar

If you've changed your mind about the calendar that you want this event to apply to, just click on the drop-down arrow next to 'calendar' and select a different one. As these are colour-coded, you can easily distinguish between them. Once you're finished, click Done.

Add a note to a Calendar event

Apply more detail to your events by adding notes

Apple's Calendar app is great for keeping track of your hectic schedule, adding events and inviting other people to attend them. When creating events that other users will be able to see, it is obviously a good idea to include as much detail as possible. However, you don't want to pepper the main event window with too many words, so what can you do? Easy: add a note. Once you have added an event you can double-click on it to bring up a floating window of information, including the all-important start and finish times, and by clicking the various fields you can then start adding invitees, alerts and notes.

Simply click on 'note' and you'll be able to write as much text as you want into a dialog box and, once you click off the box, this information will be viewable to others clicking on your event. Here's how to start adding in your own event notes.

> "Add a note to an event to give as much detail as possible"

Calendar Add more information to your entry

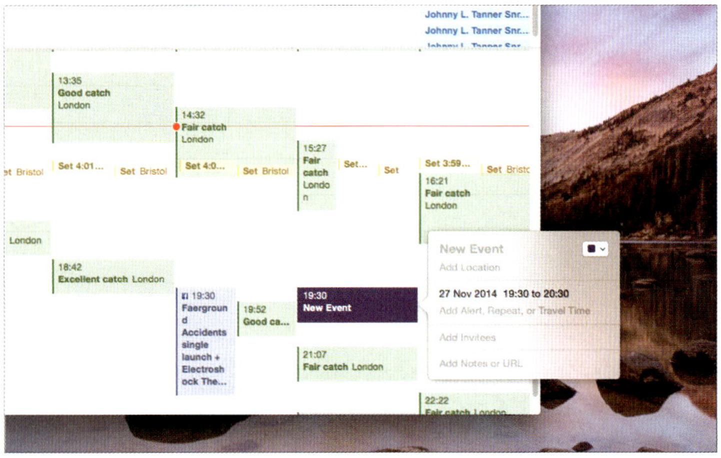

01: Double-click the event

Locate the event that you wish to apply a note to and then double-click on it to bring up an overview box of the event.

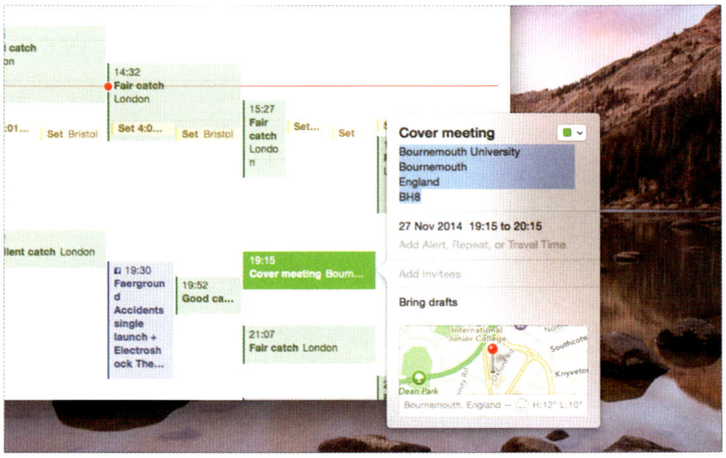

02: Click on note

In the event box will be a couple of 'Add' sections, one of which is Add Notes. Click on this section to start entering your own notes.

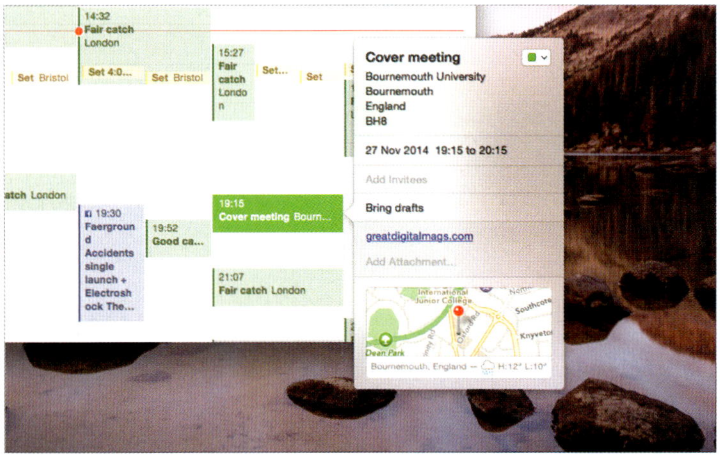

03: Enter text

Type your text into the field provided and then click off the event. The text will automatically be saved and stored with the event.

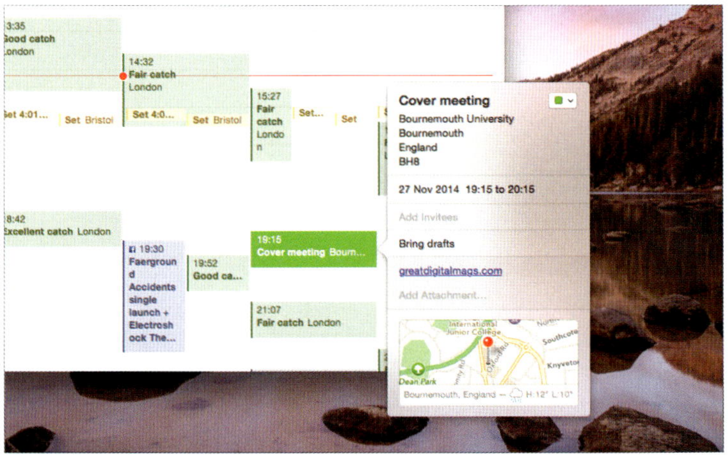

04: Finishing off

There is also the option to add a URL to your event. Simply click on the 'Add URL' field and then type or paste in the required link.

Add an alert to a Calendar event

Set alerts to ensure that you never miss an important event

For all your good intentions of adding events to your iCal calendars, they don't mean a thing if you fail to take notice and forget about them. Thankfully, to prevent this happening, you can set yourself handy alerts so that the app will inform you on the day, hours or minutes before or at a precise time and date that you determine. These alerts can consist of a message, a message with a sound, an email sent to yourself, the automatic opening of an application or, if you use AppleScript, you can set up a specific script, or action, that your Mac will perform when it needs to alert you at the specified time.

You have full freedom to determine the time and date of the alert, and you can even set up a sequence of alerts if you're worried about missing your event. Simply use the drop-down menus next to 'alert' in the event edit box.

"Alerts can inform you of an event minutes, hours or days beforehand"

Calendar Apply alerts to events

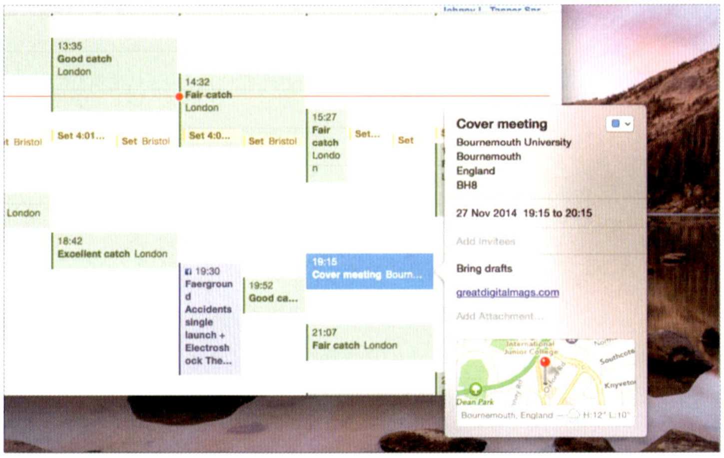

01: Double-click the event

Like before, locate the event that you wish to apply an alert to and double-click on it to bring up an overview box.

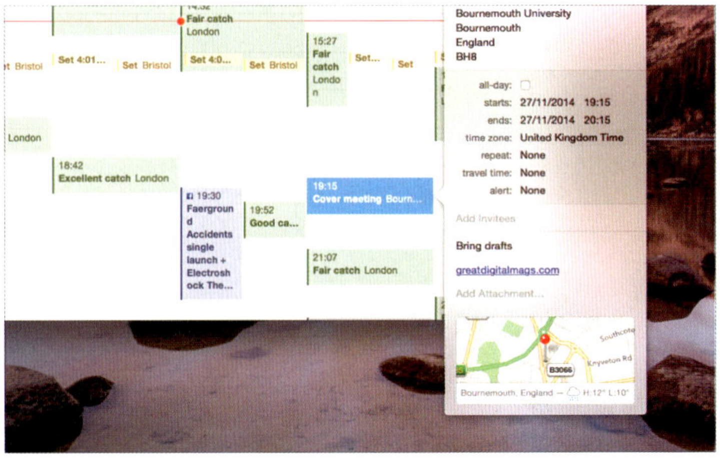

02: Click on the alert box

Now click on the time box and this will expand the window to allow you to enter start and end times and more.

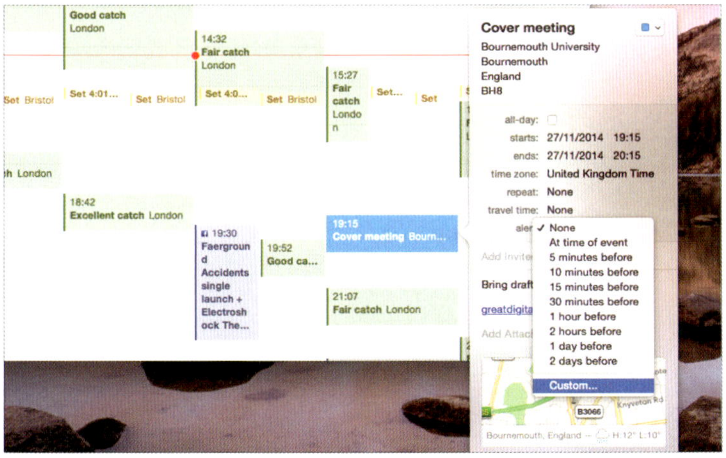

03: Set alert

Set the desired times and then click on the Alert menu. This allows you to set an alert in the run up to the event at a specified time.

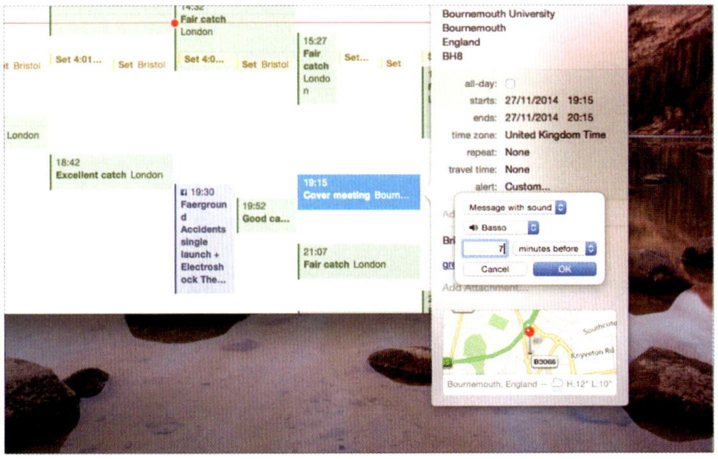

04: Set custom

Click on Custom in the alert menu and then set your own desired alert options. You can also choose to be notified via message, email or more.

Get reminders based on locations

Get location-specific reminders on any device with a little help from Reminders and iCloud

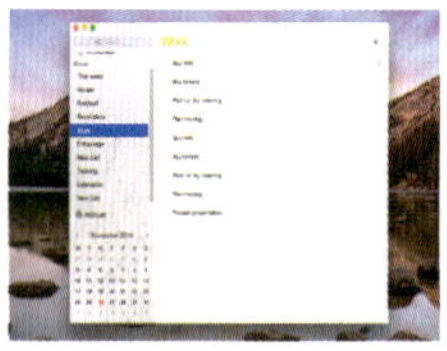

Isn't technology supposed to make life simpler? Visions of the future always seemed to depict people with lots of leisure time and everything run by labour-saving machines. However, the reality is that our lives are more hectic than ever and there are many jobs to be done, tasks to be performed and things that need organising. Mavericks can help by enabling you to create lists of everything that needs to be done, when it needs to be done by and even where it needs to be done. It's an essential feature in OS X Mavericks and you can create reminders for work tasks, jobs that need doing around the home, events like holidays, birthdays, weddings and much more. It is an essential tool for organising our lives and ensuring everything that needs to be done actually gets completed.

Reminders used to be part of the iCal calendar application, but in Mavericks it is now an app in its own right. It has a brand new look that makes reminders easier to create and view, and some great features. You can create different lists or categories of reminders and quickly browse them to see what needs doing. You can see a list of completed items, too.

In this tutorial, we will show how to create a reminder and then set a location for it. When you arrive at that location, or leave it, you will get a visual and audible message alerting you to the task or job that needs to be done. Now there is no excuse for forgetting to do something.

Setting a location for a reminder so that you are alerted when arriving or leaving a certain place is obviously useful if you have a MacBook and use it at different locations, such as at work and at home, but what about a Mac? That rarely moves. What you have to remember is that iCloud is fully integrated with Mavericks and any reminder created on your Mac automatically appears on all your iOS devices.

"Reminders is an essential tool for organising our lives"

Reminders Create a location reminder

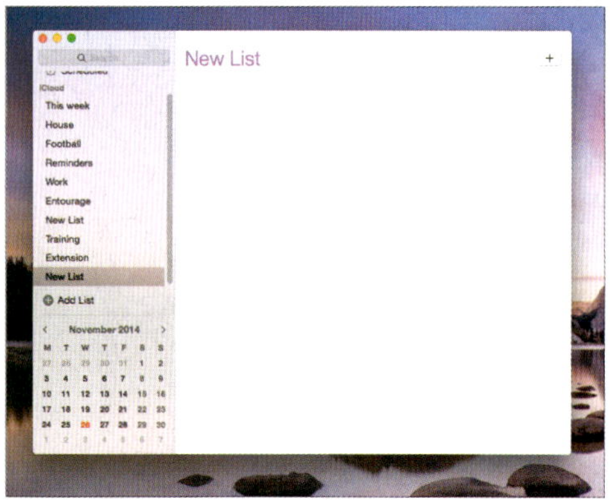

01: Make a list

Click Reminders in the Dock to see a window containing categories on the left and reminders on the right. Lists you have created on iDevices are displayed.

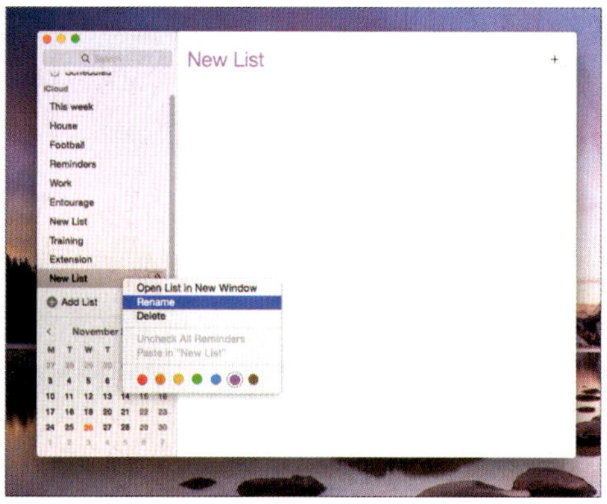

02: Rename a list

Ctrl/right-clicking on a list enables you to rename, delete or open it in a separate window. You can also double-click a list to open it in a window.

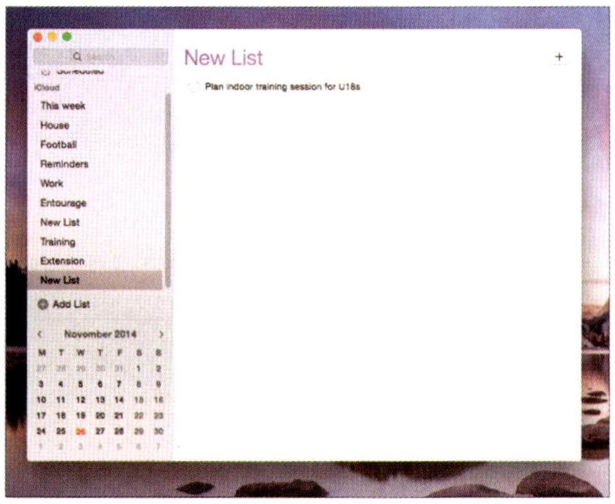

03: Add a task

If there is a task you need to do, select the appropriate list and then type it in. The tickbox shows whether a task has been completed or not.

A look around Reminders

Get to know this essential app

Create reminder lists

It is useful to create different reminder categories, such as home and work, or special events like birthdays and weddings. Double-click on a category to open it up

Deadlines and locations

To turn a to-do task into a reminder that has to be finished by a certain date and time, or done at a particular location, click this icon on the right

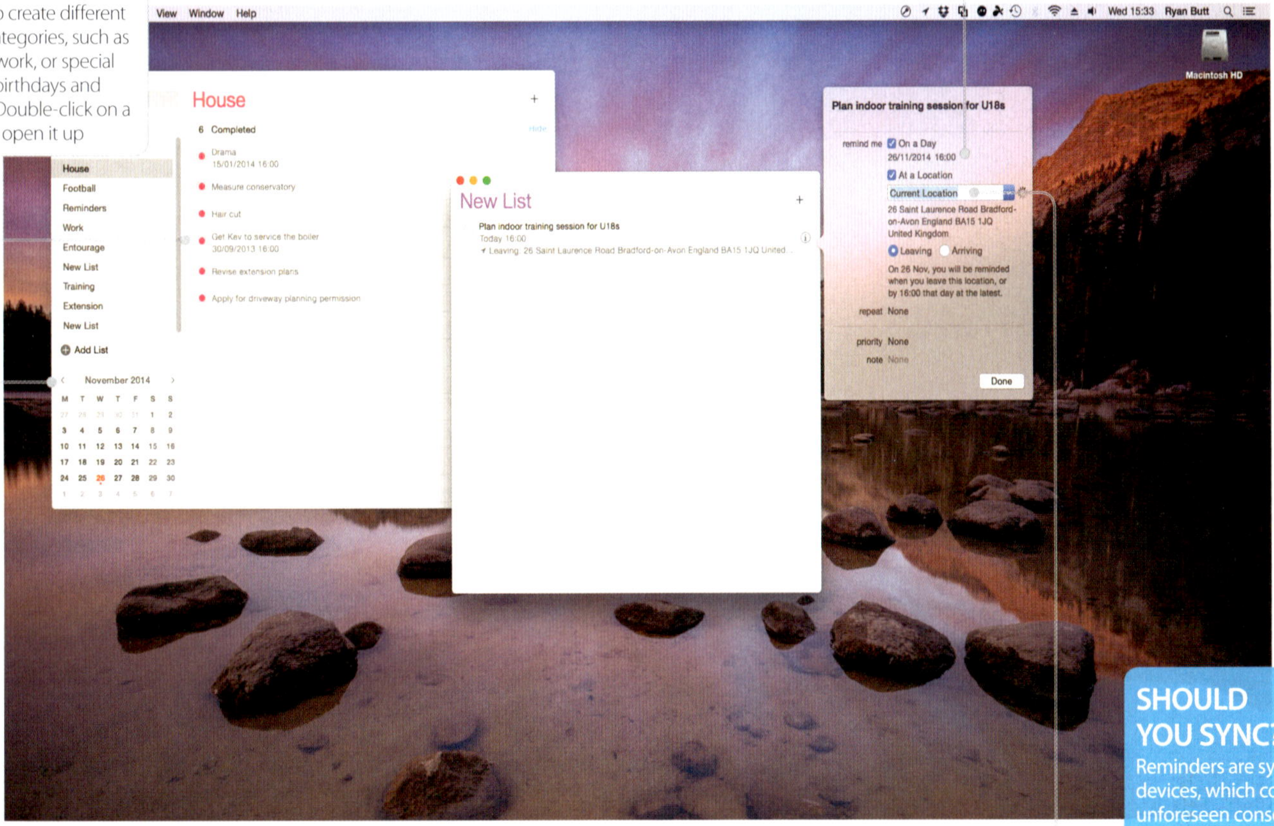

Pop-up calendar

When setting reminders, you might need to check a calendar, perhaps to see the date, but also to see when other reminders have been set. This pop-up one is handy

Set a location

Tick the 'At a Location' option and, the first time you use it, you will need to give Reminders permission to determine and use your location

SHOULD YOU SYNC?

Reminders are synced to all devices, which could have unforeseen consequences if you are planning an event such as a surprise party. Another family member might see it on the iPad! You may want to temporarily disable syncing in iCloud.

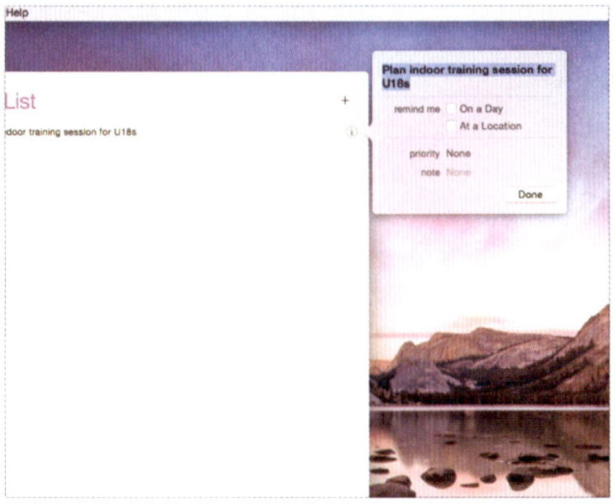

04: Add a reminder

To turn a to-do item into a reminder, let the mouse hover over it and then click the 'i' icon. Reminders can be shown on a day, time or location.

05: Remind on arrival

Tick 'At a Location' and your current location is added. When you arrive at work, home or wherever you are now, you'll see a reminder of the task.

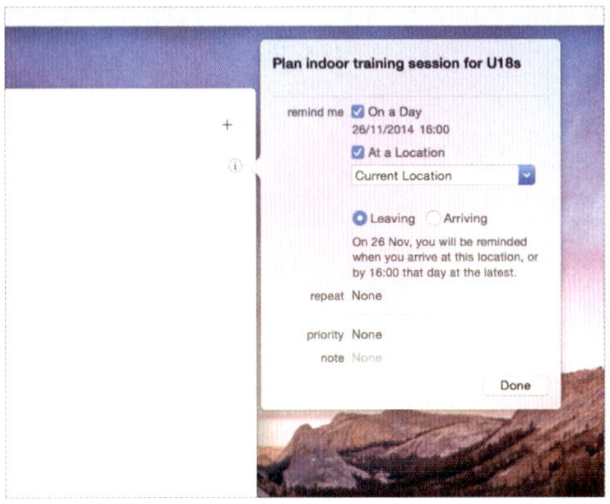

06: Enter a location

Enter a location if you want to be reminded at a particular place. Addresses can be general like a town or specific like a street. Enter one and then press Done.

Keep your contacts in an address book

Get to grips with the Contacts address book and master its iOS-like layout

Often overlooked, the Contacts app (previously known as Address Book) is an important element of OS X. While it might not be the first thing you open in your dock, it's the hub for all your contacts and makes sure that apps like Mail run a lot more smoothly. It seems only fair, then, that the address book has been given a Yosemite overhaul, too. It now sports a cleaner, simpler interface that before. It is easy to create and edit contacts and you can also share them effortlessly. Managing your database is easy too as the app can sniff out duplicates and merge them with existing contacts in a single click. You can also create Smart Groups by entering what criteria to include and omit. Read on to find out more.

"An overlooked but important element"

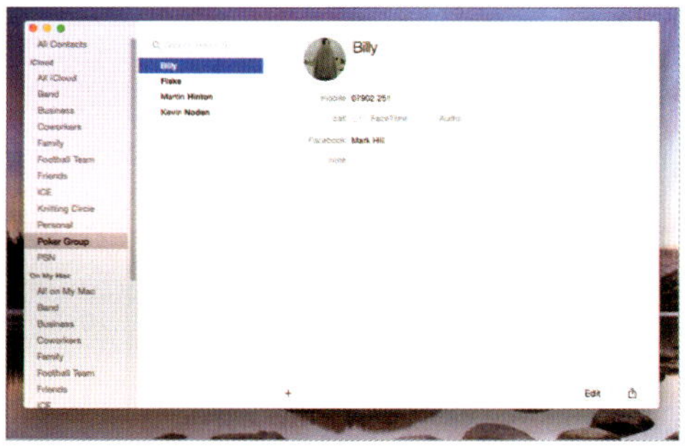

Contacts Explore your address book directory

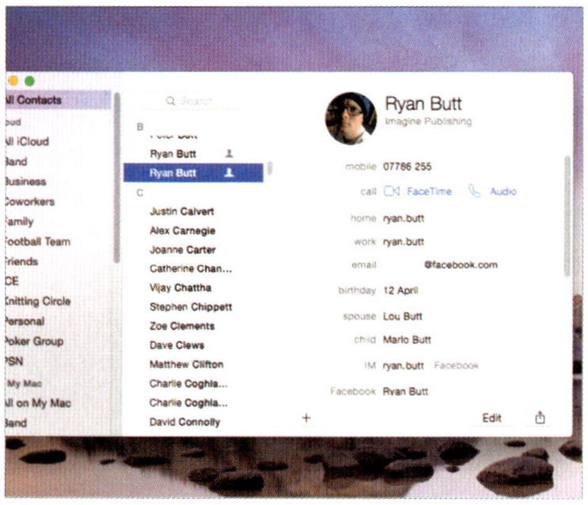

01: A whole new look

The first thing you'll notice about the app is that its view is very similar to that of its counterpart in iOS. It's looking a lot cleaner, for one thing.

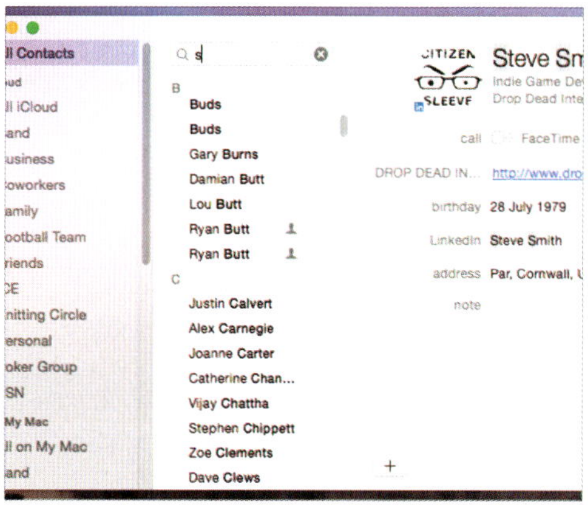

02: Find a friend

Searching is as simple as typing a name straight into the search box. Results are displayed in real time and Contacts will highlight any matches.

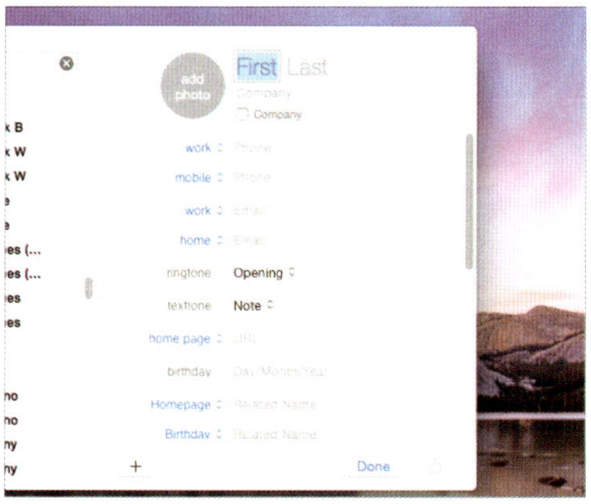

03: Add an entry

Click on the plus icon under your contacts to add a new one. You can change what the default template includes in Contacts' preferences.

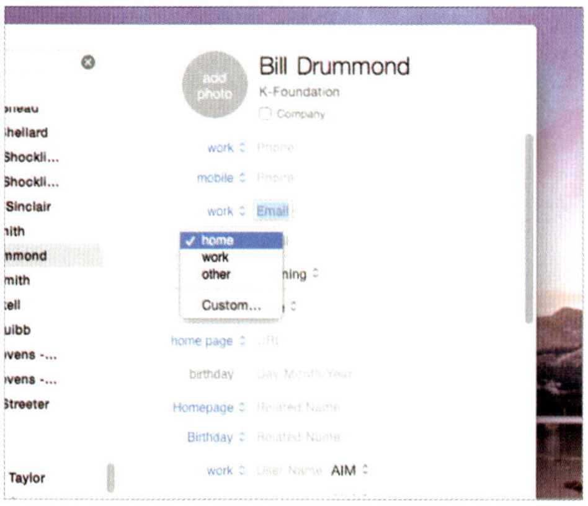

04: Business and pleasure

Contact details can be categorised by type, such as work or home. Click on the type next to the detail and select one from the list to change it.

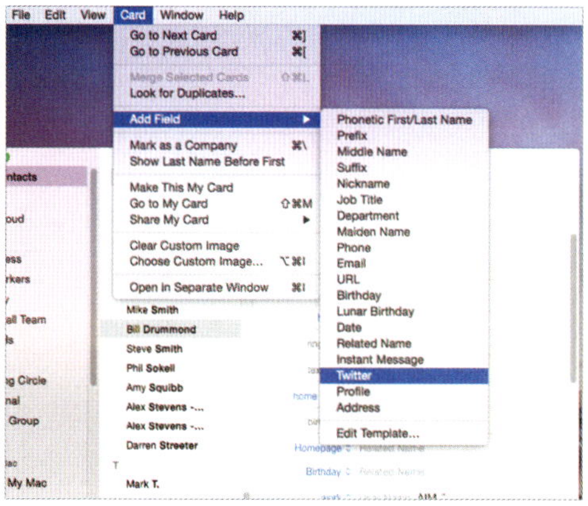

05: All a Twitter

You can add new fields, such as Twitter usernames, to this version of Contacts. Clicking on a Twitter username will take you to the Twitter app.

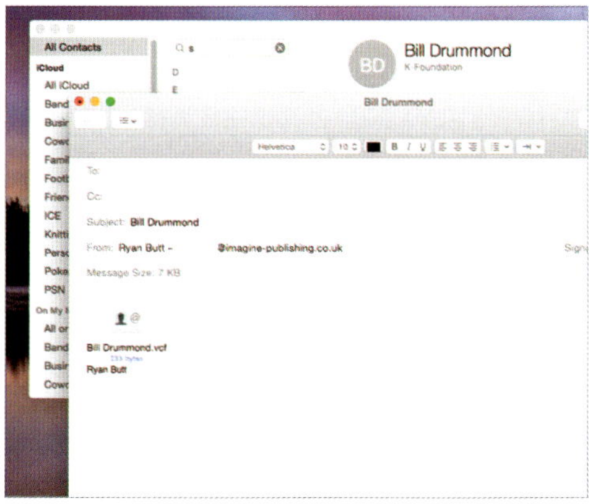

06: Share the details

Click on the Share button underneath a contact card to email that contact to somebody else. Contact cards will be attached in vCard format.

Navigate your contacts

Find your way around the address book's interface

iOS-like interface

In keeping with OS X's move to be more like iOS, Contacts sports a new interface that is very similar to the one found on the iPad or iPhone. And like iOS, it's clean, simple and textured

Getting social

OS X's Contacts includes contact detail fields such as Twitter, Facebook and Skype usernames, allowing you to easily integrate social media details into your list of contacts for quick access. They are even compatible with native Mac apps

BACKING UP

In OS X, it's fairly easy to make a backup of your contacts. Under the File menu, click Export, then 'Address Book Archive…'. Give the file a name and choose where to save it then hit Save. To import contacts from a backup, select Import from the File menu and find your backup file.

Create new contacts

Clicking on the '+' button at the bottom of the interface will allow you to create a new contact card into which you can enter all manner of details. As you will discover, building up a database rammed with contacts is incredibly easy

Sharing is simple

The Share button makes it even quicker to send contacts. It's fully integrated with Mail and certainly saves a few mouse clicks when it comes to sharing your details

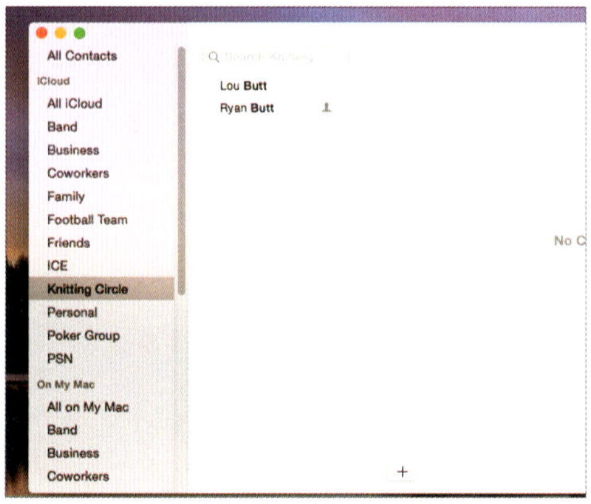

07: Get a group

Clicking on the View menu will bring up the option to Show/Hide Groups. Activate it to bring up a side column with all of your groups listed.

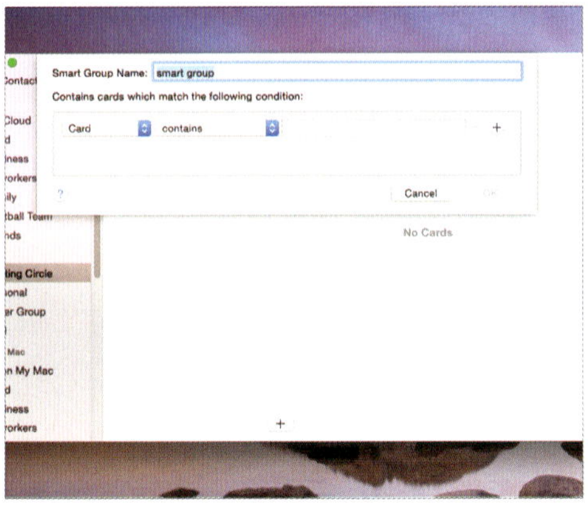

08: Smarter grouping

Smart Groups allow automatic grouping of contacts by certain details. Click 'New Smart Group…' from the File menu to set one up.

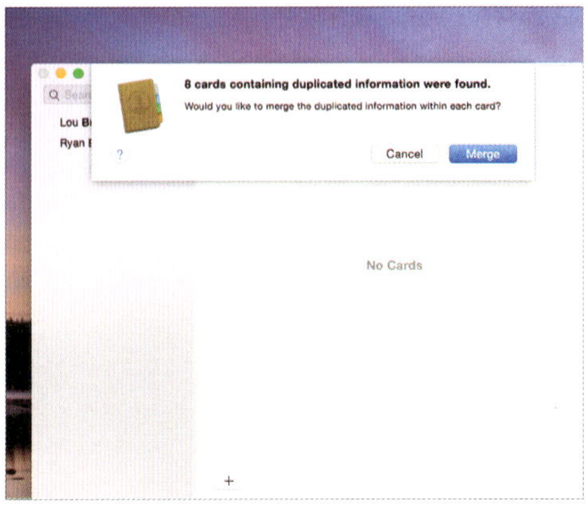

09: Look for duplicates

Click on the Card menu and choose the Look for Duplicates option to source multiple cards and merge/delete them from your database.

Set up Messages for every device

Stay in touch with iOS and OS X users via the Messages app on your Mac, iPhone and iPad

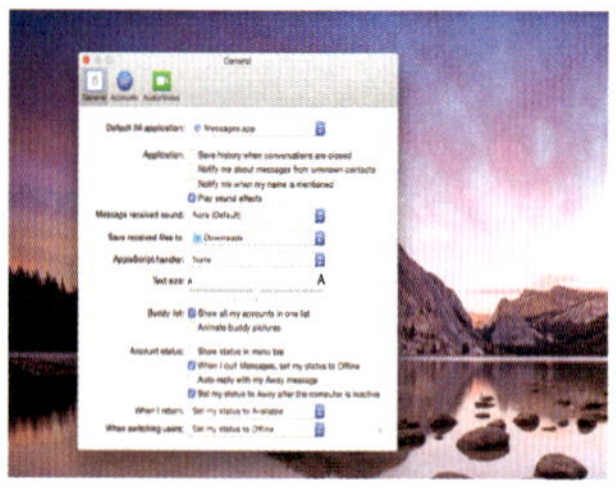

Messages is an instant messaging application that is built into Yosemite, and iPhone, iPad and iPod touch users will find it familiar. That is because it is the same messaging facility that is part of iOS. You can chat with your friends and relatives using your Mac as well as your iOS devices. In fact, you can start a conversation on your Mac and then pick up where you left off on your iPhone or iPad because they are automatically kept in sync through iCloud.

The app looks a lot like SMS messaging and at the top you specify who to send the message to. As you start typing, matching contacts are displayed and you can select someone by their email address or phone number. Down at the bottom of the window is a box in which to enter your message. It's just like sending a text message on a phone, but you can also send images. Ctrl/right-clicking in the message box enables a section of the screen to be copied and then inserted into the message, or you can open a Finder window and drag a file into it. The file will then

> "You can chat to several different people at the same time"

Inside Messages

The new way to enjoy a conversation

The conversation list
This panel on the left shows the people you are currently chatting to. Notice the three dots under one of them. This means that they are typing a response

SMS RELAY
If you are logged into the same iCloud account on your Mac and iOS devices then you can respond to text messages from non-Apple owning friends from different devices other than your iPhone. On your iPhone running iOS 8.1, go to Settings>Messages>Text Message Forwarding and decide which devices will receive text message forwarding. You will then need to enter a code to continue using the service.

appear inside the conversation window. When you receive an image, double-clicking on it opens it in a larger window and there is also the option to quickly open it in Preview.

A conversation is displayed using speech bubbles in the main part of the window and you can chat to several different people at the same time. Double-clicking the person in the left-hand list opens the conversation in a separate window, which is useful when talking to two or more people. You can also continue a conversation later because everything can be remembered.

There are some useful features in Messages, and in the top right corner you'll see a FaceTime icon if the person you're chatting to has it. Click on it and you can start a video call. There is also an option to display a notice when someone has received a message, which is useful when you don't know if they are there, busy doing something or gone. You can even see when they are typing a response.

Start FaceTime
This contact has FaceTime and so clicking this icon will start FaceTime and call them. You can then continue the chat using a video call. It is a useful option to have

Open the photos
This is a thumbnail image showing the photo that has been sent. Clicking on it opens it in a larger window and it can also be opened for viewing or editing in Preview

Type a message
The iMessage box at the bottom is where you type your message. Ctrl/right-click on it or drag a photo to the box from Finder to send it to the person

Messages Get started with Messages

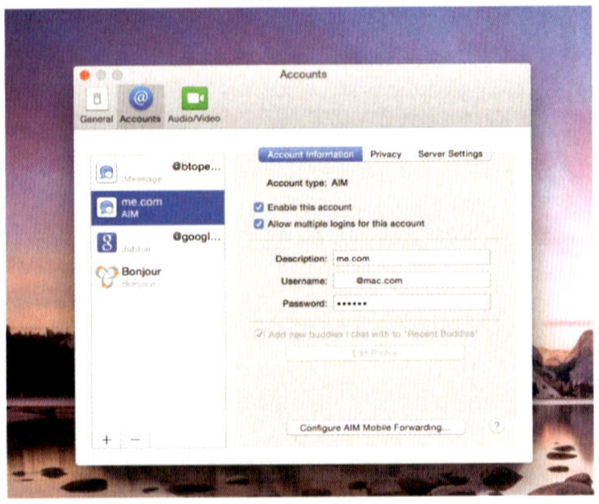

01: Enable Messages
Start Messages and go to Preferences>Accounts. You may have several messaging accounts that can be enabled and used with Messages. Turn them on.

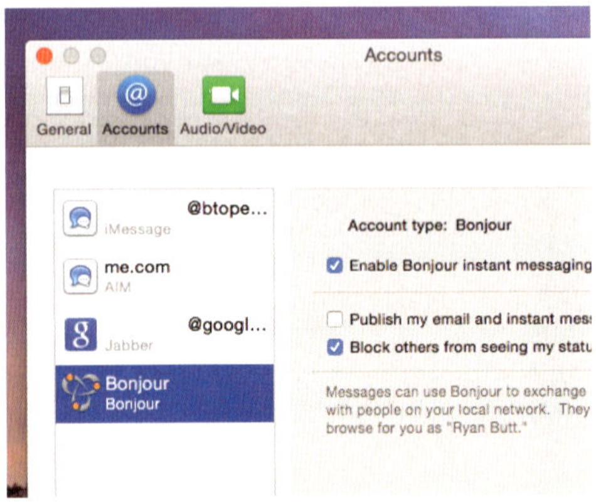

02: Local instant messaging
If you have several Macs, you can select and enable Bonjour instant messaging. This allows Macs to exchange messages and files over a local network.

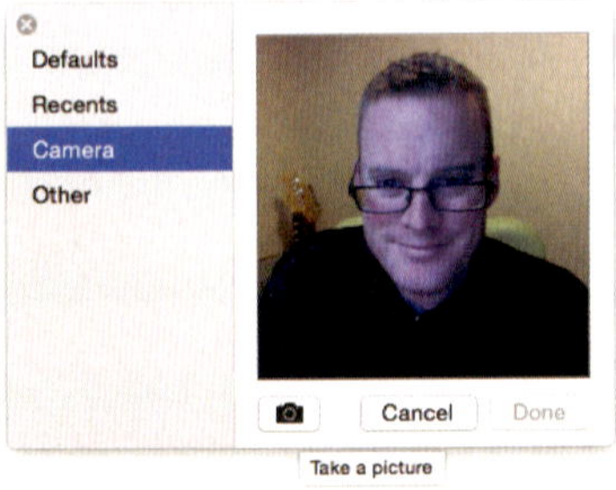

03: Change your picture
Close Preferences and click Messages>Change my Picture. Click the camera icon to take a photo using the Mac's camera, or click Other to load a photo.

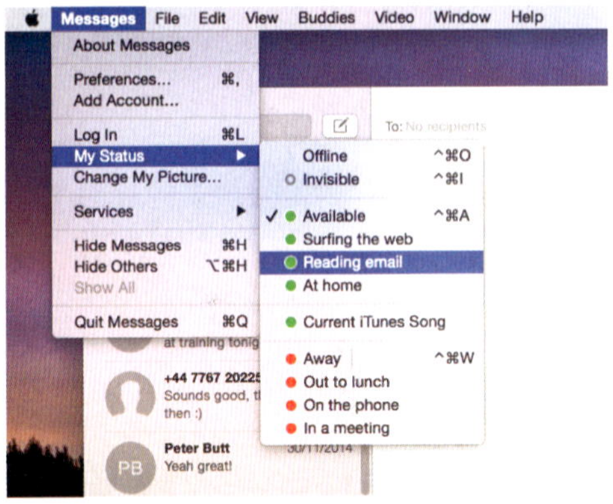

04: Set your status
You can tell people whether you are available or away from your Mac, or even which iTunes song you are listening to. Hit Messages>My Status and select one.

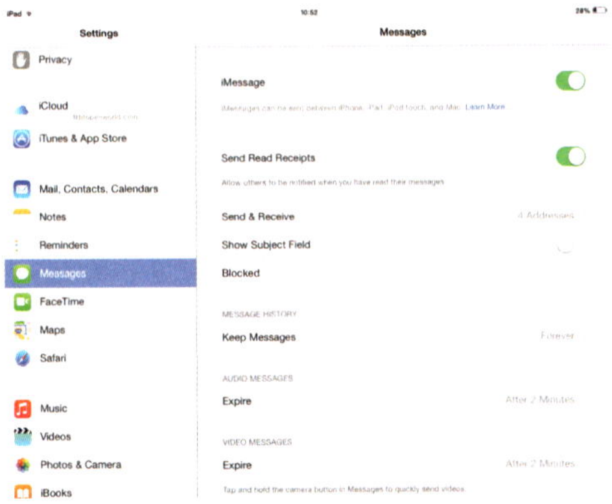

05: Set up iOS
On the iPhone and iPad, go to Settings>Messages. Turn on iMessage. It's useful to enable the Send Read Receipts option to show that messages have arrived.

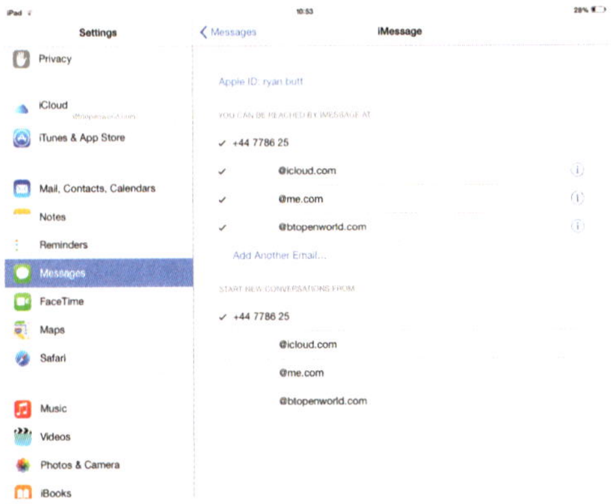

06: Add email addresses
Tap Send & Receive and you can add the email addresses people can use when they want to contact you. On iPhone they'll be able to use your number.

Discover FaceTime for Mac

With FaceTime for Mac, video calls are now only a few clicks away. Learn how to install and configure this great tool

One of the most acclaimed features of the iPhone, iPad and iPod touch devices is now available on your Mac. From the comfort of your laptop or desktop, FaceTime for Mac now makes it possible for you to have a chat or share a smile with your friends and family who also possess an iPhone, iPad, iPod touch or Mac. It is even possible to engage in video calls over your local network. With the simple further requirements of an email address and an Apple ID, a whole new world of enhanced communication is now easily accessible. The sleek, simple and powerful interface of the FaceTime for Mac application is fully integrated into your Mac OS X environment. Plus, if you have an iPhone running iOS 8, you can now even make phone calls to any number if you have your iPhone nearby.

This two-page tutorial takes you through the few simple steps needed to set up FaceTime on your Mac, and in just a few minutes you'll be calling friends all over the world.

> "With your Mac, video calls are just a few clicks away"

FaceTime Set up and use FaceTime

01: Launch the app

You can launch the FaceTime app by locating and double-clicking on the app icon in your Applications folder or by selecting Launchpad from the Dock and opening it from there. Alternatively, drag the app icon into your Dock to create a handy shortcut if you intend to use the app frequently.

02: Sign in

When the FaceTime app has been launched, you will have to sign in with your Apple ID to start using the app or create a new account, which you can do by opening System Preferences and clicking on iCloud. When you have entered your account details, you will be able to start conducting FaceTime chats.

Find your way around FaceTime

Make calls to your friends and family with ease

Search for Contacts

Click in the Search bar at the top of the left-hand bar and you can type in a name. As soon as you hit the first keys, FaceTime will start making suggestions of who you might mean, and you can call with a click

Audio or Video?

In FaceTime you can now make both Audio and video calls. Click on the two tabs to see your recent calls in each format, and quickly call a person back

Quick calling

You can right-click on the FaceTime icon in the Dock to bring up this contextual menu containing your recent calls. Click on any one of them to call that person back instantly – it's a really fast way to make calls

Contact information

To get more information about a specific contact, click the 'i' icon next to their name. a Contact window will pop up, with all their information from your Contacts app displayed

WHAT IS AN APPLE ID?

An Apple ID is a username and password used to identify you on every Apple service. Whether you want to buy software or a device on the Apple Online Store, music or movies on the iTunes Store or log in to iCloud, an Apple ID provides you with a single set of login credentials.

03: Find a contact

You'll see Video and Audio options at the top of the screen. Click the search bar and type in the name of a friend, or click the '+' button to add one from your Contacts app manually. Then click on the phone or camera icons to make an audio or video call respectively.

04: Make a Call

When your friend has been notified of your FaceTime invitation and accepts the call, they will appear in the main window of the app and you will be visible in a stamp-sized screen in the corner. You can change to Portrait or Landscape orientation by hovering your cursor over the window and clicking the arrow.

Get more out of Preview

One of OS X's staple apps has undergone a recent face-lift. Let's take a closer look…

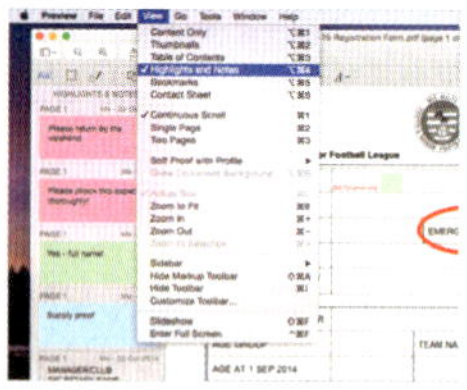

Preview is a powerful and flexible general purpose utility that is designed for viewing and editing a wide range of different file types. However, it is mainly used for viewing PDFs and images. Since Mountain Lion, it has come with additional features that make it even more useful, such as the button and menus for sharing files. It is possible to share files directly from Preview using Twitter, AirDrop, Messages and so on. Sending a file to a friend or work colleague via Preview has never been easier.

There are now more PDF editing tools and it is also possible to insert pages from other files, as well as images directly from a scanner. Notes can be added throughout a document, but they are hidden. There is a new panel on the left for viewing notes, plus any text you have highlighted too. Preview also supports iCloud and it stores files online so they are available everywhere.

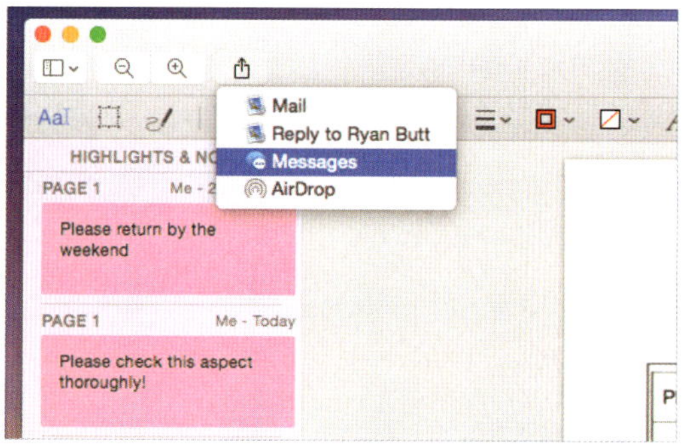

Inside Preview

The best new bits explained

Share the file

The Share button enables you to share images, PDFs and other files with your friends and work colleagues. Click on it and then choose an option, such as Twitter or AirDrop

Highlights and notes

If notes have been added to a document, or text has been highlighted, you can display this panel on the left that contains everything you have added. It is also searchable

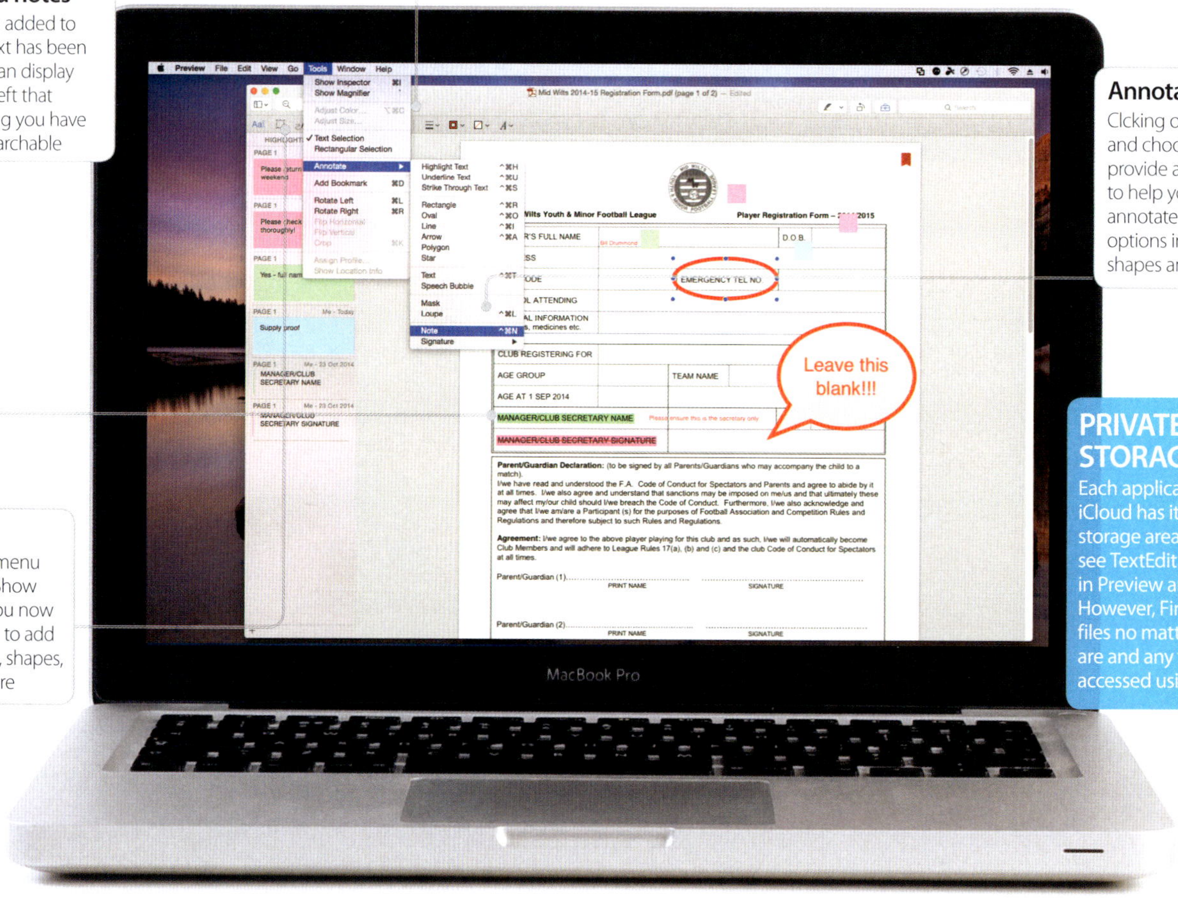

Annotating PDFs

Clcking on the Tolls menu and choose Annotate will provide a menu of tools to help you markup and annotate your PDF. These options include adding shapes and more

Markup tools

Click on the View menu and then choose Show Markup Toolbar. You now have tools to hand to add notes, annotations, shapes, signatures and more

PRIVATE iCLOUD STORAGE

Each application that uses iCloud has its own private storage area. You can't see TextEdit's iCloud files in Preview and vice versa. However, Finder shows all files no matter where they are and any file can be accessed using File>Open.

Preview Explore the latest features

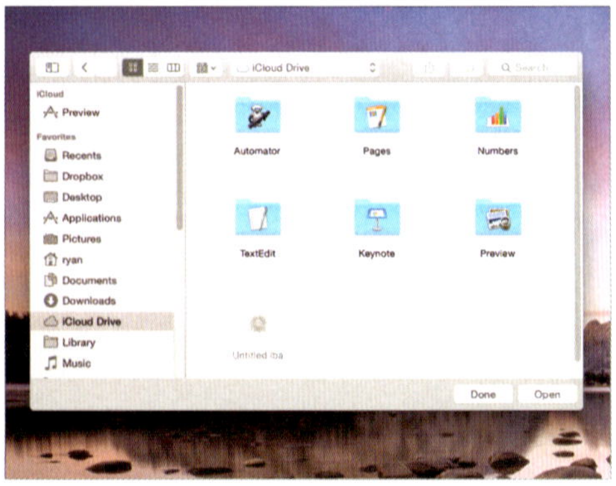

01: iCloud or disk

Start Preview in the Applications folder and select File>Open. You will now be able to navigate to picture files on your your Mac or iCloud.

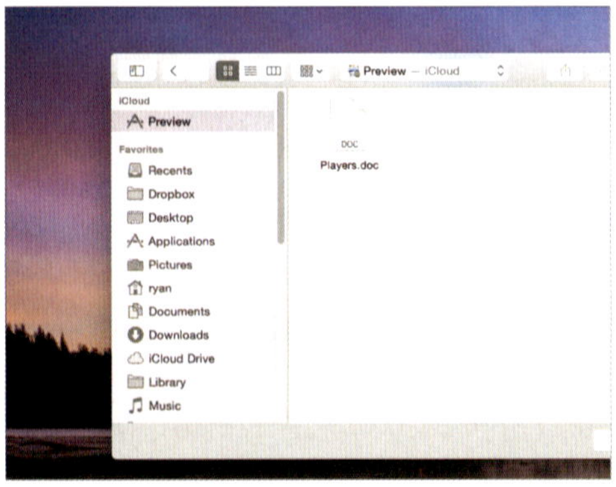

02: Upload files

Files on the Mac's disk drive can be uploaded to iCloud Drive for universal access. Open iCloud Drive and drag them to the Preview folder.

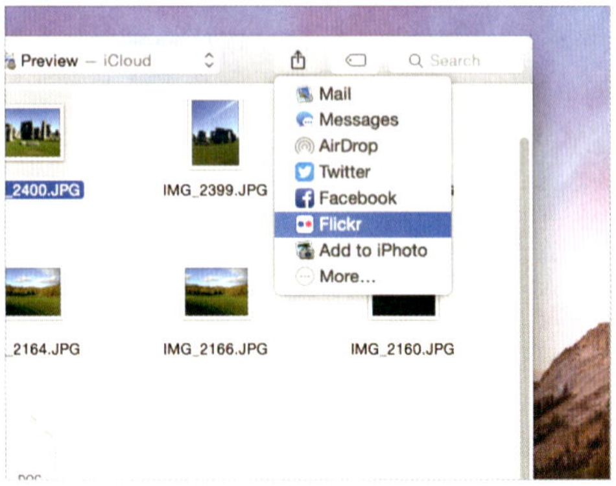

03: Share Preview files

All windows in Yosemite have a share button at the top. Click once on a file and then click on this button to share the file to a range of services.

04: Message your image

Sending files to others is very easy. Here we are sending a photo using Messages. A thumbnail is displayed and you can enter the text.

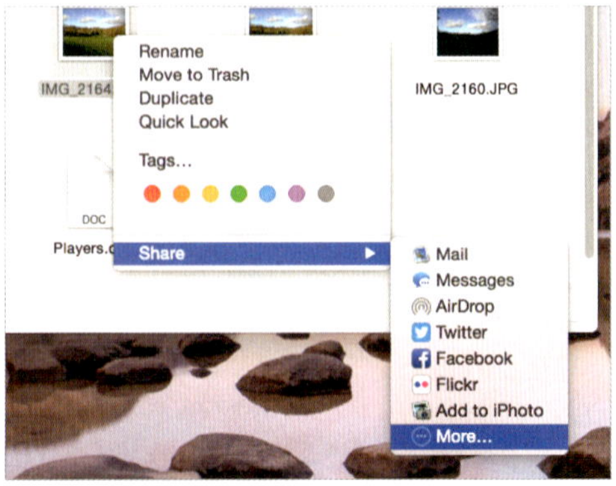

05: File management

There are full management facilities for files stored on iCloud Drive through Preview. Right-click to see options to rename, delete, viewed or shared.

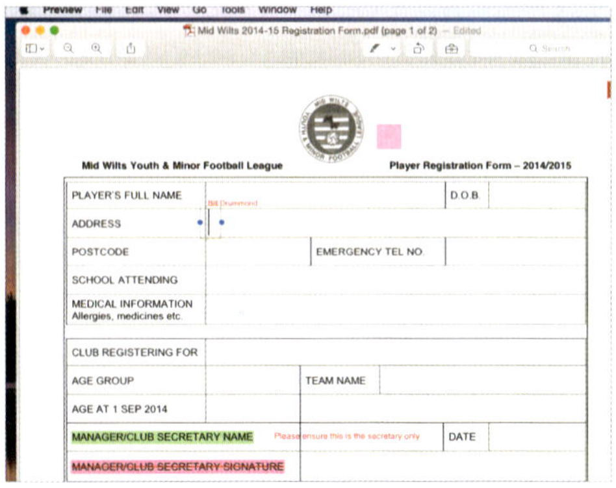

06: Fill in forms

Forms can be created and saved as PDF files, and now you can fill them in using Preview. Open the PDF file and click in the form to enter text.

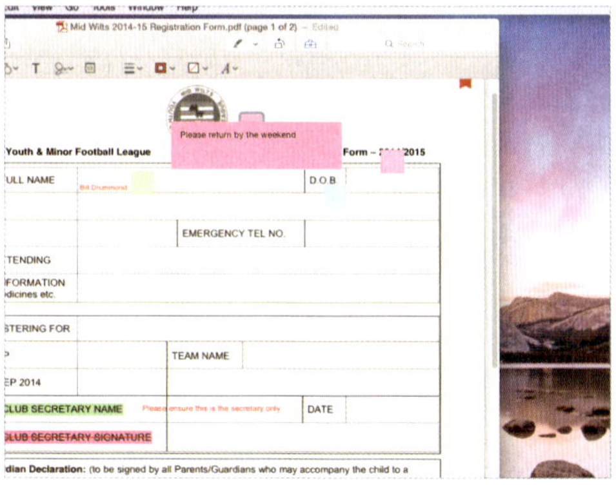

07: Notes and highlights

Go to Tools>Annotate to edit a PDF document and highlight important text, or even insert notes. Your notes are then hidden, leaving just a discreet icon.

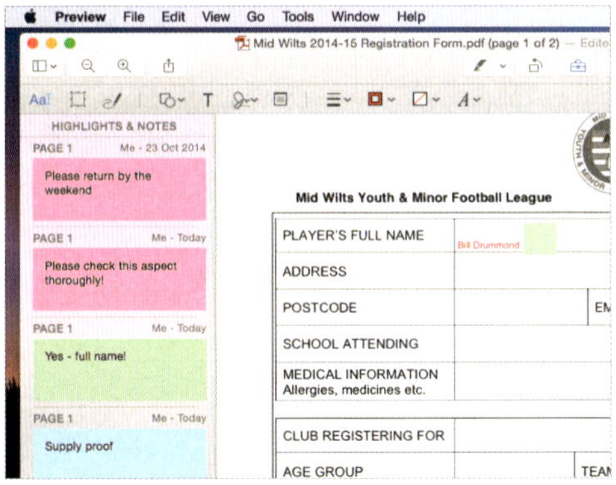

08: View your notes

The sidebar usually displays thumbnail images of the pages, but there is now an option to display all your highlighted text and notes with more information.

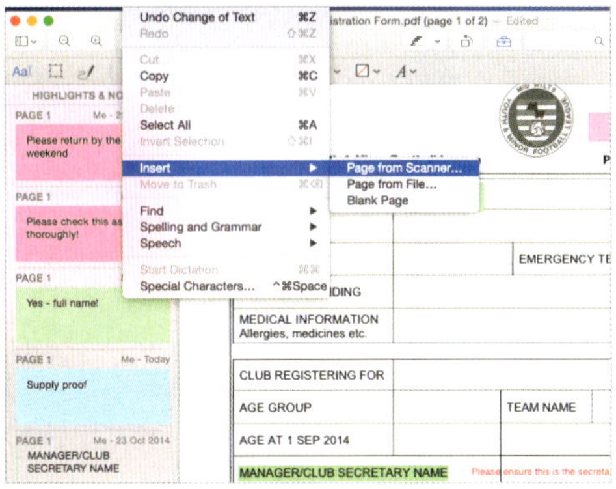

09: Insert a scan

Previously, Preview could only insert blank pages into PDFs, but there are two new options. Now, you can insert from a file or a scanner, too.

Store information with Notes

When you need to remember information, jot down thoughts and store items, Notes is the ideal app

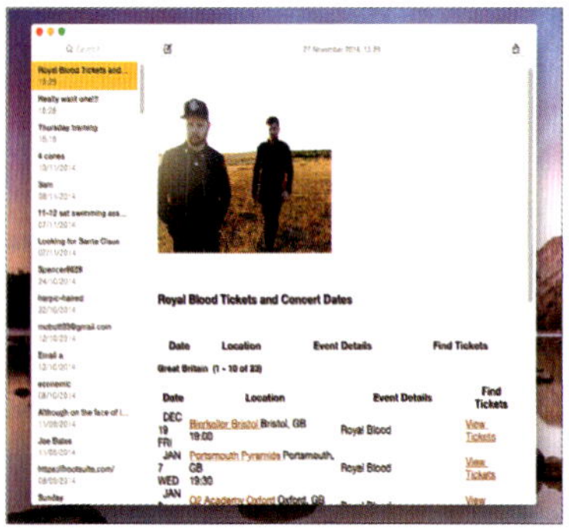

When you are using your Mac, whether for work or for fun, you will come across information that you need to remember. It may be a recipe that you see on a website, some information in an email, a file and so on. The Notes app is a place where you can store all this information and it is perfect for collecting and managing a wide range of different things you want to remember.

The Notes app lives in OS X's Dock and it enables you to create notes and store them in folders, which is great for projects you are working on, but they can also be opened in their own window. You don't need to stick Post-It notes on your Mac or desk when you can pin digital notes to your Desktop – they won't fade or get lost! Notes are synced with iCloud, too, so you can create notes on the Mac and read them on the iPhone or iPad and vice versa. Let's dive in and find out more.

> "It enables you to create notes and store them in folders"

Your virtual notebook

Adding multimedia content to notes is very simple

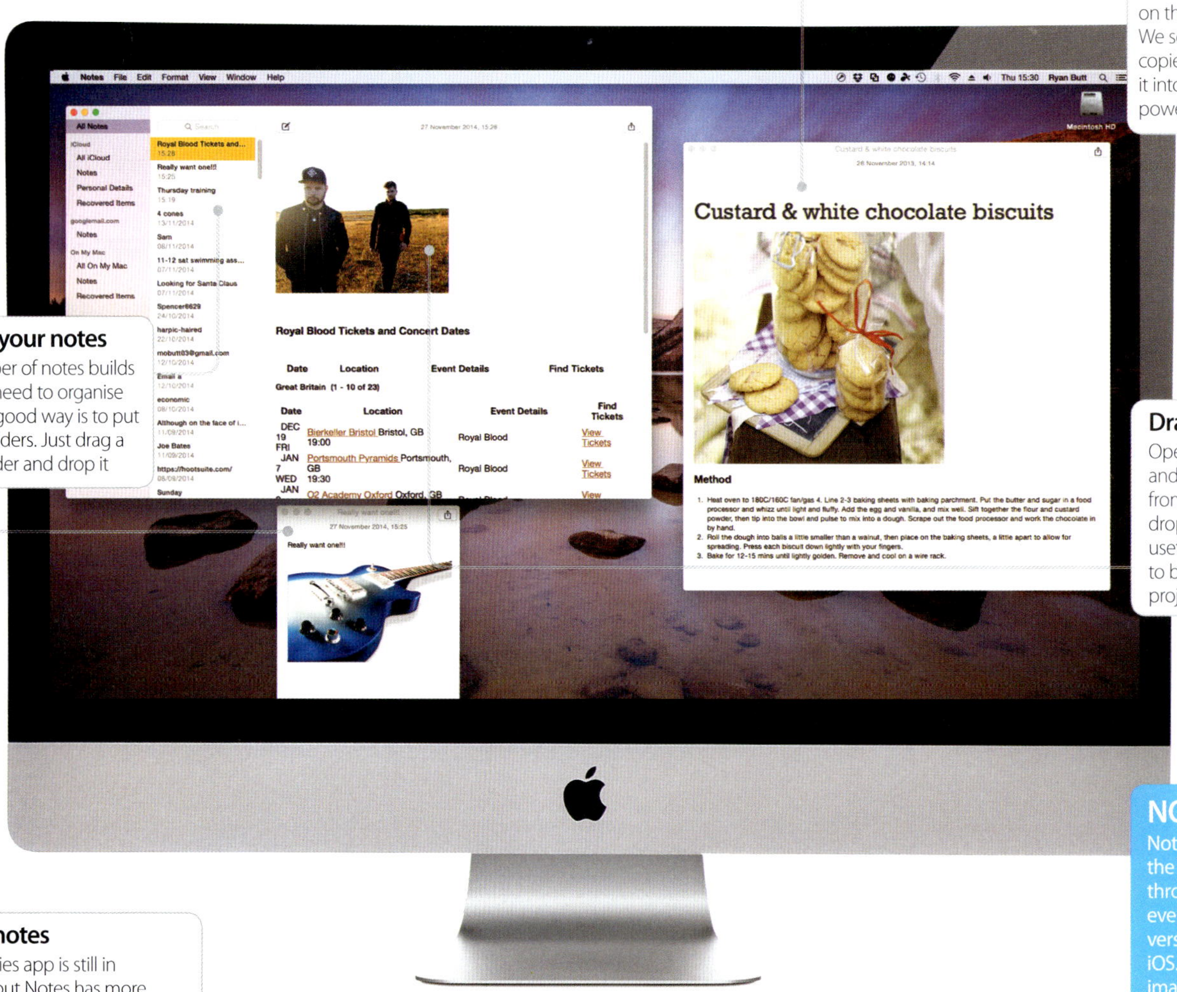

Copy web pages

This recipe from Anthony Worrall Thompson was on the BBC website. We selected it in Safari, copied it and then pasted it into a note. It shows the power of Notes

Organise your notes

As the number of notes builds up, you will need to organise them and a good way is to put them into folders. Just drag a note to a folder and drop it

Drag and drop

Open a Finder window and you can drag files from the hard disk and drop them onto notes. It's useful for collecting items to be used in reports, projects and hobbies

Desktop notes

The old Stickies app is still in Dashboard, but Notes has more features and is synced. Double-click a note in the list to pin it to the desktop

NOTES ON iOS

Notes are synced with the iPhone and iPad through iCloud, but not every feature of the Mac version is supported in iOS. If a note contains an image, for example, on the iPhone it will appear as a paperclip.

Notes Familiarise yourself with the app

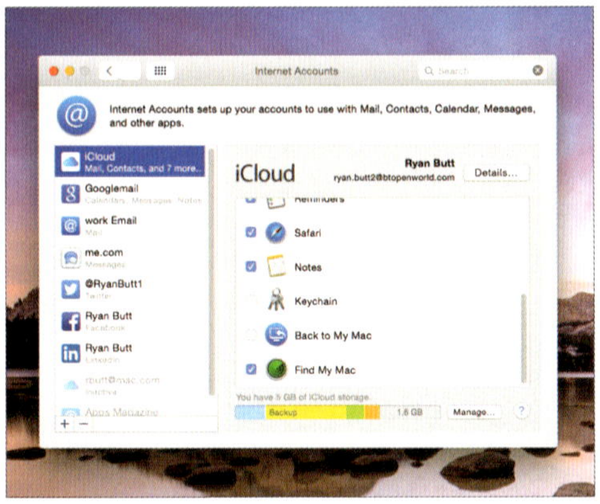

01: Add your accounts

Click System Preferences>Internet Accounts. iCloud includes Notes, but so does Gmail and other accounts. Select each one and then tick Notes.

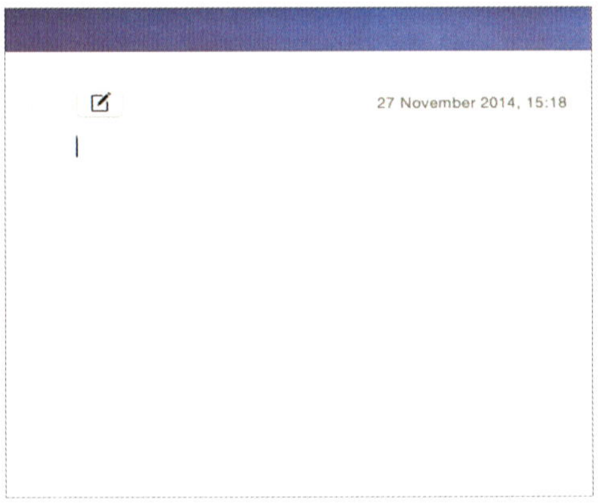

02: Create a note

Click Notes in the Dock and then click on the pen and paper icon in the top left to create a new note. Start typing. The first line is used for the note title.

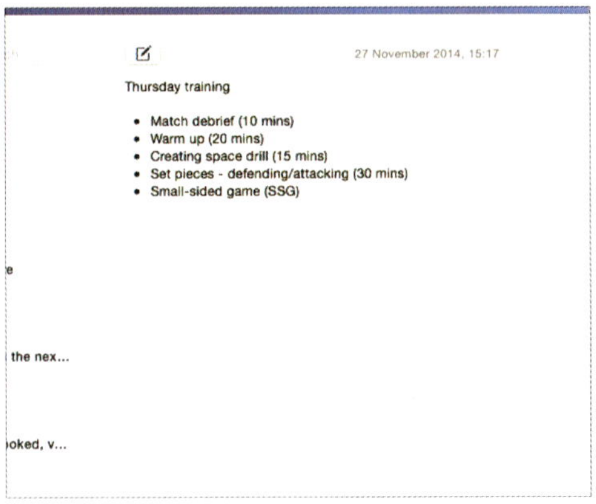

03: Make a list

Notes intelligently formats the text that you enter, and if you start a line with an asterisk (*) then it magically turns into a bullet point. Handy for making lists.

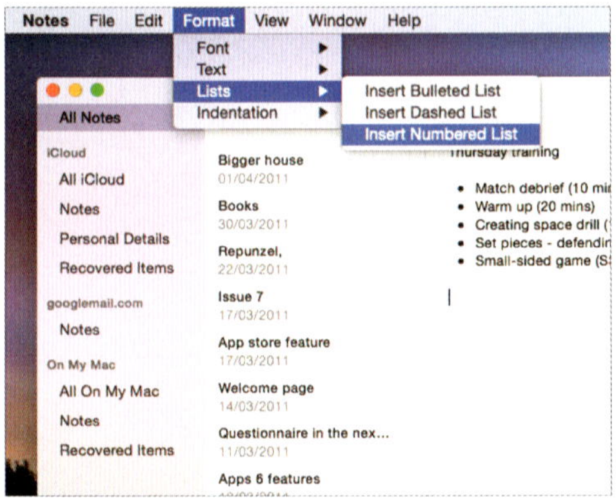

04: Bullets, dashes, numbers

There are other types of list, and starting a line with a dash (–) creates one automatically. The list types are in the Format menu, including numbered lists.

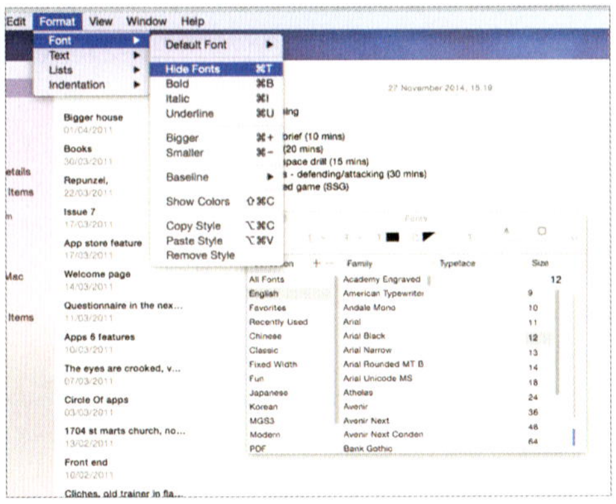

05: Change the font

There are excellent text formatting functions for notes and in the Format>Font menu is the option to show the Fonts window. Select some text and pick a font.

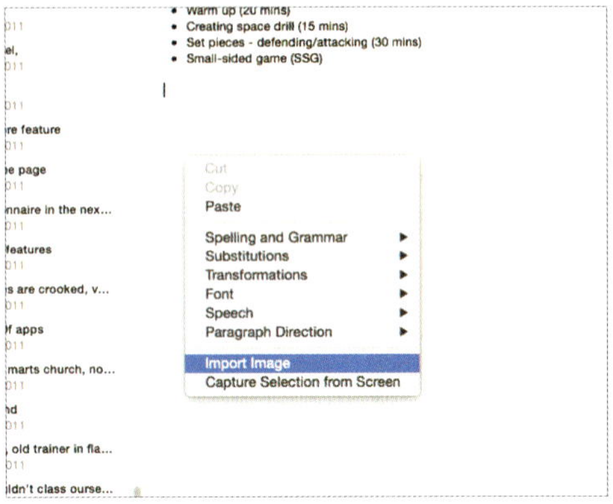

06: Insert an image

Ctrl/right-click on a note and you will see options to import an image. It can be imported from a camera or scanner, or you can even grab a screenshot.

07: Share your notes

In the lower-right corner of the note is a sharing icon. Click it and select either the Email or Message sharing options. Here's an email.

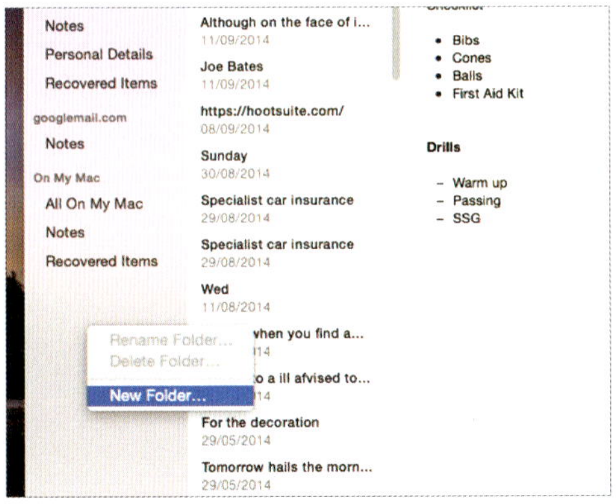

08: Create folders

Click View>Show Folders List and a panel slides out from the left. Ctrl/right-click inside it and you can create folders for storing different notes.

09: Floating notes

A note can be torn off and pinned to the Desktop by double-clicking its title in the list. Select Window>Float on Top to keep it on top of other windows.

Use Siri-style Dictation in any app

Use your voice to write in any app using Yosemite's brilliant built-in dictation tools

When Apple introduced Siri on iPhone and iPad back in iOS 5, it was expected that the system would soon be making its way over to the Mac. While we're still yet to see the full version of Siri make its way to OS X, you do have the ability to speak to your Mac and have it understand exactly what you mean.

Dictation enables you to tap a key on the keyboard and then speak to your Mac. The Mac will listen to what you say until you click Done, and then transcribe your words onto a page or into another app on your Mac. The system needs an internet connection to work normally but you can change this with a download. Read on to find out how to speak to your Mac and help it understand.

> "It enables you to speak to your Mac"

Dictation Use Dictation anywhere in Yosemite

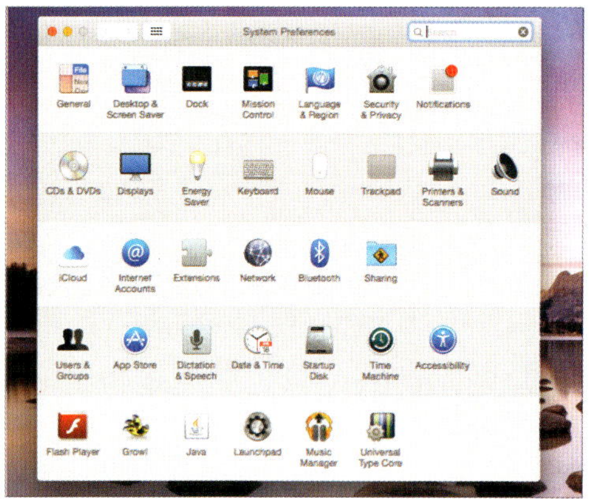

01: Activate Dictation

You'll need to activate dictation on your Mac. Go to System Preferences>Dictation & Speech. In the Dictation tab, click On beside Dictation.

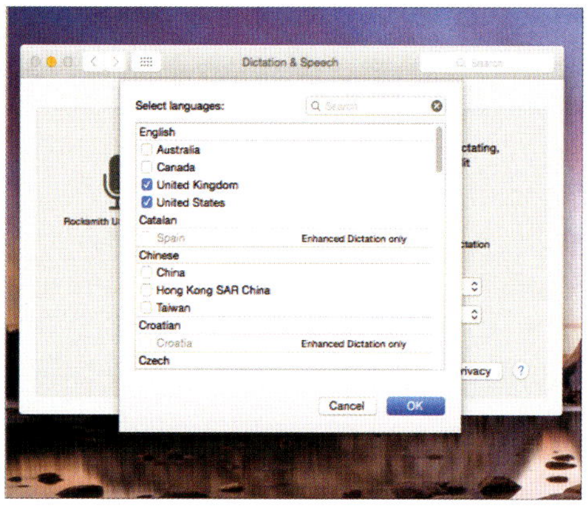

02: Choose your language

Choose your language from the drop-down. It will use your system language by default, but you can add more languages here if necessary.

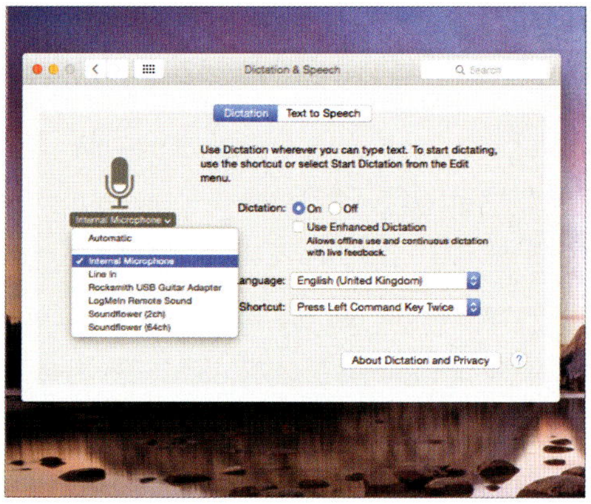

03: Set your input

If you have headphones with a built-in mic connected, you can use it as the input. Click below the mic and pick the one you want.

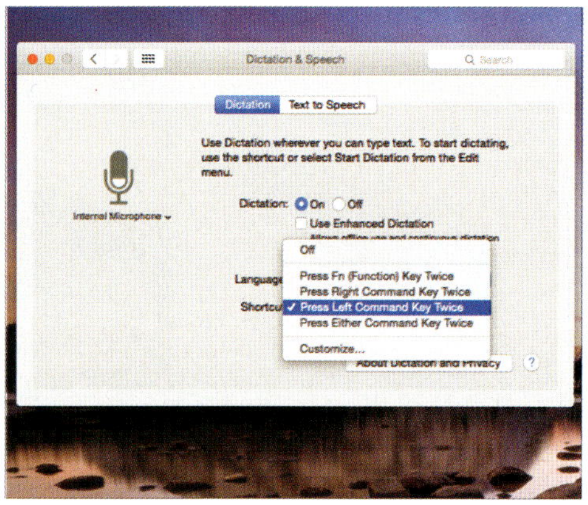

04: Choose the shortcut

You can choose a shortcut to activate Dictation quickly. Choose the keyboard combination you want, or choose Customize and enter your own.

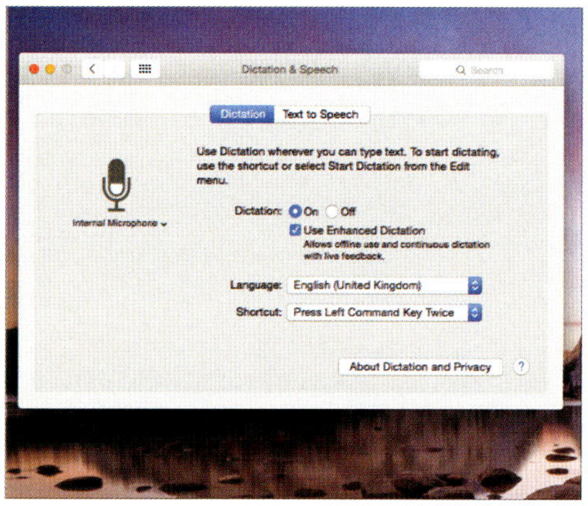

05: Enhanced Dictation

If you are using a MacBook, you may want to use it when you're not connected to the internet. To do this, check this box.

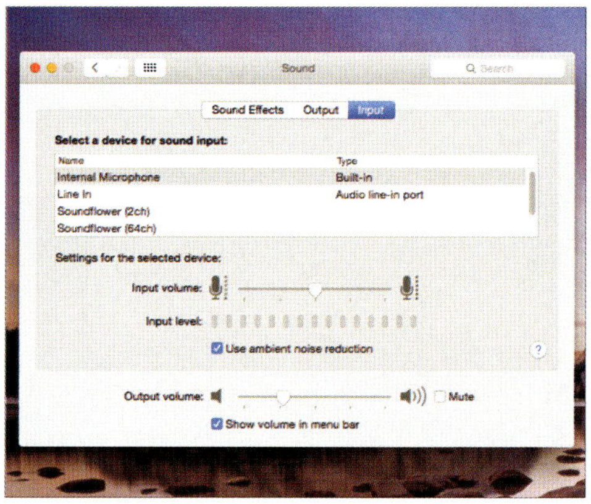

06: Check your levels

You can speak to see your input levels on the mic. If it can't hear you, open the Sound tab in System Preferences, choose Input and adjust the volume.

Talking Mac

Get more from Yosemite's Dictation feature

Sending data

When you switch on Dictation in System Preferences you'll see this pop-up box to explain that your speech is sent to Apple for analysis so the written text can come back, so click Enable Dictation to confirm

More information

If you're concerned about how your speech data is being used, you can click the About Dictation and Privacy section in System Preferences to see more information on how your information is used

I'm listening

When you activate Dictation, this small window will appear where you are typing to show you that your Mac can hear what you are saying. Three dots will shake if your Mac didn't hear anything when you click Done

Waiting time

The dictation sends all your audio to Apple for analysis, so you won't see your words appearing onscreen as you say them. After you click done, three dots will appear to show that your words are being worked out, so be patient

SIRI FEATURES

Unfortunately, we still don't have full access to Siri's features, such as sending emails and messages quickly with a voice command, on Mac. Some search options, such as movie times and restaurant information, are coming to OS X Yosemite's new Spotlight later this year, so we'll keep our fingers crossed that this can be accessed via speech when it's finally released.

Text to Speech

Along with Dictation options, which enable you to transfer your voice to text, you can also use the Mac's built-in Text to Speech options. With these options, you can select an area of text and have your Mac read it out to you in a voice you choose. This is available from any app, so no matter what you're doing, you can have your Mac read out what you're working on.

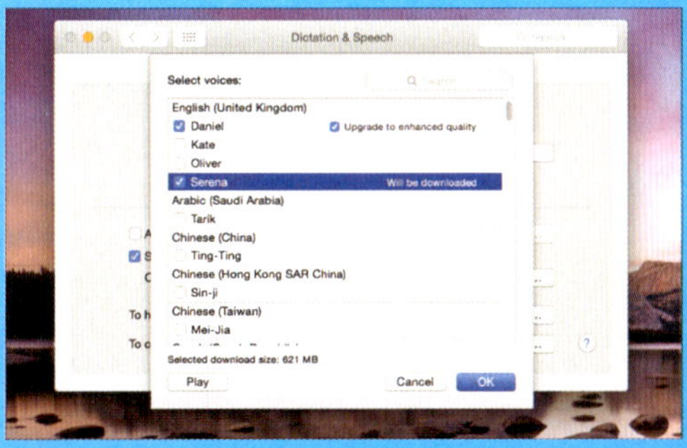

1: Choose your settings

In the Text to Speech tab of the Dictation & Speech preferences you'll see a number of options. You can choose a different voice and adjust the speech speed, or create a keyboard shortcut for activation.

2: Speak to me

In any application, select an area of text, right-click the text and choose Speech>Start Speaking. Your Mac will start reading the text; to stop it, right-click again and choose Speech>Stop Speaking.

Play with Game Center in Yosemite

Explore the new social gaming platform on the Mac and get one up on your mates

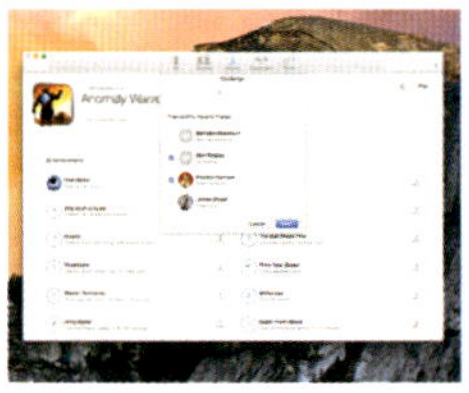

The iOS version of Game Center has been live for a few years now, allowing users with an Apple ID to connect to their friends, compare high scores and earn achievements. Apple also includes a Game Center app on the Mac, so that scores from all of your games can be stored and shared in one place.

Scores from both iOS and Mac games are displayed alongside each other, so achievements can be earned for the same profile on either device, and the social features of the app allow you not only to share scores but send challenges to friends with customised messages. You'll also get friend recommendations for those you might know, and a tally of your current score from achievements, enabling you to quickly see how you rank against your friends. To start using Game Center, all you need is an Apple ID, so let's get started…

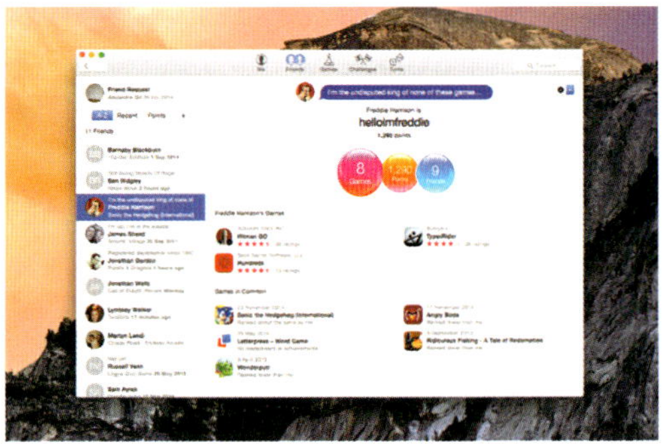

Get your game on

It's not about taking part, it's about winning…

Notifications

When you have a challenge from a friend, you can view it by clicking this icon in the toolbar. You can also see the number of challenges you currently have on your profile page in the purple bubble

Ultimate order

Down the left hand side, you can see a table of all your friends. To change the order, use the three buttons above the list to show players ranked alphabetically, by points or by the most recent players

Comparisons

The lower section in a friend's profile will show the games that you have both played and you'll also see how you rate compared to their high-scores. If they're ranked higher than you, then it's simple – try harder!

CHALLENGES EVERYWHERE

Challenges will appear on all devices, but naturally not every game is available on all platforms. Everything is linked through your profile, so even if you see a challenge on your Mac, you can always pick up your iPhone or iPad and start the game to beat your friend.

Game Center Get started with Game Center

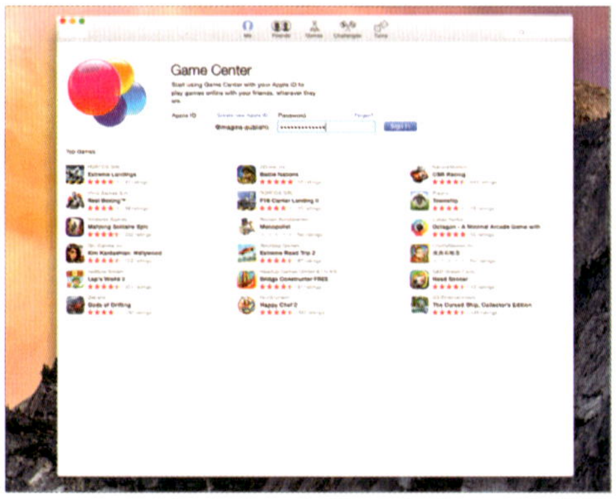

01: Sign in

First things first; you'll need to sign in using an Apple ID. Use the same address you use for buying apps, or an address your friends have, so they can find you.

02: Set a status

You'll now see your profile. If you've played on iOS devices you may have points already. On this screen, you can upload a status that your friends will see.

03: Find games

Below your profile are the Mac games that support Game Center. Click on any one of them and the App Store will open up so you can download them.

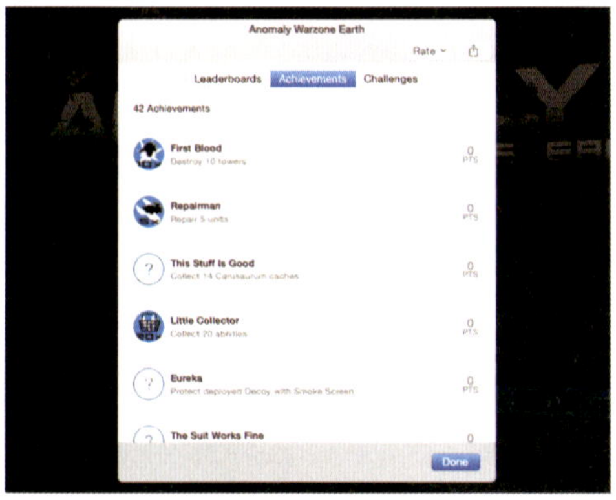

04: In-game options

If you start playing one of these games, such as Anomaly, you can view Achievements, Challenges and Leaderboards without ever leaving the game.

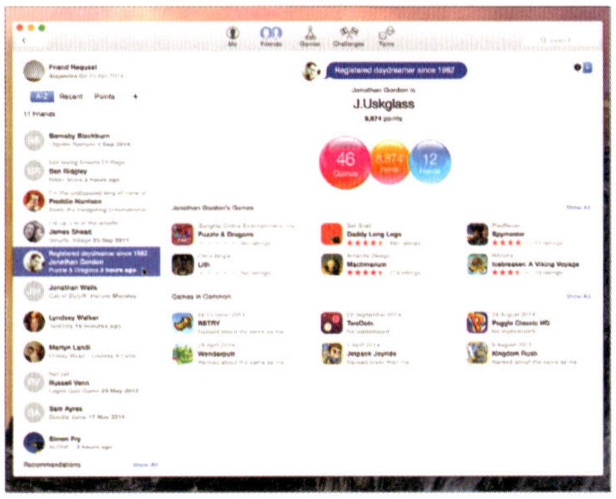

05: Friendly

In the Friends tab, you can see all your Game Center friends, as well as recommendations for those you might know. You can easily view each person's profile.

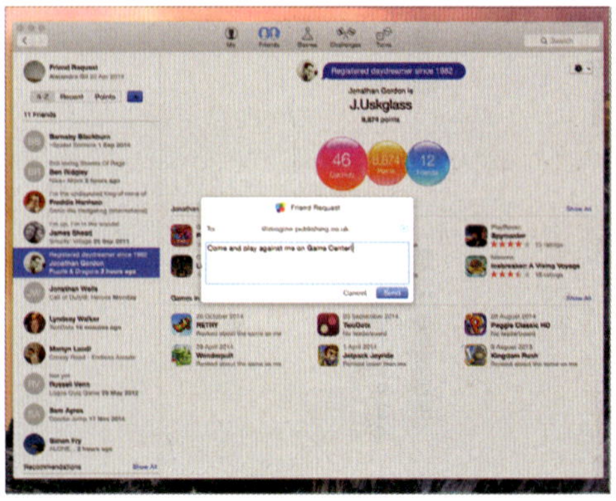

06: Find friends

If you want to add more friends, use the button on the left of the window. You can send requests to anyone you like, along with a message.

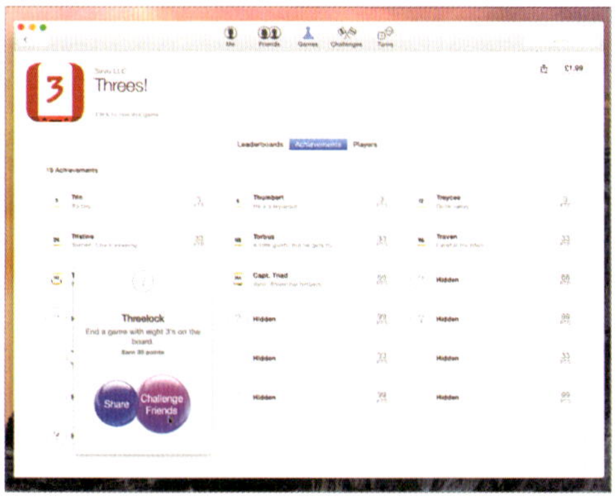

07: Setting challenges

From the Games tab, you can challenge friends. Choose a game and find an achievement; you can click it to set up a challenge with your friend.

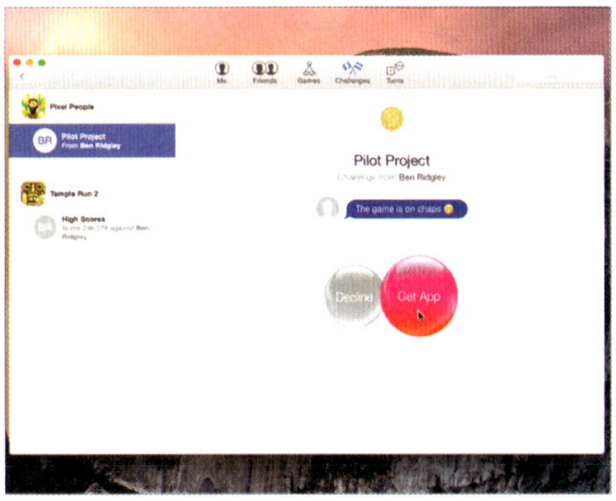

08: Beat the competition

When you are challenged, it will appear in the Game Center window with your friend's message and in Notification Center, so you can go straight into battle.

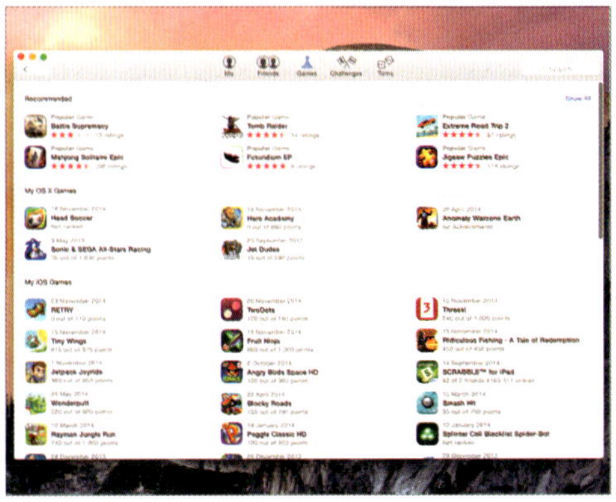

09: Games

In the Games tab, you'll see every game you have in Game Center. They're sorted by the order you last played them, and they're sorted by device too.

Convert images to other formats

Change images to your preferred format and get them suitable for uploading to the web

In a world where the iPhone 6 can produce images with its impressive 1.5 micron-pixel camera, and with hardware only improving, the snaps that we are taking are getting larger in size – both in dimensions and megabytes. While these numbers are great if you wish to share your images on a large screen – the high resolution means they'll be able to be shown on large displays without pixelation – if you're looking to put them on the web it'll take longer and may take up a lot of screen space.

Fortunately, there are several ways to convert images and reduce their size and dimensions using OS X's built-in apps. Here we look at how the Preview app and Automator scripts can work together to get you suitable shots in no time at all.

> "There are ways to convert images and reduce their size"

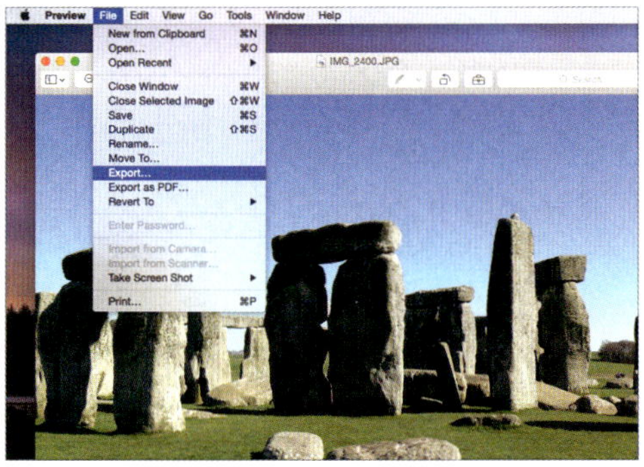

Batch convert your files

Use Automator to set up a simple script

Folder of new images

Our 'web ready' folder contains the converted images as dictated by the Automator script – all in one place and with the new file names. The originals are still on the desktop untouched

Copy Items

This order sends the converted images to a separate folder, which reduces desktop clutter and also enables you to have all your converted images in one place. It's handy for uploading to social networks

USING AUTOMATOR

To use the script you've created, simply drag as many images as you wish to convert onto the script's icon (you may have to manually open the Automator app first). If you're finding it a bit awkward to drag your files onto the script's icon on the desktop, then consider keeping it in the Dock for easy access.

Change type

This order sends the converted images to a separate folder, which reduces desktop clutter and also enables you to have all your converted images in one place. It's handy for uploading to social networks

Renaming

To further eliminate confusion between the original and web-ready images, we've decided to add a bit of text before each file name. You can also replace text or add in the date and time if you wish

Preview Convert an image

01: Choose your image

Start off by choosing an image to convert. Switch to the column view to get a thumbnail preview of each images as you click on them.

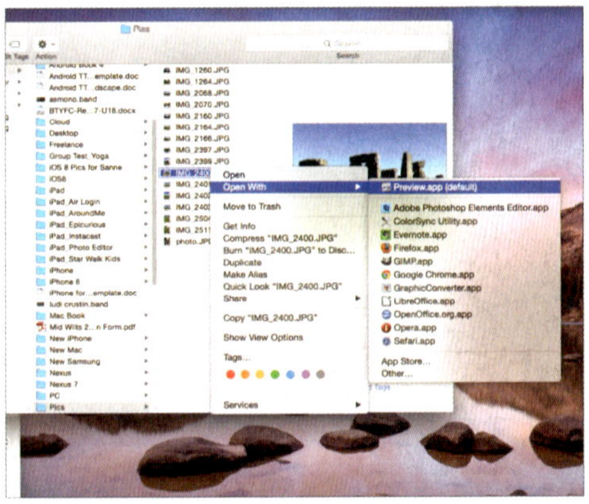

02: Open in Preview

Double-click your image. In the event that it opens in an app other than Preview. Ctrl-click the image and choose Open With. Select Preview.

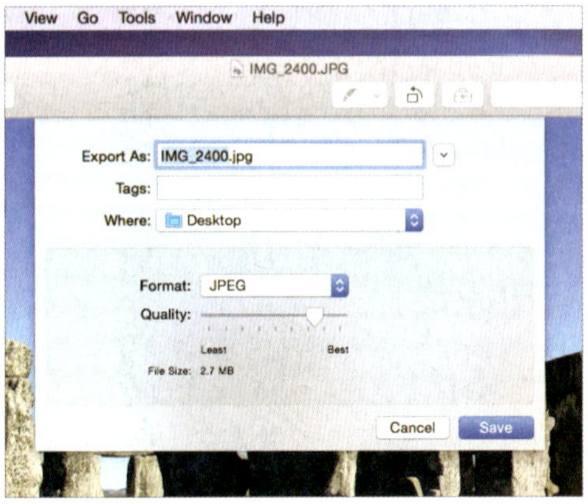

03: Convert the image

Click File>Export. Click on the Format drop-down box to select your chosen format. We've chosen JPEG, and already there's a marked drop in size.

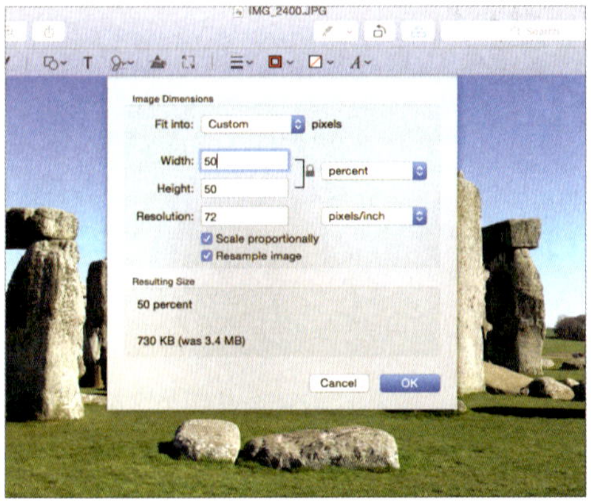

04: Reduce size

We can make the file size even smaller by editing the dimensions. Go to Tools>Adjust Size and click percent in the Width/Height drop-down.

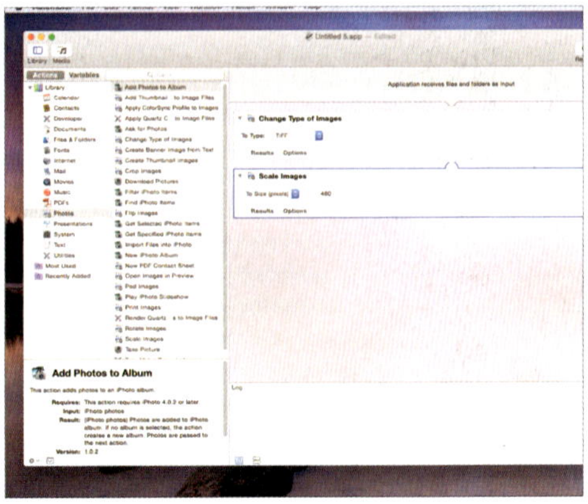

05: Batch editing

To set up an Automator script, open Automator and choose Application. Pick Photos and drag Change Type of Images and Scale Images into the window.

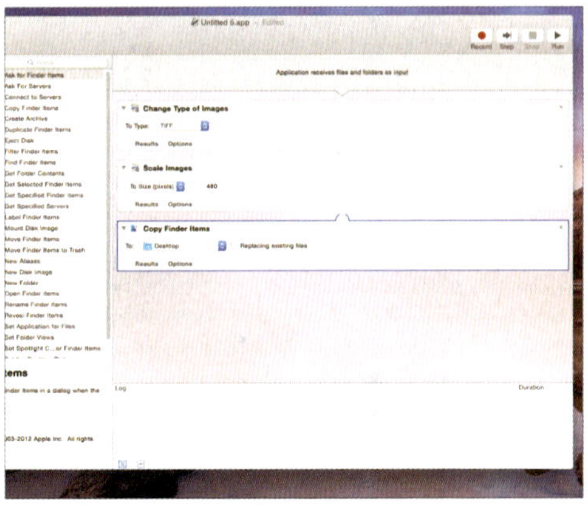

06: Tidy up with folders

You can add an order to your script that copies the resized images to a different folder. Go to Files & Folders and drag Copy Finder Items into your script.

Alternate formats

Although it's one of the most effective when looking to reduce the size of your images, JPEG isn't your only option when looking to convert on a Mac. Preview most notably offers PNG and TIFF, while ColorSync adds BMP and GIF support. You could check out open-source image editor GIMP, which offers a wide variety of export formats.

"JPEG isn't your only option when looking to convert on a Mac"

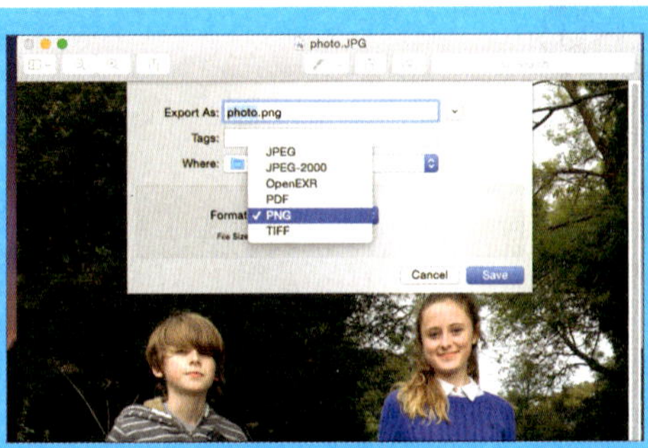

1: PNG

PNG (portable network graphics) format is a lossless compression format that's commonly used on the web. It's the format in which Mac screenshots are taken. Our 106MB psd file went down to 66MB when converted to PNG.

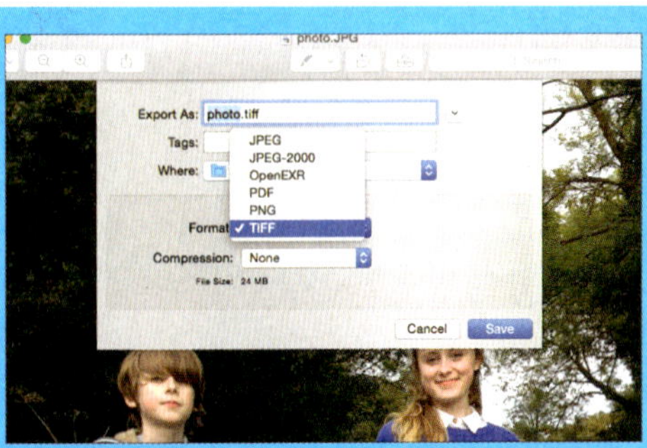

2: TIFF

TIFF (tagged image file format) is a format often used in publishing and by graphic artists. The file sizes of TIFF images do not differ a great deal from psd files, and as such are not suitable for casual uploading to the web.

Introducing iLife

Find your way around iLife with these in-depth guides to iPhoto, iMovie and GarageBand

"Apple's creative suite helps you craft amazing movies, sounds and images, while being a real delight to use"

"GarageBand allows you to record music, edit and export all with ease"

148 Blockbuster effects

150 Create your own loops

152 Use Drummer

Get perfect portraits with iPhoto

You'll be amazed at how easy it is to use iPhoto's powerful retouching tools and effects

iPhoto makes everything about your photos easier and much more fun. As well as automatically sorting them all out for you into Events, Faces and Places, iPhoto gives you some smart tools to help you improve your photos, which are simple to get to grips with but surprisingly effective. Here we shall explore a couple of the different ways that you can utilise these handy tools.

From a quick one-click Enhance button to set a good baseline for editing your image, right through to sliders that enable you to control very specific areas of your image in great detail, in order to fine-tune the look you are trying to achieve, iPhoto has it all. So dig out all those holiday photos and get ready to give your friends and family the star treatment – it's the perfect step to take before sharing them online or bringing them into another iPhoto project!

"Get ready to give your friends the star treatment"

Using the Adjust panel

There are more great tools in this area of iPhoto

Skin tones

iPhoto will protect skin tones from unrealistic manipulations by default, but if you're going for a more artistic edit then you'll want to uncheck this box so that skin can be affected too

Histogram

Usually the preserve of Photoshop, the Histogram is both powerful and fun to play with, though difficult to master. Often, the best adjustments involve bringing the end sliders in slightly

De-noise

This is a great tool to use with photos containing any grain or noise, such as old family photos you've scanned in or those that you've taken with a slightly dusty camera lens

Revert

iPhoto saves your image automatically at each step, but you can roll back to the unedited version at any time by clicking this button. Be warned – you can't undo it!

DUPLICATES AND ADJUSTMENTS

To save time when editing lots of photos at once, you can copy all of the adjustments you've made and paste them straight onto another image with Cmd+Alt+C/V. If you also want to keep the original versions too, either hit File>Export and save as JPG before you make your edits, or export afterwards and then hit Revert to Original to roll back.

iPhoto Retouch photos the easy way

01: Enhance to start

Open a photo and click Edit in the bottom-right. Select the Enhance option in the right-hand panel for an automatic boost.

02: Straighten it up

Use Straighten to either straighten up a tilted image or add a jaunty angle. Note that tilting will crop the photo, to ensure there are no blank spaces left over.

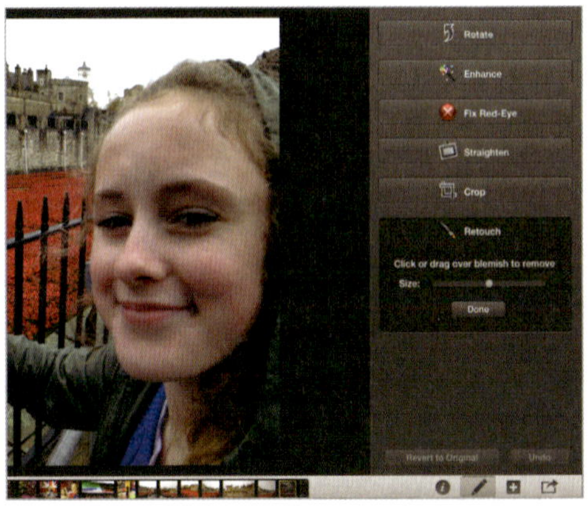

03: Smooth the skin

To remove blemishes, marks etc, click Retouch. Use the slider to change the cursor size to match the area you want to smooth over, click once to apply.

04: Improve the colours

Switch to the Effects panel and click the coloured circles to make your portrait lighter, darker, warmer or cooler, and to increase contrast or saturation.

05: Add some effects

Below the circles you'll see some squares – each is a different effect that you can apply. Here we've applied Edge Blur five times to enhance the lights.

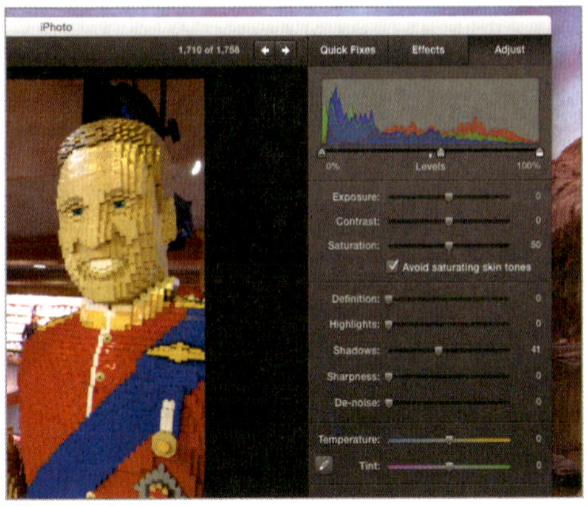

06: Bring colour to shadows

Go to the Adjust panel. Colours in the shadows are a little dark, so drag the Shadows slider up. You want to restore colour but preserve realism.

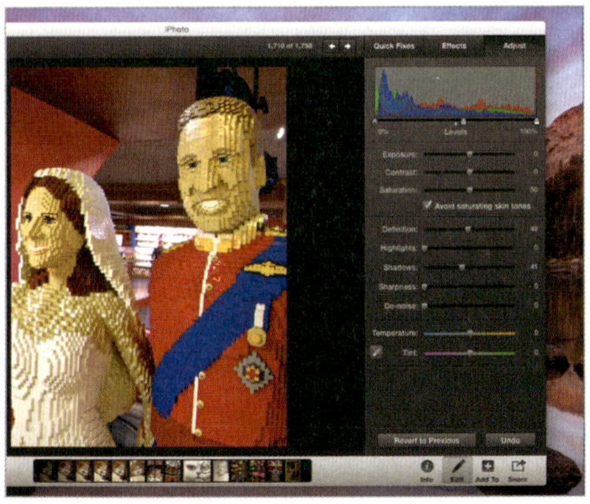

07: Add some definition

To combat the smoothing that's been introduced by the colour manipulation, increase the Definition slider a little too. Use sparingly as it's quite powerful.

08: Play with colours

Move the Temperature and Tint sliders at the bottom to taste. Try sliding them in the same and opposite directions, to compare the effects.

09: Use the eyedropper

With Tint, you can also click the eyedropper tool to bring up a crosshair. Just click on a neutral grey or white point to remove any colour casts.

Correct common photo problems

Underexposed? Wonky? Blue? We show you how easy it is to correct typical image issues

There's always room for improvement when it comes to photography. By cropping photos you can enhance the overall composition and draw attention to the focal point. By tinkering with exposure you can draw out details previously lost in the shadows or blown out in the highlights. Pumping up the saturation will make colours pop and increasing the image's definition can help to correct lens distortion and camera shake. iPhoto's Edit suite is the perfect place for making all these changes, as it's easy to use and stacked full of helpful post-shoot solutions. Its Quick Fixes section addresses typical photo flaws, the Effects tab gives users access to one-click presets and Adjust offers precision controls for enhanced editing. We show you how to turn images from mundane to mesmerising.

> "Edit is easy to use and stacked full of post-shoot solutions"

Quick Fixes

Your one-stop panel for getting better edits

Effects

The Effects tab contains a palette of preset options that attempt to resolve problems with one simple click of a button. Come here for easy-to-rectify complaints, but for more precision it's better to use Adjust

Adjust

The Adjust palette contains dozens of controls ideal for gently tweaking certain aspects of the image. They can easily be reversed by pulling the slider back the other way

Preview

Changes are shown in real-time in the Edit suite. As you pull sliders or hit preset Edit buttons, the changes occur automatically on the Preview image. Remember that you can always use Undo to go back a step

Revert to Original

If you decide you're not happy with the changes you have made, you can easily start again by hitting the Revert to Original button, or use this to dismiss all adjustments and keep the image the way it was

FIX RED-EYE

Red-eye occurs as the result of the flash illuminating the back of our retinas. Usually this isn't a problem, but when it's very dark or the subject is young, old, tired or under the influence, it can take too long for the pupil to close and so red-eye occurs. In Edit's Quick Fixes panel, use the Fix Red-Eye option to add black circles in place of the red ones.

iPhoto Fixing photos with iPhoto's Edit suite

01: Distracting backgrounds

It's all about what you want people to see. If a photo has distracting elements, the eye will drift from the subject. Use Edit's Crop tool to focus attention.

02: Orientation issues

If you shot a photo in one orientation but think it works better in the other, go to Crop, tick Constrain and select Constrain as Portrait (or vice versa).

03: Exposure

A dark image is underexposed; too bright and it's overexposed. In Adjust, tweak the exposure. Lift the Shadows and Highlights sliders to regain details, too.

04: Wonky horizons

If your horizon is a little off kilter, head into Edit's Quick Fixes followed by Straighten. Just drag the slider to perfect the result. Hit Done when satisfied.

05: Make softness sharp

A slow shutter captures soft movement, and a wide aperture creates soft backgrounds. If you want either to be crisper, drag the Definition slider right.

06: Make sharpness soft

We can use Effects' Edge Blur tool to soften edges. This is particularly useful when you want to draw attention to the centre or focal part of the frame.

07: Drab to dazzling

Sometimes images need more punch. Do this by boosting Saturation in Adjust. If there are people in the image, click 'Avoid saturating skin tones'.

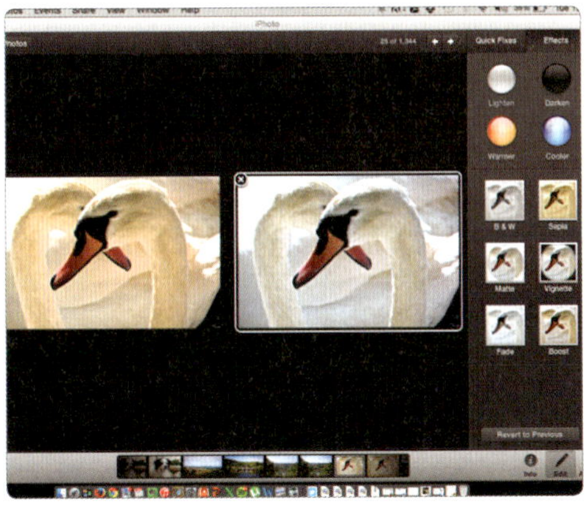

08: Colour cast

Cameras can get colours wrong, so whites looking slightly blue (cool) or orange (warm). To reverse this, take the Temperature scale in an opposite direction.

09: Go further

If you want to make more amazing images, but feel iPhoto has its limits, go check out some great photography apps on page 181.

Prepare your iPhoto library for Photos

The iPad allows users to alter the background on the lock screen as well as the main home screens, here's how…

When Apple first announced OS X Yosemite in June 2014, it also announced that it would be developing a new app, called Photos. At the time, it simply said that it would be available in early 2015, and that it would be replacing both iPhoto and Aperture on the Mac. It's recently been released, meaning many will want to make the switch from iPhoto to the new Photos.

If you're worried about switching - don't be. The new app integrates much more easily with iCloud, as well as offering new and more powerful editing tools. But to prepare for the swtich, it's time to start organising your library to make the transition quick and easy. These tips will not only help you keep your iPhoto library in top condition, it will also ensure that all your photos are sorted properly when you move over to the new app on your Mac.

iPhoto Get ready for the Photos app

01: Merge Events

One way to clean up a library is to tidy Events. A new event is created for a each new date. Drag one onto another, or right-click and select Merge Events.

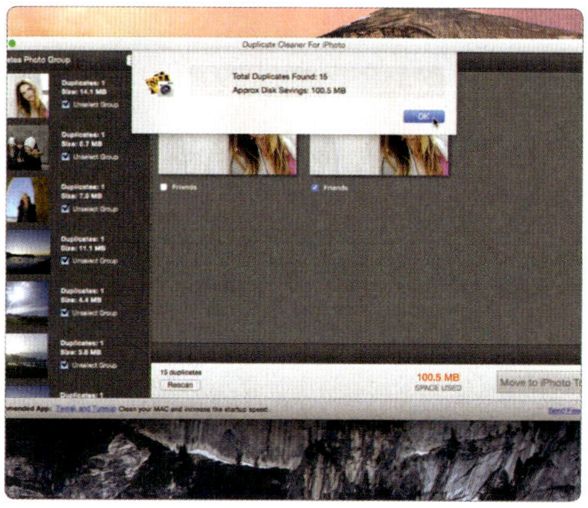

02: Remove duplicates

Grab an app called Duplicate Cleaner For iPhoto for free from the App Store to search your library for images that are duplicated, and then delete them.

03: Add keywords

Go through and add keywords to as many photos as possible. This makes it easier to search for a specific shot when you switch to Photos.

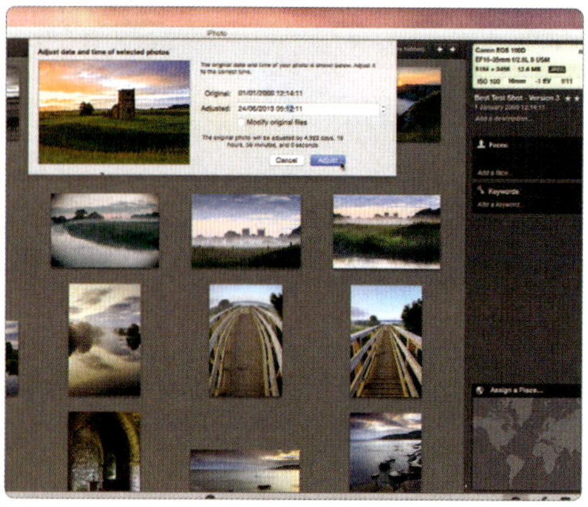

04: Change dates and times

If you took your photos on a camera that wasn't set up properly, dates and times may not be correct. To change this, click Photos>Adjust Date and Time.

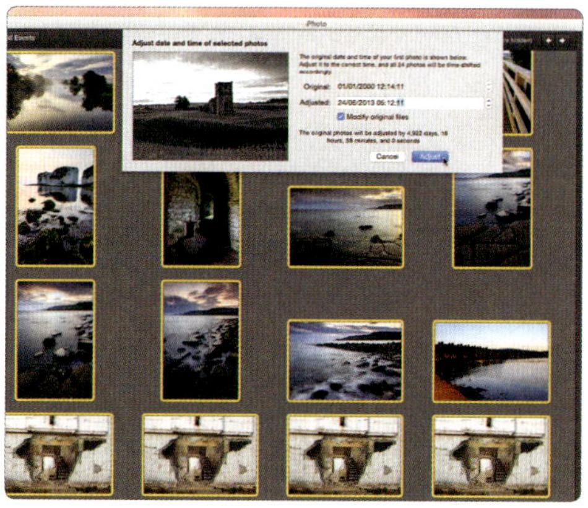

05: Update them all

You can also edit multiple shots – select all the shots and choose the same option. Set the time of the first shot and the rest will adjust accordingly.

06: Add location data

If you took photos in a location without a GPS locator, you may want to add location data to make them easier to search. Choose a photo and click Info.

The finishing touches

Perfect your library before the big migration

Safe to edit

Any edits you have made to your photos will be transferred into the new app, and they will still be non-destructive, so you will be able to revert to the original photo with a click if you wish

Titles and descriptions

Add Titles and Descriptions to all your shots where possible – the more descriptive words you use, the easier it will be to find your photos with a search when you make the switch to the new app

PHOTOS IN ICLOUD

The new Photos app will sync up with iCloud to save your shots online, so all of your images will be accessible on all of your devices. Currently, you can increase the storage space on your iOS devices by only downloading optimised versions of shots, and keeping the full-resolution images online – the same will be the case for Photos for Mac, too.

Back it up (twice)

When you're happy with your library clean-up, open your Pictures folder and back up your iPhoto library to an external drive. You can also back it up with Time Machine to make sure your shots are safe

Finish your projects

Be sure to make a backup and finish your projects before you make the switch. While nothing should be lost when you move your photos over, it will be a large amount of data, and it's better to be safe than sorry

07: Search and pinpoint

Click Assign a Place and type a location to search. Select the correct one, then click and drag on the pin, dropping it where the shot was taken.

08: Add a Key Photo

Go back to the Events view, and hover your cursor over an event. Scroll through shots by moving your mouse, then hit the Spacebar to set a Key Photo.

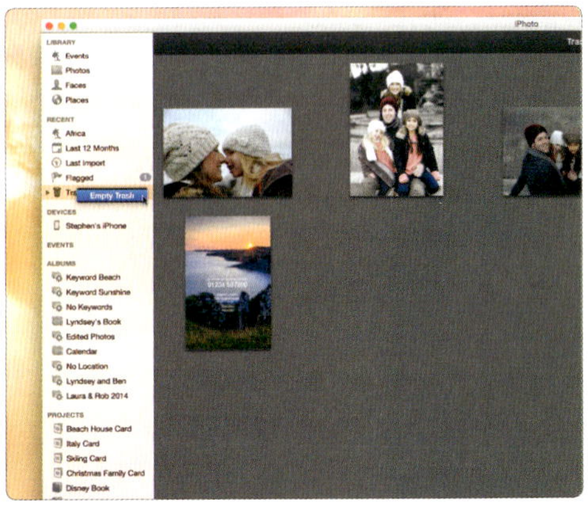

09: Empty the Trash

When you've finished cleaning your library, don't forget to empty the Trash by right-clicking on the icon for Empty Trash – this saves a lot of disk space.

Create a Side by Side clip in iMovie

Play multiple clips onscreen at the same time by modifying iMovie's Video Overlay settings

One way to make a stimulating video sequence is to play multiple clips simultaneously, courtesy of iMovie's Side by Side video overlay setting. This enables you to share a montage of clips in a more interesting way than by simply cutting from one shot to the next. The Side by Side command is perfect for creating slick title sequences, or for enhancing dramas by showing the action unfold from different camera angles.

Here, we'll demonstrate how to modify the Side by Side command to make clips slide in and out as they share the screen. You'll also learn how to swap the position of clips so that you can see the appropriate half of each inserted shot. You can download files to use in the tutorial at **www.filesilo.co.uk/bks-598**.

"Enhance drama by showing the action unfold"

iMovie Create a side-by-side sequence

01: Create new event

Go to File>New Event. Label this 'Side by Side'. Click Import Media. Browse to our source clips and select. Set the Import menu to Side by Side. Click Import.

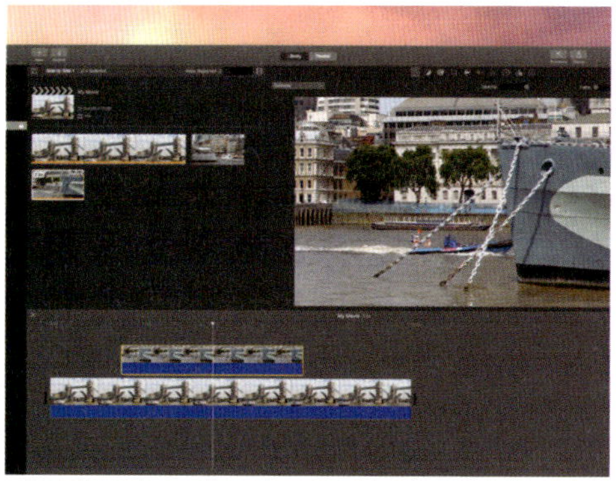

02: Add a cutaway

Double click the 'Bridge' clip and drag it to the Timeline. Double click 'Insert01' and drag that to the Timeline. It will automatically appear as a cutaway.

03: Choose Side by Side

Set the Cutaway drop-down menu to Side by Side. Click the Right button to place the inserted clip to the right of the frame. This suits its composition.

04: Make smooth transitions

Play the sequence. The two clips jump into position. Set Slide to one second. Now it slides smoothly into position as they share the screen.

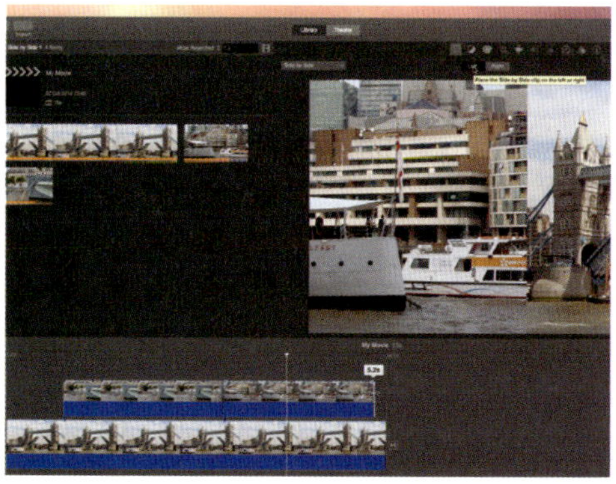

05: Add second clip

Trim three seconds from the end of 'Insert01'. Add 'Insert02' as a second side-by-side clip. Trim two seconds from the end. Click the Left button.

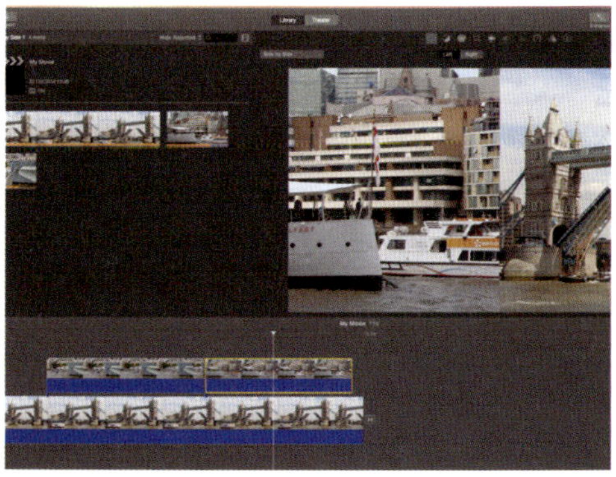

06: Make it slide

Set 'Insert02' clip's Slide value to one second. Play the sequence. The two inserted clips slide in and out as the background sequence plays.

Top dictation tips

Get more from one of OS X's latest features

Side by Side
By default the inserted clip on the top layer of the Timeline will replace the clip on the layer below as a cutaway. Click here to change it to a Side by Side clip that will share the screen

FADE IN AND OUT
To get your side-by-side sequence to fade up from black at the start and down to black at the end, go to the Content Library panel and click Transitions. Drag the Cross Dissolve transition to the start of the sequence. Drag another Cross Dissolve to the end of the sequence. This transition will create a fade up from black at the start and a fade to black at the end.

Video overlay
To make overlapping clips run side by side onscreen simultaneously, you need to first access the Video Overlay Settings in the Adjustments Bar

Slide in
By default the inserted Side by Side clip will jump into shot. Increase the Slide value to make both the inserted and background clips slide smoothly into each half of the screen

Left or right?
Use these buttons to make the inserted clip on the top layer appear at the left or right of the screen. This helps you to keep important detail onscreen when the inserted shot is cut in half

07: Add a title
Click the Titles browser and drag the Line title onto the Timeline. Position the title and adjust its duration so it appears over the inserted clips.

08: Modify the text
Modify the placeholder text to read 'River Life'. Double click on the 'Life' text field and click the B icon to make it bolder. This text adds an extra layer.

09: Add music
Click the Sound Effects browser and go to Jingles. Drag a track into the Timeline. Trim the end of the jingle to finish as the title sequences does.

Master iMovie's editing timeline

Take control of your movies with these tips and tricks for getting more from the timeline

Many of the features of the timeline changed with the latest release of iMovie. For a start, by default the timeline moved from the top-left of the interface to the bottom of the screen, making it similar to the design of Final Cut Pro X. However, there have been other changes and some new features that can help you edit movies more easily.

Support for iPhone's slow-motion video is now built directly into the timeline, and with customising tools you'll have an interface that's perfect for your workflow. Whether you're a newcomer to the app or you have some experience of creating great home movies, we've got the tips and tricks you need to get started with iMovie. You'll be editing and sharing some amazing creations in no time.

"You'll be editing amazing creations in no time"

iMovie Take control of the timeline

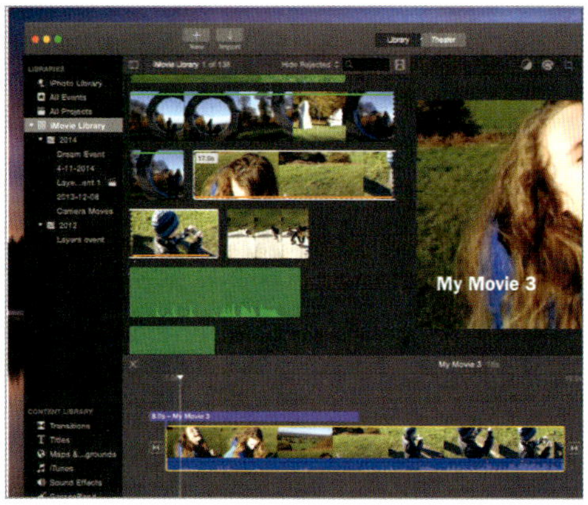

01: Add clips

Open or create a new project and the timeline will appear at the bottom. Drag and drop video clips into it from the Events Browser in the top-left.

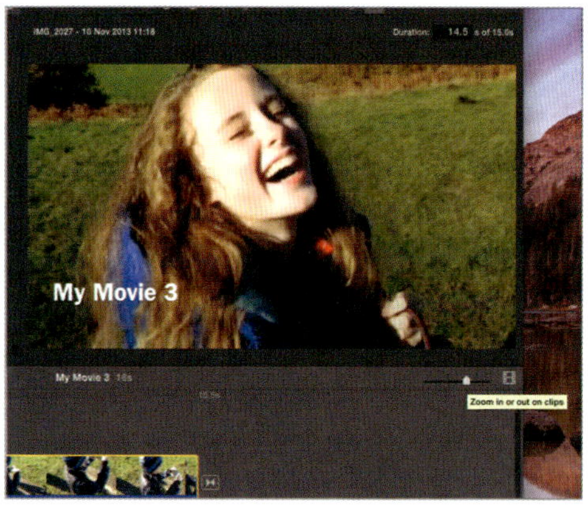

02: Expand your view

Use the slider in the top-right to adjust the length of the timeline. You can also use a trackpad like those found on MacBooks to adjust this with a pinch.

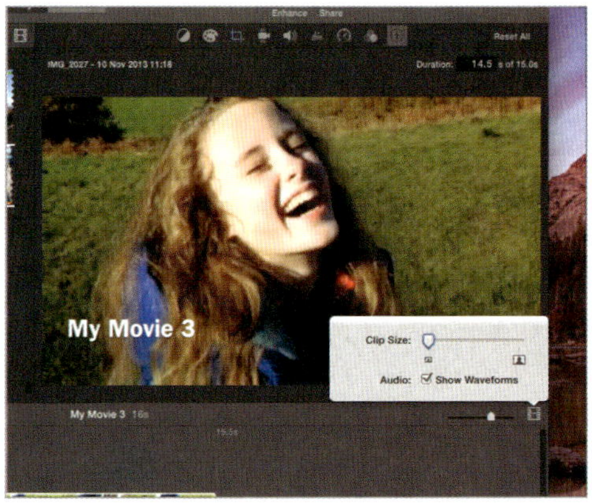

03: View audio waveforms

Click the icon next to the zoom slider and you'll be able to show the audio waveforms for each clip, you can pick out speech or reduce the volume.

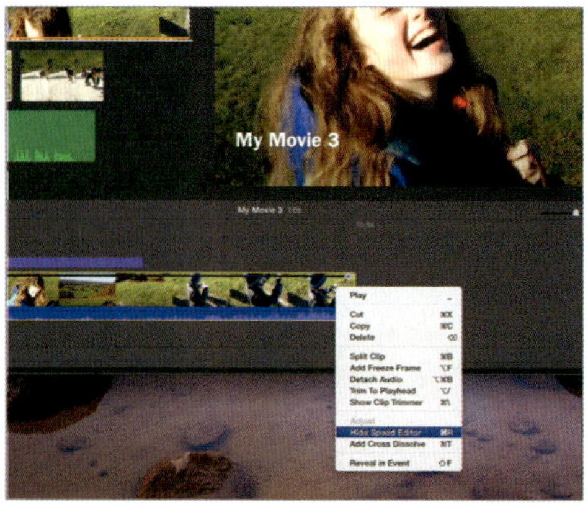

04: Slow clips down

Clips recorded in slow-motion will offer controls for adjusting the speed inside the timeline. Access these for other clips by right-clicking.

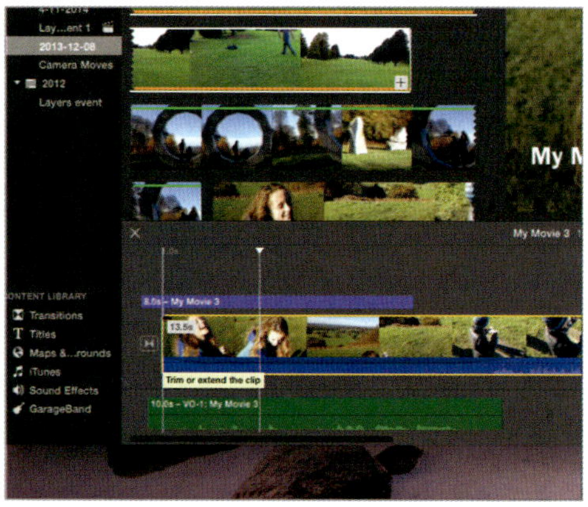

05: Clip Trimmer

Double-click on a clip and the Trimmer will open. This enables you to closely control the length of your clips; just drag the sliders or the clip to adjust.

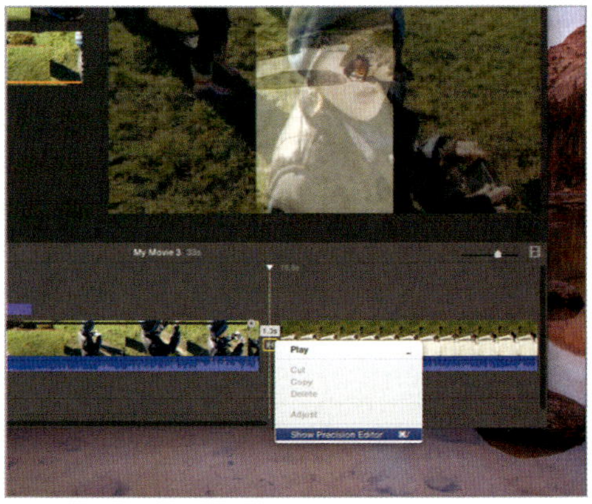

06: Precision Editor

Double-click on the space between two clips or right-click on a transition and then select Show Precision Editor to open the interface.

Customising your view

Quick tips to help you get more from iMovie's timeline

Wrapping Timeline

To fit more movie into your timeline at once, you can use the Wrapping Timeline. To activate it, simply click View>Wrapping Timeline. Clips no longer scroll off the right of the screen, but show over multiple lines

Clip size

You can adjust the vertical size of a clip using the menu in the top-right corner of the timeline. Click it and use the slider to increase or decrease the size of the thumbnails in the timeline

CLIP OR MOVIE AUDIO?

The track at the bottom of the timeline is for audio that flows throughout the clip, like music. Each clip has its own audio, but remember that you can adjust the audio levels of both, so you can hear speech from a clip over the music, or mute the clip audio to make sure the music is prominent.

Multi-track timeline

You can drop clips over others in the timeline, and then view the two clips side-by-side, use one as a cutaway clip or with a picture-in-picture setting. This is perfect in case you would want to drop a clip in but continue the main clip's audio in the background

Quick trim

To quickly trim a clip, you don't need to double-click it to open the Clip Trimmer every time. Simply grab the start or end of the clip and drag it left or right to adjust the length of the clip while maintaining its position

07: Editing transitions

With the Precision Editor, you can drag the two clips around to set the exact start and end point, and drag the middle control to change transition length.

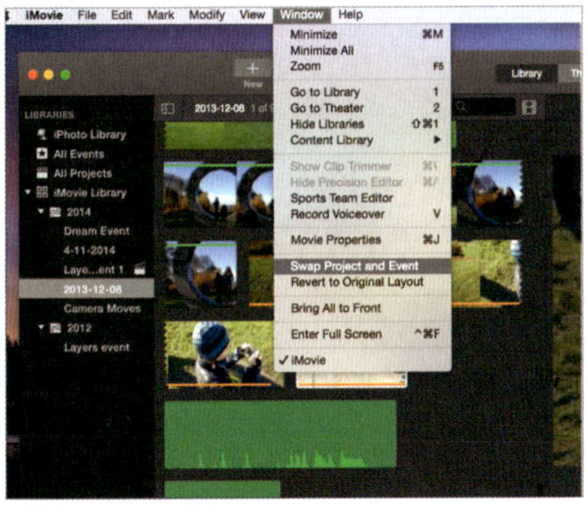

08: Flip the timeline

If you want to revert to a more classic look, you can swap the clip viewer with the timeline by selecting Window>Swap Project and Event from the menu.

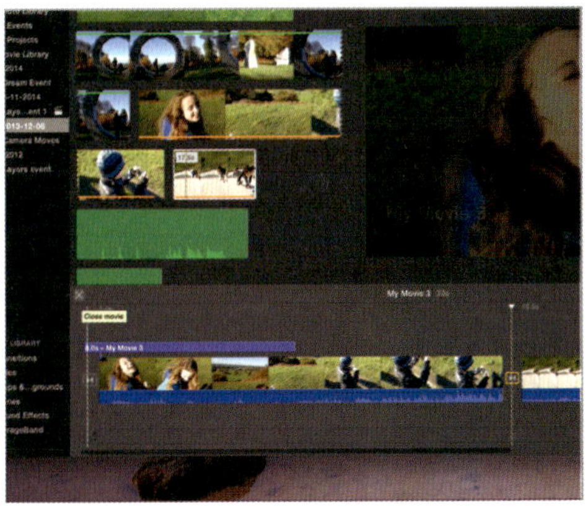

09: Close the timeline

When you're finished, you can click on the cross in the top-left of the timeline to close it. This is also perfect for viewing your events in a wider space.

Stack clips with iMovie's multi-track tool

Layer your video clips, audio, music and sound effects and make it easier to edit projects

iMovie is a core part of your Mac's creative software. The most up-to-date version of iMovie has so many different functions and tools available to you that you'd be hard pressed to find any limitations to what you can achieve. A huge benefit to iMovie is the ability to add multiple tracks to your timelines. Doing this enables you to stack your clips above one another, and by assigning your primary video track for your main clips, you can use the secondary track for your cutaways, which also makes editing a much faster process. iMovie also offers a series of tools when using multiple tracks, including Green/Blue Screen, Side by Side and Picture in Picture. You can also set up multiple audio tracks. Follow along with these six simple steps to multi-tracking.

> "A huge benefit is the ability to add multiple tracks"

Green/Blue Screen settings

Superimposing clips in iMovie

Apply effect
Click here to apply all of the changes that you have made using the Green/Blue screen tool. You can then edit the clip using other tools such as Enhance and colour correction

Cropping
You can crop a clip to remove parts of the image by clicking and dragging on the corners of the clip. Use this to remove elements of a clip or image that Green/Blue Screen can't remove

Eraser
Select this tool and then click on parts of a clip where green or blue are still showing. The eraser will remove this colour tone from all parts of the clip for you, tidying up the shot

Softness
Once you've placed a clip, use the Softness bar to better remove blue or green areas. The slider can also help to soften the edges of artefacts within the layered clip

HOW GREEN/BLUE SCREEN WORKS

Green/Blue Screen is an approach to superimposing video on video. An actor or object is placed in front of a green or blue screen. In post-production, software is then used to identify the blue or green in an image and then remove it entirely from the shot, creating a transparent backdrop so the clip can be superimposed onto another.

iMovie Add multiple tracks in iMovie

01: Side-by-side

Select a clip and drag it onto the timeline. Drag the next clip to the end of the first one. iMovie will link the clips, so one will follow onto another.

02: Add another track

Drag another clip onto the timeline above the first clip and place it anywhere on the timeline. It will be set as a cutaway, cutting to it where it appears.

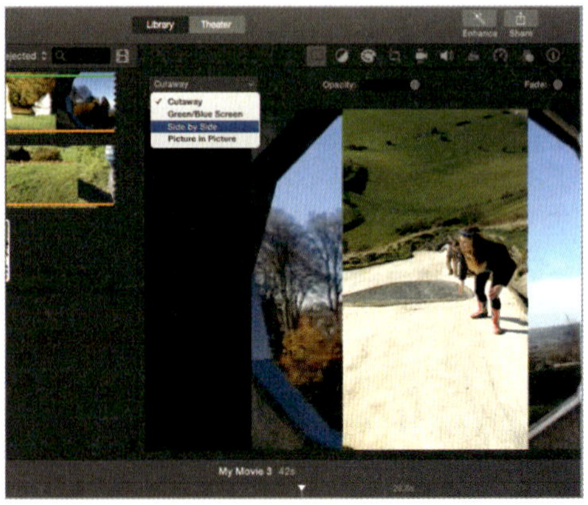

03: Video Overlay

Select this clip. Select Video Overlay settings above the viewer window. Click on Cutaway, select Side by Side. Use the slide dial to create a sliding transition.

04: Picture in Picture

In the Overlay settings menu, select 'Picture in Picture'. You can resize, reposition and add a border to the clip in the second track and add an opening.

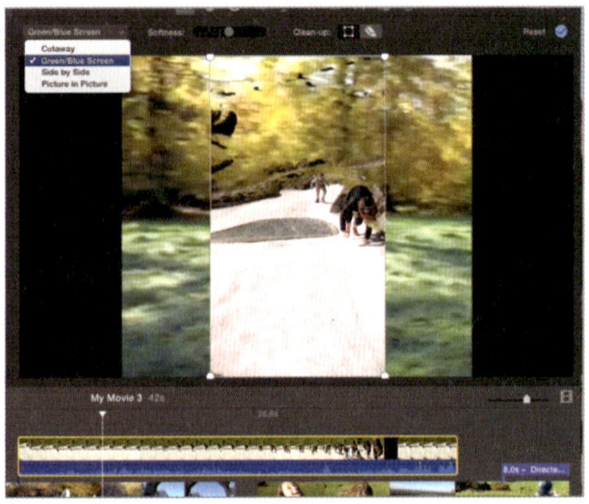

05: Green/Blue screen

Import a clip that has green or blue in it. Place it above a clip. Select Green/Blue screen in Overlay settings and use Softness to remove the green.

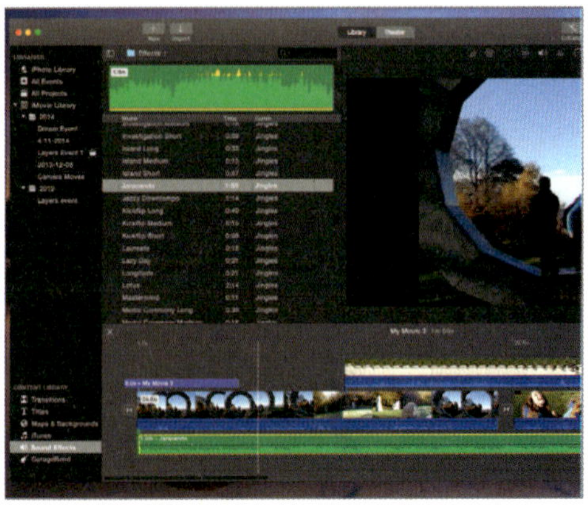

06: Audio layers

Apply multiple audio tracks as you would video. Use the bottom audio track as the primary one, on which you might want to place the soundtrack.

Editing audio tracks

When it comes to editing, if you're working with multiple audio tracks then it's important that you take the time to balance out the levels between them, so that your end movie has a nice, even mix. Audio can be edited in a number of ways in iMovie – in these two short steps, you'll see how easy it is to gain control of multiple audio tracks when you're working in iMovie.

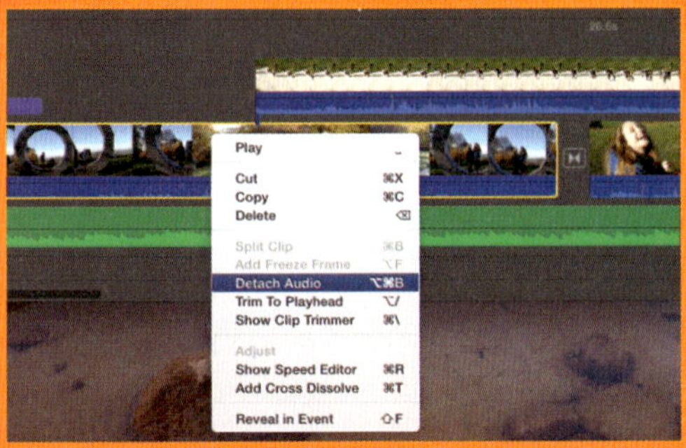

1: Detach audio

Right-click on any clips in your timeline that contain audio. Select Detach Audio. The clip's audio track will now be separated from the video and automatically placed in an audio layer above the other audio tracks in your timeline.

2: Master audio track

Once all your audio is in the timeline, select the audio track that you want to be most audibly present. Open the Adjust panel above the viewer window, click on the sound icon and select the 'Lower Volume of Other clips' option.

Adjust colour in movie clips

Correct colour problems for more attractive clips, courtesy of iMovie's colour controls

There are many reasons why you might want to adjust a clip's colours. For starters your camera/camcorder can find it a challenge to capture a scene's true colours. Different light sources (such as natural daylight or artificial indoor light) produce different colour temperatures. This can cause outdoor footage to look too cold (blue) or indoor clips to look too warm (orange). You can set your camera to use a suitable white balance preset setting (such as a Daylight, Cloudy etc), which will cause the camera to create white-looking whites and counteract any warm or cool colour casts. However, due to other camera presets you may find that your footage's colours look drab and desaturated. Thankfully iMovie can make these colours appear more vibrant as you'll discover in our walkthrough.

"iMovie can make these colours appear more vibrant"

Colour correction

Take control over problem colours

Color correction
This icon gives you access to more colour adjusting tools. You can manually boost a clip's saturation strength using a slider or click the Enhance icon to let iMovie automatically attempt to improve the colour and tone

Non-destructive corrections
You can experiment with different colour adjustments safe in the knowledge that you can always click the Reset button and restore the clip to its original state

Color Balance
Click this icon to access a host of tools designed to create a healthy white balance. Tools such as the White Balance eyedropper enable you to remove warm or cool colour casts from every frame of your footage in one click

Temperature
If a shot is too cold and suffers from a blue colour cast, drag this slider to the right to create tint-free colours. If it looks too warm (orange) then drag the slider to the left to cool things down

PICTURE STYLES
By taking control over your camera or camcorder, you can modify colour in-camera, which saves you adjusting colour using iMovie's post-production tools. Choose a white balance preset that suits the scene (such as Tungsten for indoor lighting). You can also choose picture styles such as Vibrant, which will produce clips with strongly saturated colours.

iMovie Correct and improve colours

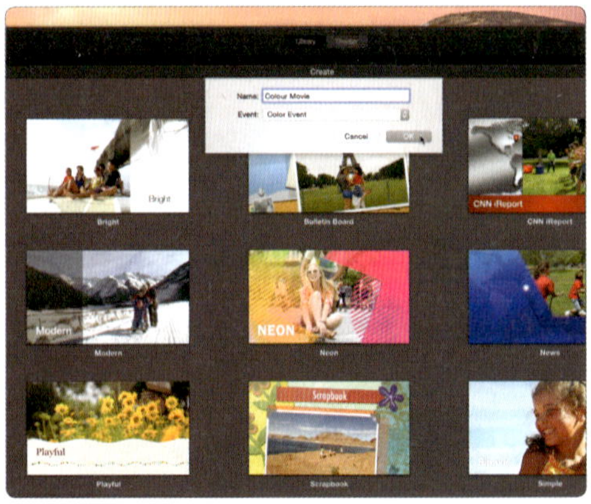

01: Create an event

Go to File>New Event. Label it 'Colour Event'. Go to File>New Movie. In the Create window choose No Theme. Click Create. Name it 'Colour Movie', click OK.

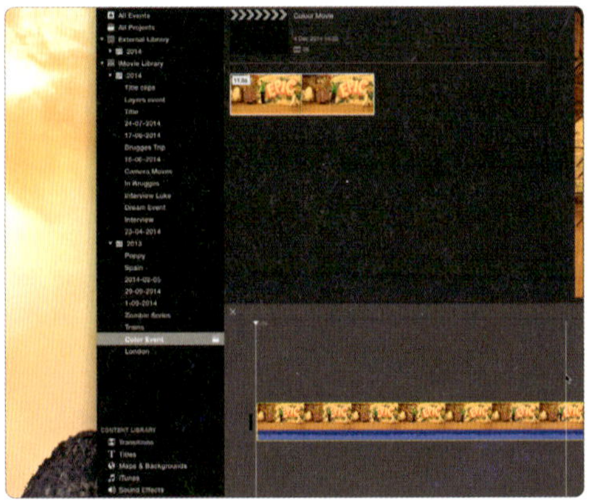

02: Import a warm clip

A new Project icon appears, and an empty Timeline. Click the Import Media button and browse to a source clip. In our example our clip looks too warm.

03: Get the balance right

Click the Color Balance icon above. There's the option to click on the Skin Tone Balance or the White Balance buttons. The latter is more precise.

04: Cool it down

Click the eyedropper on an object that should be a neutral white. If the area is too warm, the tool cools it down, creating more natural colours everywhere.

05: Weak colours

You can set some cameras to use a neutral picture style that produces drab colours. This allows you to decide how vibrant the colours will look.

06: Boost saturation

To manually boost the strength of a clip's colours, click the Color Correction icon above. Drag the Saturation slider to boost the colours' vibrancy.

07: Tweak tones

Brightening up underexposed areas can reveal drab colours, so a boost in saturation is a good plan. A contrast boost can create more vibrant colours, too.

08: Match Color

A series of clips with an inconsistent colour balance won't cut together in the Timeline. Click the Color Balance icon and then click Match Color.

09: Consistent white balance

Use the Eyedropper tool to click on the corrected clip. Click to make the problem clip match the selected frame's healthier colours and tones.

Add blockbuster effects to your movies

Use post-production techniques to give your clips a slick Hollywood-style finish

When you watch the 'making of' footage of a Hollywood blockbuster, the quality of the clip looks different when the same scene is viewed in the finished movie. This is because Hollywood spends much time and effort digitally altering the colours and tones of footage to give it a specific look. They may also add digital camera moves such as a zoom to make a statically framed shot look more dynamic, or re-time the footage to speed through the action and then suddenly slow things down to focus on a specific event.

We'll show you how to indulge in a little Hollywood style grading, add a vignette effect and create some speed ramps to give your footage a more dynamic blockbuster look. You'll also discover how to plunder extra music and graphical assets from iMovie's Trailers features. We'll then help you master the interface, making address keeping slicker than ever.

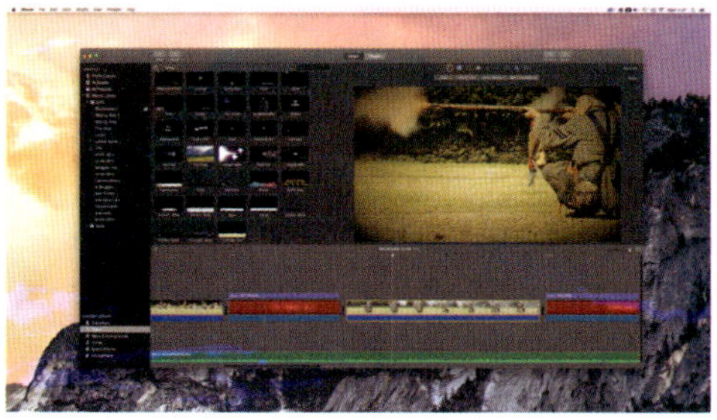

iMovie Apply blockbuster post-production effects

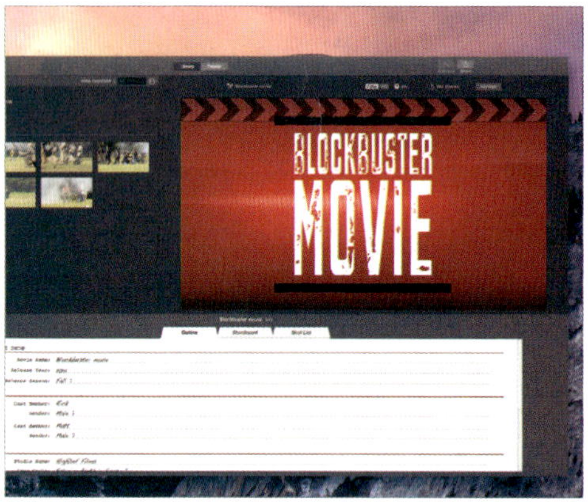

01: Create a trailer

Create a new Event, import our seven clips and choose File>New Trailer. Select the Action trailer. Click Create, label it Blockbuster movie and click OK.

02: Convert to movie

Choose Convert Trailer to Movie for access to assets such as a studio logo, graphics and music you can't find elsewhere. Delete the grey placeholders.

03: Add the clips

Shift-click to select the seven clips and drag them to just after the studio globe has finished playing. The up tempo music enhances the battlefield action.

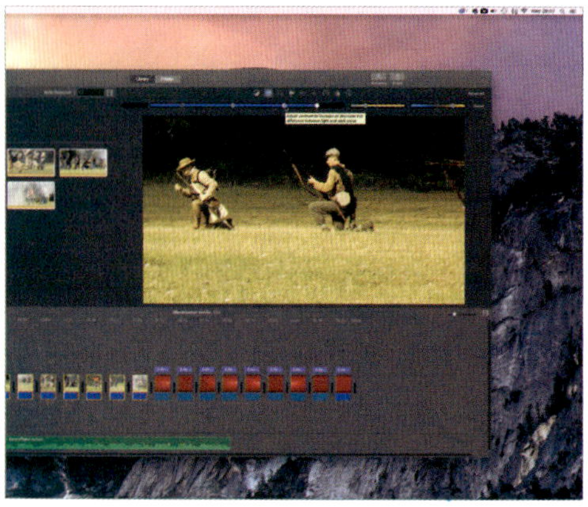

04: Grade the clip

The clips selected, click Colour correction. Increase the contrast, drop the strength of the saturation and warm up the temperature for a retro sepia tint.

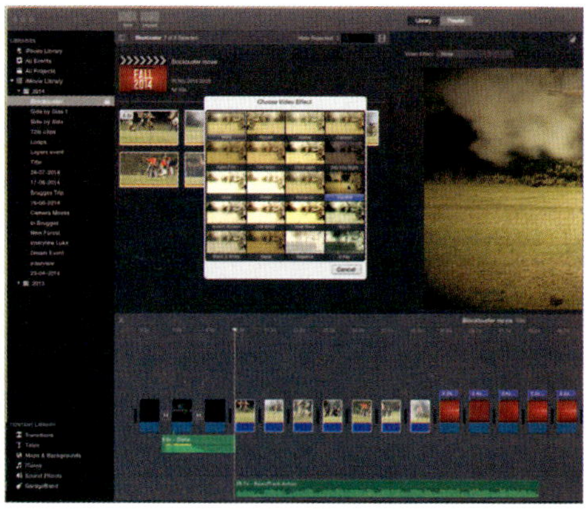

05: Add a vignette

Click the Video and Audio effects icon. Set Video Effect to Vignette to darken the edges. The grading and vignette will be applied to all the selected clips.

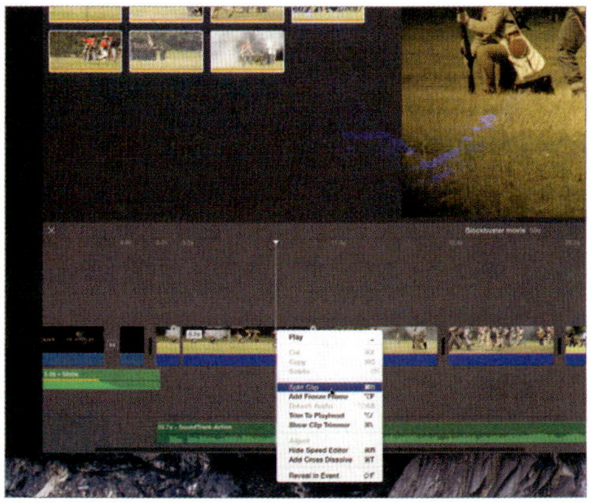

06: Split the first clip

On clip 01, scrub the playhead to just after the first shot. Choose Modify>Split Clip. Scrub forward to and split the clip again after the soldier kneels.

Blockbuster effects

Edit colour, tone and add effects

Video effects

After manually tweaking a clip's colours and tones you can add further enhancements by clicking on one of these preset video effect thumbnails. Here we've added a vignetted edge to give our retro subject a vintage look

Colour correction

Click here to adjust a selected shot's colour saturation, tone and temperature by dragging sliders. This enables you to give each clip a distinctive look (such as the warm vintage tint in this example)

COPY AND PASTE

After experimenting with colour adjustments, video effects and Ken Burns camera moves, select the modified clip and choose Edit>Copy. You can then select an unprocessed clip in the Timeline and choose Edit>Paste Adjustments. Pick All, or select to transfer a particular adjustment such as Colour Correction, Crop, Video Effect or Speed.

Speed ramps

To give your production a more dynamic pace you can split a clip into three sections and then speed up the middle part using iMovie's Fast Forward menu

Trailer effects

By converting a trailer into a movie you can access extra graphical and musical assets that aren't available in the Content Library, such as a spinning globe logo that endows your production with a blockbuster look

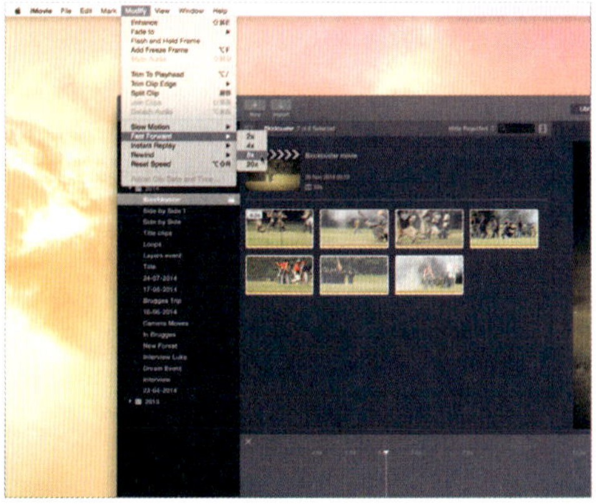

07: Add a speed ramp

Shot01 is now in three sections. Select the middle section. Go to Modify>Fast Forward>8x. This adds a dynamic burst of action to the middle of the clip.

08: Create a digital zoom

Click on Shot04 and click the Cropping icon. Click Ken Burns, then the End window. Resize, reposition it for a close-up on the canon. Click the tick.

09: Add titles

Drag and drop the animated titles between clips. Click on the text in the main window and edit it. Feel free to add speed ramps to other sections.

Create your own loops in GarageBand

How to broaden GarageBand's fruitful loops library with your own creations

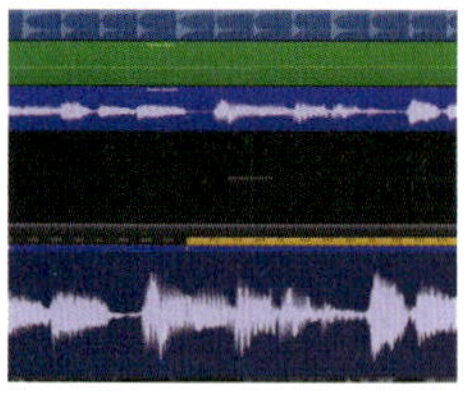

GarageBand is a loop-based audio editor by definition. It simplifies the process of composition and digital music arrangement by building up tracks in this way. Smaller modular regions of audio are replicated as 'loops' over defined bars based on tempo and time signature. The suite includes preset drum, bass, piano and many more loops – ideal for creating tracks rapidly. However, as you progress and lay on real audio recordings and input MIDI-based software instruments, you'll inevitably form your own. Luckily, GarageBand makes this so easy you might not realise it, but there are best practice techniques. We'll go through those here, from identifying suitable regions to cutting them down to size and expanding. To finish, we'll look at adding new loops to your library for repeated use.

Identifying essential loop areas and tools

Where to look on the GarageBand interface when creating loops

LOOP DESCRIPTORS

GarageBand tags your loop with the key and tempo defined by the source project. However, the 'Add loop to library' dialog does let you recommend how strictly this should be adhered to. Saved loops will adjust to match the target tempo and pitch whereas 'one-shot' examples remain fixed. Versatility will vary here, especially with real audio loops over software/MIDI equivalents.

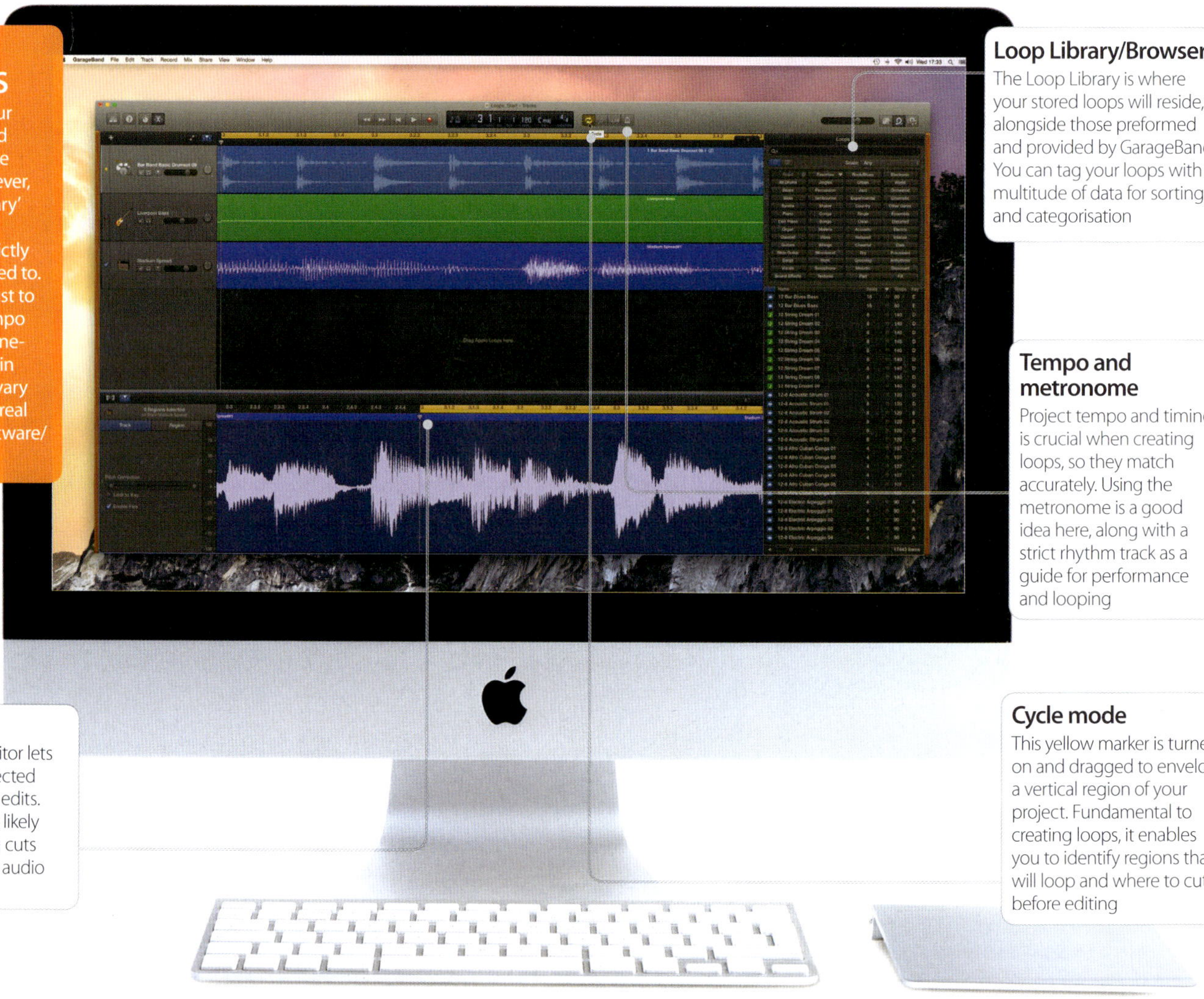

Loop Library/Browser

The Loop Library is where your stored loops will reside, alongside those preformed and provided by GarageBand. You can tag your loops with a multitude of data for sorting and categorisation

Tempo and metronome

Project tempo and timing is crucial when creating loops, so they match accurately. Using the metronome is a good idea here, along with a strict rhythm track as a guide for performance and looping

Track Editor

GarageBand's Track Editor lets you get closer to a selected region to facilitate fine edits. In looping terms this is likely to mean administering cuts or splices, isolating the audio comprising the loop

Cycle mode

This yellow marker is turned on and dragged to envelop a vertical region of your project. Fundamental to creating loops, it enables you to identify regions that will loop and where to cut before editing

GarageBand Create your own loops

01: Ready your project

Loop creation begins with an existing project. Use your own or our 'Loops_Start' project, but preferably you'll have at least two tracks, one being real audio.

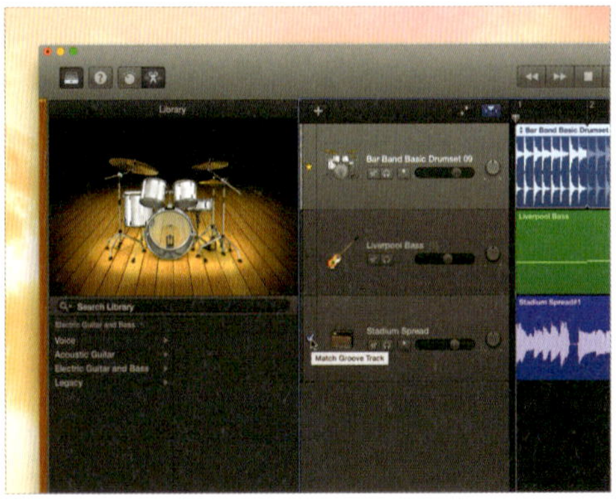

02: Tighten up timing

Before creating loops, you'll probably want to ensure your tracks are in time. Here we've set the drums as our Groove Track, matching our real audio track to it.

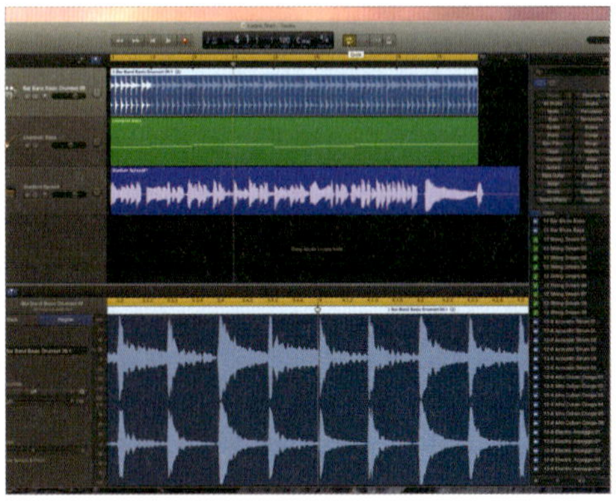

03: The Cycle mode

Toggle on the Cycle mode with the button in the top control bar. A yellow cycle bar appears in the ruler below. Drag into position to plot the loop region.

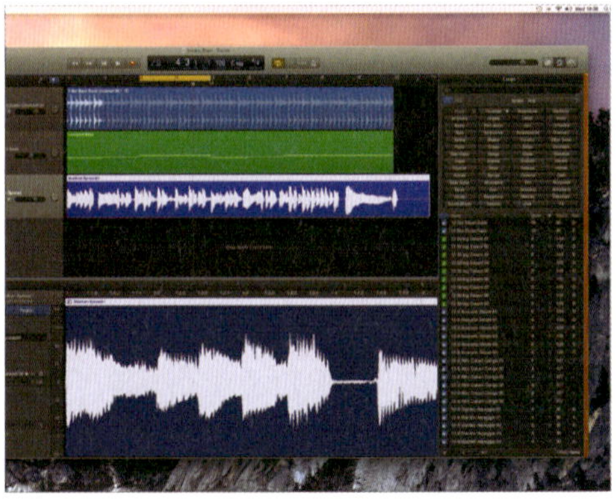

04: Seamless loop

Drag the yellow cycle marker along the ruler, until you cover a region. Play to preview and adjust until you find a perfect looping region.

05: Cutting it out

Stop playback and move the playhead to the start. Select Edit>Split Regions at Playhead or Cmd+T to cut the start point, before moving to the end to repeat.

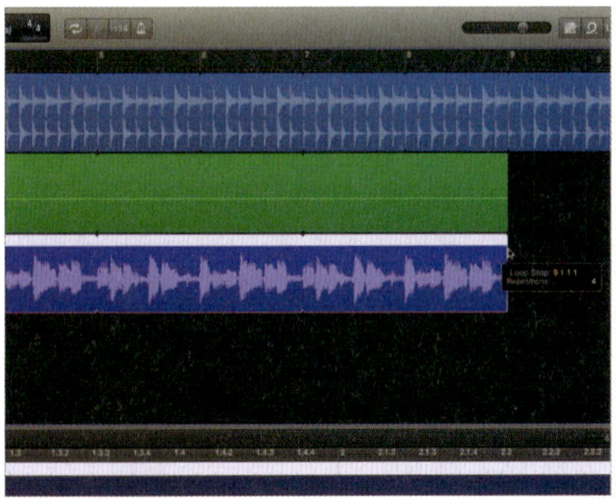

06: Dragging out to loop

Move the extracted region into position and hover over the top-right corner. A looping cursor enables you to drag the loop out over a desired duration.

07: Adding loop to Library

With your loop region selected, choose Add Region to Loop Library from the File menu. Add a description for the loop before saving to library.

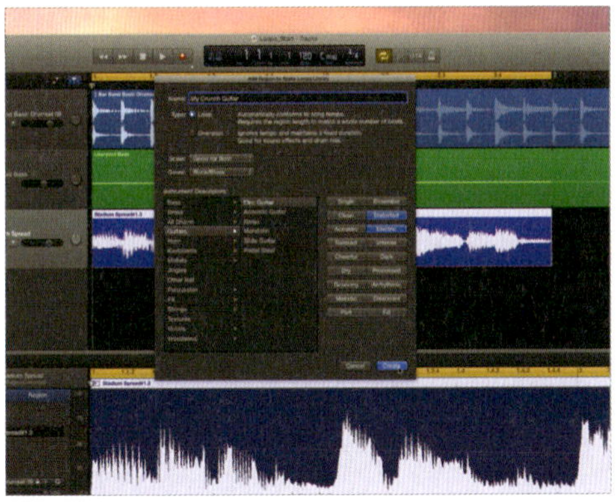

08: Add Region dialog

New loops must be given a unique name, a type, scale criteria, genre and description. Fill these in as desired before clicking the Create button to commit and save.

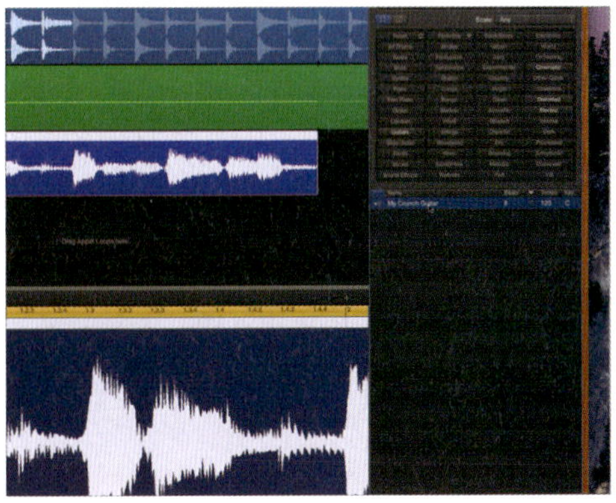

09: Browse the Library

Open the Loops browser panel and search or filter for your saved loop. It appears below for quick preview and can be dragged from the library into any project.

Use Drummer to add more natural beats

Produce more organic percussion via the roster of virtual stick twirlers in GarageBand

As you progress with GarageBand and your compositions become more ambitious, you'll hit a wall. This tends to happen most around drums because this is the hardest real instrumentation to capture. You need a big expensive kit and a seriously good microphone setup to get natural beats, when loops won't cut it anymore. Help is at hand, though, as Apple has introduced a dedicated feature to assist here, known simply as Drummer. Taken from sister music-maker Logic, composers will find a collection of 18 session player 'characters' across four popular genres. Each is fully customisable and accepts direction to fit your style, resulting in a much more dynamic and 'human' feel. Follow the steps and view the sample project to get a perfect 'kick' start with Drummer!

"Get a perfect kick start with Drummer!"

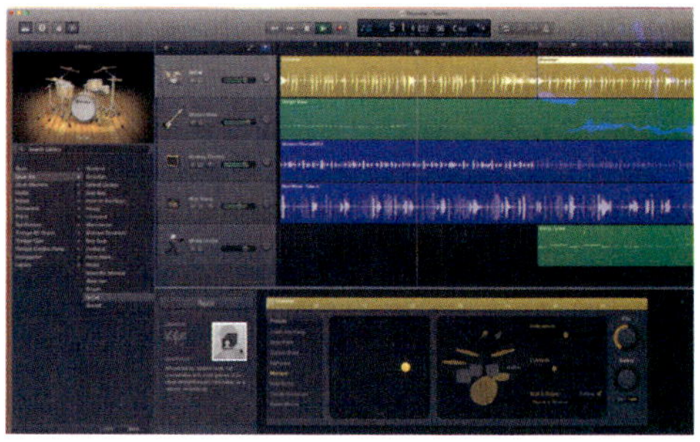

From dumb to Drummer

Wise up to the percussive possibilities that await you

Drummer track
The Drummer track is a special track type. Generated based on your Drummer preferences, it can't be edited in the same way as audio (blue) or MIDI (green) tracks but you can tweak Smart Controls

Drummer Editor
The Drummer Editor is active when the Drummer track is selected, allowing you to switch presets, tailor patterns with the X/Y pad and vary the instrumentation along with how fills/timings are used

Library
Drums and the 'SoCal' variety are applied to a new Drummer track, although you can switch this within the Library panel to the left. What's more you can even switch to other instruments like Piano!

Genre and Drummer
The genre pop-up menu provides access to the four general styles, so if you only see one you will need to download the rest. Below this is the Drummer overview showing the selected character

BANG FOR YOUR BUCK

Drummer starts out pretty limited with only one 'character' available, called Kyle. More influenced by modern rock, he's versatile enough for most initial applications and does provide a good sense of what Drummer is about. Previously the Additional Content in-app purchase of £2.99/$4.99, now free, was required to unlock the full 18 spanning styles including Rock, Alternative, Songwriter and R&B.

Garageband Add more human beats with Drummer

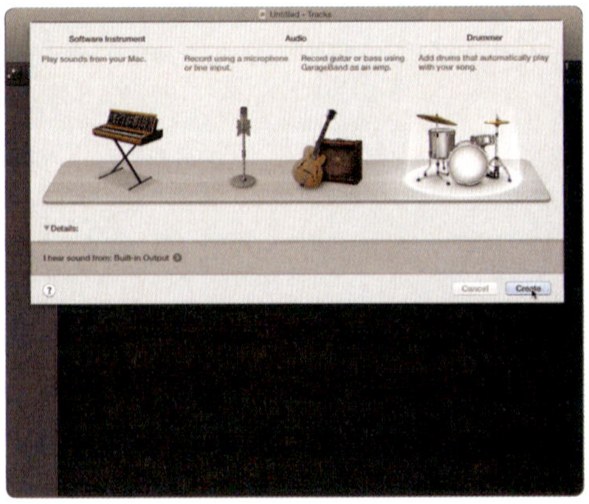

01: Add Drummer track

To start, add a yellow Drummer track - the fourth option from the New Tracks menu. You can have only one per project, or the option is ghosted out.

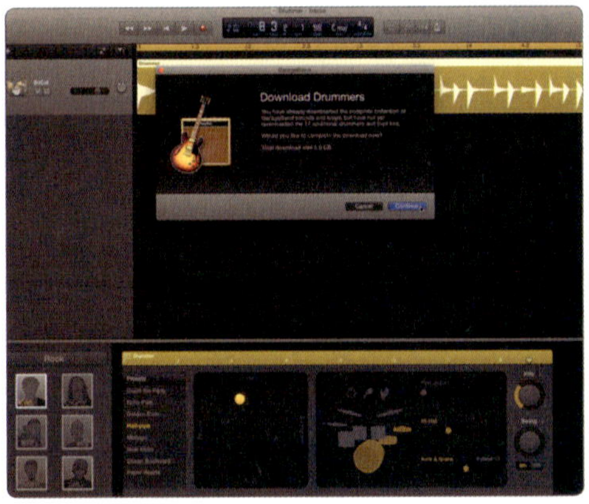

02: Download Drummers

With a Drummer track selected, click on 'Kyle' the default player. Roll over another Drummer and if it says Download you must install a 5.0GB add-on.

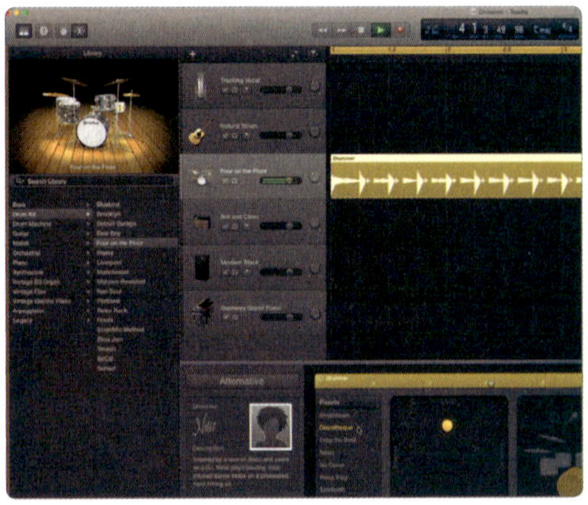

03: Pattern presets

With them all installed, you can switch Drummers within four genres. Each has some preset patterns to flick through. Preview the track with Space.

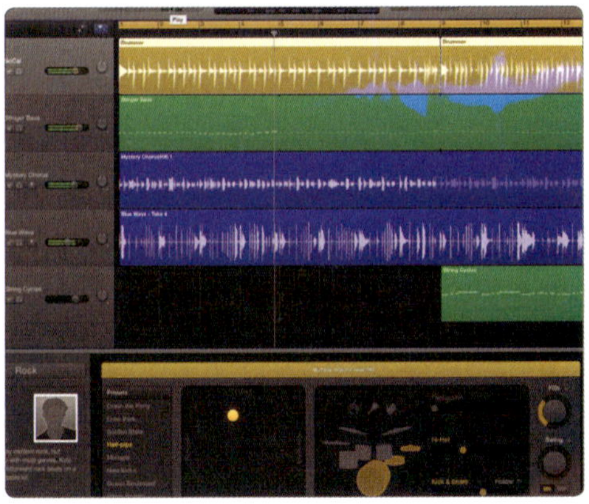

04: Accompanying tracks

Drummer works off other track recordings to be most effective. In our sample, we have bass, guitar, synth tracks and the default Kyle track.

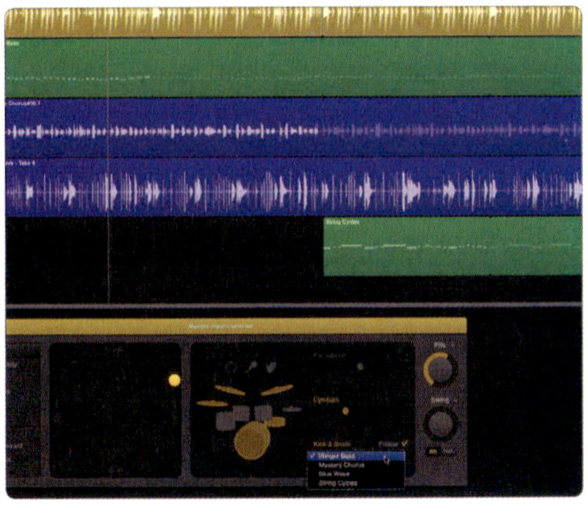

05: Presets and Follow

Choose a preset pattern - we picked Mixtape. In the Drummer Editor, check Follow and pick Stinger Bass to lock the beat to the bassline.

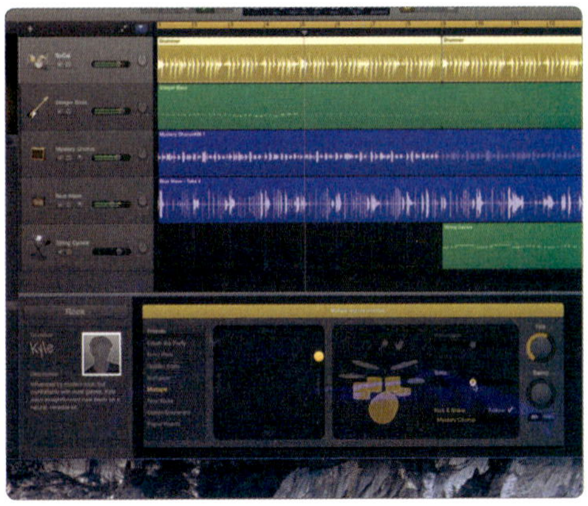

06: Using the kit

Switching the Follow track changes the timing. Use the kit diagram to isolate drum or percussion and use the sliders to dictate the amount used.

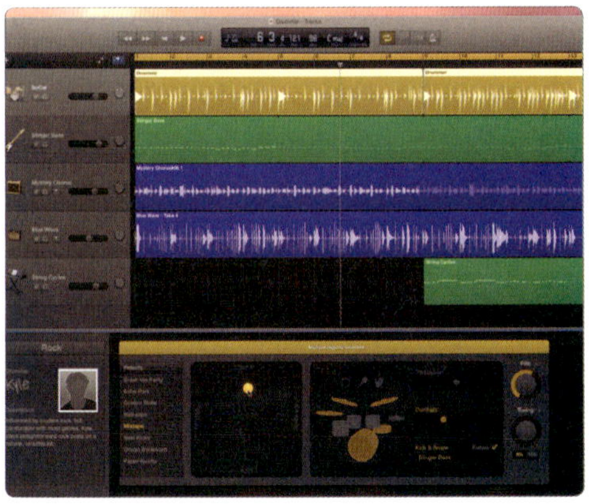

07: The X/Y pad

This bi-directional pad lets you tweak presets to control how soft/loud or simple/complex the pattern plays, changing the Drummer track.

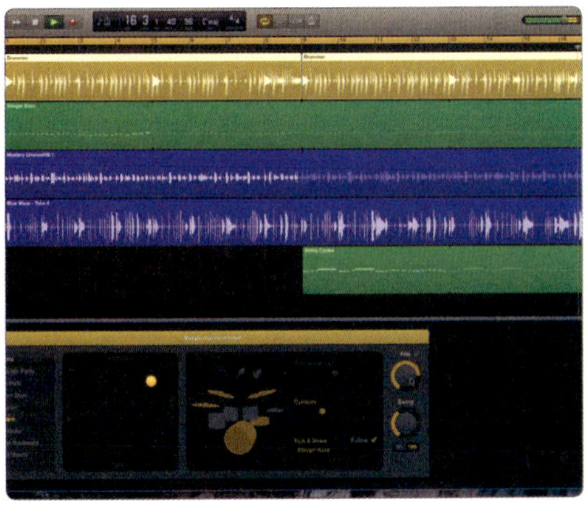

08: Fills and timing

You can use the Fills dial to increase the amount of intricate parts. The Swing control and the 8th/16th toggles affect timing and groove.

09: Divide and rule

By editing Drummer regions individually you get more human sequences that adhere to different rules – patterns, drum use, fills and timings.

Using iWork

From spreadsheets to word processors and multimedia presentations, iWork is a vital tool for any Mac user

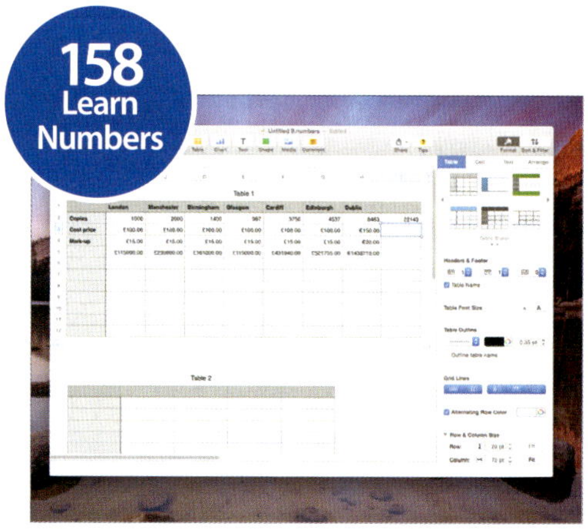

"iWork will help you become more productive with your work"

160
Learn Numbers

164
Top Keynote tips

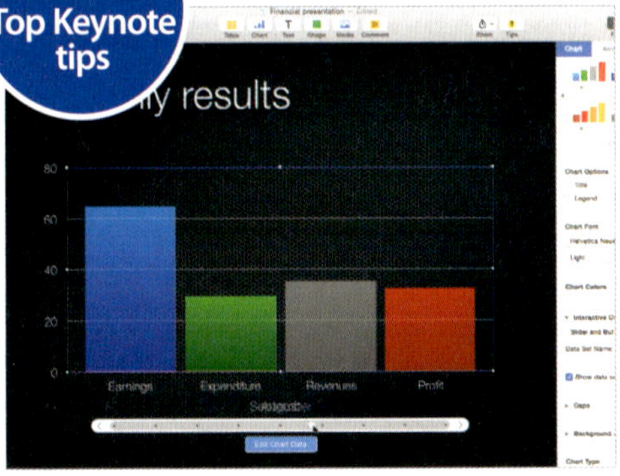

166
Use notes in Keynote

Build documents with Pages

Whether you need to create a letter, CV, work report, poster or newsletter, Pages is perfect for the job

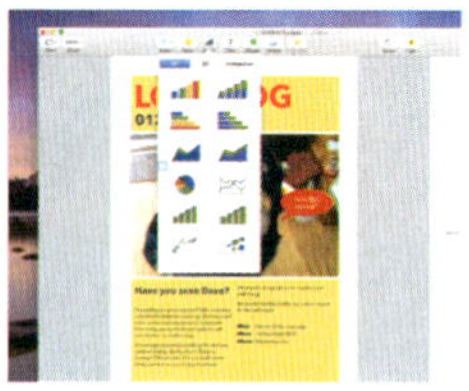

At first sight, Pages looks just like a word processor and it's true that it can create simple letters and documents. However, there is a lot more to this application, as it can create visually exciting publications such as flyers, posters, newsletters, brochures and much more. The app has been designed to make the task as easy as possible and this Yosemite edition has some great features. For example, there are some fantastic templates to get you started, as very often creating a publication is just a matter of selecting a template and replacing the text and images with your own. It's brilliantly simple. Other new features in this latest version include interactive charts, sharing facilities on iCloud and a whole lot more.

Pages Create publications from templates

01: Select a template

When Pages is started, click the New Document button to open the template browser. When Pages is open, just select File>New, then pick a template.

02: Edit the text

The template contains text and images, but it's easily replaced. Double-click on the heading, for example, and type in a new one.

03: Replace the images

Click the picture icon in the corner or Ctrl-click a photo to replace it with one from your iPhoto library, iCloud or photo stream.

04: Format the text

When text is selected, the panel on the right provides all the formatting options you need, such as font selection, alignment and so on.

05: Layout options

Select the Layout tab in the panel on the right to access features such as multiple columns to give the text a newspaper or magazine look.

06: Expand sections

Many options are hidden, so click the triangle next to each section heading to expand it. Expand Spacing, for example, for line spacing options.

Master the Pages interface

Tools and features for document design

Sharing options

You can share links to the file on iCloud where it can be accessed with a web browser. Alternatively the file can be sent via Mail, Messages or AirDrop. This makes accessing it far simpler

The toolbar

The toolbar lists all the items you can insert into a document, such as shapes, photos, music and movies, charts and tables. Hidden comments can be added too, for help during the design process

iCLOUD SHARING

These document files can be created on your Mac's disk drive, but there are advantages to storing them in iCloud. For instance, this makes your files available on all your Macs and iOS devices, so you can begin a document on the Mac and continue on the iPad and vice versa. Pages documents shared on iCloud can be accessed by anyone you give the URL to, which means you can get instant feedback.

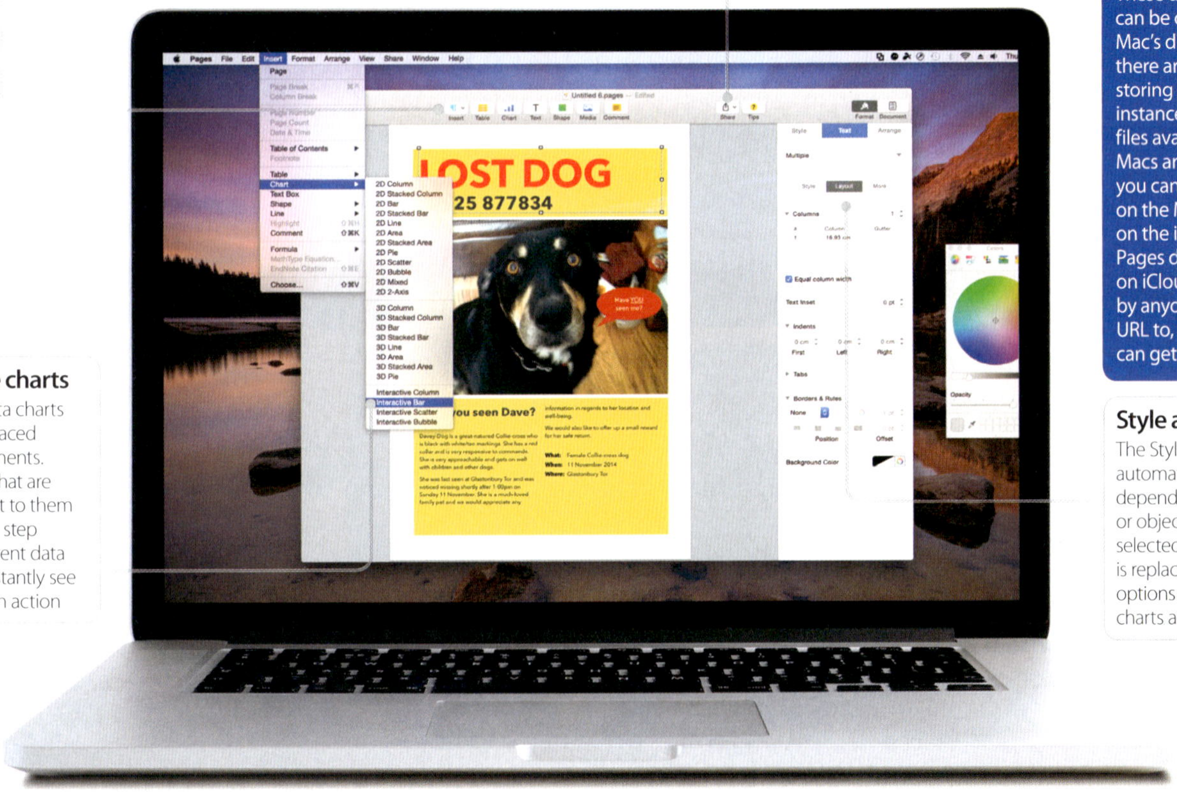

Interactive charts

Interactive data charts can also be placed in your documents. The buttons that are displayed next to them enable you to step through different data values and instantly see the changes in action

Style and layout

The Style and Layout tabs automatically change depending on the text or object that's currently selected. This whole panel is replaced with new options when working with charts and photos

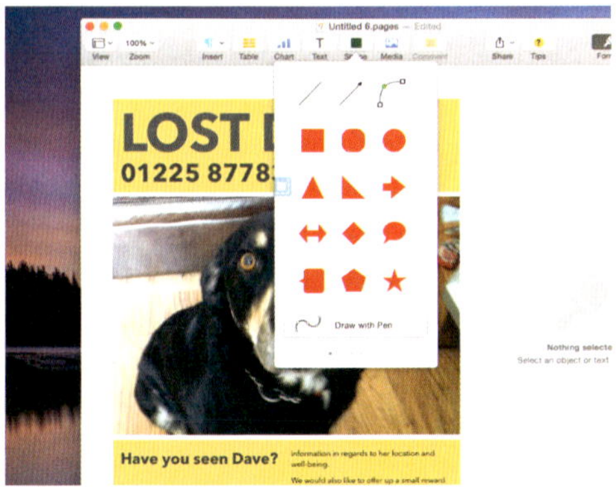

07: Add shapes

Click the Shapes icon in the toolbar to add lines, arrows, curves and predefined shapes. Click the dots at the bottom to view the items.

08: Shapes and text

Add a shape, such as a speech bubble, drag it into position on the page, click inside it and you can easily enter some text.

09: Share it

Click the Share button in the toolbar to access the sharing options. The document can be put on iCloud and links shared on Facebook and Twitter.

Create a spreadsheet in Numbers

Ensure your data is well presented and calculates perfectly with the excellent spreadsheet features of Numbers

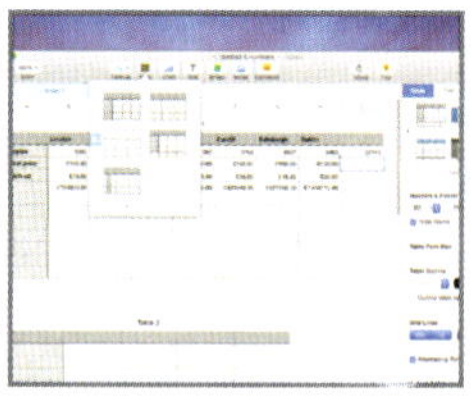

Spreadsheets may scare you and with good reason – they are not always easy to use. Microsoft Excel is a very powerful spreadsheet program, but it's complex. So is Numbers, but it delivers all of the functions you need in the simplest way possible and it even offers up explanations to help you out.

With a range of templates and the ability to add tables, resize them, calculate and choose from a range of maths options, you will soon be populating your tables with reams of data.

You aren't confined to one sheet either, as you can edit multiple ones at once by selecting the Sheet button in the toolbar. Numbers makes it easy to work with each one, providing you with a tabbed options pane.

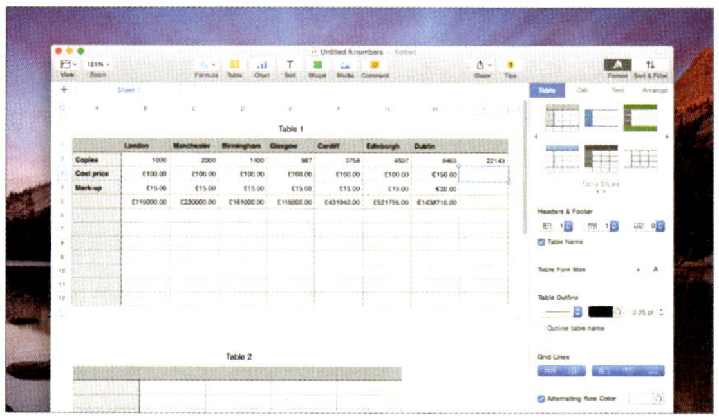

Numbers Get to grips with spreadsheets

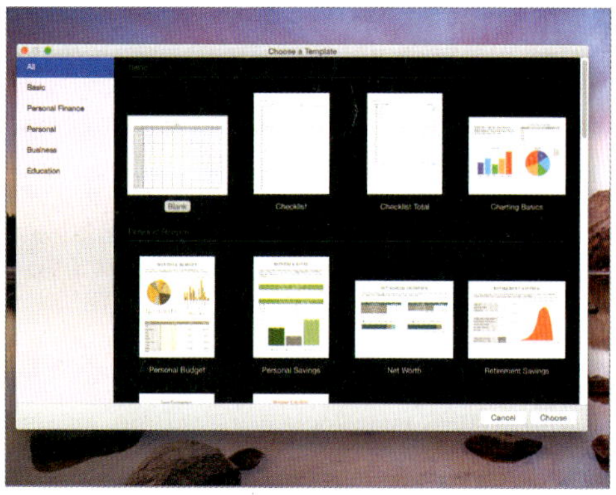

01: Choose a template

First choose from a selection of useful, presentable templates. They are sorted by categories including Business, Personal Finance and Education.

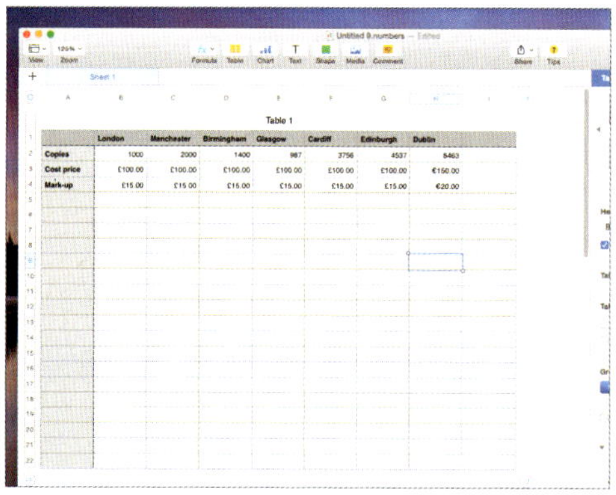

02: Input data

We've selected the Basic template. Spreadsheets have rows, columns and cells, so click each cell to add data. You can use words and numbers.

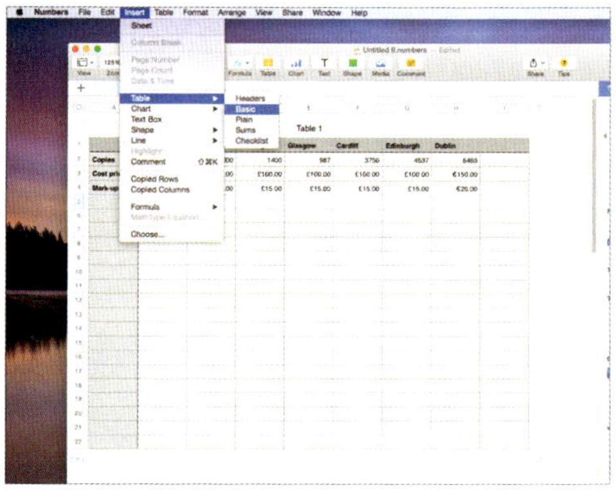

03: Add new tables

As well as using the table in front of you, try adding more via the Insert>Table navigation. Table types are shown in the right-hand box.

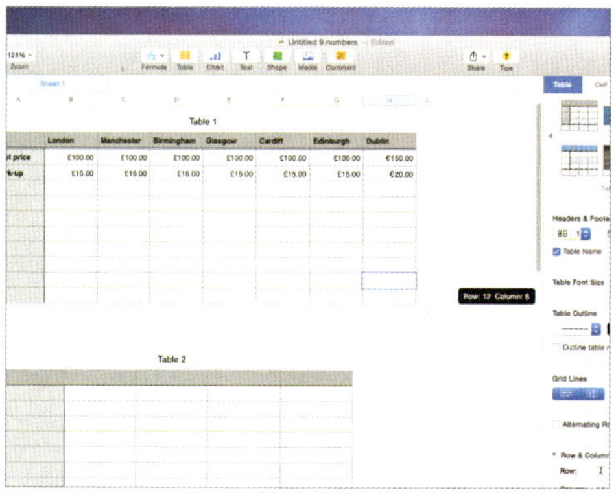

04: Resize tables

By using the arrow icon in the bottom-right-hand corner of a table, you can resize it. Refer to the row and column numbers for guidance.

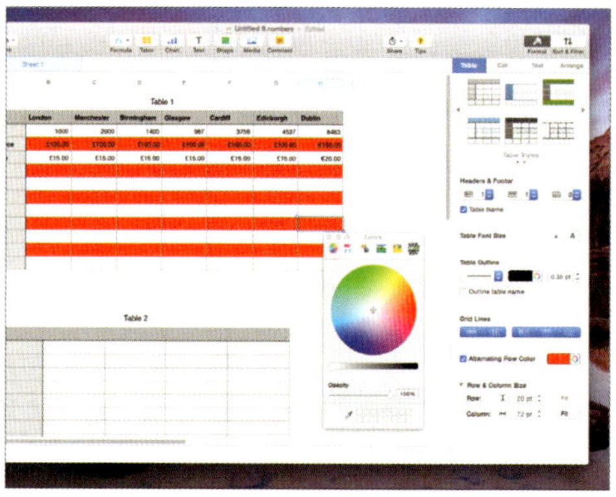

05: Alter the colours

Now choose cells to colour. Click the Cell tab, click Fill and select Alternative. To change alternate row colours, click Alternating Row Colour under Table.

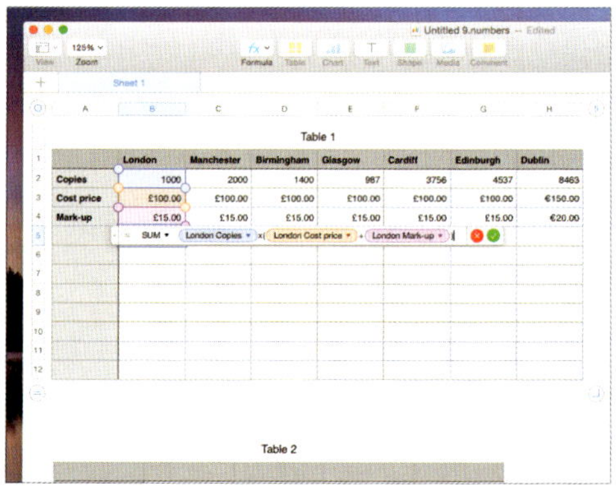

06: Add formulas

Click a cell where you want a total to be displayed. For a simple sum, type '=SUM'. You'll need to define cells to work with.

Find your way around Numbers

Make presentable spreadsheets within minutes

Title

Tap the word Untitled-Edited at the top of the screen and input a new name that best describes the project or spread you'll be working on. You can save this to the iCloud and to your Mac

The tabs

This window lets you view the options available for the overall table, cells, text and the arrangement of the spreadsheet. Try clicking on each one to discover what editing options it offers

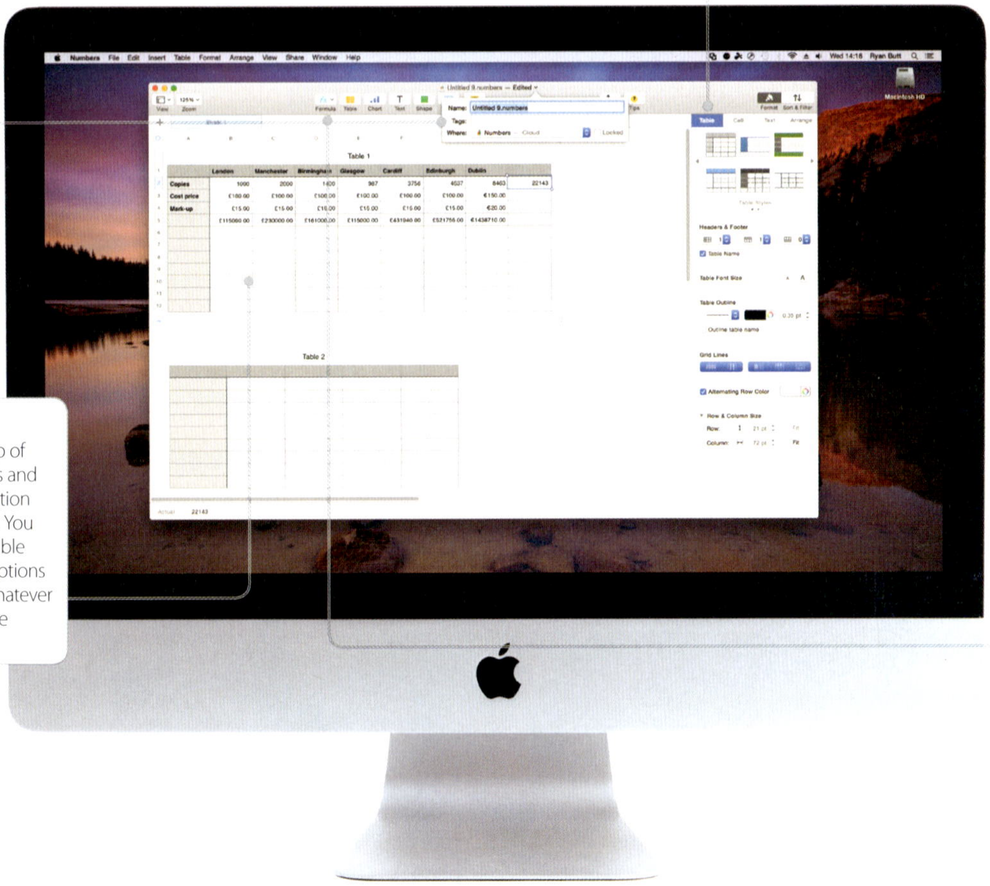

The table

A table is made up of rows and columns and can be a combination of words and text. You can change the table make-up in the Options window to suit whatever kind of table you're looking to create

HIGHLIGHT CELLS

When creating a formula for your spreadsheet, you don't have to type in the table co-ordinate (such as B2, C9 and so on). You can simply start off the formula (ie =SUM) and then click on the cell that you want to form part of the formula, similar to Microsoft Excel. This is very helpful for speeding up the process of calculations and eliminates any potential errors.

Add functions

If you want to add a particular function, a table, a chart and more, then just use the toolbar icons at the top of the screen for easy access. This makes creating and adjusting your tables much simpler

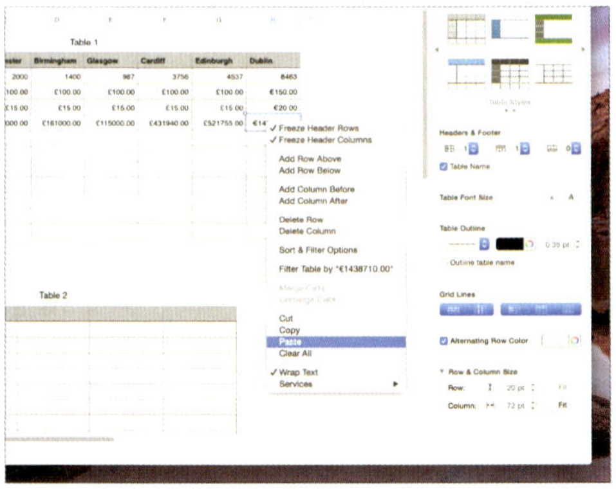

07: Produce the sum

To multiply the final two boxes by our first, type =SUM(B2x(B3+B4). Copying and pasting this cell speeds the task for the remaining calculations.

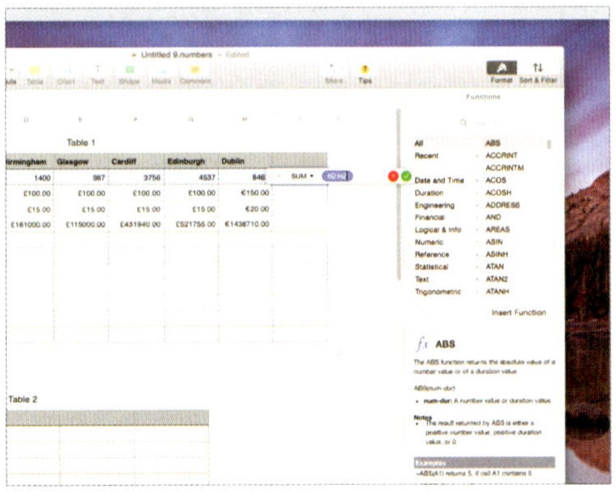

08: Calculate rows

You can also calculate rows. Available functions appear in the right-hand panel and each of them is categorised and explained in full.

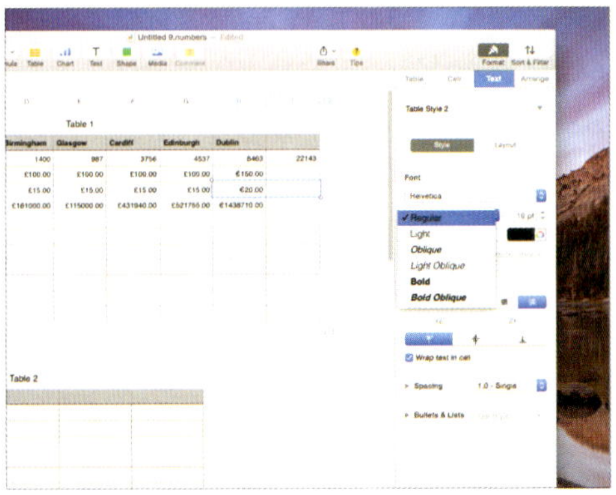

09: Change text

Of course, spreadsheets aren't just about numbers. You can control the size, font, wrapping and style of text under the Text tab in the right-hand panel.

Use date, time and duration formatting

One of Pages' new features lets you format table data into date, time and duration

Pages isn't only a platform for showcasing pretty images and compelling text, it's also the perfect place to present tables and charts; transforming a presentation into something alive with creativity and charm. One of the software's latest innovations is the ability to add Time, Date and Duration information into its range of colour-clad tables. Okay, so on the surface this might not sound like the most exciting development, but for those who are constantly creating tables, this update means less time spent on laborious data entry and more time spent on, well, anything else!

So make sure your version of Pages is completely up to date, and instead of wasting hours of your life typing out dates in full, or adding numerical units after durations, start using Pages and it will just do it for you.

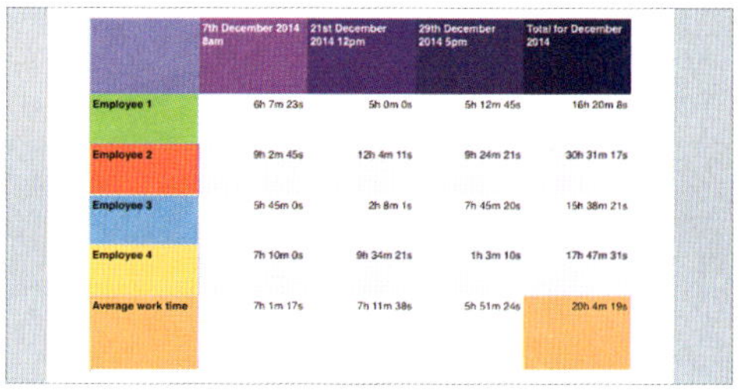

Times, dates and durations

Use the new feature for a sense of professionalism

Data Format

Use this tab to select how you want your data to be styled, as well as picking values such as date, time and durations. You'll also find other options such as Percentage etc

Style

Under the Style Duration tab, you will discover options that let you decide how these chosen values appear. Users have the options of either numerically, with abbreviations (h, m, s etc) or as fully written words

Automatic Units versus Custom Units

As always Apple makes interfaces easy to use. There's no mass of dialogue and the system breeds confidence to try more complex tasks and procedures

Date, Time or None

You don't have to include a time with a date, and vice versa. With a cell selected, pick Date & Time under Data Format then choose a styling from the Date options and select None under Time, or vice versa

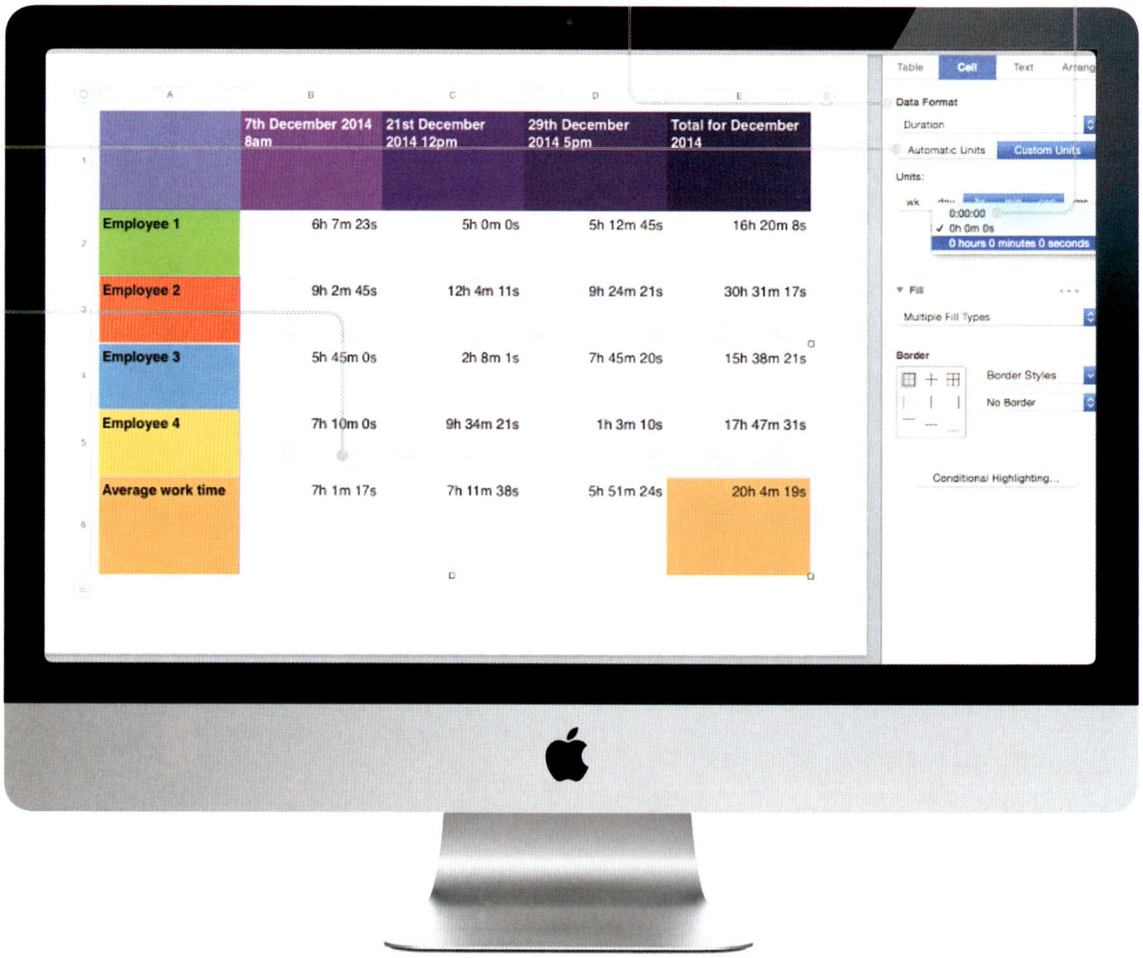

DURATION OPTIONS

When you select a styling for your duration information you can opt between Automatic Units and Custom Units. Automatic Units is a restricted, typical list of options, whereas Custom Units enables you to choose between the values you want, thus a personalised combination of weeks, days, hours, minutes, seconds and milliseconds. You can then pick from a list of styles in order to determine exactly how these units should appear (hours versus h, for example).

Pages Using date, time and duration formatting

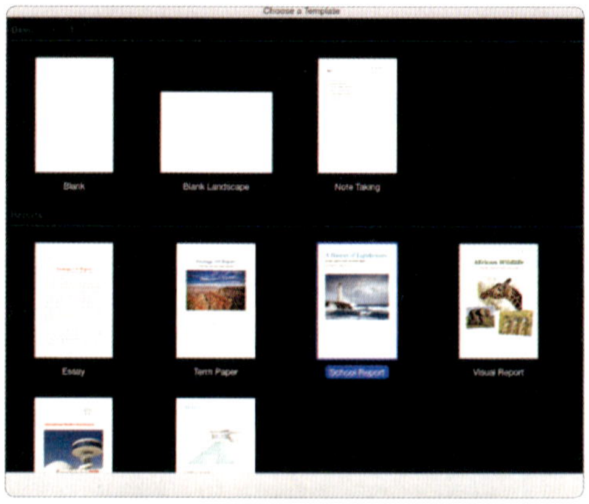

01: Getting started

You'll need to choose a template or blank page to get started. Travel up to File on the menu bar and discover New or key Command and N.

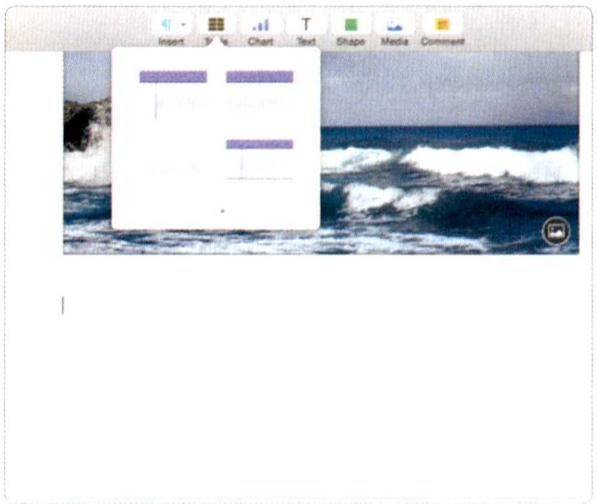

02: Choose your table

Position the cursor where you want the table to go. Head to Table and select a style and colour. Click on the top-left circle to reposition the table.

03: Dates and times

Add a date into a cell, select it and go to the Format panel. Choose the Cell tab. From the Data Format options, pick Date & Time and a styling.

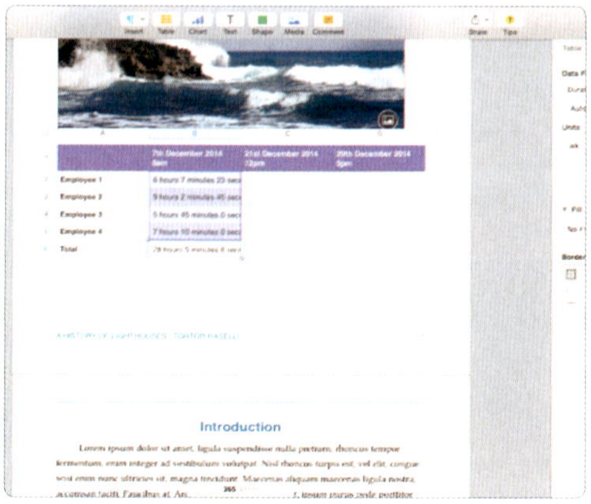

04: Durations

To create duration information, add an initial number, then with the cell selected, choose Duration and add in all the data that applies.

05: Copy and paste

A quick way to fill in the rest is to copy an existing duration, move on to the next cell and paste it in, then change the numerical date as needed.

06: In one go

You can select a number of cells and adjust the Data Format to suit. When you enter a number it will adopt the same styling as the initial unit.

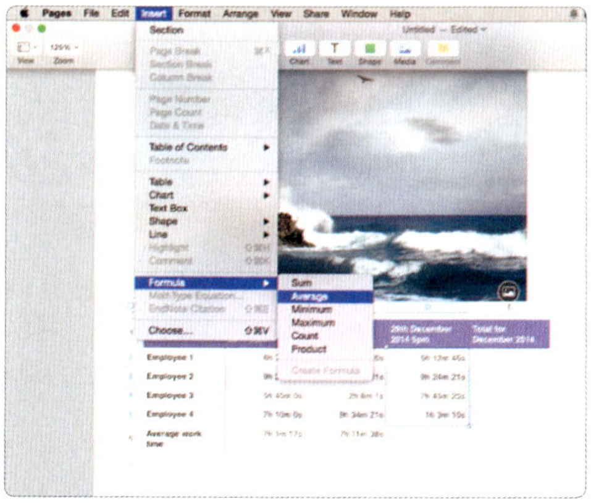

07: Formulas

You can use formulas and Pages calculates the value as a duration. Just highlight the appropriate cells and head to Insert on the File menu.

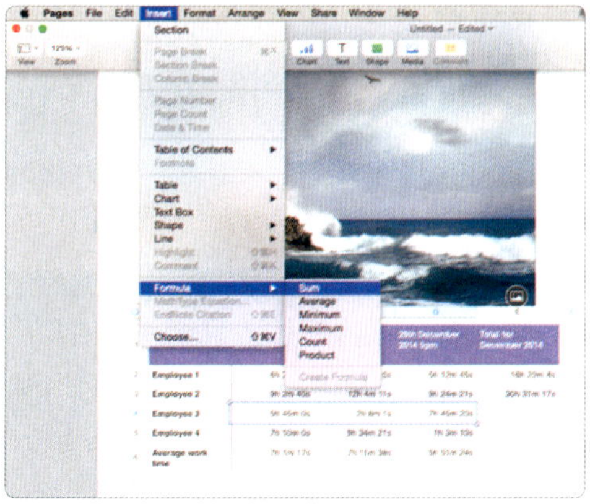

08: Formula options

From Insert, click Formula and choose an option. Sum will add up selected durations, for example, and Average calculates the Mean duration.

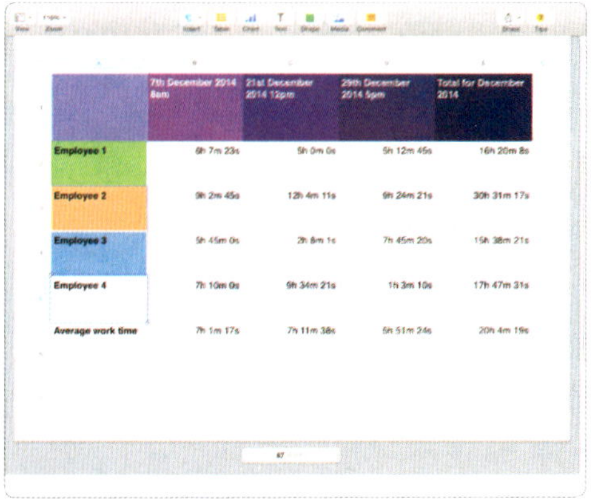

09: Finishing touches

When your table is complete you may like to spruce it up with colours to highlight cells. Select a cell and under Fill, choose an appropriate tone.

Create amazing charts in Numbers

Customise and control your charts and graphs with Numbers' advanced controls

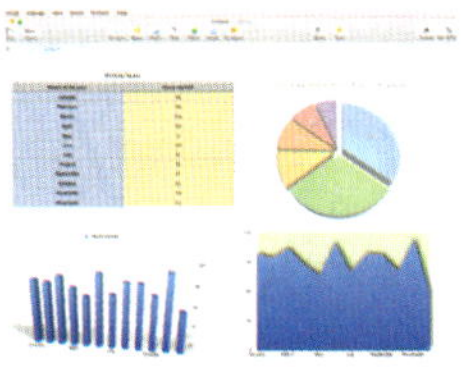

Spreadsheets are boring. They're used the world over by business people who need to show information in a professional way, which usually results in dull tables, drab charts and numbers that all blend into one. But it doesn't have to be like that, and with Numbers it's incredibly easy to make your work bright, interesting and eye-catching. In particular, you can add a huge dollop of creativity to your charts, ensuring that all of your data will jump right off the page.

With plenty of customisations available like colours, textures and 3D effects, Numbers offers you the most powerful tools possible to make your spreadsheets much more than just boring business work. Here, we'll show you how to customise your charts to fit your needs and take them beyond basic numbers to make them truly spectacular.

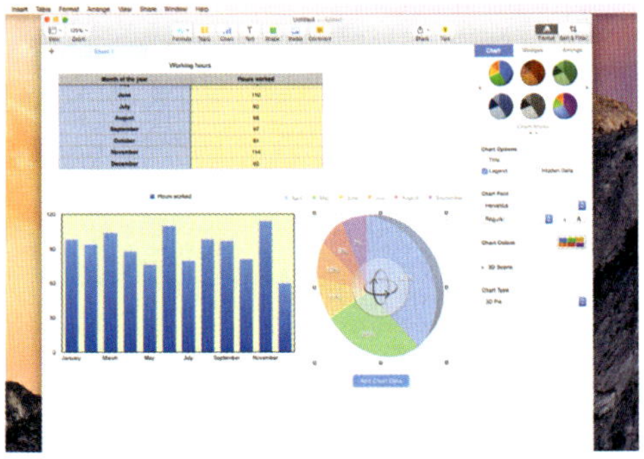

Axis of power

Control how data is displayed on your chart

On the line

You can add and adjust the gridlines on your graph manually using this section, adding minor gridlines and recolouring the lines in order to make them stand out more

Alter the labels

You can change the label designs for each axis, too – choose the label type using the drop-down box, select whether you want to show the minimum value at the lower end of the axis, and adjust the label angle

Change the scale

The axes will set their scales automatically based on the data you're choosing to display, but you can control the scales manually in this area by simply inputting the maximum and minimum values for the selected axis

BEAUTIFUL TABLES

You don't have to limit yourself to designing your graphs in beautiful ways – your tables can also look magnificent. Select the table you want and you can change the font and colour of the text, as well as recolouring all your cells and gridlines using the style controls. Pick colours that complement your graphs to create a stunning and captivating spreadsheet.

Pie design

You will see different controls in the sidebar if you choose a pie chart – here you can adjust the labels' distance from the centre of the pie, pull out individual wedges and choose how the data is displayed on the graph

Numbers Make amazing charts in Numbers

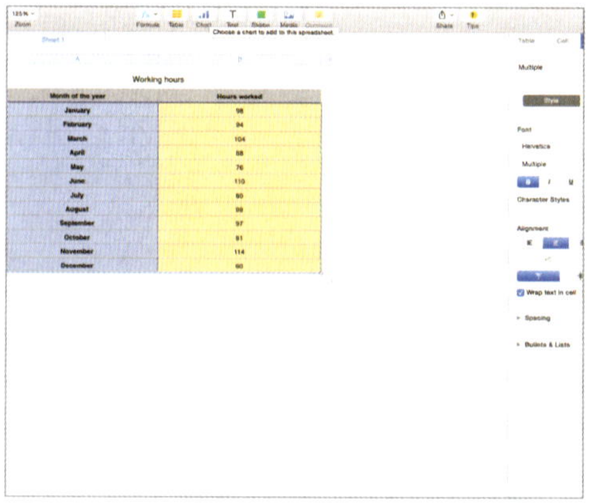

01: Create your chart

Create a table in your document with the information you want to show. Select the desired data and click the Chart button in the top toolbar.

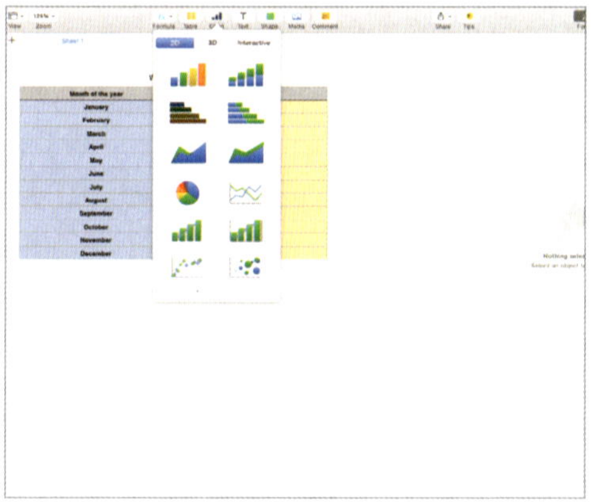

02: Pick a chart

You'll see three options – 2D, 3D and Interactive. Each one has a series of style options to choose from, so for now pick a standard 2D chart design.

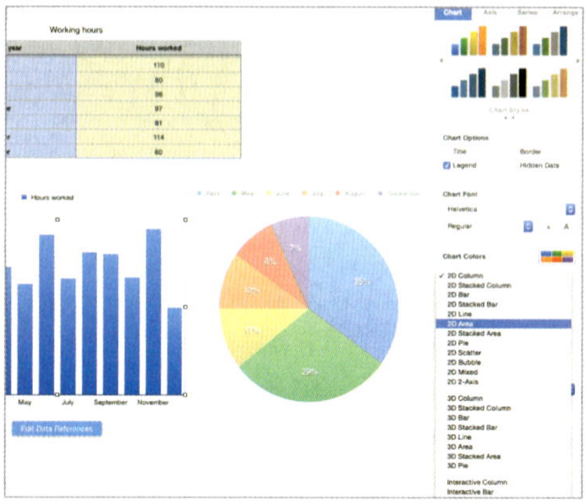

03: Choose wisely

Consider the type of chart you need for the data you have. To change the type of chart, open the Chart sidebar and use the Chart Type menu.

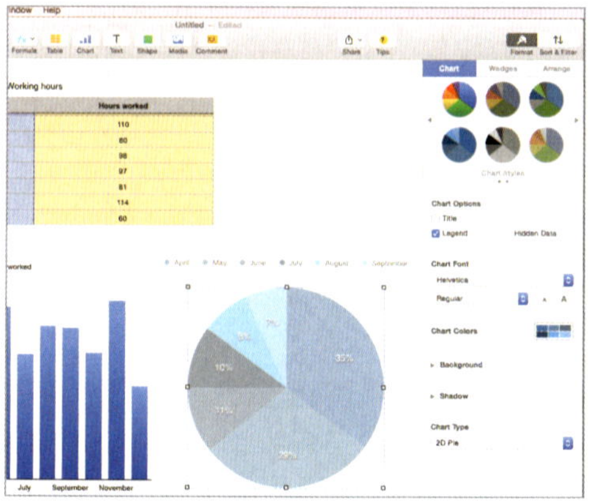

04: Change your style

Each chart has a selection of styles at the top of the Chart sidebar. Pick one of the alternative styles from here, or edit manually and save it as a new style.

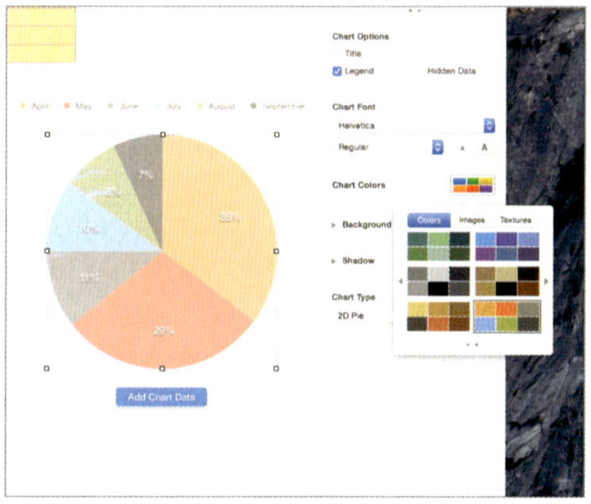

05: Font and colour

You can change the colours of your chart using the presets in Chart Colours section, and alter the font used in the chart to make it eye-catching.

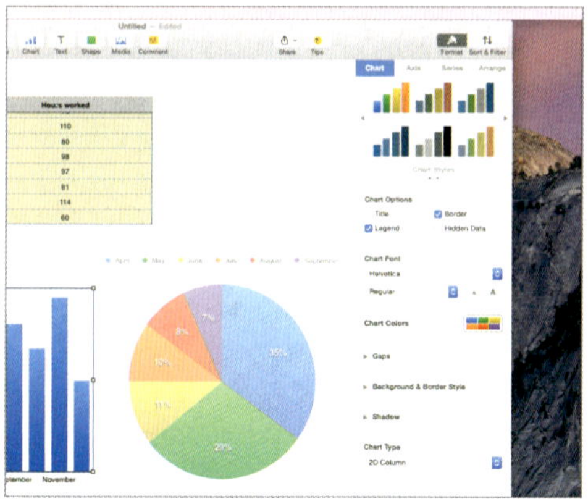

06: Change Chart Options

Depending on the kind of chart you're working on, you may want to show or hide different information – use the checkboxes in Chart Options to do this.

07: Mind the gap

For bar graphs, you have the option to customise gaps – it might seem picky, but these changes can make all the difference to the finished spreadsheets.

08: Going 3D

At the bottom of the Charts sidebar you can adjust the type of chart used. You can change the chart type, or change things like moving to 3D design.

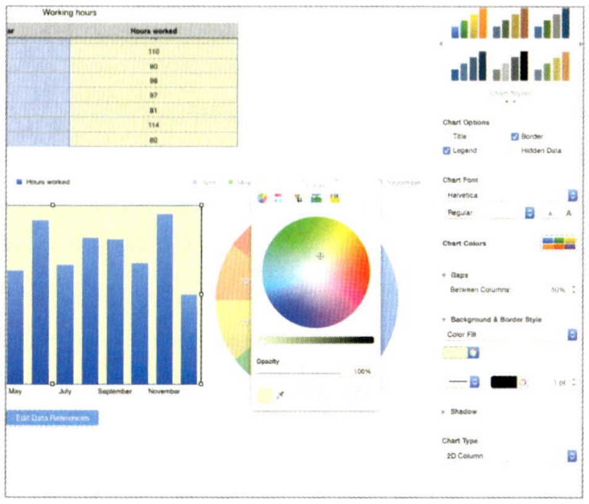

09: Backgrounds and borders

Edit the border and add a background to your chart to make it stand out. You can add all kinds of backgrounds, so experiment with the options.

Punch up data with interactive charts

Add interest to a dull spreadsheet with interactive charts in Keynote

Just because Microsoft Excel is used by thousands of workers across the world to create boring spreadsheets every day, doesn't mean every spreadsheet has to be boring. With the latest iWork apps, Apple is doing its best to make the information you present more interesting, and more eye-catching. For those times where you have to add a graph or chart into a Keynote document, you can now add an interactive chart to your slides. These charts include a bar that can be dragged along to change the data displayed. This not only helps to keep your slides uncluttered, but also offers a moving, engaging way to present the information. Even better, these charts are surprisingly easy to add to your presentations.

"An overlooked but important element"

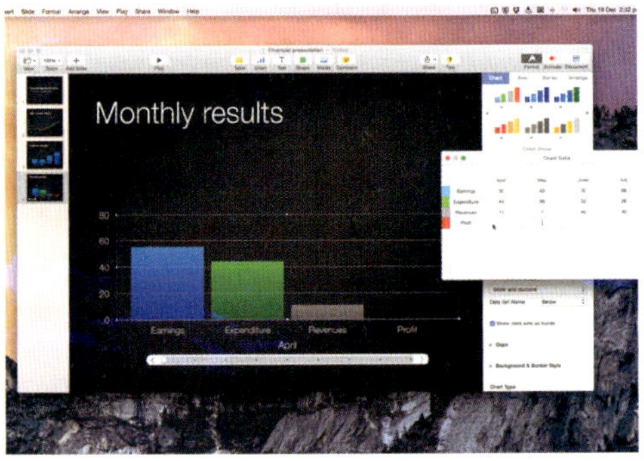

Keynote Make more engaging charts

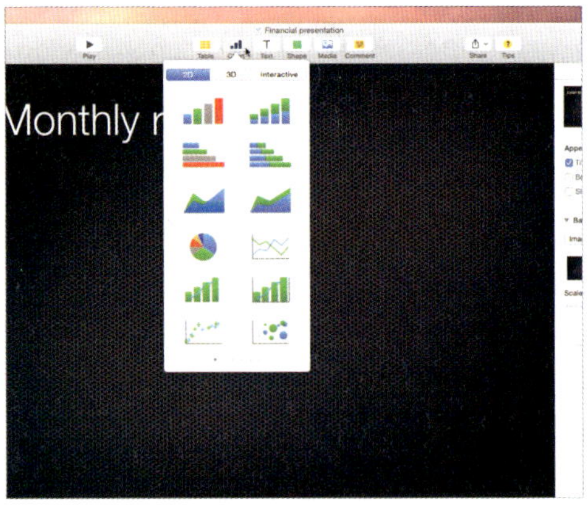

01: Add a chart

Open up your Keynote presentation and, to add a graph to a slide, click the Chart button in the top toolbar to see all the chart options available to you.

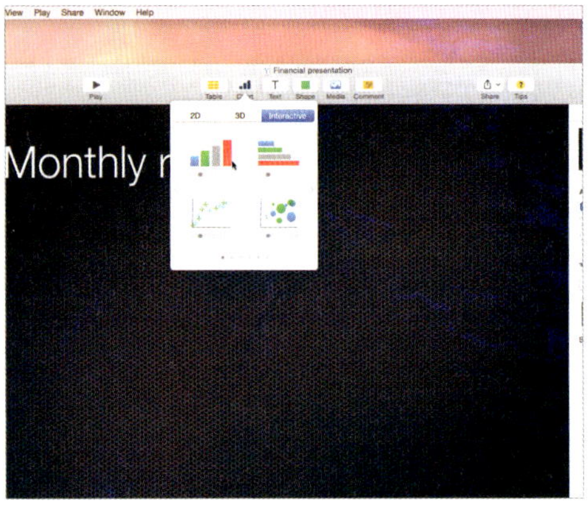

02: Go interactive

There are three options: 2D, 3D and Interactive. Choose the Interactive tab on the right and click on whichever of the four designs fits for your data.

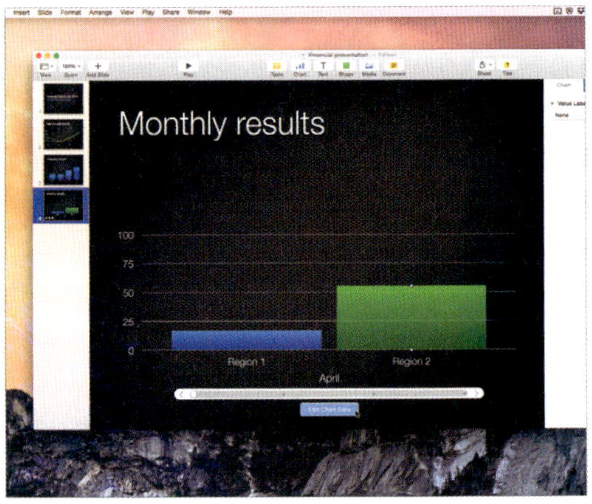

03: Edit the data

A graph is added instantly, but the data is randomly generated. To add data, click the graph then click on the Edit Chart Data button that appears below.

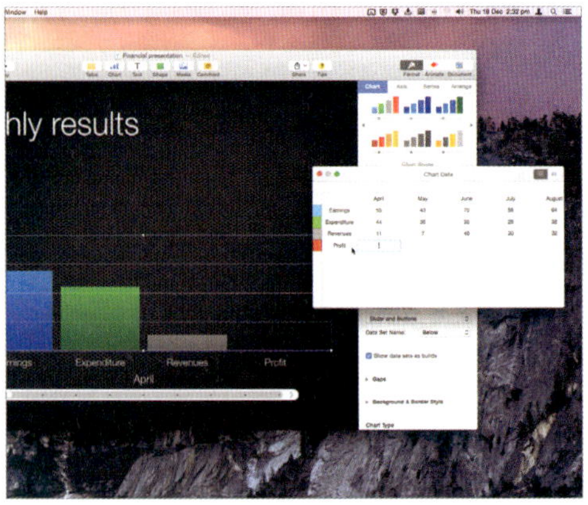

04: Add sets of data

By default, there are only two bars. To add more, simply add more rows to the Chart Data panel. Hit Enter and a new bar will appear on the chart itself.

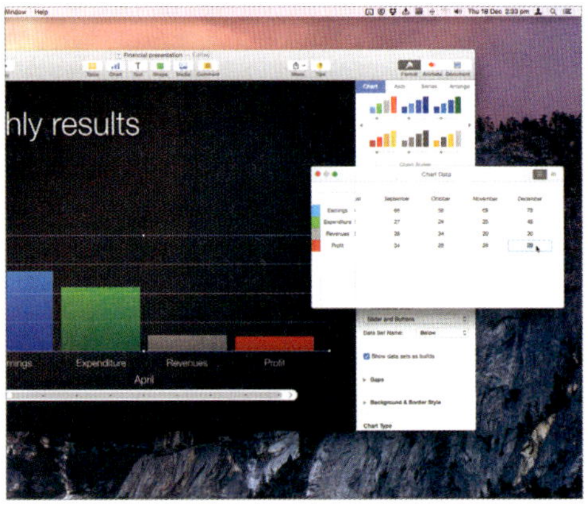

05: Expand the graph

Go right in the Chart Data window and add more titles in the top bar, then fill out the data. This adds more pages in the interactive bar below the graph.

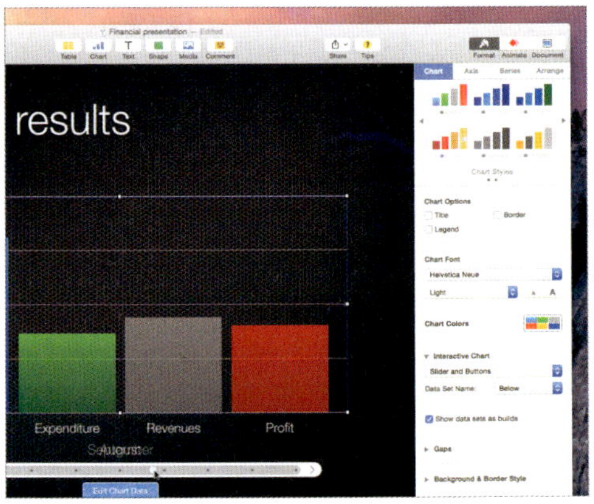

06: Check the data

Below the graph on your slide is a scroll bar – drag the marker across to preview your data, ensuring all the information is correct before hitting Play.

Customise your chart

Personalise the look of your interactive graph

Chart options

Click on the Chart tab and you can adjust the look of the overall chart. Alter the font used in the labels, change all of the chart colours quickly, or change the whole chart to a different design if you wish

Bar styles

Click the graph, then click on a specific bar and you can change the colour of just that bar. Click the Style tab on the right and you can use the controls to adjust the look of that specific part of the graph

MORE OPTIONS

If you want more options for your chart, such as the ability to use formulas, try creating the chart in Numbers originally. This, of course, includes a selection of extra options for you to use in your tables and charts, so you can create a table with complex formulas, use the data in a graph or chart, then copy and paste it into your Keynote slide and customise its look.

Chart style

You can adjust the style of the chart quickly by clicking one of the options at the top of the Format sidebar. Scroll right and you can add your own style, with custom colours and settings, so you can quickly apply it to other charts later

Interaction control

If you want to change how the interactive nature of the chart is handled, click the arrow next to the Interactive Chart option and you can change it from a slider and buttons to just buttons, as well as change its location

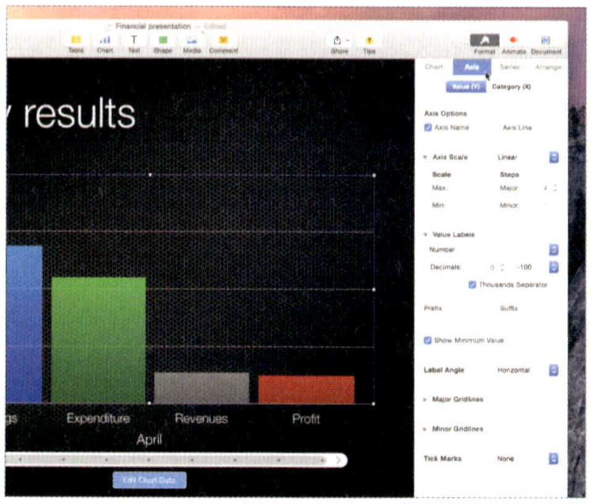

07: Axis options

Clicking on the red bookmark at the top will bring up the contact groups view. It's a lot cleaner than the columned view of the old address book.

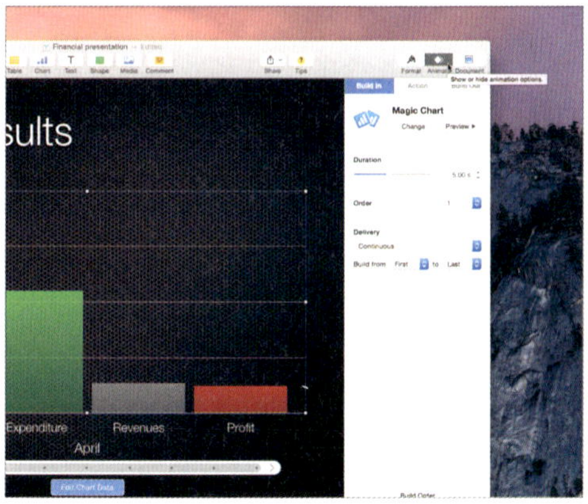

08: Animation options

With Interactive Charts, an animation is added that plays through the progression automatically. To edit the animation, click the button in the top-right.

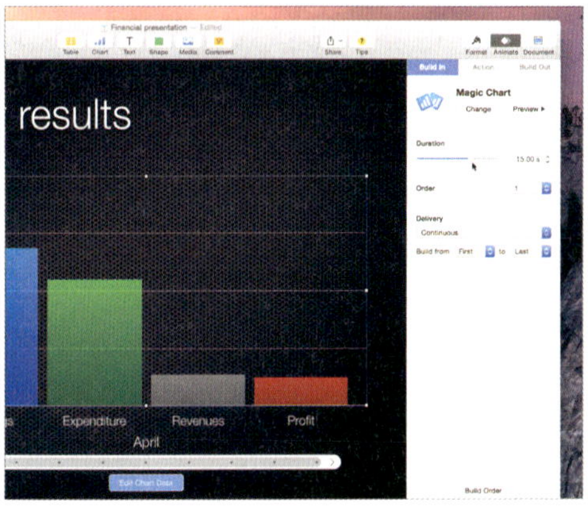

09: Slow it down

Depending on the number of entries, five seconds may not be long enough – drag this slider to the right so each entry is shown for longer on-screen.

Keep notes to help you present

Create presenter notes for you to refer to when showing off your Keynotes

Keynote makes it simple to create fantastic presentations thanks to its easy-to-use but surprisingly powerful tools. Whether you want to create a simple text-based presentation or you need something a little more creative, with images, videos and animations, Keynote gives you all the tools you need with just a couple of clicks.

But once you've created your presentation, Keynote doesn't just stop helping you. When you stand up in front of a group of people and give your presentation, it can still help you. You can use the Notes tool to write down important points that will display on your Mac's screen, so only you see them. It not only makes presenting easier, it will also make you look incredibly professional, and preparing your notes doesn't take long at all.

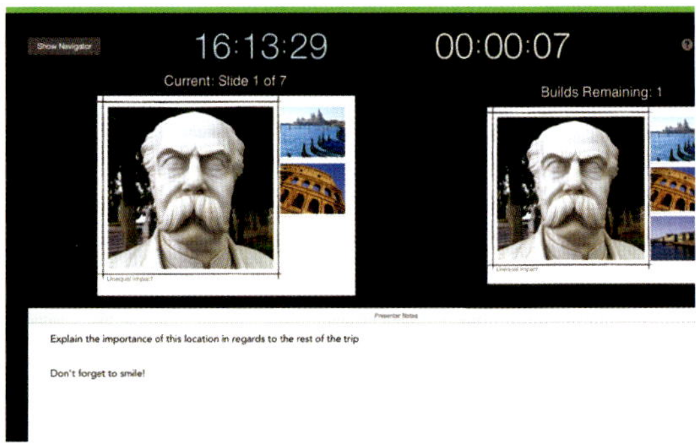

Presentation screen explained

Understanding how to use Keynote's presentation tools

Builds remaining

You can see the number of builds remaining on each slide above the right-hand box. This will only appear if you have applied animations to your slides before hitting Play

Close the presenter

If you want to exit the presenter at any time you can click the 'x' button in the top-right corner of the screen, or simply press Escape to go back to your normal Keynote window

Coloured bars

The bars at the top of the screen denote the status of your presentation. Green means you are ready to progress to the next slide or animation with a click, while red means it's in the middle of an animation

Next slide

On the left is the screen that your viewers can currently see displayed on the external display, while the right-hand box shows what is coming up next, either in terms of animations or slides

KEYBOARD SHORTCUTS

When you use this view to work with your presentation, you can use a number of keyboard shortcuts to make your life easier. For example, with a single keystroke you can pause your presentation and turn the screen white or black, or skip back and forth through individual builds or whole slides. To see the full list of commands, click the '?' icon in the top-right.

Keynote Add presentation notes

01: Open Notes

Open the Notes viewer. Open a Keynote and choose View>Show Presenter Notes to bring up the Notes section at the bottom of your window.

02: Add a note

To add a note, click in the new bar and type it in. The Notes section will remain at the bottom of the window even when you switch between slides.

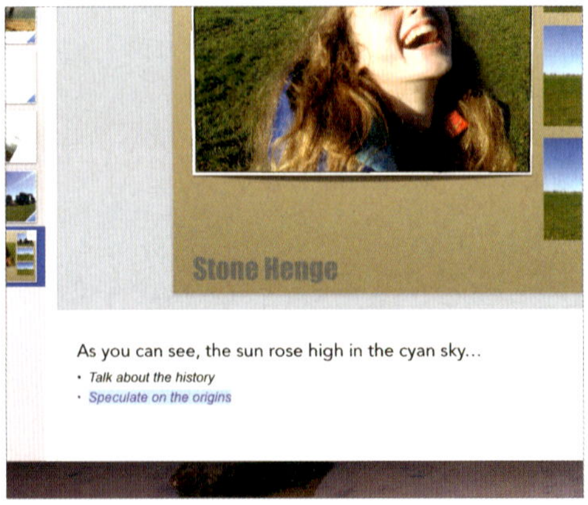

03: Format notes

Click on the Format button and you'll have options for customising your notes. You can change fonts and colours, and add bullets if necessary.

04: Start rehearsals

Once you've finished your notes, you can start rehearsing your presentation. Choose the Play option and select Rehearse Slideshow.

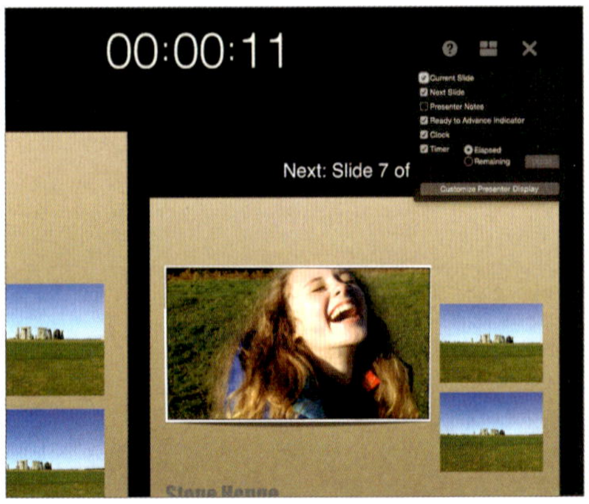

05: Customise your screen

To customise your view, click this icon in the top-right and choose the options that you want to appear on-screen while you present.

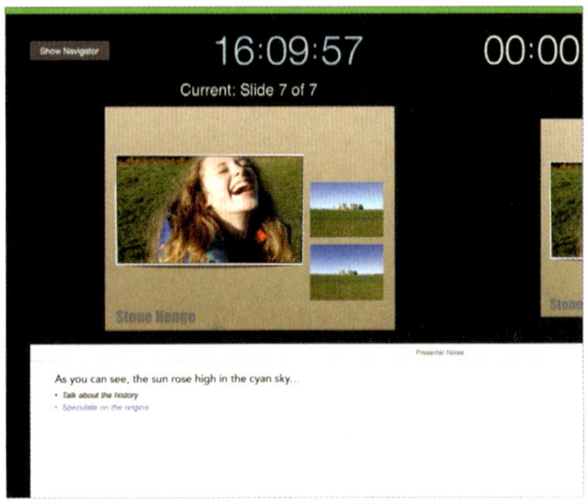

06: See your notes

Make sure the Notes section is ticked and you'll see that your slides move to make room at the bottom of the screen for the notes you previously wrote.

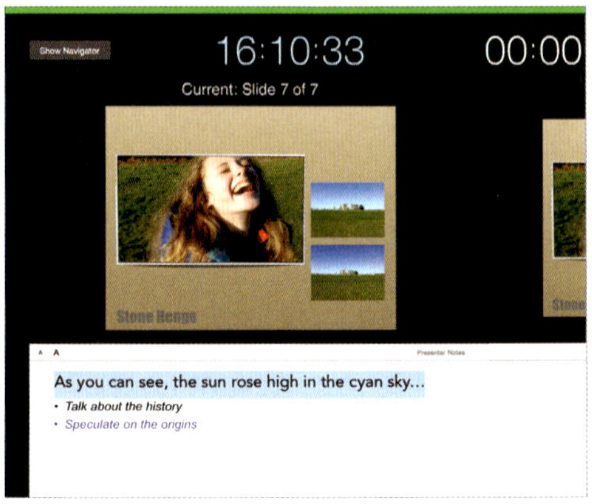

07: Edit your notes

Change the size of the notes in your Rehearsal view by clicking the bigger or smaller letters in the top-left of the Notes bar, or click Edit to make changes.

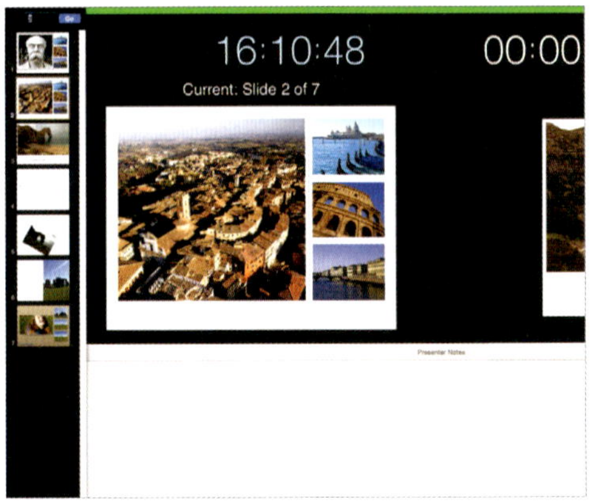

08: View your slides

If you want to see an overview of all your slides, click the Show Navigator button in the top-left and type in the slide number in the top box.

09: Play your slideshow

When you're ready to present, connect your Mac up to an external display or projector and hit Play to start with your notes appearing on your screen.

100 Essential Mac Apps

The ultimate guide to the Mac apps you simply have to have

Finding and installing Mac apps is now easier than ever, thanks to Apple's brilliant Mac App Store. It works by letting you install apps with just a click, and you can be assured that they will be safe for the Mac device you are using. You can still download and install apps from anywhere on the web, but the App Store is by far the most efficient and safe way to add new software to your setup. The apps extend the functionality of any Mac greatly, and without them your choices are limited as to what you can do. There are thousands available, and they cover near enough every conceivable subject or task that you need to complete. This feature will highlight the essential apps from every app category, and hopefully narrow down your search for the best of the best. Your choice of apps is genuinely unlimited.

Essential apps

5 essential apps

Templates for MS Office

Price: Free **Developer:** UAB "Graphic Node"

If you are a regular user of Microsoft's Office suite then this collection of templates is a great way to revitalise your work. The bulk of the templates provided here are for Microsoft Word – 50 in total – and include a wealth of personal and business designs, including letters, brochures, books and menus. For Excel, there are 15 diverse and practical templates to make everyday tasks more manageable and for Powerpoint there are seven high-quality slide designs to make your slides instantly more eye-catching and captivating.

Cobook

Price: Free **Developer:** FullContact Inc

This app provides a unified address book that brings together contact information from your Mac, all of your various social networks and other sources. It is highly efficient at drawing together every last scrap of contact information to keep your database as up-to-date as possible and allows seamless integration from a range of sources, such as Facebook, Twitter, Foursquare, Instagram and more.

friedEgg Touch

Price: £14.99/$19.99 **Developer:** friedEgg Limited

Creating and analysing complex charts is not an easy task, and often requires specialists to complete the job. This is not the case any longer, however, because this app will let you build impressive 3D charts whenever you need to, and also lets you manipulate them in real-time. It looks as good as it works, and allows anyone to create complex charts relating to any subject. A truly impressive business tool.

Splashtop Remote Desktop

Price: £10.49/$14.99 **Developer:** Splashtop Inc

Imagine being able to remotely access your PC or Mac from the computer that is in front of you. You can now do this thanks to this app which works cross-platform at high speed. You will never be away from the office again, wherever you are at any given time.

OmniGraffle 6 Pro

Price: £79.99/$99.99

Developer: The Omni Group

If you need a diagram, process chart, quick page layout, website wireframe or graphic design then OmniGraffle can help you make eye-catching graphic documents quickly and easily by keeping lines connected to shapes, even when they're moved, providing powerful styling tools with just one click.

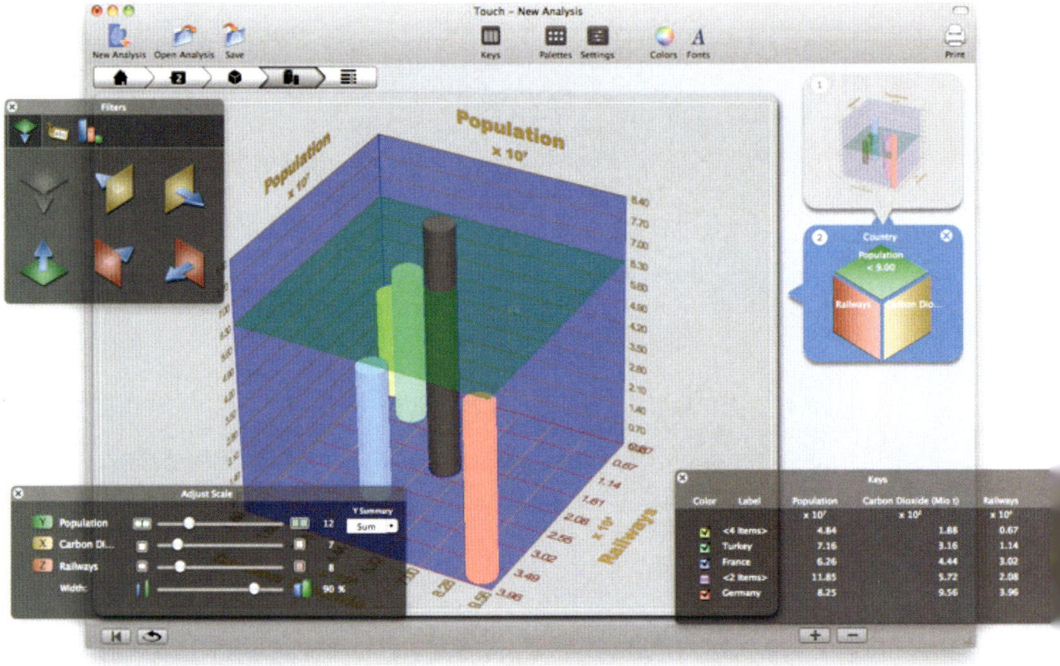

friedEgg Touch's visuals are stylish, clear and impressive

Business

Tailor apps to your work-related needs

Business apps can take a variety of forms, and cover everything from general communication to solutions for specialist industries. Despite the fact that many companies have bespoke software for their tasks, it is often possible to improve productivity by using third-party applications. Computers can be remotely monitored and used from miles away, employees can collaborate on projects using a single app, and there are solutions available for every conceivable task. With some planning and the careful selection of the right apps, anybody's Mac can be greatly extended to become perfectly functional for whatever task you need to do. Often, it isn't just the well-known or expensive apps that do the best job, because there are a variety of solutions available for every single business need. Business is a wide-ranging topic, and fortunately there is a wide range of Mac apps available to support your needs.

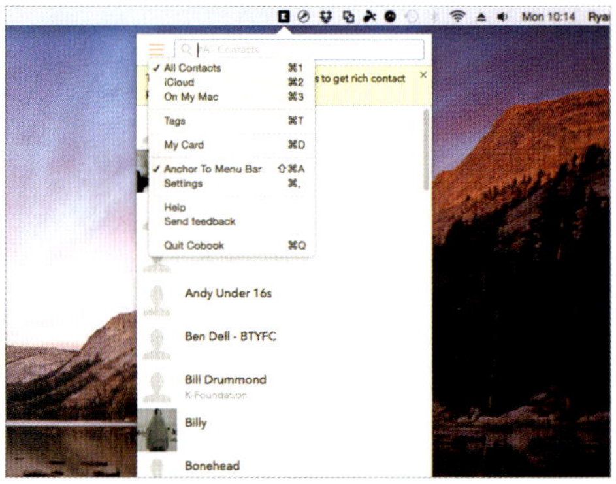

"Business apps take a variety of forms"

Splashtop lets you view videos on another computer

Templates for MS Office will re-energise your work…

Lots of information is displayed within Solar Walk's clean interface

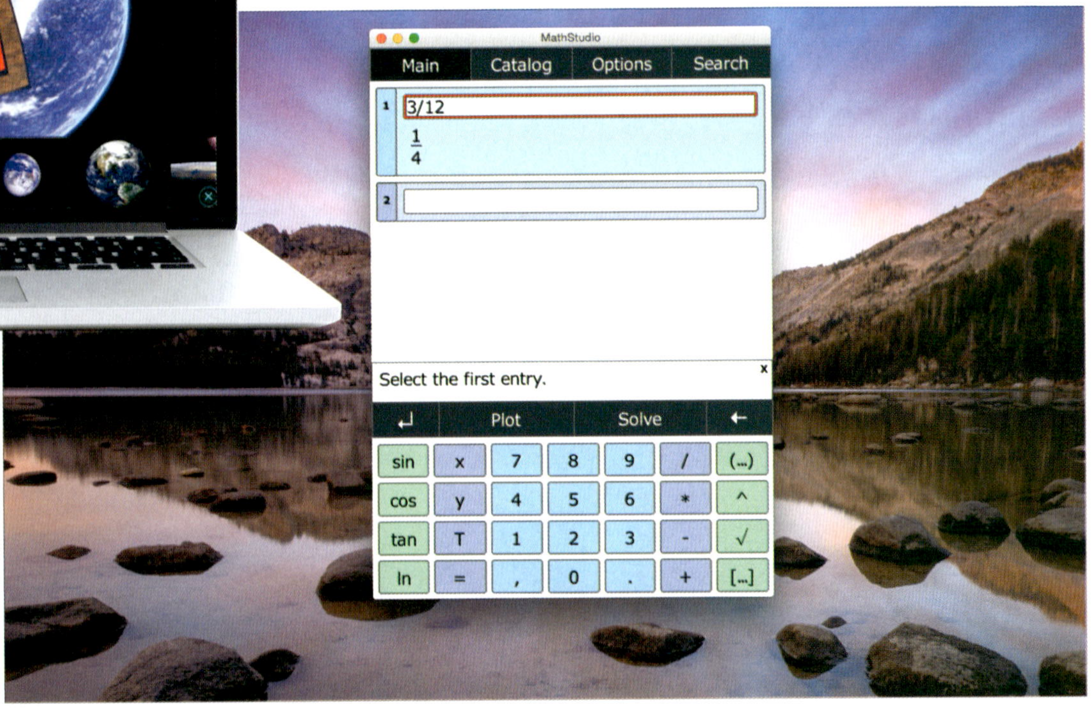

Check out the versatility of MathStudio…

AlphaBaby's vibrant colours and shapes will keep young children happy

Education

Get well and truly schooled with this collection of apps

Education is something that stays with us for all of our lives, from the day we are born to the moment we die. It doesn't matter how old you are or how clever you are; there will always be software solutions that can help you. Children can benefit from colourful and imaginative visual games, and adults can benefit from learning about the complexities of advanced topics. Education works best when it is fun, and the imagination put into many educational software solutions makes the Mac platform ideal for learning. No matter what is the topic or the individual needs, Mac apps will help you and your family learn whenever is convenient for you. This is one of the most important areas of computing today, and one that can be potentially beneficial to all Mac users, because the platform is perfectly suited to all areas of education.

Mrs Owl provides an engaging way to teach kids

5 essential apps

MathStudio

Price: Free
Developer: Pomegranate Apps

If you need a robust-feature-packed calculator to help from anything to managing your finances to assisting with your 2D or 3D graphing then this free offering is a must-have. Featuring over 200 functions, it is capable of handling anything you'd care to throw at it and features a built-in tutorial to help you every step of the way. Check it out and be amazed.

A to Z – Mrs Owl's Learning Tree

Price: £3.99/$5.99
Developer: Wayne Smith

This is a good app to aid pre-school learning and entails bright pictures and attention-grabbing sound effects – pretty much all the stuff that young children are into. You join Mrs Owl in the Learning Tree's treehouse classroom as she takes you through the complete alphabet with phonetic letter sounds. Updated regularly to include more features, this is inspiring.

Mathemagics

Price: £3.99/$5.99
Developer: Blue Lightning Labs

Mathemagics feels like a game, but there is a serious motive behind the design. You can learn tricks to impress your friends, or help yourself if you are struggling with maths. It teaches you some methods to quickly multiply, divide or find the square root, and in our tests it proved to be extremely effective. This is a map for everyone, no matter what your level of expertise.

AlphaBaby

Price: £0.79/$0.99
Developer: Laura Dickey

AlphaBaby not only works in an environment which makes it impossible for a child to play with, or be distracted by other applications, but it also serves as an excellent learning tool for children. It is probably best suited for the very young, and allows them to understand letters and shapes at a steady pace. Overall, it works brilliantly, and we wouldn't hesitate to recommend it.

Solar Walk

Price: £2.29/$3.99
Developer: Vito Technology, Inc

This 3D Solar System model enables you to navigate through space and time, observe all of the planets in extreme close-up, learn their trajectories, inner structure, history, points of interest and more. It's an eye-opening and engaging app that has plenty of information to convey and some cool methods of doing so. If you're curious to learn what's out there, this will help.

Entertainment

Have a whole lot of fun on your Mac

The word 'entertainment' can cover a multitude of things. From listening to internet radio to watching movie clips and enjoying clever screensavers, you can entertain yourself in almost any way you like. It is a broad category, and is hard to define completely, but it is also a category with a wealth of apps that will help you pass your spare time. You can learn magic tricks, watch Earth from space, or simply sit back and watch a realistic fireplace fill your Mac screen. The days of computers being used purely for business are over; now, you can use them for any activity you like. Entertainment is one activity that everyone should spend some time enjoying on their Mac – the only dilemma is choosing from the huge range of apps that are designed to make everyday life a little more fun.

The presentation of The Lost Watch 3D is stunning

Curl up in front of Fireplace Live HD

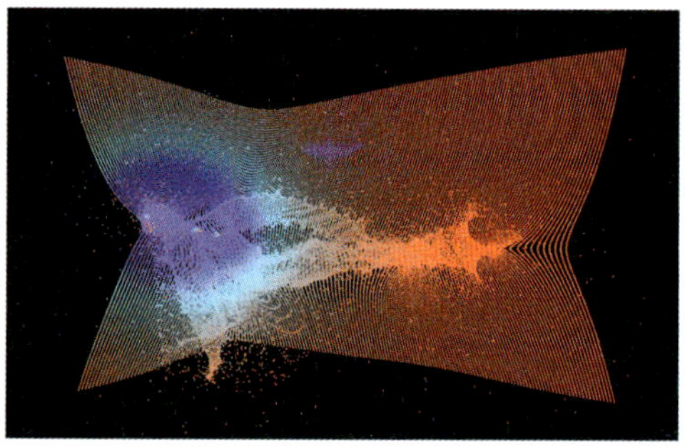

Gravilux becomes more engrossing the more you use it

"There are a wealth of apps to help you pass your spare time"

Media is recreated perfectly in MPlayerX

5 essential apps

The Lost Watch 3D

Price: £1.49/$2.99 **Developer:** Igor Panichev

Not all wallpapers are the same, and The Lost Watch 3D proves that. Besides looking beautiful, it will show you the current date and time, and also lets you personalise it in a rather creative way. It can work as a wallpaper or a screensaver, and there are multiple themes to choose from. If you want to add a personal touch, then simply choose a photo, and it will be shown inside the pendant displaying the time. However, an app like this isn't about the features, but how good it looks and how well it works, and it succeeds in both areas.

Gravilux

Price: £1.49/$1.99

Developer: Scott Snibbe Studio Inc

It is hard to describe Gravilux, because it is a combination of many things, but essentially you click the mouse to move simulated stars towards it. You can think of it as a game, or just as a simple amusement. There's science behind the app, but you don't need to worry about that. Just click on the screen, and watch the magic happen.

MPlayerX

Price: Free **Developer:** Zongyao Qu

For a free app, MPlayerX comes with an astonishing feature set. It can play or stream almost any file format, and the result is a perfectly presented media experience. Subtitles, the Apple remote and multiple monitors are supported, and it will also remember your last watched position. This app fills in some of the gaps in the Mac platform, and really should be built into every single new Mac computer that is sold.

Fireplace Live HD free

Price: Free **Developer:** Voros Innovation

When the winter nights draw in, why not turn your Mac into a visual centrepiece of the room by turning it into a living, crackling open fireplace? The effect is mesmerising and you can almost feel the heat coming off of it. There are eight fire visuals to choose from that all run in stunning HD.

Earth 3D

Price: £1.49/$1.99 **Developer:** Igor Panichev

Ever wondered how our beautiful planet looks to astronauts? This app displays the Earth as few will ever get to see it and provides more than 1,500 geographical objects to explore in glorious HD. You can also set it as your screensaver to impress others who casually stroll past your monitor.

5 essential apps

iBank 5

Price £44.99/$59.99
Developer IGG Software LLC

Personal finance is often overlooked, which is a shame, as many apps bring a simple solution to what should be a complex problem. iBank turns this on its head, by offering the ability to monitor every aspect of your money. You can track your spending, plan for the future and even deal with digital receipts, foreign exchange rates and schedules of events. The presentation maintains a personal approach, despite masking some complex calculations, and it all comes together to create an app that is perfect for anyone who wants to keep a close eye on their personal finances.

You Need a Budget 4

Price £44.99/$55.99 **Developer** Steine LLC

Although the price may seem steep, the money this app can help you save in the long run more than justifies it. YNAB aims to help you break the paycheck-to-paycheck cycle, get out of debt and save money faster by providing a simple and straightforward system to help you manage your money. It also syncs with mobile and tablet versions of the app to keep on top of your finances wherever you are.

Investoscope

Price £22.99/$29.99 **Developer** Morten Fjord-Larsen

The interface is unusual in that it just uses one screen. However, you can monitor multiple areas of your portfolio without having to continually click to find the information you need. Charts are included alongside real time trends to ensure you are always up to date, and it should provide enough information to ensure you don't lose that important trend. It is likely to become a one-stop shop for many investors.

miCharts

Price Free **Developer** Garreth Cain

If you follow the stock exchange then this app lets you monitor your shares quickly and easily through a clean and efficient interface. Quotes from all of the major exchanges are supported and they are charted using over 40 technical indicators. Charts can also be drawn as a Line, Candlestick or OHLC Chart.

MoneyWiz 2 Personal Finance

Price £14.99/$24.99 **Developer** SilverWiz Ltd

There are loads of apps that let you view and manage your accounts, but this is definitely one of the best. Not only can you view your accounts, budgets and bills in one place, you can do so through a fantastic interface.

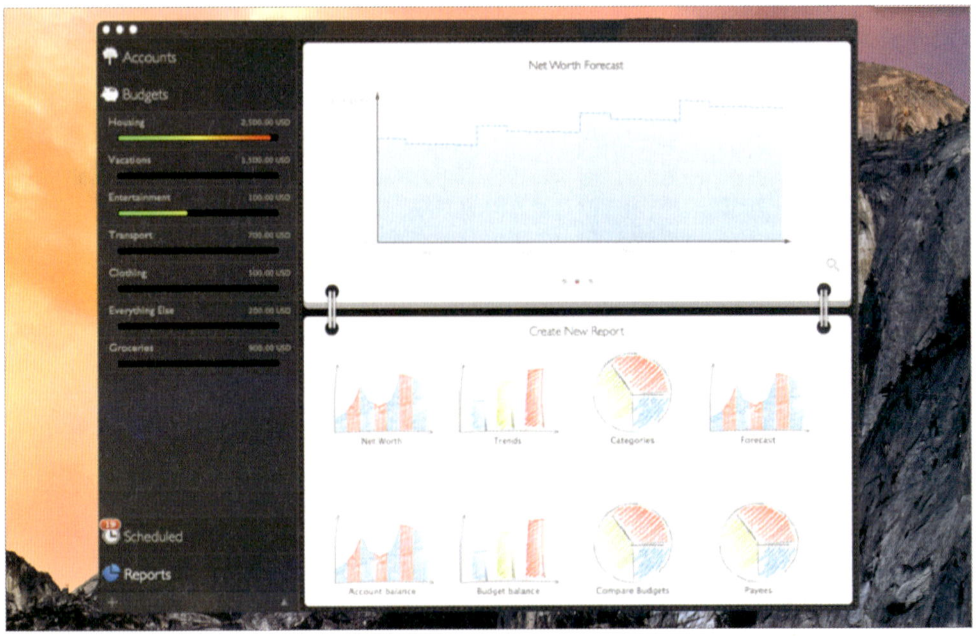

The MoneyWiz app also syncs with your iCloud

Finance

Keep track of the money side of things

From dealing with your bank account to monitoring complex share dealing, the world of finance is often a complex area. It doesn't have to be, however, because there are thousands of apps available that have been designed to make money-management that little bit easier. Accountants can deal with complex databases, a housewife can manage household bills, and even a teenager can keep track of their pocket money. If there is a need to deal with finance in any way, then the chances are there will be an app that supports the task at hand. You may also find that using a Mac to manage your money will, in the long run, save you lots more money. You can now have control over every aspect of your finances, be they for work or home. You just need to spend some time getting used to the solutions available.

> "Apps make money-management easier"

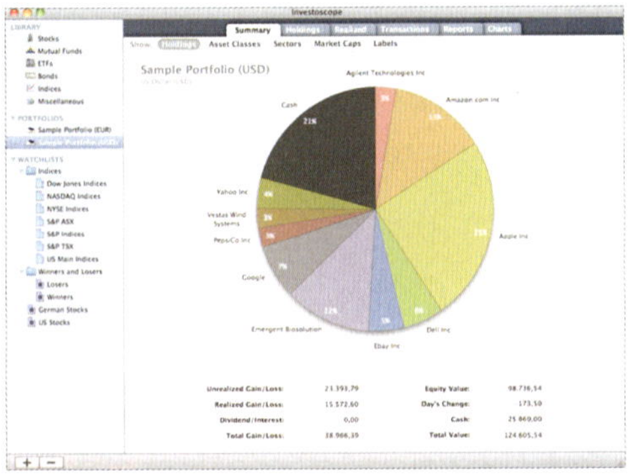

Judge investment performance visually with Investoscope

Monitor the stock market with the free miCharts app

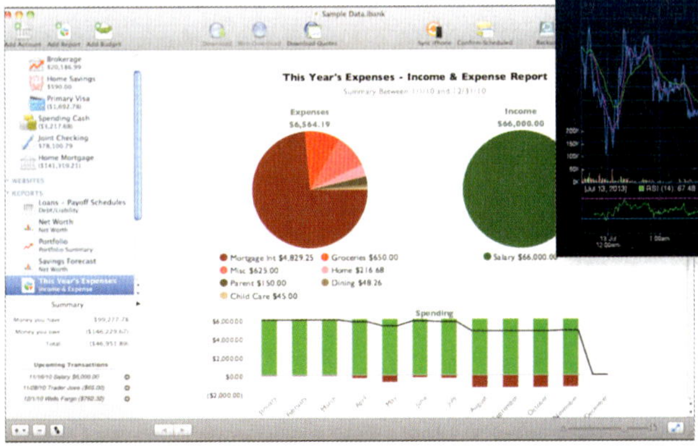

iBank's reporting feature will help you get to grips with your finances

Take in the highs and lows of life in The Sims 2: Super Collection

Games

Have fun and keep your brain engaged

Gaming has historically been somewhat lacklustre on the Mac platform, but the huge growth of iOS gaming has transferred to its bigger brother. Popular titles in the puzzle and strategy categories have long been standard, but there are now many hundreds more options available, most of which are at very cheap prices. To complement these simple titles, there is now a variety of high-end arcade titles available, some of which actually rival games consoles in terms of quality, longevity and addictiveness. You can choose almost any game type you like, depending on your preferences and the budget available, and can be sure that the games you like to play are available. Every possible genre is covered, and once you start you may find that you play games on your Mac more than anything else. Everyone needs some fun from time to time, and a Mac is the perfect tool to help you relax and enjoy yourself.

The simplicity of Rail Maze's visuals hides an immersive gameplay experience

5 essential apps

Jelly Defense

Price: £3.99/$5.99
Developer: Infinite Dreams

Jelly Defense contains visuals, a soundtrack and gameplay like we have rarely seen before. Despite falling into the tower defence category (you defend the jelly nation from invaders), it has many unique aspects, and will keep you coming back time and time again. It's addictive enough to make you pull your hair out, but it is sensational to play, and you will keep playing for hours at a time.

Machinarium

Price: £7.99/$9.99
Developer: Amanita Design

Hailed as one of the best indie games on the market, Machinarium is a point-and-click adventure in which you have to interact with objects within your reach to solve a series of complex puzzles. If you get stuck then you're permitted to one hint per level and it even comes with a walkthrough, which only consists of vague sketches accessed via a mini-game. A premier brain-teaser.

Star Wars: Knights Of The Old Republic

Price: £7.99/$9.99
Developer: Aspyr Media

Set 4,000 years before the famous films, this enjoyable role-playing game lets you evolve your very own Jedi Knight and explore seven different worlds from the Star Wars universe. You get to pick who accompanies you into battle and you get to slice and dice with your own lightsaber. This is an enjoyable and engrossing game at a very reasonable price.

The Sims 2: Super Collection

Price: £22.99/29.99
Developer: Aspyr Media (iDP)

If you're bored of your humdrum life then why not escape into someone else's? The Sims 2: Super Collection lets you simulate life from the cradle to the grave, transforming your character into a successful high flyer with the ideal life or treat them to a life of neglect to see what the eventual outcome will be. The possibilities are endless.

Rail Maze 2

Price: Free
Developer: Spooky House Studios UG

Sometimes, the most simple games are the best ones, and Rail Maze, where you build railroads, is an example where simplicity has been successfully married with superb replay value. The levels get harder as you progress, but that won't stop you stepping up to the challenge as your abilities improve. This game will certainly keep you on the right track.

Graphics and design

Don't neglect your artistic side; discover the best there is to offer on the Mac

The Mac platform has long been preferred by those who like to create, and the options available today are greater than ever before. Whether you want to annotate a simple image or produce a work of art, there will be a solution ready and waiting for you. You can have fun tweaking photos, create photo albums for the family, or spend hours producing a completely original digital painting. No matter what your budget or level of talent, you will be able to find an app that sparks your creative juices, and some of the titles are truly extraordinary. Indeed, it is now possible to create graphics that only a few years ago would have required roomfuls of computers. So it is time to have a look around to see what is available, and spend some time creating like you never have before.

> "Whatever you want to do, there's a solution waiting for you"

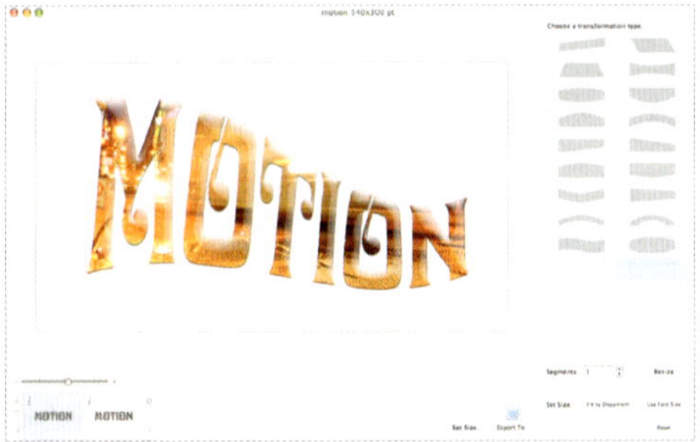

With Art Text 2 you can turn text into any design you like

Get your images looking great with Paint FX

VintageScene can produce some stunning effects

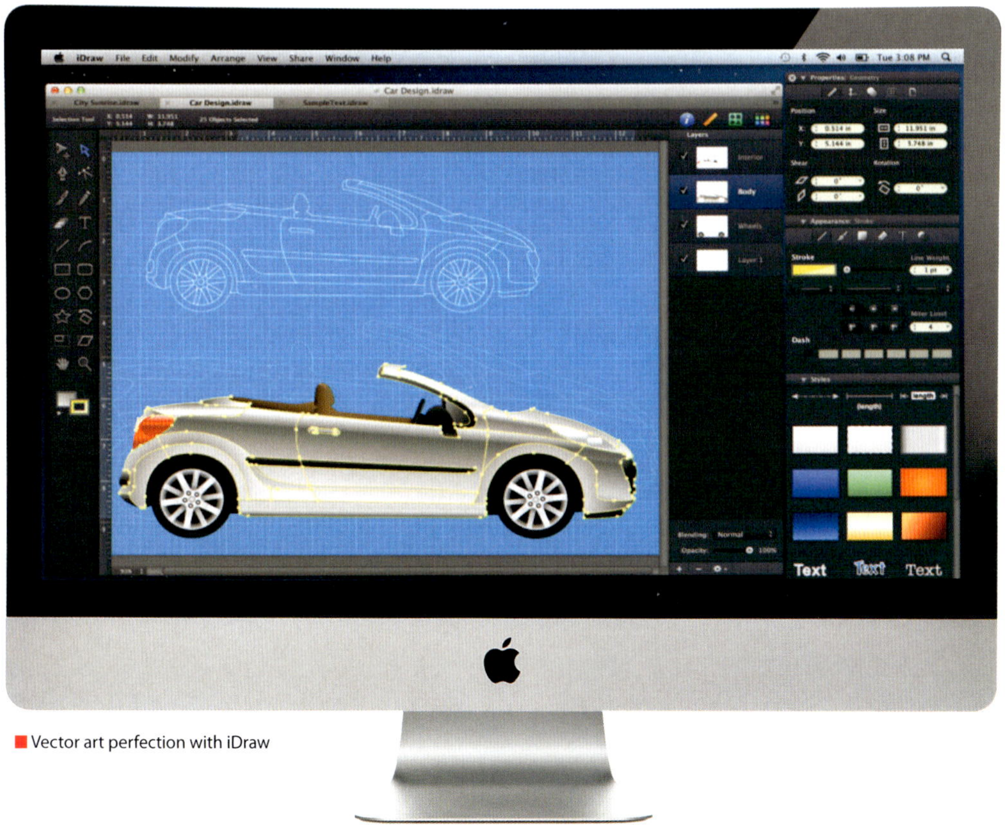

Vector art perfection with iDraw

5 essential apps

Art Text 2

Price: £14.99/$19.99 **Developer:** Belight Software Ltd

The need to make text look more creative is commonplace, and is a requirement for logos, website headers and a multitude of other tasks. Art Text 2 lets you add colours, shapes and all kinds of other effects to words to make them really stand out. You can bend text around images, and manipulate the final result in finite detail so that it will fit perfectly wherever you need to publish it. It concentrates purely on text manipulation, but it does so well, and will suit the many people who need this kind of solution.

iConvert Icons

Price: £3.99/$5.99

Developer: Mathew Eis

This app makes it easy to create your own custom icons from almost any format. Thanks to an auto-detection feature, you can simply drag and drop images, folders with custom icons and pretty much any other icon into the conversion window, choose a location to save them to and the app will do the rest. So if you are in the app-creation market, this handy download will save you a lot of time and stress.

Paint FX

Price: £2.29/$3.99 **Developer:** Kejian Jin

This is a paint app for Mac that brings with it similar tools to those of the popular Microsoft Paint app. As well as all of the basic tools you need to draw, Paint FX also allows you to combine multiple images into one, crop and resize images and apply a variety of photo effects. Best of all, you can control where to apply the effects within the images (as opposed to applying them to all of the image). A simple and easy to use app to unleash your creative side.

VintageScene

Price: £5.99/$7.99 **Developer:** JixiPix LLC

You would think that deliberately making photos look old is a bad thing, but strangely it can add a great deal of personality to your snaps. VintageScene contains a unique algorithm that really does add special effects to any photo, and the end results are marvellous.

iDraw

Price: £18.99/$24.99 **Developer:** Indeeo, Inc

This app provides a feature-packed suite for vector drawing that has all of the tools you need to create anything from detailed technical illustrations to stunning works of art. All of your creations can also be imported into Pages documents and Keynote presentations.

5 essential apps

Perfect Diet Tracker

Price: £18.99/$25.99 **Developer:** Byoni Ltd

If there is one thing you need when trying to diet, it's motivation, and this app is a very good source of this. It can track every aspect of your regime, offer advice and, crucially, show you how well you are succeeding. It is designed to take away all of the hard work, and let you concentrate on your goals. Without this much-needed motivation, you are more likely to fail, and so it's exceptional value for money. This is one of the most complete diet trackers we have seen so far on the Mac, and is highly recommended.

Optimism

Price: Free

Developer: Optimism Apps Pty Ltd

Optimism is a mood chart that helps you monitor your state of mind and develop strategies to help manage depression, bipolar or other physical and mental health conditions. By helping you monitor your mental health, Optimism will help you better understand the triggers that affect you, allowing you to gauge the early warning signs that could lead to depression and a downturn in your mental health.

rubiTrack

Price: Free **Developer:** Markus Spoettl

If you're serious about exercising, it pays to be serious about analysing what you have achieved. rubiTrack will provide you with all sorts of information, such as how far you have walked or run, and can also be used with accessories to ensure real-time tracking. The level of detail is astonishingly complex, and should provide you with enough motivation to keep running your way to ultimate fitness. Definitely one for the serious exerciser.

All-in Yoga

Price: £3.99/$5.99 **Developer:** Zeda Inc

If you want to tone your body and relax your mind then this app features over 250 poses and breathing exercises, photo, video and voice guidance, plus much more. A special algorithm will choose the best program for you according to your goals, level and time, and you can also create your own routines.

Daily Workouts

Price: £2.99/$4.99 **Developer:** Daily Workout Apps, LLC

With a database of over 100 workouts, all with execution instructions and demonstrative videos, the app plucks a routine at random on a daily basis to give all aspects of your physique an all-round tune-up.

Daily Workouts provides a random exercise to try every day

Health and fitness

Stay fit with the help of your Mac

Sometimes you need a little help to get healthy, and this is particularly true when undertaking a new diet or fitness regime. Being able to monitor your progress is often all the encouragement you need to keep going, and a Mac can help with the serious stuff such as tracking an illness or trying to stop smoking. There are apps available in every health category, and everything from specific illnesses to specialist diets are covered. It may not sound that important, but remember that when you use an app that helps you, it has the potential to greatly improve, or even save, your life. This is a category that serves as an example of the wide range of Mac apps available, as it truly does cover every possible health subject. It is time to improve your life with your Mac and a few apps.

"Your Mac can help with the serious stuff"

The All-in Yoga app is a great stress beater

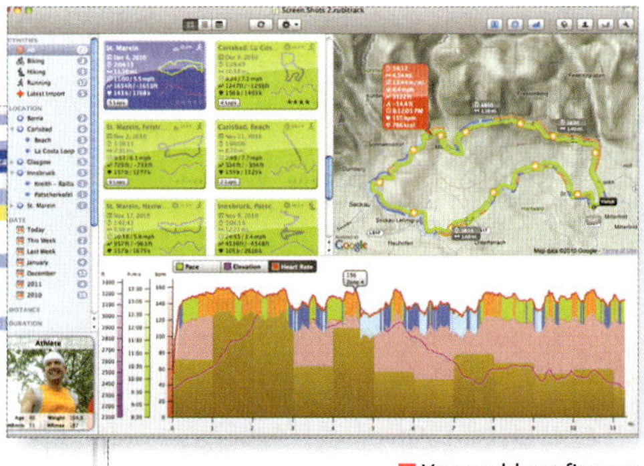

You could not fit more detail on rubiTrack's screen

You can track what you eat every single day with Perfect Diet Tracker

5 essential apps

Comic Life 3

Price: £22.99/$34.99 **Developer:** Plasq LLC

This entertaining app can help you transform your photos into cool comic layouts (and even entire books). With Comic Life 2 you can easily import images from your Mac and arrange them how you see fit using creative templates. You can then add in speech bubbles, fonts and filters to give your photos a specific look and feel. The interface is highly intuitive so that you can create cool new ways to show off your holiday snaps in minutes.

Day One

Price: £7.99/$9.99 **Developer:** Bloom Built, LLC

If you're in the market for an elegant app for inputting your daily thoughts and feelings then this fits the bill perfectly. A password-protected interface lets you write, safe in the knowledge that your words won't be seen by prying eyes. The app also utilises iCloud, so you can start writing on your Mac and then continue later on using your iPhone or iPad.

Vinoteka

Price: £22.99/$34.99

Developer: Elodie Morin-Rager

Serious devotees of wine like the thought of having their own wine cellar and, whether you have one or not, you can now experience this feeling through Vinoteka. It will let you monitor every aspect of your wine collection, and is particularly useful for businesses involved in this industry. No matter what your level of expertise or interest, this app is a true example of what can be achieved on a Mac.

Yummysoup!

Price: £10.99/$14.99

Developer: Kenneth Humbard

Yummysoup! has been created to let you bring all of your favourite recipes to one place. You can import recipes from your favourite sites or add text notes that your friends have given you. The presentation is professional, and really does help to bring the recipes to life.

Bits

Price: Free

Developer: Dmitry Nikolaev

With its simple drag and drop interface, Bits is perfect for compiling thoughts and images to make blogging as intuitive and effortless as possible. Full cloud integration also means that you can add to it whenever inspiration strikes to ensure that no idea is left by the wayside.

Vinoteka's presentation is about as good as any app gets

Lifestyle

Tailor your Mac to fit in with your life

We all have different lifestyles, hobbies and interests, and as such a wide range of apps are required to cater for the majority. This particular category is more wide-ranging than any other because it covers all of our interests. From waking up in the morning to keeping a diary, all of these and more can fit in the Lifestyle category. With the right choice of apps, and used properly, they can be truly beneficial to your day-to-day life, and it is worth checking as many as possible to ensure that you are using the ones that are right for you. It is testament to the creativity of Mac developers that even the most obscure of interests are covered by Mac apps, and it goes to show just how flexible and powerful the platform truly is. Whatever your lifestyle, there will be an app for it.

Catch those thoughts effortlessly with Bits

Recipes come to life in Yummysoup!

"The right choice of apps can benefit your day-to-day life"

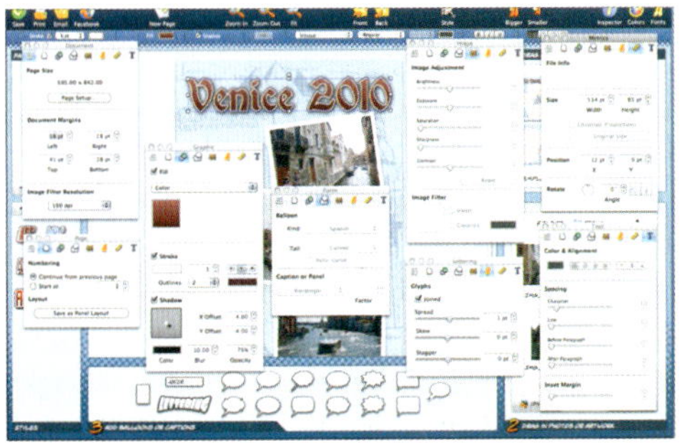

Transform your photos into comics with Comic Life 2

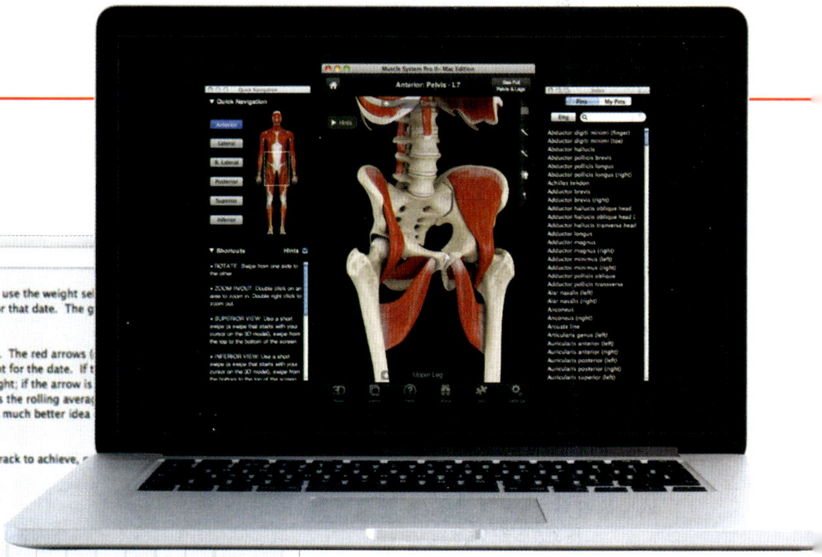

More than 5,000 diagrams are included in Muscle System Pro II

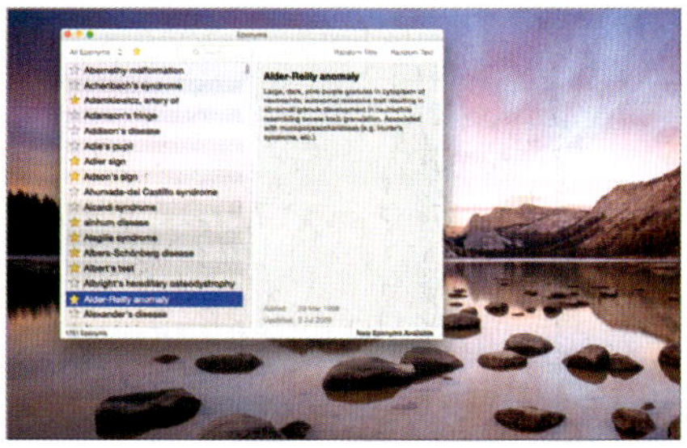

The calendar feature in Weight-Monitor will ensure your weight is managed properly

Get quick and easy access to an extensive dictionary of medical terms with Eponyms

Medical

Never let important matters like your health slide

Medical apps tend to fall into two categories: those that are designed to help the individual, and those designed to aid medical professionals. These apps can be as simple as helping you monitor your weight, or as complex as showing X-rays on a Mac screen. There are serious uses for the individual as well, and people with diabetes and asthma, as well as other ailments that require constant monitoring, will benefit from specialised apps. The way many of them have been designed makes them accessible to anyone. Doctors can quickly look up patient information, and the individual can easily understand complex medical data that is pertinent to them. It is an area that is very important, and the Mac OS is a platform that is more than capable of helping anyone who has a need for medical help, which is ultimately all of us.

The colourful visuals of Breathing Zone help you understand the exercises

5 essential apps

Muscle System Pro III

Price: £13.99/$19.99

Developer: 3D4Medical.com

Muscles are not easy to visualise, but with this app you will be able to view every single detail. It allows the labelling of specific areas, and you can zoom, rotate and manage the view in almost every way. If you're using this app in a professional capacity, there is a quiz included to check your own knowledge on the subject matter.

Weight-Monitor

Price: £1.49/$1.99

Developer: Jim Chapple

When you're trying to lose weight, you always need encouragement. That could come from friends and family, but the best way is to monitor your progress and to try to continue your success. This app lets you input your daily weight, which is then plotted on a graph. Seeing the graph drop over time is the perfect incentive, and also lets you see your average weight and work towards a specific goal.

My Medical

Price: £10.99/$14.99

Developer: Hyrax Inc

This app lets you keep all of your important medical information together in one place. You can also store information for other family members so that you have one central comprehensive database that can be called on when you need it. The app offers auto-completion for a wealth of medical jargon, such as drug names and vaccinations and the file can be easily shared with others.

Breathing Zone

Price: £2.49/$2.99

Developer: Breathing Zone Limited

Breathing is not just something that we all do naturally. Done properly, and it can greatly reduce the effects of asthma, alleviate stress-related symptoms, and offer countless other benefits. The exercises themselves are very well presented and easy to follow, and if you take the time to mimic them as closely as possible, then you will surely benefit.

Eponyms

Price: Free

Developer: Ossus GmbH

This useful app provides a short description of more than 1,700 common and obscure eponyms. Obviously the amount of detail provided may be a little vague for the needs of some medical professionals, but it is nevertheless a handy quick reference tool and a great source of medical trivia. Its compact interface means it can sit easily on your desktop alongside documents.

Logic Pro 9 is a fantastically in-depth music making app

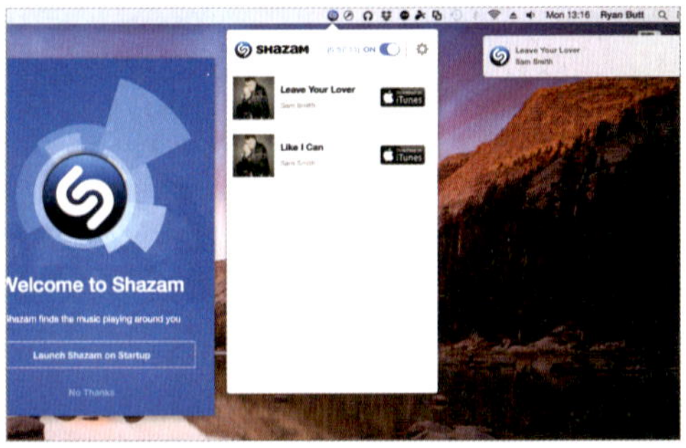

Shazam works in the background to identify music…

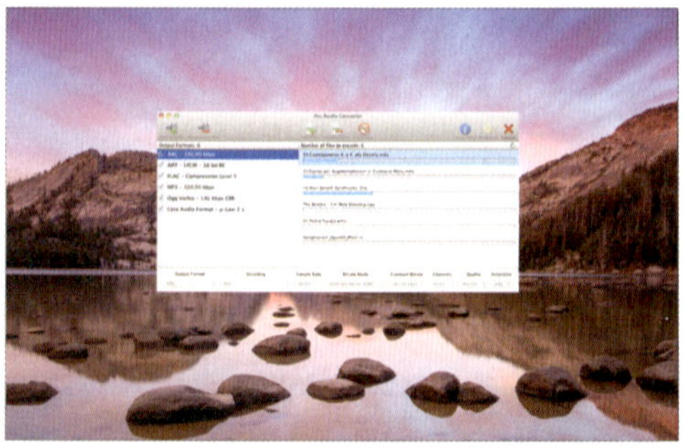

Pro Audio Coverter can convert a multitude of audio formats

Djay's authentic turntables make you feel like a real DJ

Music

Get down to the sound of the beat

The days of playing instruments and recording the resulting sounds to make music could be numbered. You can now create music in thousands of different ways, and record your output in extremely high quality. People now have the capacity to use instruments that haven't been designed yet, and have fun searching for new music using apps that understand their tastes. No matter what you want to do in the musical field, you can now do it, and some of the solutions also suit professional musicians. Songwriters, guitar players and producers can all use complex apps to create new work. DJs can mix music, and individuals can create completely original ringtones. Music has truly reached the digital age, and the digital age has brought music to anyone, no matter how talented they are. Now, we can all create music, just as we wanted to do when we were children.

5 essential apps

Logic Pro X

Price: £149.99/$199.99 **Developer:** iTunes S.a.r.l.

Logic Pro 9 is a complete set of creative tools for any musician who wants to write, record, edit and mix music. It comes with a huge collection of instruments, effects and loops, making it easy to get crisp and authentic sounding accompaniments on your tracks. Novices can get up and running quickly thanks to production-ready templates, while one-step track setup and a single-window interface allows you to work fast with easy access to all of the tools you need. With 40 built-in instruments, 80 different effects and over 1,700 samples, this is a studio boffin's nirvana.

Shazam

Price: Free **Developer:** Shazam Entertainment

Shazam is a handy service for identifying song titles and artists quickly and easily. The app listens to the track and relays all manner of in-depth information in just a few seconds. The service has already been incorporated into Siri on iOS devices and this Mac app provides a handy menu item that works in the background to listen to, identify and provide information on the music around you.

Pro Audio Converter

Price: £7.99/$9.99 **Developer:** Mark Verstraete

This app lets you covert between a wide variety of audio file formats. You can batch convert with ease and it also supports the reading and writing of metadata, including that of existing audio files without the need to re-encode. All coverted files can be added to your iTunes library.

djay Pro

Price: £39.99/$59.99

Developer: algoriddim GmbH

If you've ever wanted to be a DJ, but didn't have the confidence to try it, you now can with this brilliant app. The feature set is immense and the presentation is realistic, so you have no excuse to not play around with your music and spin some virtual discs. You can even 'scratch' them like a true pro.

SoundMate for SoundCloud

Price: £3.99/$5.99 **Developer:** SoundCloud Ltd

SoundMate for SoundCloud is a social network for musicians and music lovers, populated by big-name acts showcasing their latest projects and aspiring musicians who upload their own tracks to get feedback. The community is friendly and it is a great place to share sounds with other users.

5 essential apps

Mixtab

Price: Free **Developer:** Mixtab

There are many news apps that offer the ability to read news in a tweaked format, but few bring such a quick and easy to use interface to the experience. Mixtab includes predefined news channels, which collect news from topic-based websites, and lets you build your own topics for your own interests. Full articles are available and, in theory, you could do almost all of your browsing within this app and leave the web altogether. This is an exceptional solution, which is as well designed as many expensive alternatives.

NewsRack

Price: $7.99 (US only) **Developer:** Ole Zorn

NewsRack takes the middle ground between news readers that attempt to offer lots of clever effects and the more simple RSS readers. It strikes the balance well, and brings a speedy experience which is particularly useful if you follow many different sources. With integration to third party services like Instapaper, you may find this app to be the perfect one for satisfying your news gathering needs.

NewsBar

Price: £2.99/$4.99 **Developer:** Andras Porffy

Sometimes you want your news to be available but not dominate everything you are doing. NewsBar sits on the desktop and unobtrusively presents the latest news in a stream. You can also quickly hide news items with a swipe, or read them in full with a tap for ultimate control, and the way that it updates the feeds means that you will not be constantly glancing at the latest stories. It's a streamlined way of getting your news delivered to you.

Pocket

Price: Free **Developer:** Read It Later, Inc

Pocket provides a handy service for storing all of the web articles and videos that you don't have time to explore presently in the cloud and makes them accessible through any device. You can even read articles offline, making this idea for those long commutes.

Pulp

Price: £6.99/$9.99 **Developer:** Acrylic Software

This innovative news reader transforms your favourite news sites into your own personalised newspaper, making scanning through the news quicker and more enjoyable than ever before. By putting multiple news feeds onto a single page, Pulp lets you quickly browse through headlines to find hot topics.

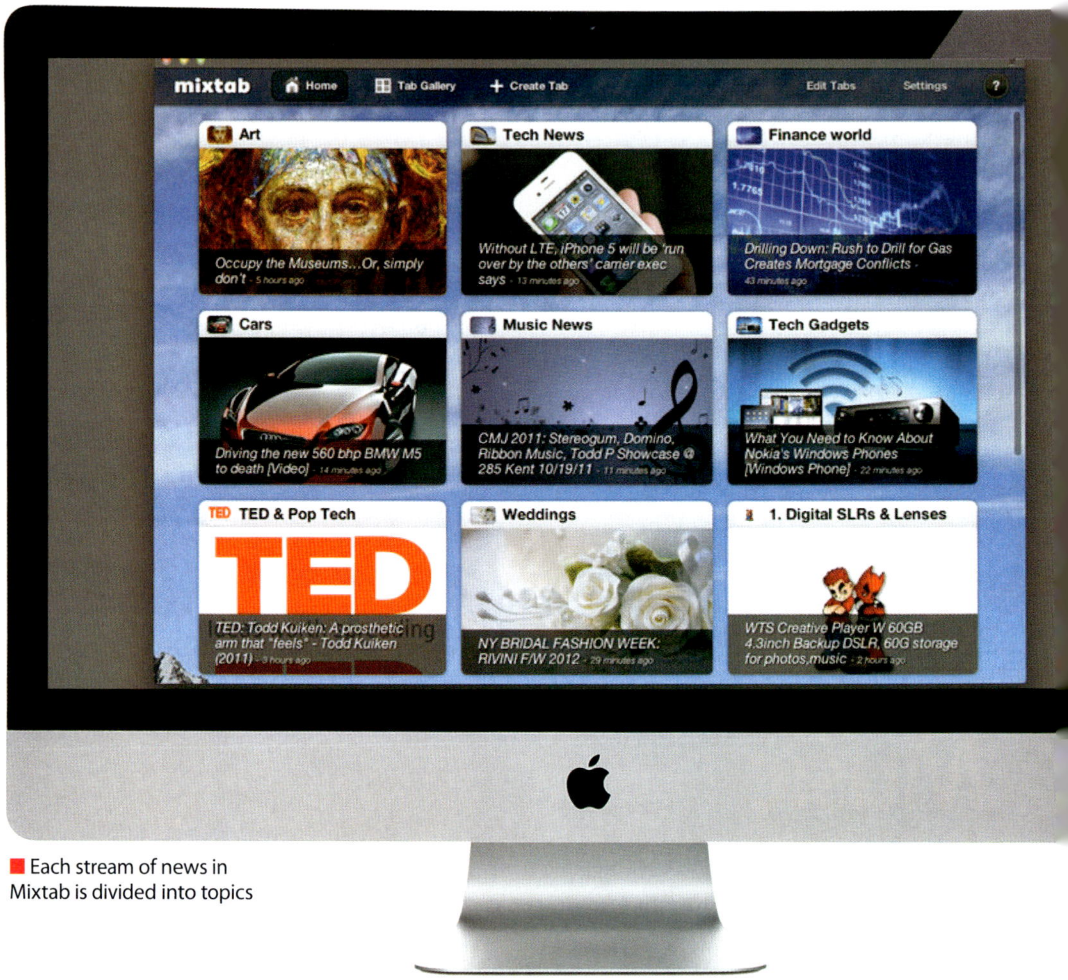

Each stream of news in Mixtab is divided into topics

News

Keep informed on everything in the world today

It used to be that the best way to keep up with the news was to visit websites. Of course, this works well for sites like the BBC, but for specialist topics it can involve hunting around for the right places. Some Mac apps are now capable of recreating news provided by websites in a way that is more friendly, logical and easier to read. Other apps will automatically grab the latest news and present it on the desktop, and the options for reading a variety of topics are almost unlimited. No matter what the topic or your visual preference, there will be a solution that suits the way you want to catch up with the world around you. Indeed, some are so good that you may never visit a traditional website for news again.

> "Some Mac apps are capable of recreating news from websites"

Whole articles can be read without leaving the NewsRack app

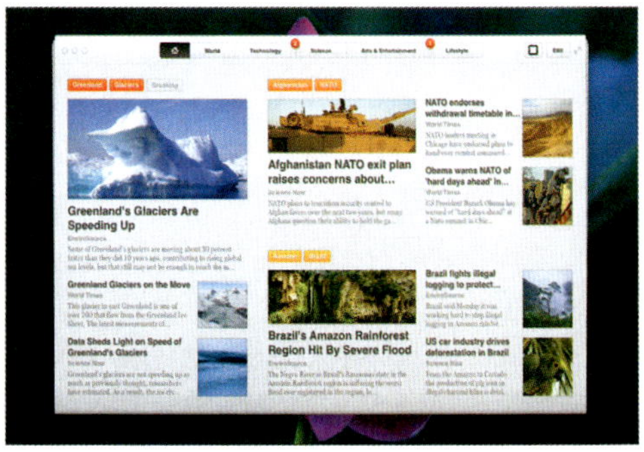

Get your news feeds in your own personalised newspaper with Pulp

The PicFrame app can make even dull photos look stunning…

Sharing the results on social networks is easy with Analog

You can create astonishing effects in minutes with Colorstrokes

Photography

Store your memories, and create new ones

Photographers will tell you that, often, a lot of the work required to create a great photograph happens on a computer after the photo has been taken, and this makes the Mac platform ideal for anyone with an interest in this field. It doesn't matter if you are experienced or new to the world of photography because there will be a solution, and the majority are designed to be as easy to use as possible.

From adding speech bubbles to making photos look like they were taken many decades ago, you can do almost anything you want with a Mac and a collection of digital images. You can take this as far as you like or just play around, but either way, the platform and available apps will offer you everything you need to get started and enjoy the world of photography for professional or personal reasons.

Aperture 3's interface is easy to grasp and can be mastered in minutes

5 essential apps

Colorstrokes

Price: £2.99/$4.99

Developer: macphun.com

The ability to add colour to black and white photos has, until recently, only been accessible by professionals with expensive equipment. Anyone can now create this effect, and all it takes is a steady hand and a mouse. The end results can be stunning and the amount of effort required is little, which is a testament to how well it is programmed. A very clever and versatile app.

Analog

Price: £7.99/$9.99

Developer: Realmac Software

Most people want to add effects to their photos without having to learn new processes. Analog takes away the learning process and lets you choose from a variety of filters. There's some clever technology behind the process, but the user need never see that. The front interface is user-friendly and you can share the results using a variety of services.

PicFrame

Price: £0.79/$0.99

Developer: Active Development

A good frame can make even the dullest pictures look attractive, and this affordable app features 67 adjustable frames, with support for up to nine photos in a single frame. Once you have composed your photo arrangements, you can share them on Facebook or Twitter, or just enjoy gazing at them on your desktop. For the price, this is a brilliant app for showing off your snaps.

Aperture

Price: £59.99/$89.99

Developer: iTunes

Aperture is primarily designed for iPhoto users who want to get more out of their photos. It includes powerful tools for refining images, showcasing your work and managing massive libraries on your Mac. Through the app's intuitive interface, you can touch up your images quickly and choose from dozens of built-in adjustment presets, or instead create your own to give your photos a custom look.

FX Photo Studio

Price: £7.99/$9.99

Developer: macphun.com

This is a neat photo touch-up app that provides an immense array of digital make-up to get your images looking great. Through a variety of 173 photo effects and filters you can transform any photo into a vintage masterpiece, a hipster snap, oil painting, sketch and more. The app also includes a collection of over 40 frames and borders to finish your photos off perfectly.

■ RapidWeaver's simple interface hides its advanced functions

Productivity

Maximise your output

Productivity takes many forms, and there are solutions that will help you be more productive, no matter what your need or speciality. Everything from creating text documents to building databases can fall into this category, and it is without doubt one of the more diverse categories, encompassing a wide range of apps. If there is any task that you need to be more productive at, there will likely be a solution available. It may require some careful searching, but a solution will arrive that could potentially speed up every aspect of your work, which can have major benefits for almost everything you do with your desktop or laptop. Sometimes, the smallest solutions offer as many benefits as the larger apps and you should take time to see if a collection of smaller apps will work better than one large app.

> "There are many great productivity solutions"

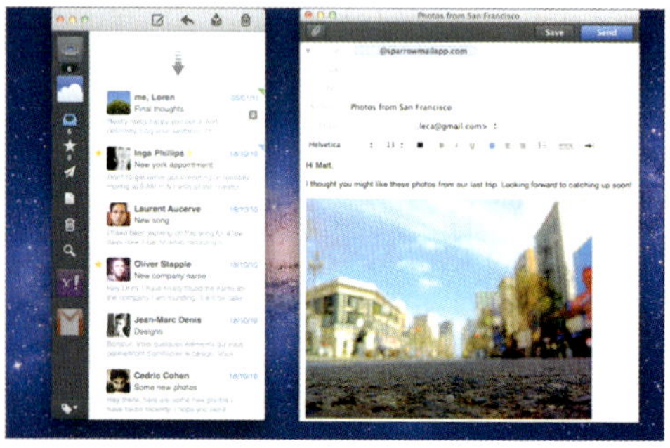

■ The emails stand out in Sparrow's minimalist interface

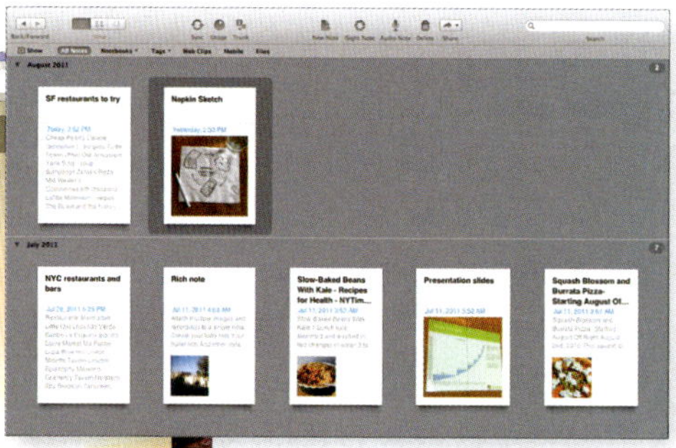

■ Multiple views are available in Evernote

■ Capture your thoughts and create to-do lists with Wunderlist

5 essential apps

Sparrow

Price: £6.99/$9.99 **Developer:** Sparrow SARL

Sparrow takes the idea of complex email management and breaks it down into bite-sized pieces, so that you can manage your emails more efficiently and still have a view of other work if you need to multi-task. Setting up is simple, and the presentation ensures that the important data is brought to the front. It follows the Mac design principles, and as such fits in with the entire operating system perfectly. It looks good, works well, and could solve your email problems.

RapidWeaver

Price: £59.99/$79.99

Developer: Realmac Software Limited

Many people want to create websites, but few have the time or knowledge to do so effectively. RapidWeaver offers a multitude of templates, and will also automate many of the site building tasks that trip up many people. It will suit the home user best, but even those who take a more professional approach will find value in this application.

1Password

Price: £39.99/$49.99

Developer: Agilebits Inc

If you want to apply extra security to your Mac and protect all of your various user names and passwords then this app works directly with your browser, saves all of your details and then effortlessly creates strong, unique passwords for each site. The app can then automatically and securely log you in, enter credit card information and fill in registration forms, all while encrypting your info with one password.

Wunderlist

Price: Free

Developer: 6 Wunderkinder GmbH

If you need an outlet for all of your creative ideas, or you just need an efficient and robust app for creating quick and easy to-do lists then this app fits the bill perfectly. Through a simple interface you can get down your notes and share them with others.

Evernote

Price: Free **Developer:** Evernote

Evernote is a hugely popular online note system and can help you manage many aspects of your life. This free app brings all of your notes and quick synchronisation to any Mac and is designed to offer all of the main features on your desktop all of the time.

Reference

Keep things at the forefront

Reference data is helpful for all sorts of reasons, and can form the backbone of many tasks we need to perform. Without accurate data, we could be working with information that makes a whole project pointless, and of course there are countless times when you will simply want to find information to help you. Whether you are writing a thesis or settling an argument with friends, reference data is required, and there are many ways in which it can be presented. Some apps will make complex data more accessible simply by stripping out the visual interference from certain websites, while others act as a layer over the major reference portals. Whether you are looking for new information or require known data to be presented more clearly, there will be ready-made solutions available which make searching and using information much quicker than ever before.

"There are many ways data can be presented"

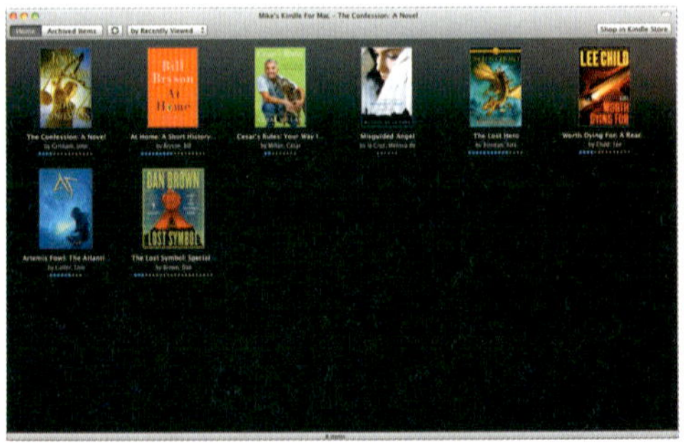

Reading books is easy with the Kindle app

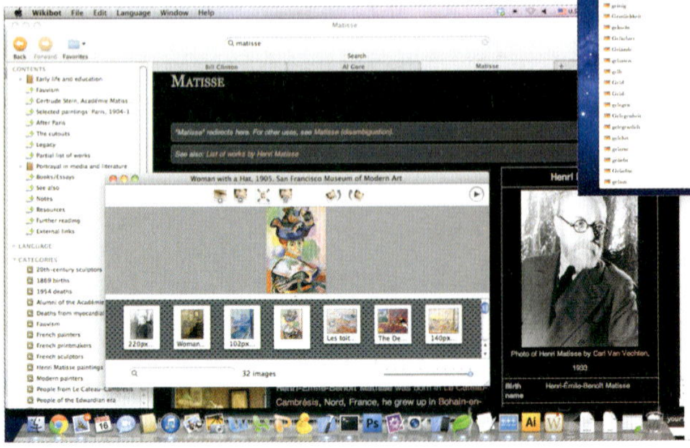

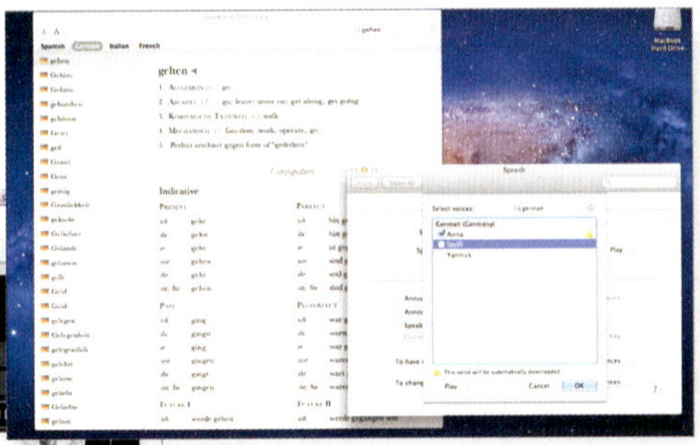

Wikipedia looks much better when it is cleaned up using the Wikibot app

You can even hear the translations in One World Dictionary

The detail in Art Authority is high

5 essential apps

Wikibot

Price: £3.99/$5.99 **Developer:** Evan Rosenfeld

Wikipedia is, of course, an excellent source of information, but it can be unwieldy in more complex articles. Wikibot strips away the visual clutter and presents each article as basically as possible. You can bookmark favourite articles, view your search history and use the app as a much better-looking version of the web for your Wikipedia research. It's beautiful, quick, and designed to bring Wikipedia closer to you than it already is.

Art Authority For Mac

Price :£7.99/$9.99

Developer: Open Door Networks Inc

If you like art and you own a Mac, you need Art Authority. With more than 40,000 paintings and sculptures beautifully rendered for the digital screen from more than 1,000 famous artists, you immediately have access to a wide range of beautiful creations. The features included and overall presentation suit the subject matter perfectly, and come together to create a solution that will be ideal for any art lover.

Kindle

Price: Free **Developer:** AMZN Mobile LLC

If you already own iBooks then the Kindle app works along the same lines by letting you read books on your Mac. You can shop for thousands of books – paid for and free – on the Kindle Store and, provided you have the Kindle app installed on your iPad or iPhone, all of your bookmarks can be automatically synced over iCloud, as well as you current page, so you can start reading on your Mac and continue exactly where you left off on your iOS device.

One World Dictionary

Price: Free **Developer:** Ascendo Inc

One World Dictionary is a good solution for those who are either learning a new language or are simply curious about particular translations. The app includes a large database for you to play with, and could potentially be used on a trip with a Mac laptop for those times when you get stuck.

Redshift Astronomy

Price: £12.99/$16.99

Developer: Oleksandr Izerkov

This eye-opening app lets you visit all of the planets in our solar system, virtually speaking, from your Mac desktop. Gravitate around 3D planets, stars and deep sky objects and learn a wide range of interesting facts and stats through a gorgeous interface.

Essential apps

5 essential apps

Twitter

Price: Free **Developer:** Twitter, Inc

Amazingly, it is only recently that Mac users have had the option to switch from using Twitter through a web browser to an actual app, but the good news is that this free download is easy to use, comes with a smart interface and has been well worth the wait. Through Twitter, you can follow your interests and get instant updates from your friends, industry experts, celebrities and see what's happening around the world. You can do everything through this app that you could through the website.

MarsEdit

Price: £29.99/$39.99
Developer: Apparent Software

MarsEdit is designed to replace the often slow interfaces offered by blog hosting services. It lets you create content offline in a setting that is ideal for quick editing or complex article writing. Compatibility with a wide range of services is also available, and once you start using it you will be able to manage multiple blogs from multiple services with ease. It takes some time to learn, but your efforts will be rewarded.

Wire

Price: Free
Developer: Zeta Project Inc

Wire is a simple app for helping you connect with your nearest and dearest. Through its efficient messaging service you can enjoy conversations on your Mac or mobile device, create groups to address multiple people at once and share links, pictures and YouTube videos. The interface is accessible and it's totally free. Obviously competition in this department is hot, but this app stands out as being a particular good means of chatting freely with others.

Pin for Pinterest

Price: Free **Developer:** FIPLAB Ltd

This app takes your Pinterest addiction to a whole new level by allowing you to instantly browse your Pinterest account without having to open your web browser. You will need Pin Pro to upload new images, but this app at least allows you to fuel your Pinterest interest whenever you need to.

LINE

Price: Free **Developer:** LINE Corporation

Also available on smartphones and tablets, LINE is a useful communication app that enables you to send unlimited free text messages and voice calls. You can also utilise the service to send photos, videos and other types of files up to 1GB quickly and easily.

Social Networking

Stay connected with a variety of fantastic apps

Social networking has grown to be one of the most used forms of internet communication, and for some people the big services like Twitter and Facebook take up the majority of their online time. Each service has websites associated with it, but rarely is the web experience as good as standalone apps on a desktop or mobile. There are apps available that can sit on the desktop and update you as they work, and others that offer more features than the social networks do officially. Other solutions attempt to bring all of your social networks together in one place, and even allow you to update multiple sites at once. If you use any of the social networks, then there are apps available that will completely transform the way that you communicate with friends and strangers. It's just a question of finding the ones that work best with the way that you like to talk.

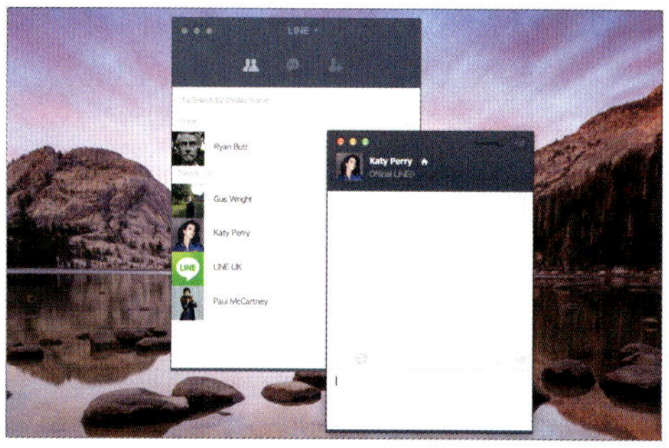

Communicate with ease thanks to LINE

> "You can update multiple sites at once"

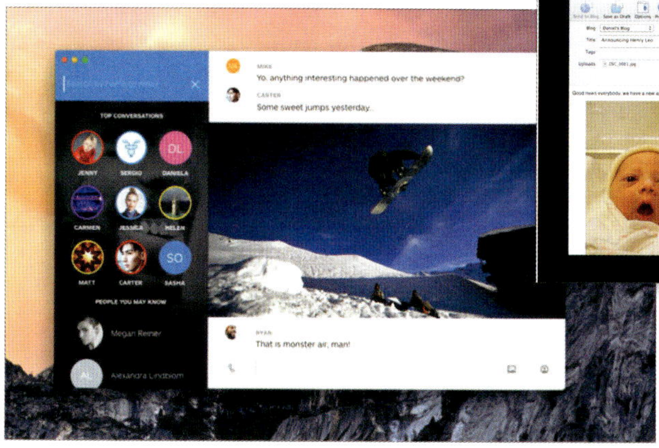

The Wire app helps you chat freely to your friends and family

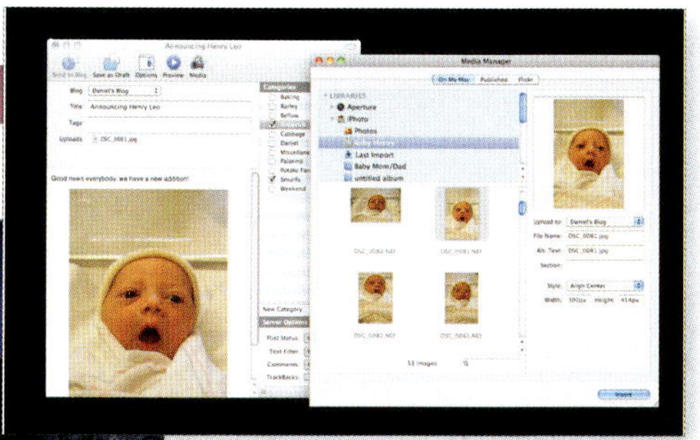

The main MarsEdit interface is much cleaner than the offerings of most blog platforms

5 essential apps

Swing It Pro

Price: £109.99/$149.99

Developer: FKE Datakonsult AB

Golf is all about the swing. Without a good technique, your scores will be higher and your enjoyment less. You can either pay lots of money to get some coaching, or purchase this app and learn at home. It uses videos to help you visualise what you need to do. You can crop the videos, create notes and work in your spare time. It isn't cheap, but compared to professional coaching, it could produce similar results, and ultimately save you money.

Marathon Pace Calculator

Price: Free

Developer: Matti Ropponen

This app helps you plan your running pace when undertaking the challenge of a marathon. Just select your distance (marathon, half-marathon, 10K, 15K, 20K, 50K, 100K or custom), set your target time and Marathonn Pace Calculator will provide you with your target split times. Once your target pace has been calculated, print out the results to refer to.

Swimming Coach's Clipboard

Price: £7.99/$9.99

Developer: PVI Maine LLC

This useful app allows swimming instructors or spectators to time and track splits of multiple swimmers across events in any race, competition or training session. The clipboard results can be stored, printed, emails and more and will always be stored within the app for easy access whenever you need them. It has all the tools you need to become a better coach.

Dive Log Manager

Price: Free **Developer:** Janice McLaughlin

One important aspect of diving is to monitor your previous dives and gauge how quickly you're learning. This app lets you do that, and will also help you monitor your diving equipment. It is incredibly feature-rich, and will cover all your diving needs.

SeaNav UK

Price: £21.99/$29.99

Developer: Pocket Mariner Ltd

This app lets you explore, plan and navigate your boating trips in real-time thanks to crystal-clear, HD vector marine charts that cover the whole of the UK and Ireland. Buoys, bridges, rocks, and anchorage areas are all displayed as layers that you can turn on and off and you can measure distances and set waypoints.

With Swing It Pro you can analyse any aspect of the perfect golf swing

Sports

Make the most of your sporting abilities

Sports is a category that is broad in that it has to cater for a wide range of different activities. Within each sport there are further groups of people; coaches, players, fans and so on. This means that app developers have to build a variety of solutions for every conceivable activity, and this category alone highlights just how popular the Mac platform is for apps. No matter what sport you enjoy, you should be able to find an app that will increase your enjoyment or participation. From getting up-to-the-minute timings on motor racing laps to building strategies and plans for a team you coach, you can do it with a Mac. As a fan, you can also find specialist apps that will present news and gossip for particular sports, and this includes information from official sources, which are presented in a unique way for the desktop.

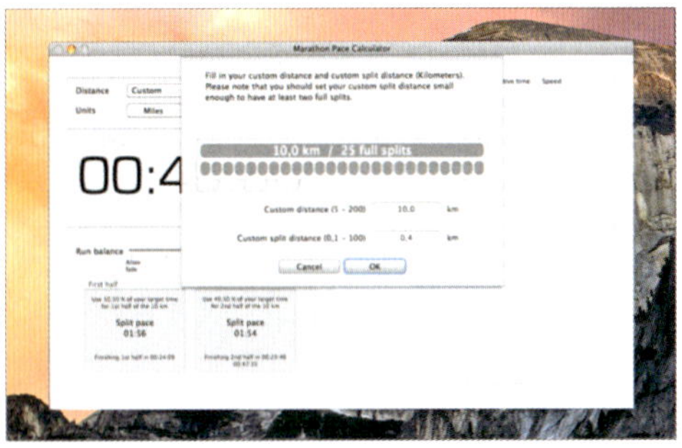

Get up to speed with the Marathon Pace Calculator

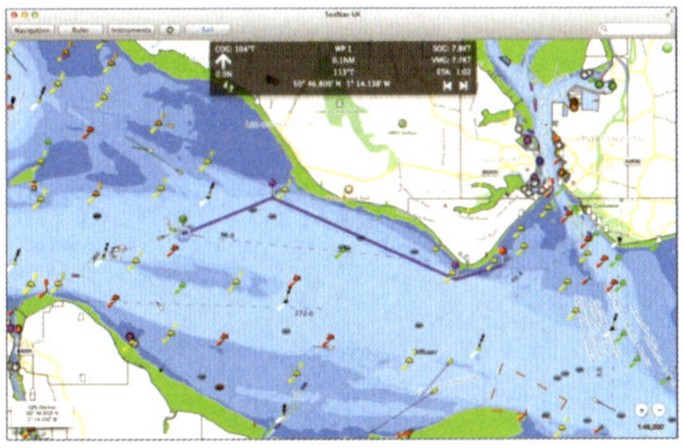

Plan your voyages with SeaNav UK

"No matter the sport, you should be able to find an app to help"

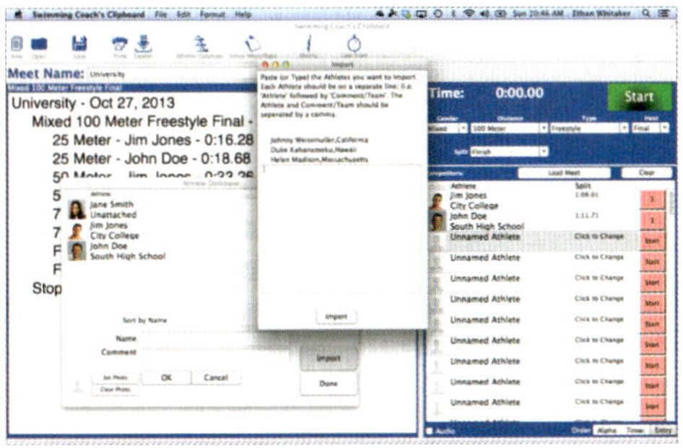

Track all aspects of those swimming sessions…

5 essential apps

Arrivals & Departures

Price: £3.99/$5.99 **Developer:** Krishna Vegesna

One of the major gripes for frequent travellers is having to continually monitor arrival and departure times. This is also true for those working in companies who need to check when people will arrive, and so this app will be a boon for them, or you. It displays real-time flight times for thousands of airports and is very accurate. You can choose favourite airports and even view flight paths if you are interested. The level of information is high and for some people it will be the perfect solution to their flight tracking needs, which they will use every day.

myTracks

Price: £10.99/$14.99 **Developer:** Dirk Stichling

Walkers and those who like to explore have a need to understand 'exactly' where they have been, and to keep detailed logs of their travels. myTracks is an advanced solution that has built-in compatibility with a number of other apps, and also works with iOS devices, which is ideal for those on the move. It is a little technical in places, but serious walkers will understand the need for this extra functionality.

Flightradar24

Price: £2.99/$3.99 **Developer:** Svenska Resenatverket AB

Already a massive hit on iOS devices, Flightradar24 is a handy app for tracking planes across Europe and the world. A smart interface monitors the planes over a Google Map and you can choose to layer on what information about the planes you with to know. This includes flight numbers, airline, registration number and much more.

Time Palette

Price: £13.49/$17.99

Developer: Xeric Design Ltd

Time Palette offers a wealth of information for thousands of cities around the world. This makes it ideal for many groups of people who need to know the weather and other specific information for particular locations. It is ideal for businesses, but potentially useful for everyone.

Offbeat Locations

Price: Free **Developer:** William Modesitt

This quirky app lists the stranger attractions in your area – the weird and wonderful places that you perhaps wouldn't normally think of visiting. As you can imagine, using this app can add some obscure spice to your standard days out.

Half flight times and half map, the Arrivals & Departures app works very well

Travel

Around the world with your Mac

Planning a trip beforehand will likely make it a more pleasant experience, and you can do this on a Mac in a variety of ways. You can build a basic itinerary or plan every single minute, which can be particularly useful for business trips where money is of paramount importance. The travel category also covers apps that will help you decide where to stay, who to fly with, and to even use the reviews of other travellers to understand if a service is worth paying for. It doesn't end there; you can use some of these services when abroad using a laptop to check on live flight times, and to see how the weather will be for days out, and as such the benefits quickly become clear. No matter what you want to do that is travel related, you will be able to do it on a Mac with the use of some clever apps.

> "Planning a trip will make it more pleasant"

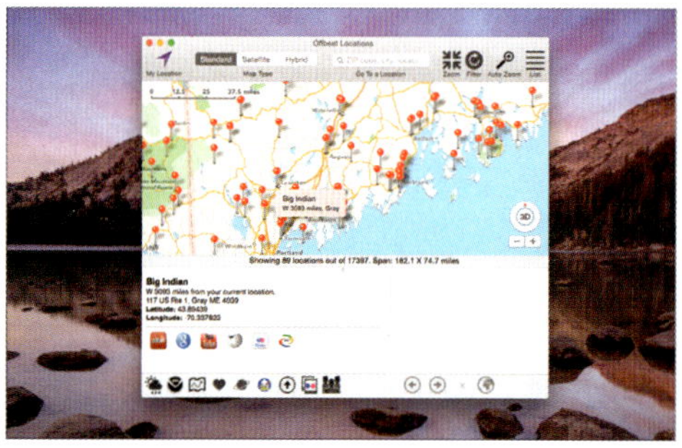

Go where you wouldn't think to with Offbeat Locations

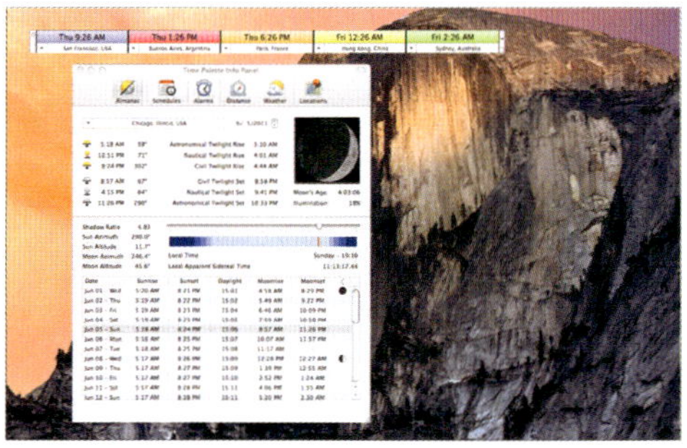

Each part of Time Palette contains comprehensive info

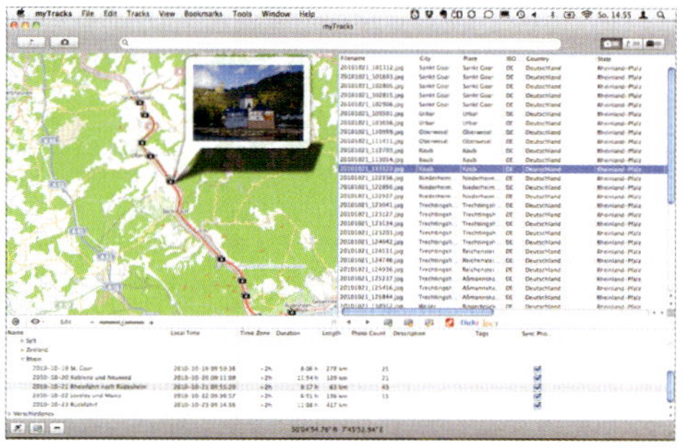

You can store as many tracks as you like with myTracks

Monitor flights and get informed with Flightradar24

The number of tasks MacCleanse takes care of is immense

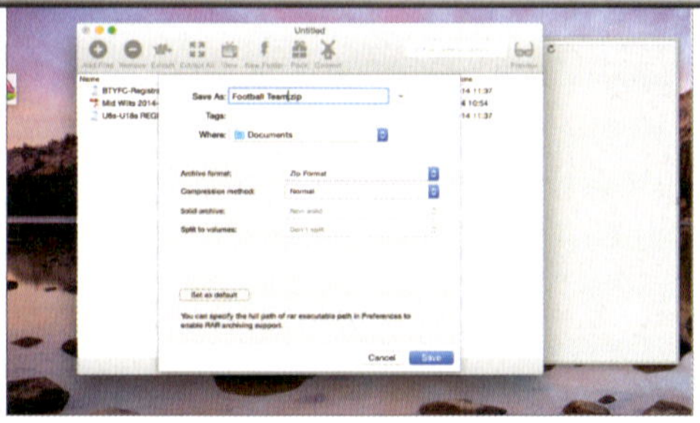

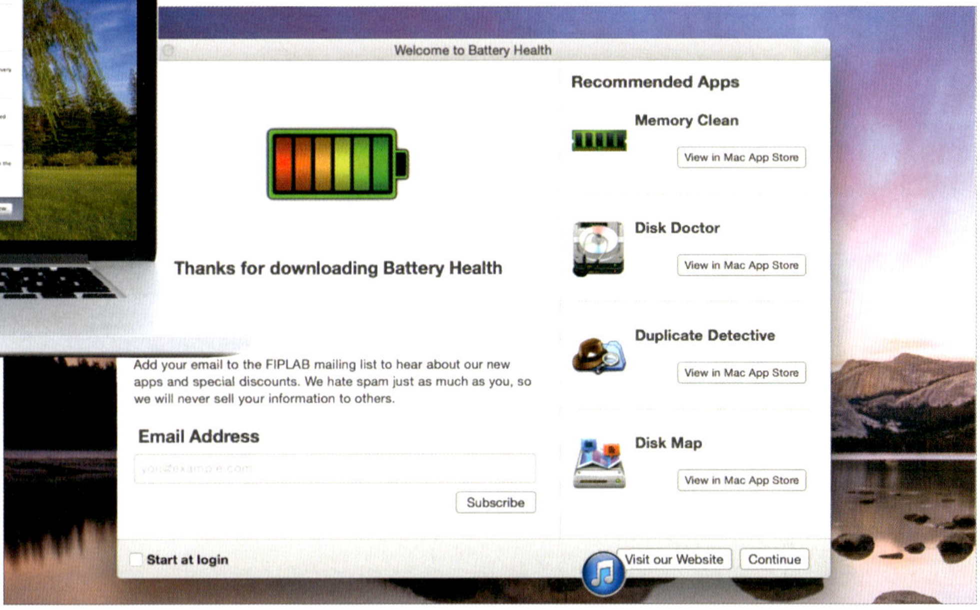

Get the most out of your charge with the Battery Health app…

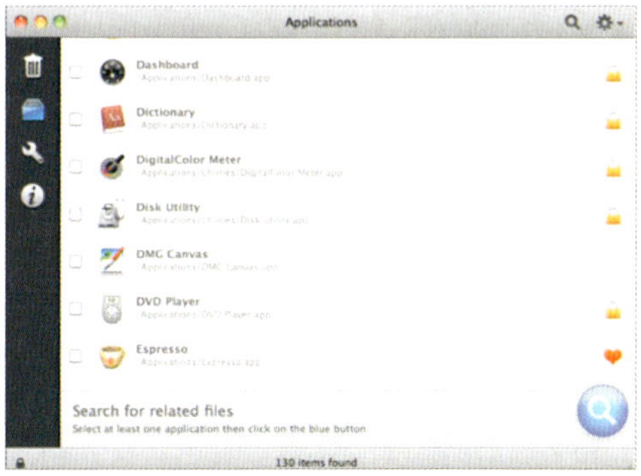

Trash Me's interface could not be any more simple

Utilities

Customise your Mac in a way that suits you best

All computers have a default configuration that is designed to let the user undertake many tasks, but there are sometimes functions you really wish it could do. Whether it is something to make your Mac run smoother or to add another level of ease to your workflow, there are missing elements from your Mac There are, thankfully, utility apps available form the Mac App Store that will not only improve stability, but also enable you to do things with a Mac that you may not have considered before. With the right utility, you can potentially complete a process you need to undertake in half the time, and then repeat this with more utilities. There are hundreds available that can be used for every conceivable task, and once you are used to them, you will able to flexibly deal with any given situation. Utilities can completely change the way you work once you have installed the ones that suit you best.

5 essential apps

iPackr

Price: Free
Developer: Hong Jiang

This free app allows you to compress and decompress zip, rar and 7z archives and even lets you preview files within compressed archives without first extracting them, which can be a great time-saver if you're unsure as to whether the archive you're dragging into the app contains that files that you need. It is also fast and ruthlessly efficient at compacting and extracting and is very easy to use.

MacCleanse

Price: £22.99/$29.99
Developer: Koingo Software

It's always good practice to keep a Mac running as smoothly as possible, but to do this you often have to follow many processes to ensure every tweak has been completed. MacCleanse automates this process, and will take care of more than 50 tasks without you having to jump through hoops. It is not an app you will even notice, but is well worth scheduling to work every week or so.

Battery Health

Price: Free
Developer: FIPLAB Ltd

Laptop batteries can be strange things – being efficient and seemingly healthy one minute and then easy to exhaust the next. This app helps you monitor the fitness and effectiveness of your MacBook's battery by providing a wealth of information. It even contains useful tips to help you maximise the efficiency of your device and get more out of each charge.

TrashMe

Price: £5.99/$7.99
Developer: Jean-Baptiste Zedda

When in the process of deleting apps, it is all too easy on a Mac to just drag them to the trash bin. The problem is that often files are left over that take up space and end up slowing the system down. TrashMe will ensure that every file has been comprehensively deleted without you even having to think about what is happening. Great for an issue that many take for granted.

Mobile Mouse Server

Price: Free
Developer: RPA Tech INC

When combined with an iPhone or iPad, this app will let you use your iOS devices to control your Mac. They can become touchscreen mice, keyboards and even dictation machines. If you use this software in conjunction with an iPhone 4S, then you can read into the phone and subsequently watch the text appear on your Mac!

iStopMotion feels like creating a home video

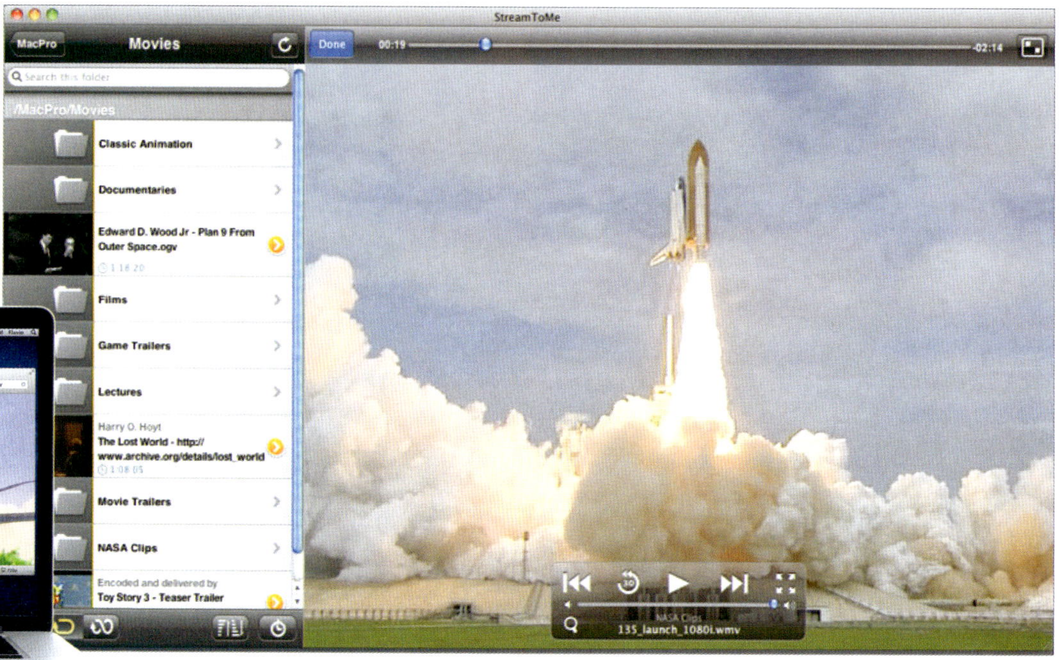

The streaming quality makes you feel like you are watching a local file while using StreamToMe

Video

Watch the latest and best videos in high-quality output

The world of digital video is a curiosity in that most people will have already been exposed to it, but few of the creators will take the time to enhance their media. It is very much seen as a static media form; you take a video and leave it as it is to view at a later date. However, you can do so much with your creations, and there are all sorts of apps to help you manipulate all of your personal and work-related videos. You can add special effects, funny commentary and even incorporate them into professional presentations. The beauty of the Mac is that even the lower-end systems are able to cope with memory-intensive video production really well. The platform is designed to cope with all types of media, even high-definition video files, and the video apps available on the Mac App Store make it all work together in an even more efficient manner.

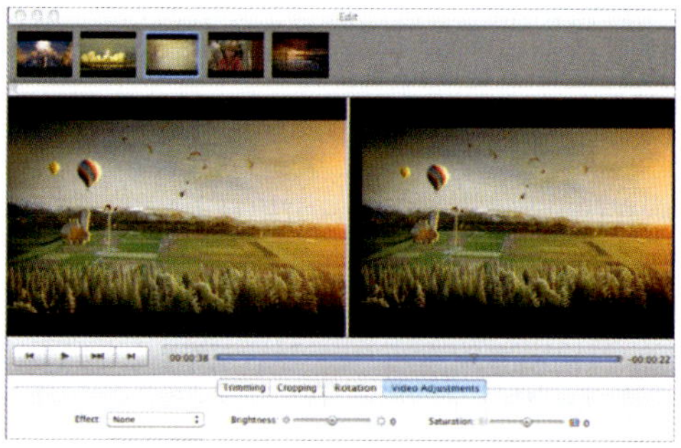

Adjustments add extra control in Video-Converter

5 essential apps

Video-Converter

Price: £14.99/$18.49
Developer: Wondershare Software Co Ltd

Varying video and audio formats cause lots of problems for Mac users who own mobile devices, as not all formats work with every device. This app caters for a variety of formats, and should cover almost every file you own. The conversion process is quite straightforward, and once you first use it, you will soon view it as something that comes in handy over and over again.

Minitube

Price: £7.99/$9.99
Developer: Flavio Tordini

YouTube is easy to become engrossed in, but not as easy to use when you watch one video after another. Minitube lets you pick a keyword and then watch a stream of videos that are related to your search without you needing to do anything else. It caters for HD, and uses QuickTime rather than Flash for efficiency. It is a solution that could change the way you view YouTube videos forever.

Movie Effects

Price: £2.29/$3.99
Developer: etinysoft Inc

This app is quick and easy to use, and it provides you with a professional standard video tool to turn any video into a work of art with a wide range of effects. Over 20 effects are included, such as flip, negate, rotation, smooth, contrast, deinterlace, cartoon, saturation and distort and all you have to do is drag your video into the window and then start applying whatever effects you want.

iStopMotion 3

Price: £39.99/$49.99
Developer: Boinx Software Ltd

Stop motion is a video effect that most people had no access to… until iStopMotion came along, that is. With this app, you can spend time creating a stunning stop-motion films, where inanimate objects can be made to move, which will surprise anyone that you show it to. The time required to become adept at using this is surprisingly low for the potential results.

Smart Converter

Price: Free
Developer: Systemic Pty

If all you require is a simple and effective video converter app then this free offering ticks all of the right boxes by being able to handle hundreds of different file types to enable that they play on all of your favourite devices. All you have to do is drag and drop a media file into the app and then choose a conversion type. It will only convert what is needed, making it one of the fastest of its type around.

Weather

Find out the forecast easily with a range of Mac apps

The weather is a subject that we are all quite obsessed with. We talk about it with friends, strangers and anyone else who will listen, but the subject is much bigger than you may realise. Besides just tracking the forecast and current conditions, you can use Mac apps for highly specialised weather-related tasks. You can track everything from local conditions to world tides and climate change, and that is just the start. There are apps for all weather-related subjects, and for most people there are more apps than they will ever need. However, the apps available will cover the needs of everyone who has interest in the subject, and you may even find some of them to be a source of learning that builds your interest even further. This category highlights the breadth of Mac apps available, and is as complete or inconsequential as you need it to be.

■ Get a quick heads-up with Weather 5 Days

■ Weather° provides forecasts through a sleek interface

■ The Sun's movements are shown in data form in Daylight

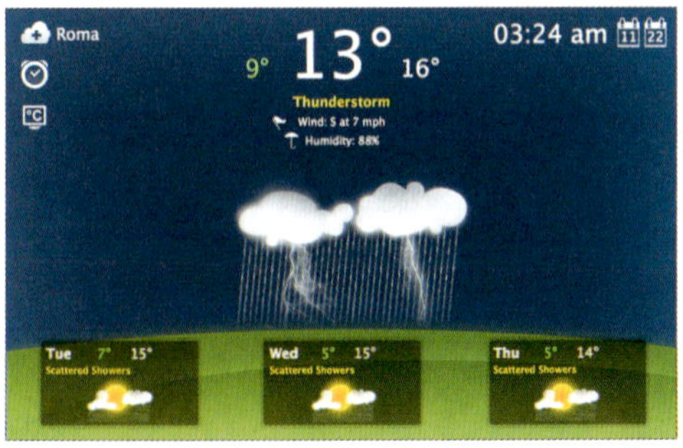

■ The Weather app icons feed the data with a quick glance

■ 3D Weather Globe's visuals are remarkably detailed for a weather app

5 essential apps

Daylight

Price: £7.99/$9.99 **Developer:** Andrew Cook

For those with a need to see what the Sun is doing around the globe at any particular time, they may as well do it in style. Daylight takes this information and displays it in a highly visual way by showing a map of the Earth with the exact sunrise and sunset times displayed as they would look in real life. Besides this, information on major cities is available and the ability to drag the night sky is an added bonus. It isn't an app that everyone will need, but for those that do it will do the job perfectly.

Weather

Price: £0.79/$0.99 **Developer:** Presselite

Sometimes you need to keep track of the weather, but not let it dominate everything you do. The Weather app is designed to keep you up to date in a minimalist way, and will sit on your desktop for when you need it. The design is clever, and lets you interpret what is happening with a quick glance. It efficiently presents details without overloading you with data.

3D Weather Globe & Atlas Deluxe

Price: £44.99/$49.99

Developer: Software MacKiev

For visual appeal, this app really does shine. It feels like you have the whole world on your desktop thanks to the splendidly detailed graphics and real-time weather information. You can tilt the globe to see natural landmarks in detail, and even if you do not need the exact weather information, it is still an enjoyable experience, and the ability to track hurricanes and other weather phenomena takes it even higher up the value league.

Weather 5 Days

Price: Free **Developer:** Regis ANDRE

If you like a quick heads-up as to the current weather conditions in your local area then this app provides a handy menu bar item that you can click on for an accurate overview for the next five days. It's certainly useful for checking if you need to take a brolly out.

Weather°

Price: Free **Developer:** IAC Search & Media

Presented through a sleek and sexy interface, Weather° displays at-a-glance stats and forecasts for your location. This free version only permits one location, but you can upgrade, in-app, to store more and get additional features such as a menu bar item and fully customisable layouts.

YOUR FREE RESOURCES

Log in to **filesilo.co.uk/bks-662/** and download your tutorial resources **NOW!**

EVERYTHING YOU NEED TO FOLLOW THE TUTORIALS AND BECOME A MAC EXPERT

FREE SOFTWARE FOR YOUR MAC

VLC Player for free

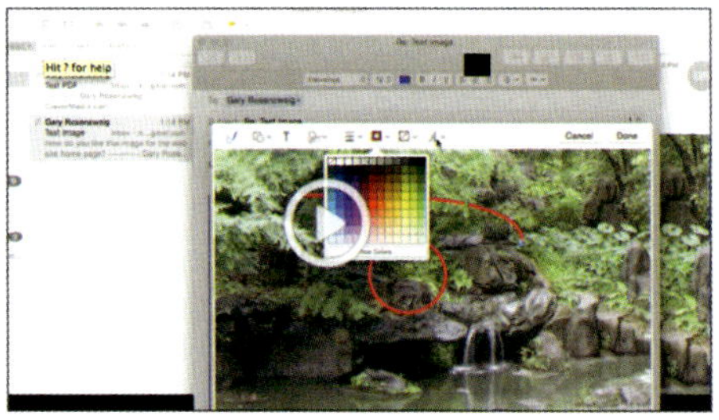

Follow great video tutorials

Everything you need to follow tutorials

PACKED WITH FREE PREMIUM CONTENT

YOUR BONUS RESOURCES

ON FILESILO WE'VE PROVIDED FREE, EXCLUSIVE CONTENT FOR **MAC FOR BEGINNERS** READERS, INCLUDING...

- 2GB of free content, including video tuition covering the Drummer function in Garageband and amazing blockbuster effects in iMovie.
- Free software to load up your Mac like the universal media player VLC.
- Additional video material to make sure you're getting the most out of your brand new Apple Mac.
- Beautiful wallpapers to grace your high res screen.

FileSilo

Go to: http://www.filesilo.co.uk/bks-662/

FILESILO – THE HOME OF PRO RESOURCES

Discover your free online assets

- A rapidly growing library
- Updated continually with cool resources
- Lets you keep your downloads organised
- Browse and access your content from anywhere
- No more torn disc pages to ruin your magazines
- No more broken discs
- Print subscribers get all the content
- Digital magazine owners get all the content too!
- Each issue's content is free with your magazine
- Secure online access to your free resources

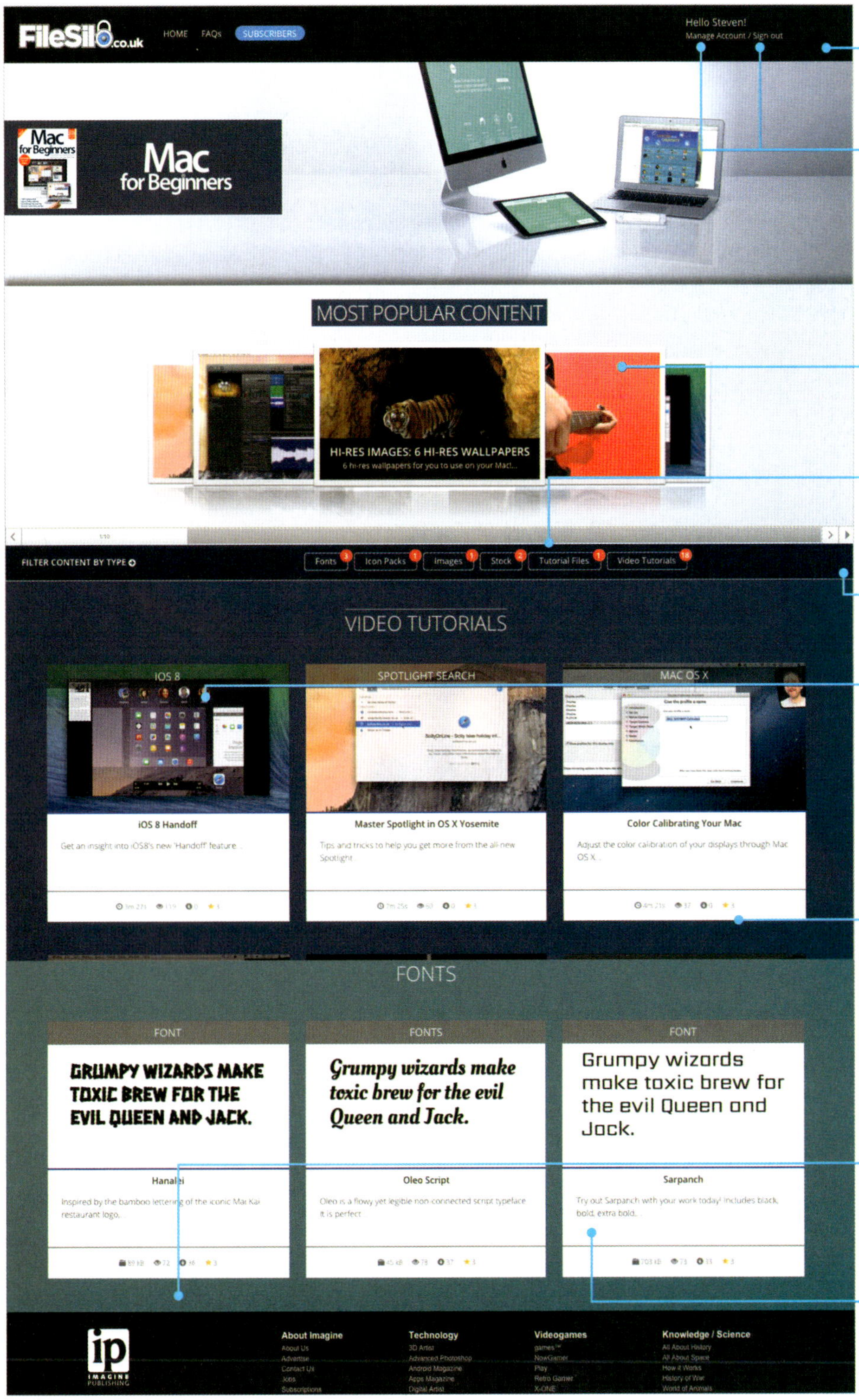

This is the new FileSilo site that replaces your disc. You'll find it by visiting the link on the following page.

The first time you use FileSilo, you'll need to register. After that, you can use your email address and password to log in.

The most popular downloads are shown in the carousel here, so check out what your fellow readers are enjoying.

If you're looking for a particular type of content, like software or video tutorials, use the filters here to refine your search.

Can't find the resource you're looking for in these filters? Click on More Types to specify what kind of resource you want (if available).

Whether it's fonts, images or video workshops, categories make it easy to identify the content you're looking for.

See key details for each resource including number of views and downloads, and the community rating.

Find out more about our online stores, and useful FAQs, such as our cookie and privacy policies and contact details.

Discover our fantastic sister magazines and the wealth of content and information that they provide.

HOW TO USE FileSilo

EVERYTHING YOU NEED TO KNOW ABOUT ACCESSING YOUR NEW DIGITAL REPOSITORY

To access FileSilo, please visit http://www.filesilo.co.uk/bks-662/

01 Follow the on-screen instructions to create an account with our secure FileSilo system, or log in and unlock the issue by answering a simple question about the edition you've just read. You can access the content for free with each edition released.

02 Once you have logged in, you are free to explore the wealth of content made available for free on FileSilo, from great video tutorials and online guides to superb downloadable resources. And the more bookazines you purchase, the more your instantly accessible collection of digital content will grow.

03 You can access FileSilo on any desktop, tablet or smartphone device using any popular browser (such as Safari, Firefox or Google Chrome). However, we recommend that you use a desktop to download content, as you may not be able to download files to your phone or tablet.

04 If you have any problems with accessing content on FileSilo, or with the registration process, take a look at the FAQs online or email filesilohelp@imagine-publishing.co.uk.

VLC

An extremely powerful yet small piece of software that can not only

Minimising Windows Versus Hiding Apps

Many new Mac users try to use the buttons at the top...

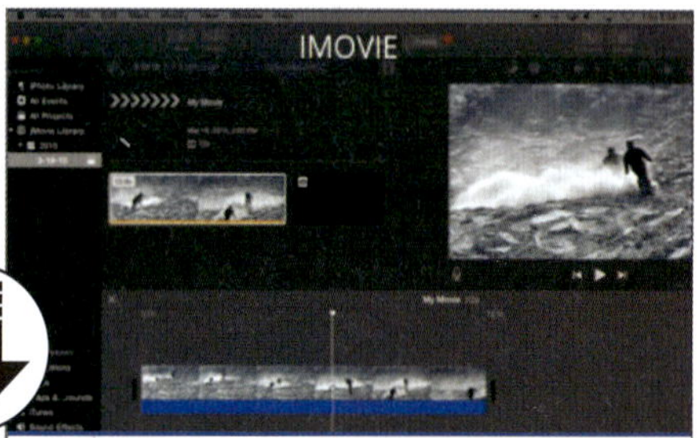

Moving Graphic Pointers In iMovie

Learn how to create a transparent graphic that you can then overlay

NEED HELP WITH THE TUTORIALS?

Having trouble with any of the techniques in this issue's tutorials? Don't know how to make the best use of your free resources? Want to have your work critiqued by those in the know? Then why not visit the Bookazines or iCreate Magazine Facebook page for all your questions, concerns and qualms. There is a friendly community of experts to help you out, as well as regular posts and updates from the bookazine team. Like us today and start chatting!

facebook.com/ImagineBookazines
facebook.com/iCreateMagazine